On Assumptions

Alexius Meinong about 1900
(photograph courtesy of
Professors Rudolf Haller and Reinhard Fabian, University of Graz)

Alexius Meinong

ON ASSUMPTIONS

Edited and Translated, with an Introduction, by

JAMES HEANUE

UNIVERSITY OF CALIFORNIA PRESS

Berkeley   Los Angeles   London

University of California Press
Berkeley and Los Angeles, California

University of California Press, Ltd.
London, England

Library of Congress Catalog Card Number: 75-27929

Meinong, Alexius.
  On assumptions.
California   University of California Press
1976
                    9-30-75
0-520-03139-3

Printed in the United States of America

1 2 3 4 5 6 7 8 9

Contents

IV
The Most Obvious Cases of Assumptions

V
The Objective and Assumptions

VI
Assumptions in Operations on Objectives

VII
Assumptions in the Apprehending of What is Presented. Intending

VIII
Assumptions and Complexes. More on Intending

IX
The Psychology of Desire and the Psychology of Value

X
Results. Steps Toward a Psychology of Assumptions

Editor's Introduction

The philosopher and psychologist Alexius Meinong (Ritter von Handschuch-sheim) was born in the Austrian-garrisoned city of Lvov on July 17, 1853. His father served in the Austrian army from about 1813, in the late Napoleonic wars, until the end of the Italian campaign of 1859, eventually attaining the rank of general. The younger Meinong never used the *von*—or its privileges, as he said in a brief autobiographical sketch.[1] All of Meinong's youth was spent in Vienna, and he studied there as well. Entering the University of Vienna in 1870, he made history his major subject, and he received his doctorate in 1874 with a dissertation on the medieval political and religious reformer Arnold of Brescia.

Meinong had been interested in philosophy for several years, and he had chosen to work on the Kantian critiques of pure and practical reason for the examination in his minor doctoral subject. That examination was the occasion of his first personal contact with the philosopher Franz Brentano, who had begun teaching at Vienna in 1874 as full professor. In 1875 Meinong decided on philosophy as his career. Brentano, under whom Meinong studied from the winter of 1875 through the winter of 1877, was not involved in this decision, but his thought and personal influence were very important in the shaping of Meinong's early philosophical outlook. Apparently Brentano felt that some-one trained in history should do a study of the 1748 and 1758 editions of Hume's *An Enquiry Concerning Human Understanding*. This unrealized proj-ect turned into Meinong's qualifying dissertation for teaching and was called "Hume Studies I: a History and Critique of Modern Nominalism." This was presented to the philosophy faculty at the University of Vienna in 1877, and Meinong taught there as lecturer in philosophy from 1878 to 1882.

In the autobiographical sketch mentioned above, Meinong speaks of Bren-tano as having been generous with his help and an altogether impressive per-son; but he also acknowledges that he was not on intimate terms with Bren-tano. The reason for this, Meinong seems to suggest, lay in his own reluctance to reveal his independent thinking, given the imposing personality of his teacher. Meinong surmises that this same reluctance provided a basis for the persistent misunderstandings about him that he discusses in the first-edition preface to the present book.

In 1882 Meinong was appointed senior lecturer at the University of Graz. Meinong spent the rest of his life in Graz, Austria's second largest city and the capital of her southeast province of Styria. In 1884 Meinong established Austria's first laboratory for experimental psychology. At Vienna, Brentano's efforts in that direction had failed. Brentano had taken holy orders, separated himself from the church in 1873, and was married in 1880 after resigning his professorship. This resignation was conceived as a formal gesture, and reappointment was expected as soon as it was established that the civil marriage of a man in his religious position was valid in Austria. Contrary to the expectations of Brentano and the philosophy department at Vienna, a protracted battle with officialdom kept him in the position of lecturer until his final renunciation of teaching in 1894.[2]

In Graz, Meinong was contending with a different sort of difficulty: gradually worsening eyesight. Eduard Martinak, who became a student of Meinong's there in 1883, reports that Meinong's eyesight was so poor that he could not be sure where he was walking, and that reading was difficult for him—impossible at the lecture rostrum.[3] Martinak's remark on the founding of a psychology laboratory under such conditions reveals that Meinong was on the way to blindness by his thirtieth year. In 1889 Meinong became full professor at Graz, and he also married in that same year. Fifteen years later, when Hans Benndorf became his student, Meinong was almost totally blind. The fifty-one-year-old man was barely able to read in strong light, and soon afterward even that was impossible.[4] Students Martinak, Benndorf, and the late Rudolf Kindinger all concur in the picture of a Meinong who moved in a strange groping way along corridors and walks, disdaining the assistance of a cane or guide, or fancying that such assistance would create a stranger impression. A picture of anxious self-reliance, it does not forbid a smile.

From the turn of the century on, Meinong used the typewriter for his writing. Printed or typed material was read aloud to him. The economizing of his working time was rigorous and thorough. From students Ernst Mally and Wilhelm Frankl, as well as the others I have mentioned, one learns that as a teacher Meinong excelled in the exposition of a subject matter through a thorough and terminologically precise discussion of its problems.[5] Neither rhetoric nor any subtler form of personal dynamics found a place in Meinong's lectures and seminars. By following an aporematic approach, he secured a striking immediacy for his subject matter. It was during the trying years of the early twentieth century, with their appealing picture of an unselfpitying spirit determined to maintain the diversity and the high quality of its professional competence in the face of blindness, that Meinong's philosophy emerged in its final form as a complementary relationship of empirical psychology and an expressly "apsychological" and aprioristic theory of objects. He died on November 27, 1920. The grave of Alexius Meinong, his wife Doris, and his son Ernst is in St. Peter's cemetery in Graz.

The published writings of Meinong date from his twenty-second year in 1875 to his sixty-seventh year in 1920. All told, these writings are some eighty in number.[6] Of these, we might mention fifteen or so as being longer writings—that is, those of seventy-five or more pages. They are as follows: "Hume-Studien I" (1877), "Hume Studien II" (1882), *Über philosophische Propädeutik* (1885), "Über Begriff und Eigenschaften der Empfindung" (1888-1889), *Psychologisch-ethische Untersuchungen zur Werttheorie* (1894), "Über die Bedeutung des Weberschen Gesetzes" (1896), "Über Gegenstände höherer Ordnung und deren Verhältnis zur inneren Wahrnehmung" (1899), *Über Annahmen* (1st ed., 1902),[7] "Bemerkungen uber den Farbenkorper und das Mischungsgesetz" (1903), "Über Gegenstandstheorie" (1904), *Über die Erfahrungsgrundlagen unseres Wissens* (1906), *Über die Stellung der Gegenstandstheorie im System der Wissenschaften* (1907), *Über Annahmen* (2d ed., 1910), *Über Möglichkeit und Wahrscheinlichkeit* (1915), "Über emotionale Präsentation" (1917), *Zum Erweis des allgemeinen Kausalgesetzes* (1918), and *Grundlegung zur allgemeinen Werttheorie* (appearing posthumously in 1923). This list excludes shorter works; but it does include the fifty-page essay of 1904, because of the essay's long standing as the only work of Meinong's available in English, and because of its importance as a guidepost in following the rapid development of Meinong's thought between the works of 1899 and 1910.[8]

Of these longer writings, the one that affords the best view of Meinong's approach to experience and its objects is *On Assumptions* (*Über Annahmen*) in the second, 1910 edition, which is translated here.[9] *Assumptions* was conceived as a psychological work, and in the second edition it is still primarily concerned with mental (*psychische*) facts or states of affairs. Such is Meinong's informal way of speaking of the primary subject matter of psychology. It was not until after the first edition that Meinong adopted the formal designation of "experiences" (*Erlebnisse*) for mental occurrences or facts. That expression appears along with the older ones in the present edition of *Assumptions*. Here and there one notes the traditional division of experiences into the complex and the elementary. The book characteristically proceeds by a type of psychological analysis. A familiar and important complex experience, *E,* is considered. Tacitly, one is presumed to have a reliable sense of what *E* is like and what one does and does not say in connection with *E*. Meinong considers the different ways that *E* might be thought *not* to contain an assumption. He concludes that *E* does contain an assumption. And so he has moved that much closer to showing that assumptions are very important elements in our experience. It is the purpose of *Assumptions* to show that.

Elementary experiences are divided into the intellectual and the emotional. On the side of the intellectual, they are again divided into representations (*Vorstellungen*) and thoughts (*Gedanken*). Thoughts are divided into judgments and assumptions. Thus, as a type of intellectual experience, assuming is somehow really akin to judgment and not really akin to representation. This becomes apparent early in chapter 1, even though Meinong has proposed to investigate "a domain of facts intermediate between representation and judgment." Nothing much comes of the intermediate-domain idea, and the position of assumptions in the following classificatory schema is in fact the position that those experiences have throughout the book.

Erlebnis, an experience
I. *intellektuell,* intellectual
   A. *Vorstellung,* a representation
      1. *Wahrnehmungsvorstellung,* a perceptual representation
      2. *Einbildungsvorstellung,* a reproductive representation
         a. *Erinnerungsvorstellung,* a recollective representation
         b. *Phantasievorstellung,* an imaginative representation
   B. *Gedanke,* a thought
      1. *Urteil,* a judgment
      2. *Annahme,* an assumption
II. *emotional,* emotional
   A. *Gefühl,* a feeling
   B. *Begehrung,* a desire for something (in a general sense); a conation
      1. *Wunsch,* a wish; or more strongly, *Begehrung,* a desire (in the usual sense)
      2. *Wollung,* a volition

Meinong's 'Vorstellung' is sometimes rendered in English as 'idea' or 'presentation'. The considerations that weighed against these and in favor of 'representation' in the present translation also allow the adoption of C. D. Broad's passing rendition, 'having an idea', if and when a more articulate expression seems appropriate to the reader.[10] If to represent something is to have an idea of it, then the representing is the *act,* the idea is the *content,* and the thing is the *object.* Brentano said that to be represented was to appear in consciousness or awareness (*Bewusstsein*).[11] Meinong uses 'Vorstellung' more narrowly. The general phenomenon that Brentano had in mind with his short definition seems to be close to what Meinong now calls "presentation" (*Präsentation*). To be presented is to be offered to judgment, Meinong says.[12] On the face of it, the thought is the same. The object makes its appearance in the inner court. But in actual usage, Meinong's 'Präsentation' does not have any such connotation of immediate presence. That a representation always presents some object through its content means only that the content more or less adequately predefines the character of an object for apprehension (*Erfassen*).

A judgment (*Urteil*) is sometimes called a belief (*Glaube*) by Meinong; less frequently, it is called a conviction (*Überzeugung*). A surmise (*Vermutung*) is a judgment in which the element of conviction (*Überzeugtheit*) is weaker than certainty (*Gewissheit*). All judgments have some degree of conviction. If one allows a limit case, something that is no longer judgment in this regard, then assumptions may be said to be judgments without conviction. At times

Meinong alters this way of looking at assuming, and it takes on instead the appearance of a core element, as one might call it.[13] Then all judgment would involve assuming, but not vice versa. This manner of regarding assumptions is sometimes adopted in the following discussion, as is the notion that judgments and assumptions are "thoughts," convinced and unconvinced thoughts, respectively.[14] Toward the end of the book, Meinong suggests calling assumptions "imaginative judgments."[15] Here he leaves implicit the specifically opposed mode of designation, "serious judgments," and in that way avoids the need to speak of "judgments in the broader sense."[16]

The concept of judgment does not receive any intensive or protracted reconsideration in *Assumptions,* although one can see already that a great deal depends on that concept. Some of the common observations about judgment that Meinong considers acceptable are Brentanoan, and none of them are anti-Brentanoan: (1) Judgment is radically distinct from representation, instead of being a complicated or otherwise special form of representation. (2) Although representation is not everything, it is the indispensable foundation for everything else—i.e., for judgment as well as for all other experiences. These two observations appear at the very start of the first section, the second of them quite explicitly. A third and fourth observation in section 1 are also quite explicit as regards judgment: (3) Judgment contains an element of conviction (and representation contains none). (4) Judgment is determinate in respect of logical quality (whereas representation is neither affirmative nor negative). Elsewhere in the book, one can pick up other contrasts between judgment and representation. Two important ones are the following: (5) Judgments are expressed in sentences and clauses, whereas representations are expressed in words and other noun phrases.[17] (6) Judgment is active, whereas representation is passive; to judge is to do something, but to represent is not.[18]

Chapter 1 ("Erste Aufstellungen") provides the first four of these observations about judgment, and then it sets forth an example of assuming.[19] One is asked to imagine (*sich denken*) that the Boers were not allowed to fight alone. If we have complied with the request, then we have made an assumption.[20] At the end of the first section, Meinong says that he is concerned with experiences in an intermediate domain between judgment and representation, and he rejects for theoretical purposes the kind of pragmatic conviction that is expressed in locutions such as: 'I can only assume that he will do as he says'.[21] Section 2 begins with the thought that perhaps imagining or representing to oneself (*sich vorstellen*) that the Boers were not allowed to fight alone is really just representation. Supposing for the time being that there is never any trouble in getting something before one's mind as "this, the positive thing," what about "that, the negative of it"? The *negativum* cannot be represented. Although Meinong has begun with a negative proposition, or state of affairs, his considerations during the remainder of chapter 1 are mostly directed to the significations of "non-" expressions, expressions of the form 'a non-A', 'a non-ϕA', and 'non-ϕ'. Even these more likely candidates for representation somehow demand more than mere representation. To begin with, Meinong notes that the things we originally perceive are represented in a positive character, and that conceiving of something in a negative character therefore cannot be treated as an imaginative or recollective reproductive representation.[22] From there on, he examines other possibilities. Rather than follow him through the intricacies of it, we might do better at this point to note a few of its connections with other things.

First, the discussion of *negativa* points back a few pages to Meinong's remark that he would offer a formal proof of the affinity of assuming with judgment, and its lack of affinity with representation.[23] He now offers it. Evidently we must keep the negative assumption about the Boers in mind. Second, the discussion of *negativa* points ahead to section 41, in which Meinong resumes the thread of discussion. Third, it served as the prospectus for four first-edition sections that have been deleted after section 44. In these sections Meinong tried unsuccessfully to move in on and to pin down the conclusion that an assumption enables one to get past the representation of a colored shape and to discriminate in thought between a red cross and a nonred cross. He tries again in the two new concluding sections of chapter 8, and with apparent success. In that way he manages to fulfill the 1902 prediction that we still see at the end of his discussion of *negativa*. Fourth, the motivation of the argument as a whole is possibly anti-Brentanoan, and one of the component arguments looks as though it were directed against a position of the Brentanoan Anton Marty.[24] Fifth and finally, Meinong thinks that his discussion of *negativa* has given him a heuristic principle: Anywhere that the opposition of yes and no comes into play, one can be sure that there is more than mere representation.[25] Since Meinong probably did not produce a decisive argument against the representing of the Boers not being allowed to fight alone, or against the essential similarity of assuming and representation, it is a good thing that the new principle is used only occasionally.

Chapter 2 ("Zur Frage nach den charakteristischen Leistungen des Sätzes") is concerned with the expressive and significative role of language, and with the expressed experience of the speaker and the understanding-experience of the listener.[26] In section 4, in a new paragraph in which the concept of presentation (*Präsentation*) first appears under that name, Meinong makes a succinct statement of his position on expression and signification. A word signifies insofar as it expresses a presenting experience (a representation would be the most obvious case), and the object presented by this experience is the signification of the word.[27]

Meinong is generally in agreement with the common view that words express ideas and sentences express complete thoughts. Sentences are the linguistic means for expressing judgments, Meinong states in the penultimate paragraph of section 5. In section 6 he notes, however, that the sentence (*Satz*) may be optative, imperative, or interrogative. It may be a "that"-clause subordinated to a main clause of wishing, desiring, commanding, disbelieving, or doubting. With such main clauses, the "that"-clause cannot be taken as an expression of judgment—i.e., as it can in 'I judge that the wind is heavy'. Neither can it be taken that way, generally, with third-person clauses of belief. Relative clauses, conditional and disjunctive clauses, and semantically empty sentences of categorical syllogistic are brought in to confirm the general point of section 6: Many *Sätze* ("sentences") do not express judgments.

In all those cases the sentence that does not express a judgment need not be understood through a judgment. In other cases one correctly sees the expression of a judgment but manages to understand without agreeing. Thus another general point in section 7: In an understanding response to the use of a *Satz,* it is not essential that the listener should make the judgment that the *Satz* expresses, even if the *Satz* does express a judgment.

What does a dependent or independent sentence express, when it does not express a judgment? What is it that will do for the mechanism of understanding, when one cannot afford a judgment? And by the way, what is the signification of a sentence, as opposed to a word? One can be pretty sure that "an assumption" is the right answer to the first two questions, but this answer is postponed to chapter 5. The answer to the last question is given in chapter 3, in connection with judgment.

Chapter 3 ("Das Objektiv") is concerned with states of affairs as objects apprehended by means of judgment, as objects upon which higher-level judgments are directed, as the significations of noun phrases of certain types as well as of sentences, and—apsychologically—as instances of being and so-being with a being and so-being of their own.[28] This chapter is the result of Meinong's rewriting of most of the old seventh chapter on objectives (same title), and of his relegating to the newly created chapter 5 all surviving material on the assuming of objectives, on judgment about assumed objectives (sections 21 and 22), and on emotional attitudes toward objectives (sections 24 and 25).

Judgment is a dependent experience. It is directed upon something that is presented by another experience. In the plainest case, the other experience is a representation; the judgment is directed upon as object that is represented, i.e., presented in that way. Then the object (*Gegenstand*) is what Meinong calls an "objectum" (*Objekt*).[29] The objectum is said to be "judged about" (*beurteilt*).[30] Thus, the judgment that there is snow outside is directed upon some represented snow, and it is a judgment about that objectum or representational object. Now, Meinong says there is also an object that is "judged forth" (*erurteilt*), and it develops that this is a state of affairs, factual or unfactual, that one apprehends through one's judgment about the objectum. Meinong calls this state of affairs an "objective" (*Objektiv*). One judges forth an objective by making a judgment about an objectum. The word 'erurteilt' is not adopted for serious use. The objective apprehended by means of a judgment is merely said to be "judged" (*geurteilt*). One judges an objective by making a judgment about an objectum. The word 'apprehend' ('erfassen') is not used in chapter 3. It is possible that Meinong wanted to avoid a complication—the distinction between mediate and immediate apprehension—in the expository work. Meinong does occasionally use the word 'present' ('präsentiern'), and it would not introduce that complication for us, though it would create the momentarily distracting association of a second-level judgment to which the judged objective was offered. If one can ignore that association for the time being, then the matter as so far developed can be summed up quickly. When one makes a judgment about an object presented by a representation (i.e., about an objectum), one's judgment itself presents an objective.

In Meinong's initial examples of the judgment of objectives, the judgments are all existential. Someone judges that no disturbance of the peace has occurred. Someone judges that there is snow outside. Someone judges that there is a (or *the*) philosopher's stone. The space at our disposal does not permit a discussion of general and individual existence in Meinong's theory of objects. The following should be noted, however. The affirmative "There is..." (*Es gibt...*) existential is almost always regarded by Meinong as expressing the apprehension of individual existence. Accordingly, if he has the judgment-expression 'There is an *A*' and he wants to name the objective in some way other than by the "that"-clause 'that there is an *A*', he will choose 'the existence of the *A*' or else make it plain that by 'the existence of an *A*' he means the existence of a certain *A*.

Objectives presented by existential judgments are regularly called "objectives of being" by Meinong. Sharing that title are the objectives presented when one thinks that "there is" such and such a plane geometrical figure or (to venture a new example) that "there is" such and such a repeating decimal fraction. One might call these objects objectives of ideal existence. But 'Existenz' is held to a real, temporal connotation by Meinong, and the ideal analogue of existence is instead called "subsistence" (*Bestand*). Existence and subsistence are taken together as "being in the narrower sense," i.e., in the sense that connotes "just plain being" as opposed to being thus and so. An objective of being (*Seinsobjektiv*) may be either the existence of a (real) objectum or the subsistence of an (ideal) objectum. The contrast between the existence and the subsistence of representational objects is less important in Meinong's twentieth-century philosophy than one would have expected at the turn of the century. The manifest reason is that not much use was found for the notion of ideal objecta, and that some of them, namely ideal relations, disappeared and then reappeared in the class of objectives. This situation allows 'subsistence' (i.e., 'Bestand') to drift into virtual synonymity with 'factuality'[31] (i.e., 'Tatsächlichkeit') for the reader of *Assumptions*. There are only a few passages in which one has to recall the original sense of 'Bestand' as the ideal analogue of 'Existenz'. Nevertheless, that sense is never removed completely, and the expression 'objective of being' or 'judgment of being' in connection with an objectum is never quite as specific as the rare expression 'objective of existence' or 'judgment of existence'.

For the sake of explicitness, it should be added that the false judgment of being and the negative judgment of being each has its objective, which is an unfactual or non-subsisting objective of being in the former case and a negative (as opposed to a positive) objective of being in the latter case. In the one case it is the negative fact that there has been no disturbance of the peace, and in the other it is the positive "nonfact" that there is a philosopher's stone.

A categorical judgment, i.e., a judgment that something is thus and so in its substantive character, or its quality, etc., is said to be a judgment of so-being. The objective that is judged or presented in that way is said to be an "objective of so-being."[32] In view of all the things that can be said in a categorical or logically predicative way, it is plain that the class of objectives of so-being (*Soseinsobjektive*) is a heterogeneous class. Leaving Meinong to make such distinctions as he cares to, we note only that the distinctions between positive and negative being, factual and unfactual being, and modal and nonmodal being apply also to so-being.

The distinction between the being and the so-being of objecta is reapplied when we ask about the instances of being in the broader sense—the objectives. Their being (in the narrower sense) is factuality (*Tatsächlichkeit*) or subsistence as a fact. Over against factuality and unfactuality stand the modalities of possibility, necessity, contingency, and impossibility, corresponding to the so-being of objectives. Thus, the list is short. The principle of exclusion, beginning with an objective's being true and presumably extending to the whole range of less venerable candidates, such as an objective's being alarming or urgent, is that the objective should be considered without reference to any experience that has the objective for an object. Meinong denies that such psychological reference is involved in thinking of an objective as a fact, and he affirms that it is involved in the thought of the objective as true or probable.[33] So it is, presumably, with the more obvious reflex concepts of alarmingness, urgency, and so on. Certainty and evidence (*Evidenz,* evidentness) constitute an interesting case; they are not thought to be properties of the objective at all.[34]

Merely insofar as a judgment is directed upon an object presented to it, it may be termed a judgment (*Beurteilung*) "about" that object. Thus, any judgment about an objectum is properly called a *Beurteilung*. But when the judgment about an object is contrasted to a judgment (*Urteilung*) "of" that same object, then the object can only be an objective, and 'judgment about' gains the narrower connotation of a judgment directed upon an objective, not upon an objectum. If this objective has been presented by a judgment J_1, then in making this judgment J_1 one judges (*urteilt*) the objective; J_1 is a judgment (*Urteilung*) "of" the objective; the objective is J_1's immediate (*unmittelbar*) objective; and J_1 itself is the objective's immediate judgment. If a modal judgment J_2 is directed upon the objective, then in making this judgment J_2 one judges about (*beurteilt*) the objective; J_2 is a judgment (*Beurteilung*) "about" the objective; the objective is J_2's mediate (*mittelbar*) objective; and J_2 itself is the objective's mediate judgment. Furthermore, any judgment-about is also a judgment-of, and so it is for this second-level, modal judgment. If it is directed upon the objective :that a is ϕ:, then it will perhaps present the modal objective :that it is possible :that a is ϕ::. It will then have this objective as its own immediate objective, and it will be this objective's immediate judgment. And since the immediate judgment of an objective is the judgment that presents it for a possible judgment about that objective, it is also easy to imagine that a further judgment J_3 is directed upon the modal objective, and so on.

What is useful for our own orientation is not so much the possibility of realizing successively higher-level judgments, but rather two facts about judgment that are apparent from the foregoing. First, judgment has a twofold bearing on objects: always a bearing of *advertence* to an object presented to it (it differs from representation in this way) and always a bearing of *presentation* upon a state of affairs involving that object. Second, an *assumption* need not have occurred for one's judgment to advert to an objective; other things being equal, the presenting experience can just as well have been a *judgment* about an objectum. These two facts are especially interesting because they jointly entail that to judge is not simply to accept or reject, to believe or disbelieve, an objective. A judgment is not an attitude to an objective. This denial is implicit in the theory of judgmental presentation in chapter 3.

Real being, existence, is temporal. Whatever exists, exists at a certain time. But this does not imply that an objective of existence (as opposed to a modal objective, for example) is itself temporal in its being. For although the objective consists in the existence of the objectum at a certain time, it consists in the whole package, one might say. The time of existence is part of the package, and we may not date the internally dated existential objective so: "It was until 1453 :that the Eastern Empire existed until 1453:." Nor is the internal past tense necessary in order to retain the sense of temporality. A chronology of events of world significance does not bother with it. The Eastern Empire exists until 1453, and this seems satisfactory to the reader. The grammatical tensing of temporal being merely reflects the attention to one's own time of existence, Meinong thinks.[35] The position taken in the reduced-type portion of section 11 is that all objectives, including objectives of existence, are atemporal in their own being or non-being. Thus, objectives are nominally classifiable among ideal objects (although ideal objecta do not have much significance anymore), and their factuality is also called "subsistence."

Chapter 4 ("Die nächstliegenden Annahmefälle") resumes the discussion of assumptions, which have not been in view since the initial remarks in the second half of section 1.[6] The uniting principle of the cases of assuming discussed in this chapter is apparently just what Meinong says, namely that these cases are the most obvious ones. But more specifically, one can see that they are familiar life situations and that a reflective person would never be at a loss concerning what one wants and says in those situations. The general reader will be ready to help with his own intuitions about the role of assumptions in science, in children's play and the work of the artist, in the bad business of telling lies, in the asking of questions, and in our own experience with the work of the artist. Thus, understandably, work moves along fairly smoothly in these sections without any large-scale use of the machinery set up in chapter 3. One major revision is made. After the third paragraph of section 17, on the liar, Meinong deletes the remaining six paragraphs of the first-edition writing. Here he had maintained that the liar makes for himself an assumptive model of the judgment he wants to produce in another, and that he "represents" to himself the other's future judgment in this way. This sort of explanation was against the main "apsychological" current of Meinong's philosophical development, and Meinong is compelled to reinterpret the liar's assumption explicitly as the liar's envisaging the objective that he wants his listener to judge. Otherwise, in chapter 4 Meinong leaves the matter of assumed objectives implicit and contents himself with the simple and interesting motif of the first edition: that by assuming, one puts oneself in the position of someone who "really sees things in that way." Nothing new is attempted with this transposition motif in the second edition; it has its limits. But in its application to the life situations discussed in chapter 4, it is within those limits.

The present chapter appeared in the first edition (as the third chapter) well before the introduction of objectives (in the seventh chapter). Consequently, it would have been possible for the reader in 1902 to understand assuming as the cause of a disposition: Imitating belief or disbelief concerning represented, complex situations, one gets to think and feel somewhat like a person who really believes or disbelieves. But given the theory of objectives, one would think that the child at play, the liar, and the dramatic actor and his audience must each have a certain state of affairs in mind if he is to gain something from the situation. Except for the liar, Meinong does not insert this point in the second edition. He evidently thinks it sufficient to have shown that our assumptions allow us to occupy the position of someone different from ourselves, someone for whom the world is as we playfully or mendaciously or otherwise pretend it to be. The book's theses concerning objectives can be applied in chapter 4 without any distortive effect, however, notwithstanding the possibility that the thinking of that chapter originally developed from a dispositional approach.

Chapter 5 ("Das Objektiv und die Annahmen") presents the long-anticipated material on assumed objectives. The presentation follows the argumentative vein of chapter 2, although it now has chapter 3 behind it: When must judgment be ruled out as the means by which an objective has been appre-

hended? Whatever the cases, the objective of each must have been apprehended by means of an assumption. In section 20, Meinong states his basic
position, which is that the judgmental apprehending of objectives (he now uses
that word, 'Erfassen') is paralleled by an assumptive apprehending of them.
Objectives can also be apprehended by assumptions, and these assumptions
are affirmative or negative according to whether they apprehend positive or
negative objectives. Meinong makes short work of this matter, and the rest of
the section is devoted to Russell's and Marty's contentions (quite differently
conceived) that the objective is somehow represented. The writing in the section is new, and section 21 also begins with some new writing. It consists of a
generalizing of the distinction between judgment of an objective and judgment
about it. In general, an experience may "immediately approach" (apprehend,
present) an objective, or it may "mediately approach" the objective. In the latter case, it is a thought or an emotion directed upon the objective as something
already presented or apprehended. That sets the pattern for the chapter: When
is there an *intellectual* mediate approach (sections 21 and 22) that depends on
an assumptive immediate approach, and when is there an *emotional* mediate
approach to an objective (sections 24 and 25) that depends on an assumptive
immediate approach? In the rest of section 21, a block of writing on secondary
expression from the first-edition chapter on objectives is brought in, and it is
worth some remarks.[37]

After the new material on "approaching," Meinong gives a more explicit
account of the secondary expression of judgment than he did in chapter 2. He
uses a sentence with an existential "that"-clause for a paradigm sentence, but
let us take instead this sentence: 'I judge (am convinced, believe, think, surmise) that the surf is cold'. The main clause "primarily" expresses a judgment
as to the speaker's mental situation. This mental situation is itself a judgment,
but it is a judgment as to the temperature of the surf. This meteorological judgment is expressed by the "that"-clause. And taken literally, the main clause
appears to express not this meteorological judgment, but just the former, psychological judgment. But for all that, the psychological main clause in cases
like this is felt to express the same judgment as the "that"-clause expresses.
Very well, then; we make room for this fact. We say that besides what it primarily expresses, the psychological main clause "secondarily" expresses what
the "that"-clause primarily expresses. Such is the theory of secondary expression as applied to sentences.

The main-clause judgment of the starting paradigm does not mediately
approach an objective. The main clause is simply what one might call an
"act"-reexpression of a "content"-expressed apprehending judgment. Thus,
we have not yet found what we are looking for in this chapter. Note that the
psychological main clause appears to communicate nothing about the logical
quality of the judgment that it secondarily expresses. This job is done by the
"that"-clause. If the "that"-clause were negative instead, then the judgment
would be negative, but the main clause would still be 'I judge'. One might say

that it secondarily expresses simply the act of thinking, minus the affirmative or negative thought content, and that its proper negative 'I judge not' expresses a "nonact" rather than a negative act. Is the act of judgment indeterminate in respect of yes and no, then? It seems that way so far, but now some new sentences weaken that impression.

The sentence 'I doubt (do not believe) that the surf is cold' does seem to give us what we are looking for. Certainly no primarily expressed judgment—"The surf is cold"—is reexpressed by the clause of doubt. Then must not that clause secondarily express the mediate approach to an objective? The objective is presented by the thought "The surf is cold," and it is mediately approached by doubting it. But then the presenting thought cannot be a judgment; it must be an assumption.

Meinong looks back to the other psychological main clauses, the ones that seem to impute neither an affirmative nor a negative quality to the judgments they secondarily express. He surmises that the appearance of indeterminacy in their psychological connotation should not be taken seriously in most cases; in most cases 'I judge' and so forth deserve to be assigned an affirmative psychological connotation.[38] He does not describe an exceptional case. His policy thrusts 'I judge that the surf is not cold' as well as 'I doubt that the surf is not cold' into the same class with 'I doubt that the surf is cold', and the only opportunity to maintain the original secondary-expression view would be with the original sentence, now seen to be an *affirmative-affirmative* one: 'I judge that the surf is cold'. Meinong sacrifices this opportunity for the sake of uniformity of interpretation.[39] Even there, an objective is mediately approached.

Then before Meinong draws his general conclusion, he adds something that will make for a very strong conclusion. He says that third-person psychological main clauses may be handled the same way, even though one cannot make a distinction between primary and secondary expression in their case. He presumably means that a sentence such as 'X believes that the surf is cold' will be the report of a believing (as opposed to a disbelieving) attitude toward an assumed objective. Thus the conclusion: It is only by way of exception that a "that"-clause concerns a judged objective and not a judged-about objective.[40]

This causes assumptions to appear important, but it is at the same time a crumbling away of the linguistic evidence for judgmental presentation. Meinong is now practically prepared to translate all prima facie reports of judgment into reports of belief and disbelief in assumed objectives. But that is quite incompatible with the way objectives were introduced at the beginning of chapter 3. He has now thrust "judgment of" into a very equivocal position by momentarily letting "judgment about" predominate in his thought.

How is it even judgment-about, though? Is that really what is expressed by psychological main clauses that have an affirmative or a negative act connotation? They are quite different from the modal and modallike main clauses of chapter 3. A judgment of direct or reflex modality about an objective was supposed to present a higher-level, modal objective for another possible judgment-about. What does it present to believe or disbelieve an objective, to accept or reject it? And if it presents nothing, why should that acceptance or rejection nevertheless be called a *judgment* about the objective?

Ockham separated apprehension and judgment, and he regarded judgment as an act of assent or dissent to an apprehended proposition, or complex.[41] Bertrand Russell's attempt, in 1904, to interpret Meinong's theory of assumed and judged objectives in an Ockhamist way[42] required him to ignore Meinong's frequently expressed opinion that objectives were apprehended by means of judgments. There was some justification for this; a reader of the first edition might almost think that Meinong's opinion was an aberration, and that Meinong was finally getting on the right track in the sentence interpretations we have been discussing. In that edition Meinong had implicitly treated judgment's determinacy in respect of logical quality as a feature of the act, and he had denied that there was any properly judgmental content.[43] In a 1905 article, the picture of judgment's structure changed, and Meinong ascribed the logical determinacy of judgment to a properly judgmental content.[44] Regarded in this way, judgment's logical determinacy, and the logical determinacy of assuming, might be said to be an "is or isn't" in what one thinks, rather than a "yes or no" in the thinking.

With that, all intellectual experiences are act-indeterminate in respect of logical quality. Meinong removed the first-edition remark mentioned above. But he also removed (in the discussion of *negativa* in chapter 1) two remarks that misleadingly stress the act-indeterminacy of representation.[45] It is no longer significant that a representation is not a yes or no attitude toward its object; for neither is a judgment that.

One might then ask what assuming and judgment have in common that distinguishes them from representation? "Their object" begs the question, and "their content" confronts one with the problem of the perceptual elusiveness (*Wahrnehmungsflüchtigkeit*) of contents of experience.[46] Meinong can fall back upon his activity-passivity principle: Representations are passive, and assumptions as well as judgments are active.[47] The locus of the distinction would obviously be the act, not the content. Therefore, representation's passivity may be regarded as its empirical mark for inward perception, and the common empirical mark of judgment and assuming is their active character. To judge or assume is to do something. The equal treatment of judgment and assuming ultimately depends on this point as well as on the change that Meinong made in favor of a properly judgmental content in 1905. Without both of these adjustments in mind, one might still see some sense in understanding Meinong's judgments as attitudes to represented objectives, with assuming being the representing. Such was Russell's understanding in 1904.

No doubt there is sometimes a phenomenon that needs explaining when language confronts us with attitudes to objectives, as it does in sections 21 and 22.

But it can no longer be regarded as centrally important for the interpretation of Meinong's theory of judged and assumed objectives. As a side problem, it most likely could have been handled effectively in a chapter on pseudo-existence. One would suppose the following to be Meinong's approach. An attitude to an objective always presupposes an assumption as the presenting, immediately approaching experience. But the assumed objective must also be related back to some real or feigned judgment, rather as it is when we say, "According to some, I suppose, . . ." The objective then appears in that intentional capacity called "pseudo-existence."[48] It does not formally exist in the mind, and its intentional existence in the mind is no existence at all; but it does serve to explicate or express what is in the mind. The objectives that we accept or reject, concede or question, and so on, are like the objectives that we call true or probable. They are pseudo-existent objectives, objectives taken not in their formal character as states of affairs but in an intentional character as propositions. We disbelieve propositions.[49] The expression "propositional attitude" is therefore excellently suited to a Meinongean approach to the issue raised in sections 21 and 22, as long as it is understood that this is a side issue. Polemical section 23 may be taken at face value. Inasmuch as sections 24 and 25 concern the mediate approach to an objective in an emotional way, they lie beyond the intended scope of the present discussions.

Chapter 6 ("Annahmen bei Operationen an Objektiven") is a study of inference and hypothetical judgment.[50] The title reflects the two main changes that Meinong has made in its first-edition prototype (chapter 4, "Die Annahmeschlüsse"). First, the question of the linguistic or psychological nature of "premises," "conclusions," "antecedents," and "consequents" is settled in principle, if not systematically, by the insertion of references to objectives, e.g., "consequent-objectives." Second, hypothetical judgments are separated from the class of "assumption-inferences" (*Annahmeschlüsse*) and treated as a different sort of "operation"—an operation, too, and not a judgment.

According to Meinong, one infers when one makes a judgment "in view of" (*in Hinblick auf;* Findlay, "looking to"[51]) another of one's judgments.[52] (Alternatively, and more in accordance with the second edition, one might say that the inferrer is one who makes his judgment by looking to the objective that he has apprehended through another judgment.) Whatever it is that one judges "in view of," that is said to be the "motive." The judgment that is made in view of the motive is said to be the "motivated." The motivational relation first of all presents itself as the mediation of conviction. If some unaccountable funds are equal to a recent debt, then that (the judgment or the fact?) will cause one to think that the debt has not been paid; or in view of that, one will think this. Evidence as well as conviction is mediated. Seeing or realizing (*Einsehen*) that the funds are equal to the debt will cause one to see or realize that one has not paid the debt. With this use of 'Einsehen', we have the normal, not-too-strong and not-too-weak sense of 'Evidenz', the sense in which the judgment with evidence is at least a seeing or realizing, but not a seeing or realizing with perfect understanding or rational comprehension (*Verständnis*). In view of one judgment or its objective, one makes another, evident judgment. Meinong discusses mediated evidence of higher and lower degrees than that of the inferentially obtained insight (*Einsicht*) in our example, and he discusses it in connection with the appropriate degrees of conviction.

The concept of inference includes the idea of belief in the conclusion, but there is clearly something like an inference when in view of one assumption one makes another assumption. It is an operation of this sort, an assumption-inference, that constitutes one's grasp of the formal correctness of an argument, or the validity of its form. The "validity-experience" is thus an inference from suspended premises, as Meinong once thought. But this inference is no longer seen as a judgment regarding the relation between represented judgments, or even regarding the analogous connection between assumed objectives. Inferring, judgmental or assumptive, does not go that far; and it hardly consists in such a judgment, as Meinong once thought.[53]

If there is something inferential, when one makes an assumption "in view of" another assumption, so too is there something evidencelike in the conclusion-assumption.[54] This creates the puzzling prospect of evidence that is mediated, or communicated, by premises that are not evident. One explanation seems to lie in the fact that a judgment is sometimes made in view of premises that are merely assumed. The person who makes such an error is responding, or overresponding, to a derivative element of reasonableness in the consequent-assumption.

A hypothetical judgment is not a judgment as to a connection, but it is also not an assumption-inference. The conclusion of an assumption inference is unqualified, but also unconvinced. The consequent of a hypothetical judgment is convinced, but also qualified. It is a judgment, but one makes that judgment in view of, or by looking to, an assumed state of affairs. This antecedent-objective is said to restrict (*restringieren*) the objective that is judged. The antecedent-objective might be said to constitute a backdrop against which one apprehends a routinely or remotely possible objective in the manner a fact is apprehended, i.e., by judgment. But the use of figurative expressions is liable to make the restricted-consequent theory of 1910 appear more innovative and momentous than it actually is. Up to a certain point, the theory is just a commentary on the interchangeability of sentences like 'If an etching is tinted, it is a spoilt etching' and 'An etching that is tinted is a spoilt etching.' The advantage of the "if"-clause over the "which"-clause would seem to be just that it isolates linguistically the objective one must assume.[55] But if the association with categorical judgment makes it less of a mystery why the antecedent-objective should be said to "restrict" the consequent-objective, it also makes it seem puzzling that a so-called hypothetical judgment should not be a judgment at all. At any event, it is not thought to be a judgment; Meinong regards it instead as an operation involving a judgment. Both hypothetical judgment and inferring are operations, and they do not go as far as the judgmental apprehending of connections between objectives, a separate matter that Meinong discusses at the end of the chapter.

Chapter 7 ("Annahmen beim Erfassen des Präsentierten. Das Meinen") consists of an old and a new explanation of the phenomenon of intentionality, understood in the specific sense associated with representation.[56] Meinong does not use this word, but it will do at the outset to cover both his old notion of the objectivity (*Gegenständlichkeit*) of representation and his new notion of intending (*Meinen*). Thus, the point of the chapter, expressed negatively, is that intentionality does not appear as a phenomenon until the representation is taken as the basis for apprehending something.

The expression 'to apprehend' ('erfassen') did not gain any serious or systematic use until later in the first edition, in connection with objectives. But in connection with representational objects, it was already clear in the first-edition chapter ("Zur Gegenständlichkeit des Psychischen," reproduced in sections 33 through 37) that Meinong was working with a generalized concept of perceptual apprehension, i.e., a concept comprehending not just perception but any *knowing of a thing by becoming aware of its existence*. It was therefore the forerunner of Meinong's present concept of the (mediate) apprehension of an objectum in an (immediately apprehended) objective of being. Thus, the epistemological tone of sections 34 through 37 must be taken seriously. The apprehending of an object was thought to be accomplished only through an evident or (internally) justified (*berechtigte*) affirmative existential judgment. Such a judgment "transcended" to something actual (*wirklich*); a similar judgment of subsistence exhibited "quasi-transcendence" to a "quasi-actuality." Although the second case need not be mentioned again here, both cases can be comprehended by maintaining that the paradigm of objectivity (*Gegenständlichkeit*) in the first edition was the cognitive apprehension of an entity (*Seiendes*) through an evident affirmative thetic judgment. Meinong adopts the retrospective title, the "being-view," for his approach to intentionality in sections 34 through 37. Only the inclusion of subsistence prevented him from calling it the "actuality (*Wirklichkeit*) view." The being that he had in mind was what he would later call factual (*tatsächlich*) being, i.e., factual existence or factual subsistence. The insistence on being as a medium of apprehension for objecta never drops out of Meinong's philosophy, but the emphasis on the cognitive awareness of factual being does drop out. Six years later, in 1910, Meinong speaks of the abandoned emphasis somewhat confusingly as the being-view.

There are occasional allusions to a definition of the notion of an object (*Gegenstandsgedanke*), or a broadening of this notion, and one is at a loss to see where the initial definition occurred, though it must have occurred in the present section 34. From a remark in the 1899 essay "Über Gegenstände höherer Ordnung,'' and from twenty lines deleted from the end of the present section 36,[57] it appears that Meinong really did think that he was defining and redefining the notion of an object in sections 34 through 37, as well as defining and redefining the notion of the objectivity (*Gegenständlichkeit*) of mental phenomena. Objectivity was cognitive transcendence to an entity, and an object was a known entity. That is what Meinong was willing to start with, in the first half of section 34, and that is what lies behind the robust epistemological realism with which the being-view begins. One does feel that something is being overstated in order to elicit a paradox, and that some sort of immanent object is in the works. It is therefore a little surprising that the being-view ultimately sticks to its emphasis on factual being and cognitive apprehension, and that only the cheapest accommodations are found for immanent objects and nontranscending experiences. But let us see how that worked. Perhaps an example of our own will not be misleading as a picture of the transition that occurs in the second half of section 34.

X judges that there is an *A*. His friend Y judges that there is no *A*. In fact, there is no *A*. Therefore, neither of the two apprehends an *A* by means of his judgment. Even after Meinong's remarks on the reliability of evident existential judgments, one hesitates to maintain that X's judgment *cannot* be evident. Nevertheless, as long as there is no *A,* then X's judgment cannot be said to transcend. He does not know of an *A* by means of his judgment. Neither does Y, by means of his judgment. But this is because a negative thetic judgment does not apprehend. It waves away or dismisses, one might say. In sum, if either judgment has an object, it does not have it by cognitively transcending to that object.

It does seem that each judgment has an object. Is it then an immanent object? Yes, one gathers that from three short observations, one near the end of section 36 and two that have been deleted from the beginnings of the present sections 43 and 44 in the following chapter (chapter 8).[58] But one can also see from those passages that by 1902 the immanent object had become a very attenuated sort of thing for Meinong. It is presumably the theoretical observers, Meinong and his readers, who "assign" (*zuschreiben*) that object to X's or Y's judgment as the entity to which the judgment does, after all, transcend (we feign that it is an evident affirmative judgment).[59] Or adopting an approach that is fictive only in a looser sense, we assign to the judgment that entity to which it *would* transcend if it *were* an evident affirmative judgment. The immanent object is therefore conceived as a fictive or would-be known, theoretically assignable to any judgment out of respect for the manifestly objective bearing of the judgment. But this fictive approach (in either its hypothetical or its properly fictive form) raises problems. Meinong gives his own version of these problems at the end of section 34. But if we were to tailor these problems to what he is actually able to accomplish, they would sound this way: What title does a judgment have to an object that it would apprehend only by being a *different* judgment? What is the actual *phenomenon* of intentionality that the theorist is marking with his "honorary object"? The work begins in section 35.

It is primarily in representations that we must look for the phenomenon of intentionality that Meinong calls objectivity (*Gegenständlichkeit*). Representations permit a dispositional way of speaking that is not suited to judgment. Any representation is so constituted that under certain circumstances (not necessarily realizable) it might serve as the basis for an evident affirmative judgment (of existence or subsistence). The foundation of this disposition, alluded to in our "so constituted," is the representational content.[60] In virtue of it, any representation is at least potentially objective. But as a phenomenon, or as the manifestly objective bearing of a representation, objectivity is actual objectivity. At first this suggests that the phenomenon appears only when the representation does in fact serve as the basis for the apprehension of an entity, i.e., an existent or a subsistent. But the theoretical demand quickly proves less stringent. Any affirmative judgment (thetic) will suffice as the cause of actual objectivity. And judgment is not even necessary. There is a manifestly objective bearing even in imaginative representations. We can see that this requires something in addition to a representation; one can give oneself up passively to representation, and experience the loss of the phenomenon.[61] The differential cause of the phenomenon is an activity; in this case it is not judgment but assuming.

Assuming thus appears in the middle of section 36 as the slightest sufficient cause of actual objectivity. Meinong then capitalizes on it for all cases of actual objectivity. If we may again introduce some expressions of our own (in quotes), the matter can be handled fairly quickly. (With appropriate changes, the following remarks will apply also to assumptions and judgments of subsistence.) The cognitive apprehension of an entity is an evident conviction, but it has an affirmative existential "core assumption."[62] That alone is the source of the phenomenon of actual objectivity in the representation. X's conviction is mistaken and presumably nonevident, but it too has that core assumption, and that alone, etc. Y's negative judgment or conviction could scarcely contain an affirmative core assumption, but it does follow upon an affirmative "preassumption."[63] A negative judgment somehow arises out of an affirmative assumption, and the way it does so is somehow analogous to adding a "not" to an affirmative sentence in order to make a negative statement. One can see that what interests Meinong here, in 1902, is merely to locate some affirmative experience that he can feign or hypothesize as an apprehending experience, out of respect for a phenomenon of actual objectivity. He is not specifically interested in maintaining that when Y says, "There is no *A*," Y means "that one," i.e., one that must have been intended through an affirmative assumption. Whatever might lie in the future, at least in these 1902 passages Meinong looks upon an affirmative preassumption essentially as the antecedent raw material for a negative judgment, and not as the antecedent targeting of something for dismissal. In any event, with core assumptions and preassumptions now in view, one might recall that "bare assumptions" also appear in chapter 7, turning mere imagery into daydreaming. In general, all actual objectivity is conceived as the result of assuming.

It can be proved that Meinong was not abandoning the notion of feigning at the end of section 34, but was instead looking for a way to give a better rendition of it. Then let us take up the notion again this way: What mental phenomenon should we and Meinong be considering when we feign that it is an evident and affirmative judgment? Is it still the subject's (e.g., X's or Y's) nonapprehending judgment? No, it seems that the observer should be considering the assumption that precedes or is contained in that judgment.[64] The assumption is actual. Thus the core of the feigned knowing is already present in X or Y. It is not the cognitive misfire or dismissal that we feign as a cognitive apprehension; it is the affirmative existential assumption. We are not feigning that it is something else; we are feigning that it is the core of an evident conviction, which is how we get to the fictive or would-be knowing and, of course, to the fictive or would-be known. So much for one of the two questions we raised. In retrospect, one can see that Meinong's opening remarks on the everyday miracle of cognitive transcendence served to discourage objection from the side of those who would maintain that a false judgment might still have the highest a posteriori justification or evidence to it. If this objection could be raised, then one could further ask whether the concept of a transcendent object *was* correlative with the concept of an evident affirmative (existential) judgment. In 1902 Meinong was supposing as much.

By considering affirmative existential assuming as the normal adjunct to a representation, Meinong was also able to answer the question about the nature of the phenomenon, the apparent "having" of an object that encourages the theoretical observer to "assign" an object. It is in the first instance the actual objectivity of the representation. Without saying anything to suggest that the change is significant, Meinong replaces the expression 'actual objectivity' with 'directedness to an object' after the middle of section 36. When he then says that affirmative assuming *is* directedness to an object (*auf einen Gegenstand Gerichtetsein*), one may understand him first as saying that assuming *is* the actual objectivity of a representation, and then that a core assumption or a preassumption *is* the objectivity of a judgment. The new expression nevertheless carries a slightly stronger connotation than 'actual objectivity', and when one is told that a representation is directed to an object by the same assumption mentioned in the last paragraph, it seems reasonable to raise the following objection. If no *A* exists, then the entity that X and Y would under certain circumstances cognitively apprehend is an entity in name only, and there is in fact nothing standing opposite X's or Y's present representation as an object of it.

Meinong's own critique of the being-view in section 38 begins at that point, and it actually does not go much further. There is not much detail in it, and the terminology is in some respects foreign to that of 1902. It is rather as if Meinong had become disused to thinking the way he once thought. He rejects the possibility of softening the starting definition of objectivity as cognitive transcendence. Here the object that a judgment "had" was an entity. Once one moves away from representations that have their objects in this way to representations that have their objects fictively, one gets representations without objects. The being-view was recondite, without question; and Meinong does not show the slightest inclination to get involved with it again. He says that when he thinks of unclouded human happiness or the perpetual motion machine, it is no less obvious to him that his thoughts are directed to "something" than it would be if the object were some everyday piece of reality (*Wirklichkeit*). The argumentative intent of that remark will probably become clear by itself in the following attempt to re-create the thought behind Meinong's movement from the being-view of objectivity into a certain beyond-being view of it.

The independence of so-being from being.[65] The third section of Ernst Mally's "Untersuchungen zur Gegenstandtheorie des Messens" (1904) contains a statement of his principle of the independence of so-being from being. This principle might have been known to Mally's teacher (Meinong) for a year. According to it, the subsistence of an object's so-being does not depend on the subsistence of its being. Significantly, for those who are interested in contrasting Meinong and Mally, the student equates an object's so-being (*die Gegenstandsnatur*) with its being an object (*Gegenstandsein*), and it is fairly obvious that Mally thinks so-being constitutes an object as "something."

The logical priority of the object.[66] This is already implicit in the being-view of 1902, but the narrow assertion of it drives Meinong into the compensating measures we have been examining. According to it, the object is a *prius* for apprehension. It is (already) there, or (*vor*)*gegeben,* for the apprehending. The apprehending (at least in the case of objecta) always consists in a thetic "There is (*es gibt*) . . ." that acknowledges the object's *Gegebensein,* its being there or objectively given. Equivalently, one may speak of the object's *Vorgegebenheit,* its advance thereness or advance objective givenness. To apprehend is always actively to get at what there already is or "is." The priority of the object is said to be "logical," presumably out of regard for the priority of timeless or temporally posterior objects. The least one may infer from Meinong's position on the logical priority of the object is that when there is no apprehension and nothing is "got at," then the hypothetical and deductive thinking out of so-being has no *prius* upon which it can work. There is nothing to think about. In interesting contrast to Mally, Meinong thinks that whatever the *Vorgegebenheit* of an object is (it seems, after all, that it is not the fact of an object's existing), it constitutes the object as "something."

From immanence to quasi-being.[67] In the writings of 1899 and 1902, Meinong had resorted to the notion of immanence or pseudo-existence when he was faced with the prospect of an object whose being thus and so was unquestionable, even though its existence was questionable. Even the decadent immanent object of 1902 is a *posterius,* although it no longer exists intentionally in thought. It is still dependent on thought, in the sense that one must determine "whither" the thought tends before one says that it tends "thither," to this or that would-be piece of actuality.

Until the true situation is worked out from the 1902 and 1903 materials that have not been published, one can only suppose that Meinong, confronted with Mally's nonexistent describables, detected not the slightest stirring of reflection upon his own experience, e.g., as he made judgments of so-being about the perpetual motion machine or an omniscient human. In this situation, I believe, it is characteristic of Meinong to reason as follows: Since the object under consideration got there without any reflection upon thought, it must have got there by being apprehended as a *prius.*

Meinong now (in section 38) wishes to rectify things by allowing that a nonentity may be apprehended, and that it, too, is a *prius* and therefore "something." He does *not* wish to discuss feigning and immanency! But no one shrinks from confessing to a prejudice in favor of actuality, and Meinong readily admits to that error.[68]

But the reconsideration originally went a little deeper, at or shortly after the time *Assumptions* was first published. Wherein lies this priority, or *Vorgegebenheit* of the object, if it does not lie in existence or subsistence? Must it not lie in a third kind of being? Or if that sounds too strong, say something being-like. But the stronger (or stronger-sounding) terminology seemed acceptable, and Meinong called this third kind of being *"Quasisein,"* ("quasi-being"). If the *Vorgegebenheit* of objects was not existence or subsistence, then it was quasi-being.

Rejection of quasi-being. The 1904 essay "Über Gegenstandstheorie" is the source of much of our information, but it also contains an argument (seemingly final) against the quasi-being postulate.[69] Quasi-being could have no opposite; nothing could lack it. Consequently, it falls out of analogy with the two recognized kinds of being. It could not really be something beinglike. This is the last time Meinong used the word 'Quasisein', but the concept under another name kept applying for readmission and eventually secured it in 1917.

Assumed being as a substitute for quasi-being. The priority of the object is up for recharacterization, but Meinong cannot and never will characterize it otherwise than as something beinglike (*etwas Seinsartiges*). In the 1904 essay, the matter is suspended. In the fourth section of the essay, Meinong finds a temporary residence for *Vorgegebenheit* in assumed objectives, or mere objectives of being, taken apart from their factuality. Meinong is not as explicit about the relation of objectives to apprehending as he is in our present edition of *Assumptions.* But he has made enough psychological observations already, by the end of the fourth section, for us to be sure that the unfactual and merely assumed existence of the perpetual motion machine is doing duty as that objectum's *Vorgegebenheit,* which must always be recognized in an apprehending.

The beyond-being status of the pure object.[70] That "pure object" expression in the 1904 essay is apparently a concession to the Mallyean way of looking at an object, viz. regarding it as the intersection node of objectives of so-being. Meinong is, of course, in a concessive mood because of his failure to find a satisfactory characterization of *Vorgegebenheit.* In the 1904 essay Meinong seems to allow that factual objectives of so-being not only constitute the *Gegenstandsnatur* but constitute the very business of *Gegenstandsein,* or being an object. Consequently, although Meinong cannot appeal to any analogue of existence or subsistence to root the object beyond being and non-being, the pure object nevertheless "stands beyond being and non-being." This beyond-being standing or status he calls *Aussersein.* The word is rendered as "absistence" in our English text, but the use of the latter word will be avoided until there is a chance to say something in its favor. The *Aussersein* concept is a typical Meinongean makeshift concept. In content it does not go beyond what the Mallyean principle of independence permits one to say (if one also accepts that so-being is constitutive of objecthood): The merest shred of factual so-being establishes an object, and this object is thereby "something" independently of the eventualities of factual and nonfactual existence. But the *Aussersein* concept is designed to fit its content rather loosely and to allow room for return to a more venturesome way of thinking. The way back to quasi-being is still impassable because of the lack of a negative. If and when Meinong circumvents that difficulty, he will not need to dust off the word 'Quasisein'; the word 'Aussersein' will do quite well. And, of course, it will also be a matter of words if Meinong finds that 'something beinglike' ('ein Seinsartiges') is a better expression than 'a third kind of being'. Twice in the present edition of *Assumptions,* Meinong experiments with a positive interpretation of *Aussersein,* one that would reidentify *Vorgegebenheit* with some ontological status, and twice he turns away just as he did in the 1904 essay, i.e., because of the lack of a negative. It is worth noting, then, that the concept of *Aussersein* that we have in 1910 not only goes back to 1904 but goes ahead to 1917, three years before Meinong's death.

Why is Sein the only window on Aussersein? We know that it is only "mere" being that is assumed in the apprehending of objecta; but why should even that be necessary if what one is apprehending is beyond being? If the golden mountain would not be more of an object by existing, then why should one have to look at it through its assumed existence? Why not a judgment of *Aussersein?* (That possibility interests Meinong, too.) The answer is probably that an attenuated judgment of real being was the best that Meinong could come up with, in lieu of a real judgment of attenuated being. Either way, by the *Seinsannahme* or by the *Ausserseinsurteil,* there would be an acknowledgment of the objectum's being there or objective givenness, but the latter way seemed impracticable because of the senselessness of a negative *Ausserseinsurteil*. Because of the strong hold that the principle of priority had over his thoughts, Meinong would always be inclined to regard the thetic "There is *(es gibt)* . . ." as an indispensable apprehending protocol. The fact that he understands it existentially results from his inability to find a weaker sense for it. Of course, when one gets away from the problem of apprehension, it is easy to pretend that one has that weaker sense, and to say that "there are" objects that neither exist nor subsist and to explain this as it was explained in 1904. The "There is" of thetic apprehension cannot be handled so easily.

The rendition of 'Aussersein' as 'absistence'. Such is our policy in the following English text of *Assumptions*. Whatever legal or other acceptation the obsolete English word might have had, it is obviously comparable to 'ex-sistere' and 'sub-sistere' in formation, and the root sense is plain. It was thought to be enough if this sense of "standing away" afforded some slight help and no hindrance to one who has anything substantial of Meinong's writing at hand. Semantically, this does not look like an unreasonable expectation. Syntactically, the case is much stronger. The only way to follow Meinong's "Aussersein" through its grammatical changes without loss of conciseness and consistency is with 'absisting', 'an absistent', and 'absistence'—the last of which, like 'Aussersein', can signify a domain as well as a status, the "beyond-being status," as it has occasionally been called here.

The concept of thetic apprehension, freed of the specifically epistemic note that it contained in the being-view and associated with the theory of objectives, is the new concept of "intending by way of being" *(Seinsmeinen)*. Let us turn to that now. In the last section of Chapter 7 it is discussed merely as "intending" *(Meinen)*.

While intending by way of being seems to be the kind of intending that comes closest to the notion of a mental reference, Meinong's later writings suggest that it is also the only authentic apprehending experience. Thus it is what —an apprehending reference? Willy-nilly we are faced with the concept of a mental directedness to something that does *not* presuppose the apprehension of the thing, but instead *is* the apprehension of the thing. It is true that Meinong seems to delegate 'fastening upon' ('Ergreifen') to carry an apprehending sense. It is also true that Meinong introduces the verb 'meinen' by speaking of its directional sense. But any attempt to separate positively the concept of *Meinen* or intending, from the concept of a fastening upon something is futile. Say that there is not an intending by way of being, which has the better claim to being called apprehension, but an intending by way of so-being *(Soseinsmeinen)*. One must still look at it as a fastening upon something, even though one would now think of the *Ergreifen* more as "grasping the type of thing which is meant" rather than as an authentic *(eigentlich)* apprehension of something of that type.

As far as *Seinsmeinen* is concerned, we have the support of one unequivocal passage. If it is someone's *second thought* about a thing portrayed in a picture (or an event portrayed in a legend) that the object is actual, then the thought is not an intending thought.[71] It is too late for that, because the intending was accomplished in the thought by which the subject fastened upon the object. The second thought is merely a consideration addressed to the object. Thus, we must be very careful about this "mental referring" of Meinong's. The objectum is intended by way of being insofar as it is mediately apprehended for "consideration," one might say; and the judgments or assumptions that constitute that consideration do not constitute the intending.

'Ergreifen', or 'fastening upon', just carries a more explicit allusion to getting at an objectum by framing it in an objective. This is called "mediate apprehension" by Meinong. One apprehends an objectum mediately insofar as one apprehends it through an objective. (As ever, the pretheoretical paradigm for this is perception: One becomes aware of a thing by becoming aware of its existence.) Unless the objectum should somehow be an incomplete object serving as an aid to apprehension (e.g., "something black and heavy") it will itself be mediately apprehended by means of an affirmative judgment or assumption of being. The objective of being will be immediately apprehended through that assumption or judgment. Such is the apprehending side of the apprehending reference called "intending by way of being." Incidentally, 'Ergreifen' is rarely used by Meinong after the present edition of *Assumptions*. After 1910 Meinong uses 'Meinen' even when he is primarily looking at intending as an apprehending rather than as a having-in-mind.

Chapter 7 is a chapter on apprehension rather than presentation (*Präsentation*). There is no hint anywhere, either in the old or the new writing, that the representational content might fall short in its function of predefining the character of the objectum that is to be apprehended. That is a presenting function. The adequacy of unaided representation in performing this function is not questioned in chapter 7. What is questioned is whether a representation alone, with merely the idea of an *A* as its content, could ever amount to the thinking of an *A*. The answer is no, of course. This negative answer is not a comment about the content. (It is assumed that the idea is *good* enough.) It is a comment about the act. A representation is passive.

Meinong's concept of apprehension becomes stricter in his later writings. The mediate apprehension of an object in an objective of *being* is the only authentic (*eigentlich*)[72] apprehension of an object, and *Soseinsmeinen,* or (as I have described it for lack of anything better) "grasping the type of thing that is meant," is assigned to the side of presentation. This, too, might help establish the contrast between chapter 7 and the chapter we shall now consider.

Chapter 8 ("Annahmen bei Komplexen. Weiteres über das Meinen") is ostensibly concerned with the representation of complexes.[73] These are higher-order objects whose *inferiora* are their constituent parts. The parts stand in a certain relation to one another. They coincide with the terms of that relation. To apprehend those terms in that relation is, in effect, to apprehend the complex. The two types of objects of higher order are therefore closely associated. The relation is not a constituent part of the complex, but it is a part of it; the idea of it is a part of the corresponding content of the representation. But here we strike the deeper and more important vein of chapter 8. Contrasting it to chapter 7, Meinong could just as well have entitled the old chapter ("Das Erfassen von Gegenständen höherer Ordnung") "The Presenting of What is to be Apprehended," for the problem of correspondence or adequation between content and object is seen everywhere, and this is a problem of presentation. The real theme of chapter 8 is not the apprehension of objects of higher order (1902) or the apprehension of complexes (1910), but the active versus the passive predefinition of the character of an objectum. Does the representational content ever really do its job in establishing that "this, not that," will be apprehended? Not so often, says Meinong. If by "this" you mean a colored shape, then yes; the content does its job. But in other cases assuming must supplement the representational content. Why is that? And how does the supplementation take place?

Sections 39 through 44 represent the remaining first half of the 1902 chapter. The two most prominent cases that Meinong works with are both liable to make one wonder if one has understood what a complex is. The simpler case is that of a red cross (39-41), and the more complicated case (42-44) is that of A and B (example of two colors) in relation R (example of *differentness*).

The red cross is understood to be a complex. Between the color and the shape obtains some relation. Meinong does not consider the relation in the case of the red cross. Therefore, it must be a simpler case in this sense: It is not an analytically transparent complex like A and B in relation R. It does not give one a chance to show that relations require thetic affirmation, not just representation. But one has a chance to show in effect that a color requires predicative affirmation and denial, not just representation in a cross shape. The disparity of these two projects undermined the 1902 chapter.

A red cross may be represented either intuitively or nonintuitively (*anschaulich, unanschaulich*).[74] The corresponding forms of designation, 'red cross' and 'cross that is red', suggest that there might be some difference between the object that is represented intuitively and the one that is represented nonintuitively. Later on, in the new part of the chapter, Meinong admits that they are not the same object.[75] Let us use that admission now. An intuitively represented red cross is a colored shape. A nonintuitively represented red cross is a cross (of some sort) that is (somehow) red. Of the representational contents themselves, Meinong says that they are composed (*zusammengesetzt*) in the instance of the intuitively represented red cross, which he calls simply the "red cross," and juxtaposed (*zusammengestellt*) in the instance of the nonintuitively represented "cross that is red."

The simpler, prima facie nonrelational case is the one that admits intuitiveness as well as nonintuitiveness. Here (in section 41) Meinong is able to resume briefly the topic of *negativa*. One cannot intuitively represent a *negativum*. Here is an improvised example. In a representational content, the ideas of a cross and a yellow color are composed (*zusammengesetzt*) into the idea of a yellow cross. But this colored shape will in the first instance be apprehended merely as that, a yellow cross. It will be no more of a nonred cross than it is a nonblue cross. Again, one cannot nonintuitively represent a *negativum* distinct from a *positivum* if there is really nothing but representing. The representation that prefigures a nonred cross is the same in content as the one that prefigures a red cross. The difference lies outside the representation in the logical quality of an accompanying judgment or assumption. The parts of the representational content may well be merely juxtaposed (*zusammengestellt*), and this is the necessary and sufficient condition for a nonintuitive representation. One may call it the representation of a cross that is not red; but there is also the cross that is red, and the representational content by itself will do just as well for that, the *positivum*.

Such is the tenor of Meinong's remarks on the simpler case. The more complicated case, as he now calls it, is taken up in sections 42 through 44. The thought is not continuous with that of the preceding sections. Meinong does not attempt a more detailed account of the simpler case, although that would have been a natural step for the 1902 edition. A red cross and a nonred cross were complexes. What was the relation in each complex, and how did judgment (or assuming) work with respect to the one relation and the other? In deferring this question and moving on to what he now calls the more complicated case, Meinong was, in at least one sense, giving himself a stay of execution. He evidently hoped that it would put him in a stronger position if he could develop the notion of the complexion or interrelation of parts in connection with some obvious case of a relation.

The findings in the more complicated case (sections 42 through 44) are negative. No amount of mere ordering or augmenting of the ideas of a constituent A, a constituent B, and a relation R will by itself adequate the representation to the object "A and B in relation R." Meinong rejects the recourse to a metarelation that ties R to A and B. Roughly, the notion is that as soon as this metarelation or tie of betweenness had been admitted, with R as one of its terms and A and B as the other two, the betweenness of this betweenness would begin to plead its own cause, and there would be no end to the ties one would have to represent in order to represent the complex. In 1899 Meinong had dismissed this ligamental regress as a paper problem,[76] but now, in a 1902 passage, he shows that he has changed his mind.[77]

"A and B in relation R" is a curious way of naming a complex. It is undoubtedly intended to exhibit the complex analytically, to show its works. But it is also a way in which something that is not a complex could come in. Perhaps there is no trouble about X and Y in a relation of musical accompaniment. That would be the XY duet, the complex. But what about green and yellow in a relation of differentness?[78] What sort of complex could that be? It is not at all apparent that the terms of a relation must coincide with the parts of a complex, although the converse might be readily admitted.[79] It is possible that Meinong was determined to risk such an objection as this, and that he was in fact regarding the ideal relation of differentness as a means of solving the problem of *negativa*—i.e., however awkward it might look as a principle of complexion. 'This bell is different from that one' is a relational sentence. On the face of it, 'This is different from a bell' is a quite different sort of sentence. But mightn't something be a nonbell in virtue of some relation?

After the negative findings that are reproduced in sections 42 through 44 came the four last sections that have now been deleted. Here Meinong pursued the subject of "*A* and *B* in relation *R*" instead of adopting the logically predicative approach to synthetic presentation that we see in the new sections 45 and 46. Judgment made its appearance, but not categorical judgment. The judgment was thetic judgment, specifically an affirmative judgment of existence or subsistence. (As a substitute for it assuming was allowed, even though Meinong had not yet appointed assuming as an apprehending experience.) It was directed primarily to the relation *R* (represented) and secondarily to the *inferiora* (also represented) between which *R* existed or subsisted. The judgment was not on the order of "Blue and green are different"; it was more like "Differentness obtains between blue and green." Meinong was apparently persisting with a Brentanoan legacy in this case, namely the disinclination to let any fundamental analysis hinge on the concept of categorical judgment. By a thetic judgment alone, it seemed, one should be able to represent blue and green in the relation of differentness, or again, *A* and *B* in relation *R*. Such, in its barest essentials, was Meinong's nonpredicative approach to synthetic presentation.[80]

Meinong supposed that in principle he had also explained how one represented *A* and *B* *not* in the relation *R,* since his previous example could also be taken as blue and green *not* in a relation of *sameness.* He therefore anticipated that if his present success could be transferred to the nonintuitive representation of a cross that is red, it would be all over but for a few strokes of the pen as regards the representation of a cross that is *not* red.[81]

Then how was the *positivum* nonintuitively represented? How did assuming or judgment assist in the nonintuitive representation of a red cross? Meinong's foraging expedition into *A* and *B* in relation *R* had not helped him. He still was not ready to answer this question. The original state of affairs showed itself for what it was: There really did not seem to be any relation between a cruciform thing and its shape. But might there not be a predicative tie (*prädikative Verknüpfung*)?[82] Meinong declined this option, no doubt because "ties" had caused him enough problems earlier with regard to relations and their terms. When he rejected the predicative tie, one could see from the wording of it that he was recalling the 1899 idea of the logical monotony or subject matter indifference of metarelational ties.[83]

But then the project that Meinong had hurried to announce in the section on *negativa* became a fatality. What hope could there be for showing the role of assuming in the representation of a nonred cross, if not even the "simpler" case of a *red* cross would yield to his chosen approach? And one could see that the intolerable being-view had prevented Meinong from introducing assumptions in a straightforward way. The closest he could get to his project was to show what cognitive judgment could do, and then to suggest that something similar was accomplished by assuming. But not even the knowing of relations between terms will work when one of the terms is a property and the other is the bearer of the property.

In the new last sections 45 and 46, it is assumptions that figure as the agents of synthetic presentation. And it is categorical assumptions, i.e., assumptions of so-being. The thetic, "Differentness subsists between blue and green" approach is given up and the categorical "Blue and green are different" approach is taken. Affirmative judgments and assumptions of being are indisputably important in Meinong's twentieth-century writings; nevertheless, the being of relations is dissolved as an integral topic, and it is replaced with the relational so-being of the terms. And this is just a topic of so-being. Monadic so-being, e.g., a cross's being red, no longer hangs back until things are settled with relations. It steps forward as the truly simplest case, and polyadic so-being now trails after it as a mere complication.

Because the apprehending of complexes and relations has become a subtopic in the theory of intending, no further consideration will be given to it here. Meinong takes up that topic again, however, once he has established the principles of the new theory. It should also be mentioned that the following remarks are concentrated on the concept of the more remote object (*entfernterer Gegenstand*) to an extent that is not characteristic of sections of 45 and 46. Again, the contrast between the concrete individual as an ultimate object (*Zielgegenstand*) and the more remote object as an auxiliary object (*Hilfsgegenstand*) is barely implicit in these sections, although stressed in the following remarks. Conceivably it might have been better to reckon with what we have, in sections 45 and 46, instead of letting *Möglichkeit und Wahrscheinlichkeit* (1915) regulate the interpretation of these sections; however, the latter course has been followed.[84]

All intending involves the immediate apprehension of an objective and the mediate apprehension of another object in or through that objective. (Typically it is an objectum; let us disregard the exceptions.) In intending by way of so-being, one apprehends an objectum as the primary material, or subject, of one or more objectives of so-being.[85] The objective of so-being establishes the fragmentary substantive character of an objectum, e.g., as something that is red, or as something that is not red.

Intending by way of so-being, as far as the present remarks are concerned, can be regarded as the result of amplifying the presenting function of the representational content with an assumption of so-being. There is always an intending by way of so-being when imagination or perception brings a concrete, many-faceted individual under consideration. Even if we demand merely adequacy of the representation in its presenting function and are willing to leave the activity of apprehending to existential judgment or assuming, the concrete individual is still out of range for the representation. It cannot present something that is red in a way that leaves a place or space for ulterior determinations. It can only present red or a red, an object that may or may not be abstract,[86] but that in either case is just as incomplete as the character in which it is apprehended when one thinks "There's that." Meinong calls such an object a "proximate" object (*nächster Gegenstand*).[87]

If an affirmative judgment or assumption of being follows directly upon a representation, then contrary to what one is led to believe in chapter 7, it will be merely the proximate object that is intended by way of being.[88] If it does not suit one's purposes to have, say, a colored shape under consideration, then one will have to resort to the amplified presenting function we are now considering. In intending by way of so-being, the proximate object is passed over or exchanged for a more remote object (*entfernterer Gegenstand*). If the proximate object is the color red, then by an affirmative assumption of so-being one will apprehend "something that is red," a more remote object. At the same time, one will also generally intend red things by way of their so-being. If an intending by way of being then occurs, one will mediately apprehend something that is red, and not the more remote object "something that is red." Nor did one intend this object by way of so-being; one intended with it. It was an auxiliary object (*Hilfsgegenstand*, 1915), not an ultimate object (*Zielgegenstand*, 1915).

The more remote object is an incomplete object (*unvollständiger Gegenstand*, 1915), i.e., an object that is incompletely determined in its so-being. In the foregoing example, it is merely "something that is red"; but it is not "something that is merely red." If the more remote object may be said to be intended, despite the policy adopted in the last paragraph, then the matter may be put as follows. The more remote object *may* be intended closed (*geschlossen gemeint*) to ulterior determinations in the latter way, but in its present capacity of auxiliary object it must be intended open (*offen gemeint*).[89] It must contain the place or space for those determinations. Like the proximate object, the sheerly incomplete object, "something that is merely red," lacks that place or space.

To the limited extent that intending by way of so-being qualifies as an apprehending rather than a presenting function (1915), it does so by the active character of the assuming that constitutes it. It presents something that is red to be apprehended by way of being, or it predefines the character of what is to be apprehended that way. Yet Meinong quite commonly speaks of the "apprehension" of the more remote object by way of so-being, and I followed this usage with regard to "something that is red." At one point (1915) Meinong speaks of intending by way of so-being as an "apprehending presentation," although his eventual term for it is 'mediate presentation' ('mittelbare Präsentation').[90]

It is apparent that besides pure *Seinsmeinen,* in which one apprehends the proximate object, there is a *Seinsmeinen* that depends on the apprehension of the more remote object by *Soseinsmeinen.* This is the normal kind of *Seinsmeinen,* which Meinong calls "the intending by way of being of something intended by way of so-being" (*das Seinsmeinen eines Soseinsgemeintes*).[91] It is seen in the paradigm case of *Seinsmeinen,* the perception of a physical object. Notwithstanding the picture of perception that chapter 7 provided, perception of physical objects involves more than evident affirmative existential judgment. There is an implicit *Soseinsmeinen* in the perception of a physical object. Presumably X is communicating only a small portion of the formal and empirical content of his representation, and not quite all of the content of his judgment, when he turns to Y and says, "There is something metallic on the hillside"; thus we might not have to worry too much about the specious generality of his statement (which we are now supposing to be the expression of a veridical perception). But one might think it antecedently improbable that X perceives the metallic object by excogitating the more remote object "something metallic," and that X does this by assuming an objective analogous to the propositional function '*x* is metallic' or the gerundial expression 'being metallic', and that it is only on the basis of this ideational intending that X ventures the remaining judgmental portion of the compound intending. If it does look a little improbable, it is nevertheless an interesting prospect and well worth trying to confirm. In contrast, it turns into a grim affair when one follows certain passages of Meinong's and concedes that the apprehension by way of so-being of "something metallic" is the function of an existential assumption that there *is* something metallic.[92] From that point on, we are no longer afield hunting for new facts; we are trying to understand what is wrong.

The *Seinsmeinen* of the proximate object or the ultimate object is always affirmative, and it may be either judgmental or assumptive. In contrast, a *Soseinsmeinen* cannot be a judgment, but it may be negative as well as affirmative. By a negative assumption of so-being (the preceding paragraph might make one wonder about its logical structure) one apprehends a *negativum,* a more remote object such as "something that is not red." One intends by way of so-being (in this simple and nonperceptual case) everything that is not red. The difficulties about the *negativum* seem to cease with the notion of an incomplete object determined by a negative objective. A nonmiser (i.e., "that") would be determined by the objective :not living miserably in order to amass wealth: or perhaps :that *x* does not live miserably in order to amass wealth:. Regarding such objectives and their positive counterparts, which were alluded to in the preceding paragraph, we note incidentally that they are indeterminate in their primary material, or in what they are about. Following Ernst Mally, Meinong calls them "determinations" (*Bestimmungen*) in the present edition of *Assumptions*.[93]

The more remote object, incomplete though it is, is most naturally regarded as a nexus of positive and negative determinations of so-being. The number of distribution patterns of negation will also be the number of more remote objects. That may be inferred, and it is worthwhile noting it because of the presupposed constancy of the representational content. But Meinong interests himself in a different sort of pluralization of the remote object, the pluralization into more specific forms, and here the representational content and the proximate object (whatever that might now be) cannot be held constant.[94] In this connection one senses that the distinction between the intensional plurality of more remote objects and the extensional plurality of concrete individuals is not as sharp as it could be, and that Meinong is commenting on the one when he should be commenting on the other.

Finally, not every assumption of so-being constitutes an intending by way of so-being, which is implicit near the beginning of section 45. Instead of taking a purely formal example, let us consider the sentences 'X is well' and 'X is not well'. Say that the former expresses my assumption, and I intend X by way of so-being by making this assumption; say also that the second expresses my judgment. Then it would appear that I intend X by way of so-being by making this judgment. There would seem to be no sense to Meinong's restriction of intending by way of so-being to assumptions, in this case. Furthermore, the same object would have been fastened upon, had I assumed that X was not well rather than that X was well. On the other hand, if it is "well X" that I fasten upon by my assumption that X is well, then it is presumably "unwell X" that I should have fastened upon, had my assumption been negative. But, then, why have I not fastened upon unwell X anyway, through my present negative judgment? Again our own preconceptions conflict with Meinong's restriction of this type of intending to assumptions. And as one proceeds with other types of logically predicative sentences, one begins to realize that one is encountering no sentences that could express intending assumptions, or at least none that could express an intending on the subject side. Intending by way of so-being would therefore appear to depend upon assumptions that are "shadowy" in at least this way: that their syntactical signature is somehow hidden behind "something that is ϕ," the signature of the auxiliary object. Still, consider the case where someone asks a question of the type, "What's the word for a person who . . . ?" The listener repeats the definiens: "Someone who sets up and adjusts factory machinery for production runs?" For whatever reason, it seems that the listener (who may not know the word for it) has already apprehended something through a nonexistential "thinking." And because of that, one is reluctant to dismiss intending by way of so-being, even though its constitutive assumptions seem to be syntactically elusive.

Chapter 9 ("Zur Begehrungs- und Wertpsychologie") is little changed from the first edition.[95] Christian von Ehrenfels did not persist with his side of the public discussion of value theory, and Meinong left his 1902 critique of Ehrenfels's theory substantially as it was. In 1910 Meinong's psychology of emotion and valuation was the only lagging portion of his philosophy, and in the laconic footnote 91 to chapter 9 we are told, in effect, that something will have to be done about the "emotional psychologism." In keeping with the decision to attempt nothing with the material on value theory and emotional psychology in *Assumptions,* we can end our main discussion here, noting only that there are substantial changes in the summarizing and speculative chapter 10 ("Ergebnisse. Bausteine zu einer Psychologie der Annahmen").[96]

Meinong's way of working has been called "philosophy from the bottom up,"[97] and it has even been asserted that Meinong is free of concern with system construction.[98] True it is that Meinong brings great abilities and very little distortive pressure to bear on experienceable facts, and it is this that should be remembered when Meinong is compared with Aristotle.[99] In *Assumptions* one meets a philosopher who is obviously little inclined to intimidating remarks about what is possible or rightheaded, or to lengthy asides on matters of procedure. It is also plain that Meinong considers it his business not primarily to explain what is on his mind, but to come to grips with his subject matter, to get as close as possible to the truth of it, and to prove what he says.[100] He does not approach the task with very strong opinions about how things should eventually look. What he brings to the task is a very good feeling for the manifest character of experience and its objects. He also respects this manifest character; it comprises much of what he calls "the facts." Our own feeling that the investigation is not a nominal investigation but a real one, driven this way and that by incoming facts, may have something to do with a certain outdoors atmosphere in Meinong's work. The work recommends itself not just by the solid virtues that have been mentioned so far but also by a quality of intelligence that English philosophers early recognized as Meinong's acuteness. This involves a good measure of intuitive finesse in grasping a phenomenon in a concept. In this important and widely acknowledged parameter of intellectual genius, Meinong is unexcelled among twentieth-century philosophers.

The foregoing expository and critical comments, and the work of translation, are dedicated to the honored memory of Hofrat Rudolf Kindinger (1884-1968), a resourceful and thoughtful proponent of the philosophy of his teacher Meinong and a good friend to English-speaking visitors to Graz between and after the two wars.

NOTES TO THE EDITOR'S INTRODUCTION

References to Meinong's works are by page numbers of the original publication or the separate print. This pagination is always retained internally in the texts of the *Alexius Meinong Gesamtausgabe.* The *Gesamtausgabe* adds parenthesized bottom numbers when volume-length continuity requires it, but these numbers are not used; neither is the volume-length top corner pagination of *Gesamtausgabe* I and II used. Wherever possible, references to the works of Brentano and Meinong are followed by titles of English translations. For example, *Psychologie,* vol. 1, p. 114 [*Psychology,* p. 81].

The *Alexius Meinong Gesamtausgabe* consists of seven (I-VII) numbered volumes edited by Rudolf Haller and Rudolf Kindinger in collaboration with Roderick M. Chisholm (Graz: Akademische Druck- und Verlagsanstalt, 1968-1978). As will be seen from the following list, there is an eighth, supplementary volume; this *Ergänzungsband* was published by the same press in 1978, and its editors are Reinhard Fabian and Rudolf Haller.

I. *Abhandlungen zur Psychologie*
II. *Abhandlungen zur Erkenntnistheorie und Gegenstandstheorie*
III. *Abhandlungen zur Werttheorie*
IV. *Über Annahmen*
V. *Über philosophische Wissenschaft und ihre Propädeutik. Über die Stellung der Gegenstandstheorie im System der Wissenschaften Über die Erfahrungsgrundlagen unseres Wissens Zum Erweise des allgemeinen Kausalgesetzes*
VI. *Über Möglichkeit und Wahrscheinlichkeit*
VII. *Selbstdarstellung. Vermischte Schriften. Ergänzungsband zur Gesamtausgabe: Kolleghefte und Fragmente. Schriften aus dem Nachlass.*

Valuable assistance in the problems of the English edition of *Über Annahmen* was provided by Roderick M. Chisholm, Reinhard Fabian, J. N. Findlay, Rolf George, Udo Strutynski, Dallas Willard, and Robert Y. Zachary. The editor is especially indebted to professors Rudolf Haller of the University of Graz and Helen K. Heanue of Los Angeles Trade-Technical College for their many-sided help.

1. See Meinong's "Selbstdarstellung," as it is customarily called, in *Die deutsche Philosophie der Gegenwart in Selbstdarstellungen,* ed. Raymund Schmidt (Leipzig: Meiner, 1921) 1:91-150. In *Gesamtausgabe* VII. The first part of the "Selbstdarstellung," entitled "Leben und Streben," is an autobiographical sketch. A translation of this sketch can be found in Reinhardt Grossman's *Meinong* (London: Routledge and Kegan Paul, 1974), pp. 230-236.

2. See Oskar Kraus, "Biographical Sketch of Franz Brentano"; Carl Stumpf, "Reminiscences of Franz Brentano"; both in *The Philosophy of Franz Brentano,* ed. Linda L. McAllister (London: Duckworth, 1976). (Includes Roderick M. Chisholm's bibliography of published writings of Brentano, pp. 248-254.) See also Antos C. Rancurello, *A Study of Franz Brentano* (New York: Academic Press, 1968), pp. 1-21. (Contains a critical bibliography, pp. 134-169.)

3. Eduard Martinak, *Meinong als Mensch und als Lehrer* (Graz: Lubensky, 1925), p. 5.

4. Hans Benndorf, *Persönliche Erinnerungen an Alexius Meinong* (Graz: Kienreich, 1951), pp. 10-11.

5. Wilhelm Frankl, "Alexius Meinong. Ein Gedenkblatt," *Archiv für Geschichte der Philosophie,* n.s. 27 (1922):42-46. Ernst Mally, "Alexius Meinongs philosophische Arbeit," *Deutschen Idealismus* 2 (1921):1, of separate reprint. See also Martinak, *Meinong,* pp. 5-6; Benndorf, *Erinnerungen,* pp. 7-9.

6. A complete bibliography of works by Meinong can be found in the *Gesamtausgabe* VII:325-342, bottom pagination. See also Michele Lenoci, *La teoria della conoscenza in Alexius Meinong. Oggetto, giudizio, assunzioni.* (Milan: Università Cattolica del Sacro Cuore, 1972). A critical bibliography on pages 305-369 includes valuable references to writings about Meinong through 1970.

7. *Ueber Annahmen,* 1st ed., supplementary vol. 2 to the *Zeitschrift für Psychologie und Physiologie der Sinnesorgane* (1902). The table of contents and pages 76-92 and 129-211 are reproduced in the *Gesamtausgabe* IV.

8. "Über Gegenstandstheorie," in *Untersuchungen zur Gegenstandstheorie und Psychologie,* ed. Alexius Meinong (Leipzig: Barth, 1904), now in *Gesamtausgabe* II ["The Theory of Objects," in *Realism and the Background of Phenomenology,* ed. Roderick M. Chisholm (Glencoe, Ill.: Free Press, 1960)].

9. *Über Annahmen,* 2d ed. (Leipzig: Barth, 1910), *Gesamtausgabe* IV, which also includes the selections from the 1902 *Annahmen* mentioned above (n. 7), a critical rejoinder to Anton Marty ("In Sachen der Annahmen"), and the German text of the note slips translated in this book. The *Gesamtausgabe* volume was prepared by Rudolf Haller. A third, unrevised German edition was published in 1928 by Barth.

10. C. D. Broad, review of *Über Annahmen,* 2d ed., *Mind* 22 (1913):92. Consistent with this, Reinhardt Grossman occasionally lets "idea" stand for the content of a *Vorstellung,* and the same informal policy is adopted here. See Grossman's *Meinong* (London: Routledge and Kegan Paul, 1974), p. 55.

11. Franz Brentano, *Psychologie vom empirischen Standpunkt,* ed. Oskar Kraus, 2 vols. (Hamburg: Meiner, 1955), 1:114; 2:34 [*Psychology from an Empirical Standpoint* (Kraus edition), ed. Linda McAllister (New York: Humanities Press, 1973), pp. 81, 198].

12. *On Assumptions (Assumptions* henceforth), p. 27.

13. Ibid., pp. 143-144, 175, 206.

14. Ibid., pp. 263-264, 268, 270-271, 273.

15. Ibid., p. 273.

16. Ibid., pp. 264, 271.

17. Ibid., p. 29.

18. Ibid., p. 243.

19. *Remarks on the text of chapter 1.* In section 1, the fourth paragraph (p. 10), concerning positing representations, is new. The polemical content of the eighth paragraph (p. 12) is new. In section 2, the third paragraph (p. 14) has some new material at the end, i.e., after the question. The fourth paragraph (introducing "non-*A*") and the fifth (division into production and reproduction) are rewritten paragraphs. Additional new material: the beginning of the sixth paragraph (p. 15), concerning the possibility of perceptual representations of *negativa*; the first half of the seventh (p. 16), concerning the possible representation of *N* through production; the beginning of the eighth, concerning the plurality of *inferiora*; and the first third of the twelfth (p. 18), after the first block of reduced-type paragraphs. The thirteenth paragraph (pp. 18-19) is new, as are the fifteenth (pp. 19-20) and sixteenth paragraphs. The seventeenth, next-to-the-last

paragraph has a new opening. The paragraphs in reduced type represent old as well as new excursuses of Meinong.

20. *Assumptions,* p. 11.

21. Ibid., p. 13.

22. Ibid., pp. 14-15.

23. Ibid., p. 12.

24. Brentano, *Psychologie* 2:65-66 [*Psychology,* p. 222]. See also *Vom Ursprung sittlicher Erkenntnis,* ed. Oskar Kraus (Hamburg: Meiner, 1955), pp. 18-19 [*The Origin of our Knowledge of Right and Wrong* (Kraus edition), ed. Roderick M. Chisholm (London: Routledge and Kegan Paul, p. 17)]. In connection with the eliminability of categorical form, representations of immortal humans and unlearned humans, and of bad-acting people who do not hurt themselves, see Brentano, *Psychologie* 2:57, 60 [*Psychology,* pp. 214, 218]. For Anton Marty, see "Über subjektlose Sätze und das Verhältnis der Grammatik zu Logik und Psychologie," *Vierteljahrsschrift für Wissenschaftliche Philosophie* (1884), p. 188; (1885), p. 71.

25. *Assumptions,* p. 20.

26. *Remarks on the text of chapter 2.* Section 4 is rewritten from the end of the third paragraph (p. 26) on. In section 5 the last third of paragraph three (p. 29) is new. In section 6, the mountain-path example (p. 31) is added.

27. *Assumptions,* p. 27.

28. *Remarks on the text of chapter 3.* Exceptions to the rewriting of the chapter on objectives may be found in sections 8 and 9 (in the examples and the comments on them on pp. 37-41—disturbance of the peace, snow outside, philosopher's stone, harmonically correct, case closed); in section 9, the first three paragraphs (old, pp. 40-41); in section 10, middle of paragraph two through paragraph six (old, pp. 45-47); and in section 11, paragraphs six, seven, and eight (old, pp. 51-52) up to the "thundering" and "being together" examples.

29. Following J. N. Findlay, *Meinong's Theory of Objects and Values,* 2d ed. (London: Oxford University Press, 1963), p. 67.

30. Following Findlay, *Meinong's Theory,* pp. 68-69. See also C. D. Broad's review of *Über Annahmen,* 2d ed., in *Mind* 22 (1913):93.

31. Following Findlay, *Meinong's Theory,* p. 32.

32. Following Findlay, *Meinong's Theory,* p. 44.

33. *Assumptions,* pp. 65-73. See the discussion of this point in Findlay, *Meinong's Theory,* pp. 87-89, 186-187.

34. *Assumptions,* p. 73.

35. Ibid., p. 54.

36. *Remarks on the text of chapter 4.* In section 15, the fifth paragraph (p. 82) is lengthened by a few final lines on scientific fictions, and then a new (sixth) paragraph on *negativa* and on the "Put yourself in my position" request is inserted (p. 82), showing that Meinong is still on good terms with these two first-edition topics. Section 15 on the lie is rewritten after the third paragraph (pp. 87-89). This will be worth a few remarks as we proceed with the chapter. In section 18 on questions, in the new remarks within the third paragraph (concerning the "object of the decision-question," p. 91) and at the end of the fourth paragraph (p. 92), the objective slips into the old writing. After the beginning, the fifth paragraph (pp. 92-93) is new.

37. *Supplementary remarks on the text of chapter 5.* Section 21 ends with a short new

paragraph (p. 111). Another block of material from the old seventh chapter appears in section 22, after the third paragraph (p. 112). It concerns the position of agreement or disagreement that we take with regard to someone's view, or to a possible view. The seventh paragraph (p. 113) and the first third of the eighth paragraph present new material on so-being judgments about objectives. The ninth paragraph (p. 114) is also new. The material immediately preceding it (pp. 113-114) and following it (pp. 114-115) is especially relevant to the troublesome section 21. Section 23 is new. Section 24 opens with a new paragraph (p. 119); the remainder of it, except for the comments on Stephan Witasek's aesthetic views, is also from the old seventh chapter on objectives. Section 25 also opens with a new paragraph, and a new paragraph is placed at the end (p. 125) to orient the reader to the new chapter sequence. See editor's note *k* to this chapter.

38. *Assumptions,* p. 110.

39. Ibid., p. 110.

40. Ibid., p. 111.

41. William of Ockham, *Philosophical Writings,* ed. Philotheus Boehner (Edinburgh: Nelson, 1957), pp. 18-19.

42. Bertrand Russell, "Meinong's Theory of Complexes and Assumptions," *Mind* 13 (1904):338-352.

43. *Ueber Annahmen,* 1st ed., p. 257.

44. "Über Urteilsgefühle, was sie sind und was sie nicht sind," *Archiv für die gesamte Psychologie* 6 (1905):40 (see *Gesamtausgabe* I).

45. *Ueber Annahmen,* 1st ed., pp. 7, 14. Brentano's emphasis on the act-indeterminacy of representation appears in his *Psychologie* 1:65-66 [*Psychology,* p. 222] and in his *Sittlicher Erkenntnis,* pp. 18-19 [*Knowledge of Right and Wrong,* p. 17].

46. The notion of the content as perceptually elusive appears in Meinong's "Über Gegenstande höherer Ordnung und deren Verhältnis zur inneren Wahrnehmung," *Zeitschrift für Psychologie und Physiologie der Sinnesorgane* 21 (1899):188-189 (see *Gesamtausgabe* II) [Marie-Luise Schubert Kalsi, *Alexius Meinong. On Objects of Higher Order and Husserl's Phenomenology* (The Hague: Martinus Nijhoff, 1978), p. 143]. See also Findlay, *Meinong's Theory,* pp. 28-35.

47. The contrast of activity and passivity appears in Meinong's "Gegenstände höherer Ordnung," p. 201 [*Meinong. On Objects of Higher Order,* p. 151]; in *Über die Erfahrungsgrundlagen unseres Wissens* (Berlin: Springer, 1906), p. 58 (see *Gesamtausgabe* V); and in *Assumptions,* p. 243.

48. The concept of pseudo-existence appears in Meinong's "Gegenstände höherer Ordnung," pp. 186-187 [*Meinong. Objects of Higher Order,* p. 142] and in his *Erfahrungsgrundlagen,* pp. 54-57.

49. The exegetic treatment of propositions as pseudo-existent objectives appears in Findlay, *Meinong's Theory,* pp. 86-89. A different and nonexegetic approach to the same general thesis (that propositions are states of affairs looked at in a certain way) may be found in Roderick M. Chisholm's *Person and Object* (La Salle, Ill.: Open Court, 1976), pp. 122-124. See also Chisholm's *The First Person* (Minneapolis: University of Minnesota Press, 1981), pp. 9-12, 123-132.

50. *Remarks on the text of chapter 6.* In section 27, the fifth paragraph is new, except for the definition of inference at the end (p. 130). New in section 28 are the second half of the first paragraph (p. 131), the end of the seventh paragraph (p. 134), concerning precision-objects, and the end of the next-to-the-last paragraph (p. 135), concerning

evidence from premises without evidence. The following new section 29 receives some material from a deleted section on "relative evidence" (pp. 136-137). Section 30 is new in its opening sentences (p. 137) and in its sixth through next-to-the-last paragraphs (pp. 140-144). The changes consist in the insertion of material on objectives and the deletion of material associating hypothetical judgments with assumption-inferences. The concluding sections 31 and 32 on hypothetical judgments are new writing, except for a sentence here and there and the rejection of negative hypothetical judgments in the third paragraph of section 31 (old, pp. 145-146).

51. Findlay, *Meinong's Theory*, pp. 190-191.

52. *Assumptions*, pp. 130, 136.

53. Meinong, "Hume-Studien II: Zur Relationstheorie," *Sitzungsberichte der philosophisch-historischen Klasse der Kaiserlichen Akademie der Wissenschaften in Wien* 101 (1882), part 2, chap. 5, sec. 6, which in the table of contents is entitled "Verträglichkeitsrelationen vorgestellter Urteile; der Schluss und das hypothetische Urteil"; see *Gesamtausgabe* II. [*Meinong's Hume Studies: Translation and Commentary*, ed. Kenneth Barber (Ames: University of Iowa, 1966).] See note *c* to chapter 6.

54. *Assumptions*, pp. 142-144.

55. Ibid., p. 150.

56. *Remarks on the text of chapter 7*. In opening section 33, the second paragraph (pp. 159-160) is new. An important deletion of twenty lines occurs at the end of the present section 36 (p. 167). In those lines Meinong showed that he had been working within the concept of an object as a known entity, and that he was prepared to weaken that concept, but not to give it up. Internal editing is virtually nil. The word 'being' ('Sein') is inserted for clarity's sake in the third paragraph of section 34 (p. 161). Section 38 is new, as can be gathered from the title.

57. Meinong, "Gegenstände höherer Ordnung," p. 187; (see *Gesamtausgabe* II) [*Meinong. On Objects of Higher Order*, p. 142]; *Ueber Annahmen*, 1st ed., p. 104.

58. *Assumptions*, last paragraph of section 36, especially "immanent" and "transcendent" objects and "the assumed as such." The 'as such' is a pseudo-existence signal; cf. p. 119. The identification of immanence with pseudo-existence is explicit in note 76 to chapter 3. The deleted observations are in *Ueber Annahmen*, 1st ed., beginnings of sections 29 and 30.

59. *Assumptions*, pp. 161-162; *Ueber Annahmen*, 1st ed., beginning of section 30.

60. *Assumptions*, p. 164.

61. Ibid., p. 166.

62. Ibid., p. 170. It is probable that the doctrine of *a poteriori* implicit assuming guides Meinong here, near the end of section 37. As for the doctrine itself, see, e.g., p. 143.

63. Ibid., pp. 168-169.

64. Ibid., pp. 166-167, 169.

65. Ernst Mally, "Untersuchungen zur Gegenstandstheorie des Messens," in the *Untersuchungen zur Gegenstandstheorie und Psychologie*, ed. Alexius Meinong (Leipzig: Barth, 1904), pp. 126-127; Meinong, "Gegenstandstheorie," ibid., pp. 11-12 ["Theory of Objects," pp. 32-33].

66. "Gegenstandstheorie" ["Theory of Objects"], section 4; *Assumptions*, p. 62; "Über emotionale Präsentation," in the *Sitzungsberichte der philosophisch-historischen Klasse der Kaiserlichen Akademie der Wissenschaften in Wien* 183 (1917):17,

22-23, 67; (see *Gesamtausgabe* III) [*On Emotional Presentation,* trans. Marie-Luise Schubert Kalsi (Evanston, Ill.: Northwestern University Press, 1972), pp. 15, 19-20, 62]; *Gesamtausgabe* supplementary volume *Kollegehefte und Fragmente,* pp. 150-154, 358-359, 397-398.

67. *Kolleghefte,* p. 92; "Gegenstandstheorie" ["Theory of Objects"], section 4; *Assumptions,* pp. 62, 176.

68. *Assumptions,* pp. 159, 170.

69. "Gegenstandstheorie" ["Theory of Objects"], sections 3, 4.

70. Ibid., sections 3, 4; "Emotionale Präsentation," pp. 22-24 [*Emotional Presentation,* pp. 19-20]; *Assumptions,* pp. 62, 175-176.

71. *Assumptions,* pp. 177-178.

72. "Emotionale Präsentation," pp. 5-6 [*Emotional Presentation,* pp. 4-5]; *Über Möglichkeit und Wahrscheinlichkeit* (Leipzig: Barth, 1915), pp. 194, 250 (*Gesamtausgabe* VI, prepared by Roderick M. Chisholm). The rendition "authentic" is from *Emotional Presentation* (Kalsi translation).

73. *Remarks on the text of chapter 8.* In section 42, the first and second paragraphs (pp. 187-188) are new, except for the beginning of the second. In section 43, the third and fourth paragraphs (pp. 190-191) are new. Sections 45 and 46 replace four deleted sections. Comments on this major change follow.

74. *Assumptions,* pp. 179-187. The rendition "nonintuitiveness," as opposed to "unintuitiveness," was suggested by J. N. Findlay.

75. *Assumptions,* p. 205.

76. "Gegenstände höherer Ordnung," p. 194 (see *Gesamtausgabe* II) [*Meinong. Objects of Higher Order,* p. 147].

77. *Assumptions,* p. 188.

78. Ibid., p. 188.

79. Discussed by J. N. Findlay, *Meinong's Theory,* pp. 138-142.

80. *Ueber Annahmen,* 1st ed., pp. 129-136 (see *Gesamtausgabe* IV).

81. Ibid., p. 136.

82. Ibid., pp. 142-144, 147. The predicative tie, p. 144 (bottom).

83. Ibid., p. 145 (top). See n. 76 above.

84. *Möglichkeit,* chap. 2 (*Gesamtausgabe* VI).

85. Ernst Mally, *Gegenstandstheoretische Grundlagen der Logik und Logistik* (Leipzig: Barth, 1912), p. 64.

86. Meinong, *Über die Stellung der Gegenstandstheorie im System der Wissenschaften* (Leipzig: Voightländer, 1907), pp. 120-123 (see *Gesamtausgabe* V).

87. *Assumptions,* pp. 200, 203, 205-206.

88. Ibid., p. 203.

89. Ibid., pp. 196, 200.

90. *Möglichkeit,* pp. 194, 250.

91. *Assumptions,* p. 194; *Möglichkeit,* p. 186 (bottom).

92. *Assumptions,* p. 199; *Möglichkeit,* p. 186 (bottom).

93. Mally, "Gegenstandstheorie des Messens," section 6 (see n. 65); *Assumptions,* p. 47.

94. *Assumptions,* pp. 199-200.

95. *Remarks on the text of chapter 9.* In section 54, the first two-thirds of the second paragraph (p. 222) consists of rewritten material, and the third and fourth paragraphs

(p. 223) are new. Section 55 is new. In sections 53 and 56, and in the last paragraph of section 57 (p. 234), references to positive and negative so-being are inserted.

96. *Remarks on the text of chapter 10.* In section 59, the third paragraph (p. 242) is a rewritten paragraph, sacrificing the active-passive distinction along with the thetic-synthetic and immanent-transcendent distinctions. At the beginning of the fourth paragraph, an equation of the judgmental content with the representational content is dropped. The fifth paragraph (p. 243) reinstates and reworks the activity-passivity distinction. The remaining paragraphs are new; some of the material on probability, however, is old. In section 60, the second paragraph (p. 246) is new, and the third paragraph is changed. The sixth paragraph (pp. 247-248) is new, except for the end (freedom of assuming). The very short ninth and tenth paragraphs (p. 249) on mediate and immediate evidence also contain some new writing. Thereafter, all the writing in section 60 is new. In section 62, the last four paragraphs (pp. 260-261) are new. In section 63, new thoughts on apprehension and presentation fill the middle of the second paragraph (p. 262). The fifth paragraph (p. 264) is new. The short seventh paragraph (p. 264) involves a characteristic substitution of "thoughts" for "thinking." The polemical section 64 is new. The second and third paragraphs of section 65 (p. 269) are new.

97. Ernst Mally, "Alexius Meinongs philosophische Arbeit," *Deutsche Idealismus* 27 (1921):1.

98. Rudolf Kindinger, "Grundzüge der gegenstandstheoretische Betrachtungsweise," *Unser Weg* 13 (1958):373.

99. Franz Weber, "Meine Beziehung zu Meinong," in *Vom Gegenstand zum Sein,* ed. Rodolf Trofenik (Munich: Trofenik, 1972), p. 165; Frankl, "Alexius Meinong," p. 43.

100. For a consideration of Meinong under the aspects of science-oriented philosophy and a specifically Austrian philosophy, see Rudolf Haller's "Ludwig Wittgenstein und die Österreichische Philosophie," *Wissenschaft und Weltbild* 21 (1968):77-87. Haller's "Wittgenstein and Austrian Philosophy" can now be found in *Austrian Philosophy. Texts and Studies* (Munich: Philosophia Verlag, 1980).

Preface to the First Edition

The preceding dedication page[1] may serve as an expression of the fact that the name it bears should really stand next to mine under the title of this work, both by the nature of the situation and by my own wishes. In June 1899, Miss Mila Radaković directed my attention for the first time to the facts which, in the present work, I have called assumptions and have subjected to an initial investigation. That lady then kindly agreed to assist in carrying out this investigation. She actually began a monograph dealing with the areas in which these new facts had first become apparent to her, primarily in the areas of play and art. The work was almost ready for printing, when my esteemed co-worker was compelled to forego continuation of her inquiries temporarily, because of a long and severe illness that required a hero's courage and strength to withstand, emotionally as well as physically. It is now to be hoped that she will again be able to lend her uncommon ability to the pursuit of knowledge in the not too distant future. Yet I have had to do without her help in carrying out the present work, as far as that help would have consisted in independently preparing certain sections of the book, sections that are now omitted. However, this cannot alter the fact that it was she who provided the impetus to the investigations set forth here and that she has given unstintingly of her suggestions and encouragement during the course of this investigation. And if, as I have good reason to believe, a large and important domain of facts should be opened up to scientific inquiry by this work, then it must not be forgotten who is ultimately responsible for this gain.

As to the present discussions themselves, it need hardly be explicitly stated that the attempt to deal with a domain of facts hitherto unnoticed in theory can provide only a bare start, not a settled theory. This is rather apparent even in the subject matter arrangement. This arrangement was not imposed on the subject matter through some "principle"; it was thrust upon me by the facts. I must report that, like many other aspects of the present effort, this one has turned out quite contrary to my original expectation. At the time I took my first steps in this new domain of facts, I had no idea that I should encounter so many well-known problems along the path—some known to everyone, and at least some known to me. A certain aspect of these problems, one that promises to be most conducive to their solution, also came unexpectedly into view. All this has undoubtedly been detrimental to the formal unity of the present discussions. Yet I can regard it as an additional reason for confidence that, in these discussions, observation has not been reshaped in accordance with a preconceived theory. Rather, a thesis has been derived from observation and has taken shape in accordance with a variety of facts crowding in from all sides.

Answering more or less to the variety of these facts is the diversity in the nature of the preliminary investigations that in certain chapters of this book lead us to assumptions. The justification for the existence of these investigations will hopefully become apparent in what they themselves yield, and not just in their relation to assumptions. This applies especially to the seventh chapter.[2] If I am not mistaken, the theme of this chapter has a fundamental significance for knowing and, via knowing, for the whole of our mental activities. It is true that this significance became especially clear to me from assumptions; by no means, however, does it on that account depend more on assumptions than on judgment. On that score, what I initially treated under the name of "objective" in this chapter would have ultimately required a special handling, one quite independent of the subject of assumptions. Under such circumstances, it will hardly seem unwarranted that, while this initial attempt to lay the foundations for the theory of objectives has never gone beyond mere foundation-laying, it has repeatedly gone beyond what would have been absolutely indispensable soley in regard to assumptions.

The eighth chapter[3] has to do with the significance of assumptions for the theory of value and the theory of desire. This chapter, too, has proved more extensive than would have been necessary, had I restricted my discussion to assumptions. A short explanation is called for at this point. My *Psychologisch-ethischen Untersuchungen zur Werttheorie* contains the injunction, which I have already carried out within appropriate limits, that ethics be based on the theory of value and the theory of value on a psychological investigation of value-facts. This injunction has given rise to a series of publications by other scholars which I welcome as the promising beginnings of a psychological theory of value and of an ethics based on the theory of value. I am firmly convinced that such an ethics and no other is the scientific ethics of the future. Among these publications, the two volumes of Christian von Ehrenfels's *System der Werttheorie* unquestionably occupy the foremost position, and not just because of their scope. Without putting too slight a value on the other works, I see in Ehrenfels's the most successful continuation by far of the investigations in the theory of value that I initiated.[4] But, as is obvious, or at least should be, Ehrenfels's work is a "continuation" only in the sense that it is also the freest expression of a different scientific personality; and this expression has led to a difference of opinion between us on some important matters. I have hitherto had no opportunity to comment on this difference of opinion on an adequately sound footing. The opportunity is now provided me by the fact that the two areas which claimed my attention almost exclusively, the major area of intellectual psychology and theory of knowledge and the minor area of emotional psychology and ethics, have manifested an unexpectedly close connection over the whole range in which assumptions appear. If I am not mistaken, then, assumptions might play a substantial role in any settlement of my difference of opinion with Ehrenfels. Hence, it is quite proper to bring up this difference of opinion in the present work. In fact, I thought I had a right not to exclude matters relevant to the discussion even when they could not be brought into any direct connection with the theory of assumptions. In any case, at the outset of the eighth chapter, the reader will find sections 47-51[5] expressly designated as being those most remote from the real subject of this work.

At this point, however, the reference to the beginnings of the psychological theory of value provides me with the desired occasion for an observation in a personal matter, a matter that I associate in the first instance with the recent report on ethical literature in the *Archiv für systematische Philosophie*. There Ehrenfels and I are casually referred to as "value-theorists of the school of Brentano," although Brentano has not the slightest connection with our respective efforts in the theory of value and hence his "school" has presumably long since rejected our ideas as false doctrine. Not long before this report, a sort of centenary issue of the *Zeitschrift für pädagogische Psychologie* described me, this time along with Alois Höfler, as the representative of a "scholastic method" in psychology. The allegation was made in connection with Brentano's intimate knowledge of scholastic philosophy, even though I must sadly confess that I am totally lacking in such thorough knowledge—a knowledge from which various advantages assuredly might be drawn, even for modern science. Now of course, I can only find it accurate if certain surveys of the present state of philosophy should, so far as they think it appropriate to speak of me, mention the connection between my professional orientation and that of Franz Brentano. And I am certainly not lacking in gratitude toward Brentano, whose favorable attitude at the time encouraged and supported my first efforts in the field of philosophical inquiry. The risk that I might minimize the extent of this debt of kindness is reduced by the growing number of those to whom I subsequently tried to render some similar service, and by my concern that the memory that these students of mine carry with them of the time of our working together is not an indifferent memory. Still, I should have to regard it almost as though my fate had been sealed by the circumstances under which I once entered into scientific work if, even as much as a quarter century later, enemies as well as friends of Brentano were constrained to hold something against me. For the former, it would be *that* I learned from Brentano. For the latter, it would be that I have not learned *everything* from Brentano and that instead, through honest effort in the course of my scientific activities, I have learned some things by myself—or properly speaking, from the facts. I should think that by now I had established a claim to count for something in my own right and to be rated according to the measure of whatever I have been able to contribute to my science through my own honest effort. That is not said to hurt Brentano's friends, and it is said even less, if possible, to please his foes; but as certain as it is that an impersonal goal was previously set for my life's work and will remain set for it in the future, just as certainly am I entitled to the fervent hope that I may encounter no difficulties or hindrances other than objective ones in the pursuit of this goal.

And so, it is hoped that what the present work has to offer will meet with an impersonal reception and that it will be tested for its serviceability by the facts to whose knowledge it is intended to contribute. As far as I know, there is no literature proper to the subject dealt with here; I believe that there has not yet been any work on it, at least not *ex professo*. Yet, the host of things to which assumptions are relevant is naturally mirrored in a host of apposite writings, so that to adduce the latter in any completeness would be a quite hopeless undertaking. From the small number of works that are expressly taken into consideration in my book it should not be concluded that I am indebted just to these works for what is profitable to our theme, let alone that I attribute value just to them. I cannot deny, of course, that I have found it especially easy to refer to publications by authors I was once fortunate enough to call my students. It is simply a fact, however, that these very authors are the ones whose accord or disagreement has primarily fostered the progress of my work up until now.

Graz, October 1901

The Author

Preface to the Second Edition

The eight years that have passed since the first publication of the present investigations have seen further developments along the lines that I had mapped out. The primary task confronting a new edition was that of implementing these investigations with whatever light had been shed upon their sphere of problems—and of bringing new material to bear upon the clarification of these problems, wherever possible. It was especially important to begin by considering the extent of the influence that was generated by the initial theoretical as well as practical attempts to establish a legitimate domain for the theory of objects. It is clear now that objectives deserved a quite different position in the foundation of the theory of assumptions than the position I saw fit to allow them at the time. It was just at that time—oddly, not until I was already drafting the first edition—that the special character and the significance of the objective became apparent to me. That realization has led me now to introduce the former seventh chapter at an earlier point in the book and to expand it into the present third and fifth chapters. The most natural thing seemed to be that the former third chapter should appear between these two as the fourth chapter. The remaining chapters have retained their serial order as well as their thematic content in which, notwithstanding the partly altered headings, some questions that were previously cloaked in the intricacies of detail now appear in the foreground. Such is the case with the present sixth, seventh, and eighth chapters, where I have made alterations in the views formerly expressed. I have been compelled to make these alterations, in part rather fundamental ones, by deficiencies in the first treatment that became perceptible to me in the intervening time. I have not managed to reach a settlement which is satisfactory in all points. I should hardly have taken the floor again in these particular matters, even today, had it not been unavoidable in responding to the need for a new edition.

On the whole, I would be inclined to say this: The material from the older thoughts that has held up under renewed scrutiny will hopefully reappear before the eyes of the reader in clarified and maybe even simplified form. But, as is inevitably entailed by the progress of a living inquiry, enough new material has supervened to afford plentiful room for even new crudities and new needs for improvement, and to afford opportunity for lenient judgment on the part of a reader who thinks that honest endeavor warrants a sympathetic reception. Such leniency might, as a matter of fact, come in especially handy in connection with my apportionment of new material into the old, which is not a thing that can be managed without some irregularities slipping through. Particularly the added material on "content and object" and on the "self-presentation of experiences" might perhaps better have been set forth in special chapters. But in that case, the real theme of the book would have been thrust further behind the preliminary considerations than it already has, by chapter 2 and especially chapter 3.

It will also be understood that a new edition has the general duty of continuing the written discussion that the old one had stimulated. My attempt to discharge this duty has not been without a feeling of distinct gratitude for the assistance of dissenting opinions. Under favorable circumstances, as we know, the effect of such opinions is even more helpful that that of agreement. I am thinking especially of such favorable circumstances as those occasioned by the work of Gustav Spengler,[1] Bertrand Russell,[2] and most recently D. H. Kerler,[3] not to mention the inquirers with whom I share closer personal relations. The position is more awkward when it comes to polemics in which it seems impossible not to sense more *"ira"* than *"studium."* Since the first edition, the "friends of Brentano" have at least taught me not to take a more optimistic view of that "fate" to which I alluded in the preface to that edition.[4] Yet on that side,[5] so much work and space have been employed in recent years to set my many errors in a sufficiently clear light and, in particular, to disallow even the possibility of assumptions, that it did not really seem feasible for me to abandon all thought of defense. I have to admit, though, that this thankless task became all the more tiresome to me in the course of the present work, since it came to mean overburdening this new edition with polemical material —material of the sort that can only by way of exception be of genuine interest to a reader concerned solely with the primary subject matter. Against many an attack, therefore, there may have been no defense; and it need not be cited as a crushing attack, simply on that account. At any event, I have as far as possible thrust polemical considerations into footnotes. Excursuses that did not easily admit of removal from the text have been distinguished by means of reduced type.

Returning now to focus on the question of whether assumptions are at all possible, it is easy to doubt that those who have already exhausted themselves in the attempt to prove their impossibility "antecedently" have actually hit upon the most troublesome things about the theory. Assumptions would at least have a companion in misfortune on which they could well pride themselves: psychological experimentation. There used to be, and there still are, a fair number of very reflective men and very serious organizations diligently pondering the question as to why experimental psychology is impossible. Alongside them, rooted in theoretical as well as practical needs, there arises one workshop after another for experimental psychology, and thousands of arms are at work capturing sector after sector of psychological territory for the experimental type of treatment. Will there be any success in bringing the theory of assumptions into this domain, too? One cannot prophesy anything on this score; overnight, a felicitous thought could open the way to success. But even now, the theory of assumptions can pride itself in the success of having been chosen as one of the mainstays for a new theoretical edifice, namely that of genetic psychology—the latest, most arduous, and most promising of the special psychological disciplines. This choice has occurred in the manner of a development peculiar unto itself, and not in the manner of a mere taking over of the results, however modest, which were afforded by the first investigations devoted to the theory of assumptions. Serious work should be ready to respond with a wholly impersonal goodwill to similar work, wherever it may occur. Yet such goodwill is, as we know, sometimes more readily extended across the ocean than from one country to the next. This is particularly true of my role in the development of the present knowledge of assumptions, which has received a doubtless undeservedly high appraisal. All the less reason for reservations of my own, then; I may use it as a testimonial to the importance of the facts treated in the present book, when an inquirer of the rank of J. M. Baldwin grants a fundamental position in his "genetic logic" to the contrast between a judgment and an assumption.[6] Again, the newest treatment of the basic problems of the theory of value,[7] one which is both comprehensive and of considerable merit and which likewise gives prominence to the genetic point of view, reveals itself intent on the consideration of assumptions and the experiences dependent on them.

All in all, then, I am surely entitled to think that I may have accomplished some useful things by the first edition of this book. And we can send the second edition on its way "out into the cruel world" with the accompanying wish that it be granted a destiny no less favorable in this regard. Let me at this point, however, express my cordial thanks to the esteemed friends who, in word and deed, proved helpful to this revision—especially to my fellow workers in seminars and at my institution, ever and again proving their value. At the head of the list is Dr. V. Benussi, who among other things was so very kind as to attend to the compilation of the new index of subjects.

Graz, Pentecost, 1910

The Author

I

Initial Theses

---

§1

A Domain of Facts Between Representation and Judgment

Representation has long been recognized as the prerequisite of anything that occurs in the realm of thought. Unless a thought-occurrence is itself a representation, it presupposes a representation. This has stood as something obvious, offering little occasion for serious doubt. And that is precisely why there have been so many examples, over the years, of the tendency to overrate the role of representation in the activities of the intelligence. It was thought that anything that necessitates a representation should itself be regarded as a representation. Even today, while the distinct nature of judgment has been pointed out emphatically to British psychology by David Hume and John Stuart Mill, and to German psychology by Franz Brentano, the prevailing opinion in psychology and epistemology is still nowhere the unanimity that befits the obviousness of the situation. However, it is not the task of the following investigations to offer a renewed theoretical treatment of the problem of judgment. If these investigations can help eliminate certain difficulties encountered in this problem of judgment—difficulties more often subjective than objective—they will do so merely in an indirect way, by attempting to show that judgment is so far from *being* representation that it does not even border on the domain of representation, and that the two domains are separated by a group of intervening facts. Thus, a sufficiently sharp characterization of this group of facts as distinct from representations as well as from judgments would prove just as fruitful for the knowledge of the one domain as for that of the other.

Naturally, I do not intend to take an entirely neutral position in the matter of judgment. What I have to set forth has its origins in the direct, intuitive apprehension of a reality presented by means of inward perception. So that in tracing the pattern of facts that confronts us here, it would hardly be feasible to leave off with something unintuitive in respect of part of this pattern, i.e., something that would still leave room for rather widely divergent opinions as to the nature of judgment. On the other hand, since the characteristic features

[9]

of judgment—things that will be of decisive importance to me in what follows
—seem really plain to the point of obviousness, I cannot but hope that the unbiased observer will be on my side in acknowledging these features, however he
may be inclined to see things in other respects.

There are, namely, two things which, in my opinion, anyone will grant as
being present in judgment, but lacking in representation. A person who judges
believes something, or is convinced of something;[1] it is only by a quite obvious
extension of verbal usage that we can speak of judgments in which the subject
leaves his conviction *in suspenso*. Furthermore, every judgment, by its very
nature, occupies a definite position within the antithesis of yes and no, of affirmation and negation. If I have a definite view, a conviction, in regard to *A* or
in regard to its connection with *B,* then this must necessarily either be to the
effect that *A* is (or is *B*) or be to the effect that *A* is not (or is not *B*). And this
holds true not only in the case of judging with certainty, but likewise in the
case of uncertain judgment: Even when I merely surmise, the surmise ineluctably has an affirmative or negative character.

Implicit in what has been said, though, is something else that I think should
now be brought quite explicitly to the fore. Namely, among the characteristic
features of judgment, I do not include the peculiar dichotomy that is typical of
the so-called categorical judgment and which shows up in the opposition of
subject and predicate, as with *A* and *B* in the formal example above. To judge
is to believe, and there is also a believing when one utters the sentence "*A* is"
["*A* ist"], at least under normal circumstances. It is true that this dichotomy,
whose peculiar character will not pass unappreciated in the following, even
now appears to a number of people to be so basic to the judgment that, in a
case where it is lacking, they prefer "to speak of positing and non-positing representations..."[2] I do not believe that this designation is appropriate. It may
well be that the *A* of the paradigm "*A* is" is initially apprehended with the help
of representations; but however current the metaphor of "positing" has become, in the end the *A* is still no more than apprehended, and to "posit" it
does not lie in our power, at least not in our cognitive power. Besides, how
would the representation itself manage to "posit"? Surely, *A* is represented in
exactly the same way, be it "posited" or "not posited" or neither of the two.
If, nevertheless, someone does not want to let the belief that *A* is—or is not—
pass as a judgment, then he may be fairly required to bear in mind that in the
following I shall use the term "judgment" in a somewhat different way, and
he will not be entitled to raise the objections to my theses that arise when my
verbal usage is replaced by the one that I have rejected.[3]

In everything that is entitled to be called a judgment, I find, therefore, without exception, the two factors mentioned above, the element of conviction and
the position within the antithesis of yes and no; and I cannot help thinking that
no theory a person has could ever prevent him from likewise meeting with these
factors. For a long time, though, I regarded the two of them as being simply

one; or at least, I regarded the second as a sort of determination of the first—and this as one of those determinations that cannot be found apart from what they determine. I would have always thought it obvious that any conviction had to be affirmative or negative, but I would never have expected to find affirmation or negation in any case where conviction was lacking. That this is nevertheless possible and, indeed, anything but rare in its realization—this point, along with the consequences of it, constitutes about the most important thing to be shown by the following discussions. As soon as it can be agreed that not only the element of conviction but also the opposition between affirmation and negation creates a fact that is essentially different from representation, then our approach to convictionless affirmation and negation will also lead us directly to the previously mentioned intermediate domain, the one between representation and judgment.[4]

Yet before we enter upon a more exact investigation of this matter, it might be well to try a firsthand examination of one of the various cases belonging to the intermediate domain in question. This is much easier with facts of the present sort than with many other events, mental or physical. Here, if one makes a reasonable effort, one can assemble the appropriate facts with total accuracy. Here, also, the suggestive power of the spoken or written word is almost always retained. I shall attempt to make use of this power now. I ask the reader to imagine, say, that the Boers were not obliged to yield to the superior force of the British, or that they experienced not just admiration and sympathy from the peoples of the European continent, but also politically effective support. The reader's justified surprise at seeing past political matters of the day brought up all of a sudden in the present context will hardly have prevented him from complying with my request. Nor, it is hoped, will he consider the request out of place, if I now see fit to add that, in complying with my wishes, he has brought about one of those mental facts that will be our concern in the following chapters.

One of the main purposes of this initial example is to help us find an appropriate name for the objects of this investigation; another is to help us achieve an initial characterization of these objects. In the first regard, it helps that we are dealing with a matter whose familiarity to us in the business of daily life just about matches the theoretical neglect that it has thus far received. When the demand that was just made upon the reader is characterized in the following way, everyone understands: It was a matter of inducing the reader to make a specific *assumption*. Secondly, as regards the word's signification, the thing that strikes us as most prominent is undoubtedly the note of opposition to judgment, as far as the element of conviction is concerned. How could I really ask the reader to believe something that he knows only too well to be false? Our "assuming" is manifestly something that is not influenced in the slightest by the presence of a contrary conviction. Another characteristic factor is perhaps not quite so palpable, in that it does demand something more in the way of psychological insight. Yet it is not too much of a demand, if I see the matter aright. For when I consider what sort of thing we have here, in an "assumption," two facts strike me as being quite satisfactorily plain. First of all, while we do not have quite the same situation as in judgment, it is still in some way cognate or similar to the judgmental situation. Again, there is something here that is entirely different from the business of merely representing something, e.g., as when one represents a color or musical note—or again, a melody, a landscape, or whatever. That is, it is entirely different as long as the representation is not a nonintuitive one; the justification for this reservation will be found in later remarks.[5] Nevertheless, in spite of the plainness of the situation, this latter point, the difference from representation, may not be immediately convincing to everyone; hence, in what follows there will be an attempt to provide a formal proof of this point. This requires a somewhat more detailed investigation, though, and so it will be appropriate to make the proof, or this investigation, the subject of a separate section.

In what follows, the word "assumption" will be used as a technical term for all those experiences which, as I hope to show, belong to the previously mentioned intermediate domain, the domain between representation and judgment.[6] As for defining the sense in which we are to speak of assumptions here, it will be obvious to anyone who has given any serious attention to this matter of definition that the foregoing is no more than provisionally adequate, adequate for the purposes of preliminary guidance. Further details will have to come from a more thorough acquaintance with the relevant facts, the securing of which is the aim of the following investigations. I find it necessary, however, to lay great stress on the avoidance of any critical approach to the following in which one operates with a definition of an assumption (or a definitional stipulation in its stead) formed *before* the investigation, only to find then that the following does not square with this definition.[7] After all, by its very precedence to the investigation, it could only be either a report on linguistic usage or a quite arbitrary nominal definition. The latter, naturally, would lack any authoritative signification. The former, however, assuming that it gets by uncontested, would certainly deserve to be considered as to its practicability, and in the choice of the word "assumption," I myself have been anxious not to lose contact with linguistic usage. But my subject is not primarily whatever it is that is called an "assumption," to the extent that it is called that; my subject is certain experiential facts. Among the available words, the designation "assumption" seems best suited for these facts. Yet only a closer investigation can yield their characteristic properties, in such a way that there can also be a clear understanding about the scientifically elucidated meaning of the word "assumption" and about the domain of employment that goes along with this meaning.

It can already be observed, incidentally, that there is a certain disadvantage in the expression that we are going to employ as a technical term. Together with all similarly employed expressions, as far as they are drawn from the vocabulary of daily life, it has the disadvantage that in regard to its accepted domain of employment it does not fully agree with what it is now supposed to mean, in its theoretical use. Even a person who judges is said to "assume" one thing or another, if his conviction or opinion is consciously, and so somewhat of his own volition, derived from inadequate reasons.[8] In this sense one can "assume" that the authority to whom one has been referred for guidance in a practical matter will be in possession of sufficiently precise information; similarly, the proprietor of a store may rather often have to be content to "assume" that a new customer to whose house he sends a valuable article on approval will not let the article get damaged; and so on. No doubt it will be seen that in these "assumptions" in the second sense of the term there is a feature that assures them a certain affinity to the experiences for which we shall exclusively reserve the word in the following. This feature is the receptivity to volitional influence, a feature that is as a rule conspicuously absent in judgments. But beyond that, these "assumptions" in the second sense are simply judgments, and it would be to deprive the word's presently advocated technical meaning of one of its most distinctive elements—nay, to obliterate the whole theoretical plan of approach advocated here—if one were willing to use the expression so broadly as to include cases of this second sort.[9] I trust that in explicitly excluding these cases, theory will not be making illicit use of its vested right to subordinate the available means of expression to its own needs.

§2
The Negative as Opposed to the "Merely Represented"

As mentioned, it is probably obvious to everyone as it stands that we are not dealing with a judgment in the initial example of an "assumption" given above. Such obviousness might not attach to the second thing that we maintained about this example, namely that the possibility of a mere representing is also out of the question. On the contrary, if I may judge for myself, there is hardly anyone who is at all accustomed to considering his inner experiences from psychological points of view who has not already, in regard to the most different of such assumptions, arrived without any particular deliberation at the opinion that it is all simply a matter of representations, nothing more. I simply represent to myself that the Boers got not just words to hear, but also deeds to see; in quite the same way, I can represent to myself that I am twenty or so years younger or that psychology can expect nothing but helpful assistance from its extraphilosophical neighboring disciplines or goodness knows what other unbelievable things. Certainly, as already maintained, I am now of the opinion that direct perception enables me to know that there is more in all this than mere representing; I should also not hesitate, were it necessary, to base the position that I take here solely on the testimony of direct observation.

Nevertheless, I regard it as a welcome safety factor that there is a standpoint from which one can prove in all strictness that "mere representing" is inadequate to the presently given situation. Also, for one who is devoting his attention to assumptions for the first time, the fact that there is such a standpoint will be a particularly emphatic indication of the peculiar character of that situation.

This standpoint comes into play when assumptions are negative. Our initial example, which on closer inspection is easily seen to constitute not just one assumption, contains an illustration of this. And of course, it is generally just as easy to form negative assumptions as affirmative ones. For negation is *never* a matter of representing, although it will naturally never occur without a representation; hence, wherever a negation is present the range of mere representation is quite certainly exceeded. This, too, will perhaps be evident to many a person even at first glance. In view of the importance of the matter, however, a closer consideration seems to me in order, although it will risk accomplishing something superfluous and although we shall be entering into a preliminary investigation that leads us temporarily away from the real object of these discussions.[10]

The assertion just now declared to be almost self-evident, the assertion that negation lies beyond representation, seems to be opposed by an extensive as well as familiar group of facts about representation. We do speak quite unforcedly of negative representations or better yet of "negative concepts"; and logic has long accorded them a very careful treatment. But if I can simply represent "nonred," "unextended," and "infinite," then one might well ask why an assumption that it is not raining or that there are people without faults could not be brought about by means of mere representing, too. What are we to think of "negative representations", then? To many, it may seem palpably obvious that we are now dealing with facts that have rather little in common with those designated above as "assumptions." As to whether this appearance might be deceptive, that will have to come out later on.[11] For now, it would be sufficiently in accord with our interest in assumptions if we could show that every apprehended *negativum* points to something other than a representation, even in cases where the situation presents itself to the observer as being markedly representational, as it were.

In this there is a preliminary question that cannot altogether be ignored. In the various cases in which a person may speak of "negative representation"— aside from whether he does so with greater or less correctness or preciseness— where is the "negative" really to be found? In every such case, as I am apprehending an A, I also apprehend a non-A in some sense.[12] So we have to do with a difference regarding what is apprehended—or in other words, a difference regarding what stands opposite [gegenübersteht] each intellectual experience as its object [Gegenstand], understanding this word in its broadest sense.[13] In this sense, infinity and immortality are doubtless objects; likewise limit, gap, and even the notorious nothing [Nichts]. In the non-*A*, then, there is a further objective factor, the "non," as it were, supervening on the *A*. Just for the moment we may designate this factor as the object *N*. Then while it may be justifiable to say of *A* that apprehending it is the business of representation, we must now answer the question whether this may be said in the same way of *N*.

The question will not be difficult to answer, if we remember beforehand that our representations fall into two major groups, according to the manner in which they come into our possession. We experience what blue or green is; we cannot likewise see similarity or difference with our eyes or hear it with our ears. But when we compare things seen, then through this activity we generate or produce representations by means of which we apprehend similarity or difference quite as we apprehend blue or red by means of sensations. Representations produced in this way, or production-representations, range themselves alongside perceptual representation;[14] reproduction will seize on representations of the one kind as well as those of the other. Aside from that, production-representations and perceptual representations are so typically different with respect to the objects naturally apprehended by means of them, that it will do well to keep an eye on the contrast afforded by their origin, even in the case of reproduced representations; for reproduction leaves objects unaffected. So the case of reproduction can simply be taken as included, as we begin this way: Any representation apprehending our object-factor *N* would have to follow either the pattern of perceptual representations or that of production-representations. This disjunction is as sound as our psychological knowledge that there are no representations other than perceptual representations and production-representations, except the reproductions thereof.

The question that we must first of all ask, on the basis of this disjunction, is this: Can the apprehending of our *negativum N* somehow be charged to a perceptual representation and thus, in some way or another, be reduced to perception? The evident nature of perception permits no doubt that the question is to be answered only in the negative. A danger of failing to recognize this—incidentally, anything but a serious danger—lies in the fact that when we hear words whose primary signification is negative, we can and not too infrequently do react with positive representations or, more precisely, representations having positive objects. This is true, moreover, not only in the case of inseparable compounds like "unwise," let alone uncompounded expressions like "blind" or "deaf," but in other cases, too. If I am to represent to myself a "knife without a blade," then the representation of a knife-handle will supply an equivalent that is entirely positive. It is easy to represent a "soft note" instead of a "note that is not loud," and so on. This is an expedient that surely suffices in many cases, and sometimes it even goes so far as to offer an advantage; yet in view of the words initially given, one makes one's self guilty thereby of an unquestionable inaccuracy—to be sure, the sort of inaccuracy that is anything but rare in our behavior toward linguistic expressions in general. So in view of such facts, it is actually not legitimate to speak of the perception of negative objects.

It is less easy to make a decision about the second and still remaining possibility, the possibility that we might perhaps attain to the representation of the object N through production. We are prohibited from rejecting this second possibility *a limine,* as we did the first, when we remember the character that was mentioned as being proper to the objects of produced representations; some of this character is immediately discoverable in our N, when one takes the natural sense of the expression non-A into consideration. If I am thinking of nonred, it is admittedly not the same as when I think of red; yet it is almost equally as obvious that I am no more able to think of nonred without thinking of red than I would be able, say, to form the idea "similar to a bell" without the idea of a bell. Referring the reader to my relevant statements on this matter elsewhere,[15] I can say briefly right now: Negative objects (of the form non-A) are always built [gebaut] on positive objects (of the form A), the latter being their *inferiora.* The negative objects themselves are objects of higher order.

The analogy provided by the example of similarity goes still further. True, an object of higher order normally requires a plurality of *inferiora*—there could be no question of similarity, if besides the bell, in our example, there was nothing else to consider. But the position in which this places the formula "non-A" is no worse than that of a formula such as "similar to A." If I cannot form even the *slightest idea* of similarity with the help of A alone, neither is there any reason why I should be able to form an idea of the *negativum* merely with the help of what is negated. In the idea of the non-A is contained surely not only the A, but also—nay, really to begin with—precisely that which is not the A. So the state of affairs would present itself more precisely as follows. The idea of the *negativum* does not develop originally from the A alone; instead, there is also given an X, of which it may be or at least is asserted that it is not A, in quite the same way that the similarity must, to begin with, be established between A and some other, second object Y. And just as abstraction then sets to work on the special complex $A\ Y$ formed by means of comparison —so that from the idea "Y similar to A" there is formed the idea "similarity to A" or "similar to A"—so too might an abstract representation "something that is not A" or simply non-A develop out of a complex of another sort, $A\ X,$ or out of the idea "X is not A." Along with the original duality of the *fundamenta,* the matter of the producing activity is also settled: What is accomplished by comparison in the other case is here accomplished by judgment— negative judgment, naturally. At that event, one can say that the *negativum* or, more precisely, the negative object is in the first instance apprehended with the help of judgment, though in the last instance it is itself not a pure judgmental object, but a representational object, one which, if need be, can also be apprehended without judgment. One can then press the semblance of agreement further, bringing in differentness[a] instead of similarity for the comparison. The ideas "non-A" and "different from A" give such an appearance of affinity, not just as concerns form, but also in respect of subject matter, as it were, that one can actually try to take the one idea to be the other.

Yet the unacceptability of the foregoing buildup becomes manifestly obvious right here, in its last step. The attempt to regard differentness and negation as being essentially the same may very well have suggested itself to more than one reduction-minded theorist already, but this has been merely with the intention of reducing differentness to negation, not with the intention of reducing negation to differentness. And an undertaking of the latter sort would do such unmistakable violence to the facts that the express reference to these facts can hardly escape being reproached with superfluousness. Nevertheless, we shall now devote at least a few words to recalling the relations between differentness and negation.

In following out the thought that the judgment "A is different from B" might be replaceable by the judgment "A is not B," one immediately meets with the difficulty that in differentness there are degrees, whereas there are none in negation—the latter being by its very nature quite incapable of gradation.[16] But then, it is easy to satisfy oneself that besides the relation in question, which is capable of gradation,[17] there is also a relation that is incapable of it and which can be called "differentness" in perfectly good accord with linguistic usage. It is the opposite of identity, nonidentity—the relation that subsists between yellow and orange as well as between yellow and red or, for that matter, yellow and blue, albeit the three differentnesses in these color-pairs are by no means equal, in the gradation-capable sense of the word "differentness." It may be that in the theory of relations the employment of the word "differentness" in the second sense, the sense in which differentness is incapable of gradation,[18] should be avoided, as something inexact and misleading. Yet it doubtless remains true that this differentness incapable of gradation is the only one whose separate character vis-à-vis negation is open to question.

There is in fact a good deal to be said for the conjecture that in categorical judgment this "differentness" might be to negation as identity is to affirmation. But what if one attempted to conclude from this, not that in a certain sense such a differentness originates in denial, but on the contrary, that denying is at bottom merely the representing (and naturally affirming) of such a "differentness"? One need only think of an existential negation to be aware of the utter untenability of this interpretation. Who would even feel tempted to see a judgment of differentness in the assertion, say, that there is no perpetual motion machine?[19] Another angle of approach is more useful, though, as it is directly applicable to the case that we have before us here, that of the categorical judgment. Suppose that as someone thinks first of iron and then of nickel, he utters in due order the two sentences, "The metal of which I am now thinking rusts" and "The metal of which I am now thinking does not rust." The listener, who has no reason to doubt the correctness of the two judgments enunciated for him and who therefore trustfully judges in the same way, connects the objects "metal" and "rusting" in his own two judgments. Who, then, however carefully he compared these judgments with each other, would in the case of the second normally be capable of detecting the appearance of a further object "differentness," granted now to the metal in the way that rusting was granted to the metal in the first judgment? Thus, it remains an obviously unpromising business to pretend to interpret away the negation, as it were, from what might be called a living negative judgment. But then could it be much more promising to attempt something similar in the case where we are met with negation in the form of a "non-A"? This is a somewhat more rigid form, after all. Nevertheless, it remains intelligible that if one is thinking of the "differentness" which itself reduces to negation, as indicated above, then "non-A" can be replaced everywhere by "different from A" or, as the case may be, "something different from A."

So it will by no means do to see an instance of differentness in our *negativum N*. But for all that, the apprehending of this *negativum* might still originate in the production of representations, as does the apprehending of differentness. Information on this score can be found in the connection between production and founding. The connection consists in this, that where two or more representations are employed, and a specific operation produces a new representation, the objects of the producing representations, as one might call them, serve as *fundamenta* for the object of the produced representation. The latter object is always an object of higher order, and it is one of those for which the designation "founded objects" ["fundierte Gegenstände"][20] may have sufficiently proved its value.[21] We find ourselves faced with the question, therefore, as to whether our *negativum N* can be regarded as a founded object [Fundierungsgegenstand]; and if it can, this still permits us to consider the possibility that once its representation has been produced, N might then also be apprehensible without a new productive process—or in other words, just reproductively—just as one can also think of sameness or similarity despite the fact that one is not right at the moment doing any comparing. But now, for the answering of this question we have at our disposal a consideration that is as simple as it is decisive. Founded objects are connected with their *fundamenta* by necessity.[22] Red and green are not just different; they must be different. Likewise, 3 is not just as a matter of fact greater than 2, but also necessarily thus; and so on. Now, there are certainly also negations that hold true necessarily. It is certainly every bit as necessary to negate sameness between red and green as it is to affirm differentness between them. But it is every bit as certain that there are negations in which necessity has no part. That a released stone goes in the direction of the earth and not away from it—that is a piece of information which, at least before the forum of human knowledge, could make no more claim to necessarily holding true on its negative side than it could on its positive side. So to the non-A *as such,* there still does not attach any necessity; and in that case, what we have here is not a founded object, either.

With that, it seems to me, we have furnished the proof that a representation which has our *negativum N* as object cannot be found even in the domain of produced representations and their reproductions. In that case, there seems to be no representation of this object at all; and while this result is admittedly not better attested to than the exhaustiveness of the disjunction between perceptual representations and production-representations or their respective reproductions, it is at least as well attested to.[23] Moreover, this result already has the epistemic sense of the person innocent of these matters on its side, if I am not mistaken. Without special reflection, such a person senses how *toto genere* different this object N is from all that representation is able to offer us, notwithstanding the inexhaustible variety of its objects. Further on,[24] we shall have the job of gaining a theoretical command of this pretheoretical impression.

Admittedly, there is a reservation that ought not to go unmentioned in this connection. If we occupy ourselves with something common in the representation of the A and that of an X, then whatever this common factor may be, it naturally establishes a relation between the two representations; and with that, there is also a relation between the objects A and X, primarily as pseudo-existences.[25] So it is, among other cases, when I affirm or negate X of the A or A of the X; if the judgment is justified, then on the strength of that it makes perfectly good sense to speak of a relation between A and X that consists simply in the occurring or holding true of that judgment. To that extent, then, there is a kind of relation between X and A even in the fact that X is not A. This relation may *cum grano salis* admit of representation; and in that case, a way to attain to something like a representation of non-A by means of abstraction has actually been found. But now let us consider what kind of apparatus a representation of that sort presupposes, if we may express ourselves so. In order to think of a "nonround thing," I would have to conceive the thought, "something of which the judgment that it is not round holds true." Any unbiased person would suppose himself to be operating in the domain of shapes, here, in his representing; and yet, besides round, one would in truth have to think also of something quite different from shapes, namely of the negative judgment and its relation to that of which it "holds true." This is possible, of course; but the drawing of psychological and logical considerations into a thinking generally turned to quite different interests is such an obtrusive thing that, where it happens, it can hardly escape even casual observation. And with the possible allowance of quite rare exceptions, not even the keenest attention is capable of discovering in so-called negative representations anything of a roundabout way of the sort just described. To all intents and purposes, therefore, the possibility of this roundabout way is wholly out of the question, and it will be left out of the question also in the following.

Yet, one must still allow for the possibility of reducing the described complication by getting rid of the psychological component and retaining only the logical one. It is in reality an anticipation of later investigations,[26] but it will be straightway clear to any experienced student of cognition, that one who says (and thinks), "It is true that X is not A," does not at all have to think of any judgment-experience in doing so. As to what it really is, then, that he must be thinking of, this can be left undecided for the present. Certain it is, however, that he just as little need think of judging if he says, "It is false that X is A." And so, in this thought of falsity, we would have found the means for apprehending the object N, the non-A without the employment of a negation.[27] But then this holds true only on condition that the thought of falsity does not iself somehow have a negative character. And it actually does have such a character, as we shall have further occasion to mention;[28] so this way is impassable, too. As a matter of fact, the testimony of direct observation should probably not be left entirely out of account in this matter, either. The thought of falsity or incorrectness might be just about as familiar to everyone as that of truth; but for that very reason, everyone will be in possession of quite reliable information as to approximately how often he has thought of falsity in connection with the words "nonsmoker" or "nonalcoholic beverage." So even this "reduction," if there were such a thing, would not as a rule actually be employed, and there would have to be something else in its place, something that is presumably identical to the subject of the present book.

While it admittedly does not yet have any value in the way of proof, let us in passing call attention to the fact that by this interpretation it would in any case be conceded that the apprehending of a *negativum* draws in something to which the attributes "true" and "false" are applicable. Thus, one who has become accustomed to regard the domain of this opposition as the province of judgment is faced with the question as to what it might mean to apprehend the notion of falsity where judgment is absent, as in the case of the "represented" *negativum,* and where something sufficiently judgment-like probably would be able to do the job best.

However, to return for the present to the normal instance of the things customarily treated as "negative representations," we can probably now regard it as settled that these things are not representations at all. Of course, this gives rise to the question as to their real nature; and the opportunity to try to answer this question will present itself later.[29] For the time being, all that is to be deduced from what has been set forth is our right to infer, in any case where the antithesis of yes and no plays a part, that there must in such a case be something more than mere representing. The advantage of this principle is not just that it provides a new and supplementary justification for assigning a position between representation and judgment to the experience for which, above, the technical designation "assumption" proved suitable. Also, this principle will prove useful as one of the handiest leads, as we now try to get clear about another question. This is the question as to whether and where in the course of psychological observation we might encounter more of such intermediate experiences, experiences that would then likewise have a fair claim to the designation "assumptions." It should not be too surprising if the relevant inquiry proves especially profitable precisely on those points where theoretical treatment with the help of the hitherto current conceptions has not quite been able to succeed. In any case, there would be a particularly auspicious confirmation of the theoretical importance of the concept of an assumption if, in the face of the old psychological or epistemological difficulties, this concept proved capable of contributing to their disentanglement.

Naturally it will be appropriate to seek out the fact of the assumption, to which we have only now been introduced, above all in those places where it most willingly offers itself to observation. But then, as with other experiences, so too with assumptions: There are cases where they do not make themselves apparent to direct observation or at least do so in an insufficiently sure and clear-cut manner, so that their presence is more easily established in a roundabout way. In the matter of assumptions, as is so often the case in other matters, this roundabout way takes one through the linguistic expressions by which the experiences in question betray themselves; and it often takes one through objects that are by their very nature dependent on assumptions for being apprehended. Accordingly, before we follow the emergence of assumptions in somewhat more detail, we must carry out a few preliminary investigations. These may have some usefulness in their own right, we might add. On the one hand, they will have to deal with linguistic matters; on the other hand, they will have to deal with a class of objects hitherto not sufficiently appreciated in their peculiar character. The next two chapters will be devoted to these preliminary investigations.

II

On the Question of the
Characteristic Functions of the Sentence

<hr/>

§3
On the Sign and Its Signification

At the outset, we can comply with the custom of considering the functions of language mainly from the standpoint of signs. Let us turn to Eduard Martinak's *Psychologische Untersuchungen zur Bedeutungslehre.*[1] I shall attempt to go a step further with that writer's precisive approach to the relation between sign and signified—or the sign and its signification, since I take it that the latter already coincides with what is signified.[2] Now if I see the matter aright, it is just too colorless a way of defining this relation when one merely adverts to the signification's correlation with the sign,[3] unless one is willing to sacrifice everything distinctive in this relation for the sake of universality. For a start, one cannot help saying just this:[4] If I can infer the presence of B from that of A,[5] then A is a sign of B, and B is the signification of the sign. Admittedly, it would be exact to say that the being of B, in the first instance its existence,[6] is the signification.

What all this really amounts to, ultimately, is the relation of the epistemic ground to the epistemic consequent. Naturally, this is most clearly apparent where said relation is in no danger of being obscured by any sort of complicating circumstances—or in other words, where the sign does its own functioning as sign, as it were, without there having been any purposive arrangements with a view to the giving of a sign. In such cases, Martinak speaks of "real signs." But of course, even the sign that he calls "final"[7] is by nature just something that is made with a real sign in mind. In other words, it is something that stands to the ordinarily conceived real sign roughly in the way that an experiment stands to a fact naturally offering itself to theoretical handling. It is just that the presence of subjective factors associated with purposiveness entails a certain possibility of disruption. This possibility can be realized, e.g., by the sign-giver choosing a sign that actually does not have the ability to serve as the *ex definitione* requisite epistemic ground. Be that as it may, there should not be

[22]

too many disruptions appearing on the record. There needn't be any at all, of course, so far as one limits one's self to the minimum of what one can determine to show by means of a sign, namely to the intention of "communicating" something. At this point, without doubt, more than one reason will suggest itself for speaking of a "conative" sign in the special case where what the sign-giver intends to communicate is his wish, perhaps even his will—or in general a conation [ein Begehren],[a] and the conation can be inferred from the sign. Then, in all those cases where the sign-giver has something different to communicate, we can speak of "communicating signs" in a somewhat narrower sense, opposing these signs to the "conative signs."[8] But by the same token, every final sign is at the same time a communicating sign in at least a broader sense, and in this fact we have no small part of the starting material for an important extension of the concept of signs or signification. It is an extension to which we must give special attention, in view of the tasks occupying us in the present investigations.

So let us suppose that the situation regarding final signs has been correctly interpreted in what has just been set forth. Then in the first instance, it is always a mental fact that stands over against this sign [Zeichen] as that which is designated [als Bezeichnetes], and therefore as the "signification" ["Bedeutung"] of this sign. As for real signs, under the right circumstances the same thing can apply to them, leading to the same result. This result consists in a second correlation, one which originates in the mental fact's having a content and, hence, also an object. If A is the sign that has a mental fact B—best let this be a representing, a judging, or a conative experience—as its "signification," and if B has the object C, then by this means A is connected not only with B but, in a new way, also with C. This does not mean that A can be taken as the epistemic ground for C in the same way that it can, *ex definitione,* for B.[9] It may be that when we set C over against A as the latter's "signification," this usage does not at all deserve to be called an extension of the concept of signification, and that it is just a new way of employing the word "signification." At all events, one must not treat B and C as being on the same footing, in their relation to A.

The importance of this consideration will be immediately clear to anyone who notes that the facts of the present case, for the time being set forth in a quite general fashion, are realized in language—in the first instance, in its individual words. Because words have their "signification" ["Bedeutung"], we have become accustomed to treat them as "signs" ["Zeichen"], all the more so as a word usually makes its appearance accompanied by a mental state of affairs whose presence may be inferred from the presence of the word, in accordance with our above definition of a sign. In consequence of this, it has often been left unobserved that what one may infer from the presence of a word does not at all coincide with what the word "signifies"—and doubtless also unobserved that word and signification are by no means always held together by a sign relation in the original sense, a relation of the word to a mental fact. It may be that the first of these two situations represents one of the many cases in which inadequacy in the distinction between content and object[10] has been harmful; nevertheless, the deficient discrimination remains especially remarkable here, since in the present case language itself has provided for clearly discriminating terms. For our purposes, there is special value in making plain the sense of these terms and the distinction they convey. For the present, therefore, they will have to concern us a bit more closely. Further on, when the understanding of words and sentences will have to be briefly entered into, we shall return to the second of the two connections between word and signification.

§4
Expression and Signification in the Word.
Secondary Expression and Secondary Signification

It is both customary and justifiable to credit language with a special measure of aptitude for "expressing" our thoughts. Whether a speaker does want to express his thoughts, whether he reveals them apart from or even against his own intentions, or, finally, whether someone is there who does really take cognizance of what the words reveal—these are details which it will not hurt to leave out of account here. It is also true that in the phrase "expression of thought" a one-sided limitation to the intellectual domain is apparent, while language is by no means about to be separated from its function of giving expression to feelings and desires.[b] For the present, it will not hurt to leave this out of account, too. On the contrary, this very one-sidedness lends itself particularly well to our present needs, insofar as in intellectual operations, what a word "signifies"[11] stands out in sharp contrast to what it "expresses." What it signifies is the *object* of the intellectual event in question, in the first instance the object of the representation that makes up this event or at least forms its basis. Thus, a person who utters a word such as "sun" normally gives *expression,* whether he really wants to or not, to the fact that a definite representation is occurring in him—a representation which can, of course, just as well be a perceptual one as a reproductive one.[c] As to what representation this is, that is in the first instance determined by what is represented by means of it—or in other words, determined by its object; and this object is simply that which the word "sun" *signifies.* It must be admitted that when there is a question about the signification of a word, the word one has in mind is not apt to be a certain word uttered just then by a certain individual. It is *"the word"* in general that one has in mind; and by the signification of a word, therefore, we understand not what this or that person means by it, but what the totality or majority of speakers mean and, hence, what the individual speaker reasonably "should" mean. But this does not carry any further implication for the natural sense of the contrast of expression and signification. No one hesitates to admit that one and the same word can "signify" different things at different times, in different places, for different social classes, for different families, and, finally, even for different individuals. And so it will probably be permissible to put the matter quite generally and say that a word always "signifies" the object of the representation it "expresses" and, conversely, that it expresses the representation of the object it signifies.[12]

It is useful to the elucidation of the relation between expression and signification to recall the facts in which this relation has its origin. "Signification" ["Bedeutung"], as especially deserves to be noted in the case of a "-tion" ["-ung"] word, is not the same thing as "to signify" ["bedeuten"]; rather, it has the latter as its source, in that it is the thing which "signifies" that has a "signification." Within our immediate sphere of consideration, that which signifies is a word, and we may ask what signifying really consists in, in the case of words. In answering this question, one cannot let one's considerations terminate in the word; one must stick with the person who utters it meaningfully. As a part of life, signifying is surely always a signifying for someone. Now as is immediately evident from the foregoing, this signifying is tied to the fact of a word's being an expression. It is tied to this fact not in the manner of a consequent fact, but in the sense that a word signifies only as far as it expresses. More precisely, a word signifies only to the extent that it expresses an intellectual experience, the object of the experience in that case constituting the signification of the word. This state of affairs is obscured just a bit by the fact that along with the actual signification of the word, as we might call it, there goes a certain potential signification. Independent of the actual signifying and expressing, it clings to the word, as it were; and with the word it gains acceptance into the dictionary. And in the course of this, naturally, the peculiarity of the individual cases from which this potential signification has arisen is stripped away wherever possible.

In that case, though, one could also speak of expression in the potential sense. In any event, the following proposition holds true, understood with enough circumspection. That which has signification is also an expression and moreover, as one may add, a primary expression as opposed to a type of secondary expressive capacity which, under certain circumstances, can belong to a word by virtue of its signification. This is not infrequently the case when the object constituting the signification belongs to the domain of inward perception. If someone complains about pain, then what the word "pain" expresses in the first instance—or in other words, primarily—is the representation[13] of pain, at least according to the customary interpretation. But on this occasion, it can also be gathered from the word that the speaker really is in pain. To that extent, the word also expresses a feeling; but it does so in a roundabout way, as it were, and in that sense secondarily. If, as we saw, signification somehow has primary expression as its prerequisite, then secondary expression accordingly turns out to be grounded on a fact of signification, as it were: No secondary expression without signification.

This proposition cannot be broadened into the converse of the above principle, though. Although it was permissible for us to say above, "no signification without expression," here, on the contrary, the following holds true. There is no need at all that something also have signification, if it is an expression. This is clearly apparent in expressions for experiences that are primarily emotional, e.g., "oh," "bah," "hey," and the like. But then it is also clearly apparent in expressions for intellectual experiences; words such as "yes" and "no" certainly express something. Yet it might be hard to say what they signify for the one who utters them, as long as we are continuing to speak of signifying in the same sense as previously. Functioning much more frequently in this way are words that by no means lack a signification in the beginning, ones whose signification has in fact enabled them to become secondary expressions in the manner touched on above: By dint of exclusive employment as such, they have, in practice at least, lost their signification. This assumes that the converse is not the case and that the significations of the words in question have not grown out of their original use as significationless expressions, which is a matter for linguistic science to decide. At any event, in the case of interjections like "woe" or formalized civilities such as "I have the honor" and so forth, no one thinks of the "sense" ["Sinn"] of these words. But it naturally should not be forgotten, when one therefore concedes that there really are significationless expressions in language, that "signification" is being spoken of here in a limited, technical sense. With that, it goes without saying that an expression which in this narrower sense has no "signification" can, merely by the fact that it is an expression, very well have a signification in the broader sense, the sense in which a signification [Bedeutung] appertains to the sign [Zeichen] as such; so that the expression may also have a certain importance or noteworthiness or however one may care to put it. Actually, it is quite alien to the traditions of grammar to flatly deny "signification" to words of the type in question; but from that it follows, as far as I can see, just that grammar does not under all circumstances adhere to the sense of the word "signification" just now characterized as the technical one.

In light of such cases of expression without signification, we can now make a somewhat closer approach to the nature of signifying. The view that signifying is lacking not only in expressions for emotional experiences but also in certain expressions for intellectual experiences, such as "yes" and "no," is traceable to an opinion which, for many, will have stood as something perfectly obvious from the outset. This is the opinion that signifying occurs only where what is expressed are representations. But to take the case of secondary expression characterized above, if a person says, "I have a headache," no one will deny signification to the word "headache," even though it is not at all obvious that one who knows of his headache would also, on that account, have to represent it. In another place, I have attempted to prove[14] that in such cases the experience itself offers itself to apprehending (which is then introversion[d]). Without failing to recognize how much in this interpretation may still be unclarified and unsettled,[15] I can accommodate our account both to it and to the needs that will arise in the course of the following investigations by characterizing significations not specifically as represented objects, but as objects *apprehended* in any way whatsoever. In that case, signifying attaches to a word not merely so far as the latter expresses a representation, but in a quite general way, namely so far as the word expresses an experience that offers an object to thought or, as I wish to say technically, *presents* it to thought. This will include the case where the presenting experience coincides with what is presented. In summary, then, we can restate the matter as follows: A word signifies something so far as it expresses a presenting experience; the object that this experience presents is the signification.

From the standpoint just introduced, that of presentation, it is immediately noticeable that there are on the one hand experiences that are by nature such as to present objects to thought, as long as the latter is somehow functioning, and on the other hand, experiences where this is not the case. Experiences of the former type are doubtless always representations; among experiences of the latter type one can include, e.g., feelings. These, too, as we saw, can be made to present; but for that, it requires a procedure which is on the whole an artificial one, as introversion is. By such a procedure, expressions that were originally significationless gain signification, by way of addition, as it were. So these are expressions in which the signifying function can only be a supervenient one; and to the extent that they are not as closely associated with this function as are expressions for representations—expressions in which signifying will hardly ever be lacking—a certain contrast seems quite feasible. Taking the latter expressions as instances of primary signification, we can contrast them to all the rest as to instances of secondary signification[16]—as far as the coining of special terms is at all requisite in this matter. In no case, however, ought one to set too high a value on the analogy between this contrast and the contrast between primary and secondary expression.

With an eye to the progress of these investigations, let us take immediate note of a certain fact, though it will be only later on that we shall want to enter into its details. There are experiences whose nature is preeminently to present an object, viz., representations; and there are also those experiences that do not have a proper object coordinated with them at all,[17] so that they can at most, like every experience, present themselves. But in addition, there are experiences which, although they do not lack a certain relationship with a definite object, are of such nature as not to present the latter. But suppose that they are enlisted into presenting, as it were. Then as far as they are linguistically expressed, there is again accomplished the transition from significationlessness to signifying, in the relevant means of expression; and the signification can differ according to whether the experiences present themselves or their object. We shall see that the words "yes" and "no," characterized above as significationless, belong in this class. Even at this point it is recognized that "ifs and buts" and "the why," as well as "the yes and no" of a matter, can be spoken of in a thoroughly significant manner, along with much else of this sort.

§5

The Sentence as Judgment-expression

As is natural, our statements up to this point have had to do mainly with individual words. But of course, the contrast of signification and expression also has its validity in the case of word-*complexes,* and we may reasonably expect to find that what already makes such complexes unified wholes before the tribunal of grammar is generally either a unity of signification or a unity of expression—i.e., at least the latter, where signification and expression are not found together. It goes without saying that we shall thereby be dealing mostly with objects of higher order and with the operations directed at the conceiving of them. But while word-complexes exhibit practically any amount of structural variety, in grammar it has long been thought appropriate to grant an obviously special status to one such complex, in opposition to all the others. And it does seem that nothing presents itself more cogently, even to the consideration of an utter layman, than the wholly distinctive nature of the *sentence*[e] as opposed to what one could take to be a mere word-combination in the broadest sense. Though the latter can attain any degree of complexity, it always seems to maintain an essential affinity to simple or uncompounded words. It will prove conducive to the goal we have set for these discussions, if we attempt an inquiry into the reasons for the special status of sentences—this fact that is apparently so obvious to everyone.

First of all, it is certainly to be expected that linguistic science will find the subsumption of the sentence under the concept of a word-complex all too superficial—nay, not even sufficiently founded in fact, since there are after all sentences that consist of only one word. A finite verb like "credo" actually has every claim to be regarded as a sentence; and even in comparison with its infinitive "credere" it immediately exhibits the distinctive state of affairs that we are accustomed to see in the sentence in contradistinction to the "individual word." But for all that, the special position occupied by sentences of this type is obvious enough for us to be able to regard them safely as exemplifying the limit case. Moreover, the present subsumption, performed here only in passing, will be harmless anyway, in that no theoretical consequences are to be drawn from it. What does have primary importance for our purposes, however, is this: that the question as to the nature of the sentence becomes only the more pressing, if not even the notion of something composed of a plurality of words can be brought in to lend intelligiblity to what is in any case forcibly apparent to us to begin with, namely the fundamental difference between word and sentence.

Accordingly, as it is scarcely any longer feasible to look for what is essentially characteristic of sentences elsewhere than on the mental side,[18] we find ourselves immediately faced with the choice between what a sentence might signify and what it expresses. But even as it comes into view, the first member of this dilemma promises to yield little profit. To be sure, there is normally never a lack of significations where there is a sentence. These significations seem to consist in the significations of words, the words united into a complex in the sentence, and to consist in the objects of higher order that are based on these word-significations and which have them as their *inferiora*. Concerning the number of *superiora* of the sort in question, a more exact determination may be dispensed with in the present context. But in the fact of the unlimited variety of such significations, there is no common element that also proves bound to the sentence. Moreover, it is possible to transform any sentence into a word-complex that is no longer a sentence but which still has all the object-related material that could be met with in the sentence according to the customary interpretation. If I say, instead of "This metal is light," simply "this light metal," all the object-related material seems to have been carried over, although the sentential form is given up and, along with it, the peculiar function of the sentence. The function, consequently, does not seem to admit of a characterization in terms of objects. But then with this sort of characterization ruled out, so is the factor of signification, in the sense that has now been established.

Thus, we find the second member of the dilemma suggested to us. A certain preconception about sentences makes it easy for us to follow this suggestion, i.e., as we set out to seek the characteristic features of the sentence in what it expresses. I mean the preconception according to which one does not hesitate to assign a quite definite function to the sentence, in respect of what it expresses. But there is also unusually clear-cut information on this point, supplied by experience of the most commonplace sort. If I say, "The sky is blue," I thereby express an opinion, a judgment, and this is something that can in no wise be gathered from the words, "the blue sky." Whatever one may think of the psychological nature of judgment, in every case it seems perfectly obvious that where the main thing is to express a judgment, a sentence must always be used and that there is simply no other way for us to express our conviction regarding a certain object.[19] With that, we seem to have found our answer in the simplest way, the answer to the question concerning the nature of the sentence. The sentence would be essentially characterized so: What we have here is the special arrangement, as it were, which language makes just for the expression of judgments.[20]

It will hardly be objected that such a definition gives an impression of artificiality or that it fails to adduce a sufficiently important and tangible factor, in trying to do justice to the obviously special status of the sentence. On the contrary, the definition presents itself as something so natural, and the grasp of it seems to require so little reflection expressly directed to it, that many a person will have almost unconsciously adhered to it, even after meeting with more than one experience that could not be brought into accord with this definition. With a little attentiveness, however, one can catch sight of an inexhaustible host of such experiences, and we cannot avoid the task of getting a general view of the most important of the relevant cases.

§6
Independent and Dependent Sentences
That Do Not Express Judgments

To begin with, it is easy to see that the great majority of sentences that really express judgments are so constituted that the grammarian can designate them as independent sentences. However, if one wanted to conclude from this that all independent sentences, at least, fitted the definition that has been tentatively brought into consideration above, then he would already be in considerable error. Interrogative sentences in their most natural form all make this perfectly obvious. I do not mean the ones in which the object of the question appears in a dependent sentence, as it does in "I now ask whether one can rely on that statement." Here we have an example of what I called "secondary expression" above. Primary expression is afforded by the following sentence: "Can one rely on that statement?" What is expressed here would normally be a conative experience [Begehren]^f, which might just be a wish but also might be an injunction. That it is certainly not a judgment may be taken as particularly obvious in this case; for under ordinary conditions, the thing that the questioner desires [begehrt] first of all will be a knowing or conviction or, in other words, a judgment about the object designated in the sentence. Accordingly, he will *not* yet have it, much less be able to express it. For one thing, then, we have the interrogative forms in language, forms that make their appearance in the rising and falling intonation of a sentence, if in no other way, and which reappear in a written or printed mark. Along with these, there are the much more distinct optative and imperative forms, which call attention to the fact that independent sentences can on occasion express another sort of conation [Begehren] than that of a questioner. Here too, of course, we are not considering the many cases of secondary expression, where what one wishes or enjoins is communicated in dependent sentences, sentences dependent on "I beg you," "I wish," and so forth. Yet where we have primary expression in the use of an independent sentence, it is true that the exclusion of a judgment as the thing possibly being expressed is not quite so outwardly recognizable as in the case of a question: but for all that, it is hardly less indubitable. For here too, a person can scarcely be judging something as already realized, if he is only now desiring [erst begehrt] it. Thus, it is at most a negative judgment that a request such as "Come to me" could be supposed to express. This would be the conviction that the person addressed is not near me—an interpretation that is to all intents and purposes adequately refuted by the lack of any negation sign.

In the case of dependent sentences the situation is considerably more unfavorable for the attempted characterization of the sentence by means of judgment. Certainly, there are also plenty of dependent sentences that can be taken as expressions for judgments. Thus, if I say, "The heat was so great that no one cared to leave the house at midday," then from the subordinate clause one may unhesitatingly infer the presence of the judgment, "No one cared to leave the house at midday." The case is no different when I say, "As the bells of the nearby church chimed, there was a persistent and distinctly audible common overtone." Here too, what is expressed includes a judgment, one about the bells sounding together. But the situation is surely quite different if, for example, one says of a dangerous place on a mountain path, "The one who loses his balance there is a dead man." By that, it is certainly not meant that already somebody has actually lost his balance at this place. But one can see even more clearly how things stand in this particular matter of relative clauses, when the latter belong to negative main clauses. If I say, "There are no faultless people," surely no one would think of finding the object "faultless people" affirmed thereby; indeed, the sentence expresses the very opposite of such an affirmation. But in that case, it will naturally not do to understand the merely superficial variation, "There are no people who are without fault," differently. And if someone says, "We do not find a single case in the whole area of psychological observation where judgment is not connected with representation," here too,[21] no one would think of looking in the subordinate clause for the judgment that there is judgment without representation. At the same time, this case will call attention to the importance of the subjunctive,[g] which appears to enter in readily wherever there is a disagreement between what the subordinate clause would have to convey as a judgment-expression and what it really conveys according to the intention of the speaker.

Sentences introduced with "that" might merit special attention here. No doubt, instances favorable to the interpretation of these very sentences as expressions of judgment might be sought among such locutions as "I am convinced (I affirm, believe, expect) that...." But it must immediately seem somewhat strange that the judgment should find expression twice, once secondarily in the main clause, particularly in its verb, and then once again in the subordinate clause, in primary form. Furthermore, the subordinate clause will now occasionally seem to say more than the main clause really allows. In order to see this, compare two sentences such as "I am convinced that it will still rain today," and "I surmise that it will still rain today." If in the first case the subordinate clause is an expression of a judgment, namely, "It will still rain today," then so too is it analogously, in the second case. And naturally, if in the first case the subordinate clause is an expression of a judgment made with certainty, so likewise in the second case. And so it is in general: Any sentence, when it expresses a judgment and nothing about certainty appears noted in it, may be taken as the expression of a judgment with certainty. But in fact, there is no certainty in our second case; there is just a surmise [Vermutung], as the main clause shows. Regarded as an expression of judgment, the subordinate clause would in this case give the lie to the main clause, as it were. But the disagreement between the main clause and the subordinate clause, namely with the latter taken as an expression of judgment, can become a much more considerable one. After all, I can also say, "I don't think that it will rain today"; and although one may sometimes experience a slight feeling of inexactitude in speaking this way,[22] we know that it usually means the same as, "I think that it won't rain today"—and thus the exact opposite of what the subordinate clause was supposed to express. Even locutions like "I doubt that..." and "I don't know (doubt, can offer no opinion as to) whether..." stand in fairly clear opposition to the disputed interpretation of the further, subordinate clause. To the above "I affirm," the further, we could with utter strictness of expression oppose an "I deny that..."; and if the subordinate clause in this case were supposed to convey, besides what is denied, also the denial once again, then for our rain example the dependent sentence would inevitably have to have a negative character. From this I conclude that in none of the presently adduced cases of secondary expression of judgment in the main clause, i.e., not even where the interpretation in question is not already ruled out in advance by virtue of the special situation, has a judgment been expressed, except *per accidens,* as it were.

A type of verification for this is afforded by cases that differ from the ones just discussed only in that the views of another are spoken of, instead of those of the speaker. If someone says, "My friend X is of the opinion that the problem of determinism and indeterminism is insoluble," the speaker himself can just as easily as not be a convinced determinist. In the present case, all that he would be expressing for his own part is a judgment concerning the opinion of his friend and not one concerning the question of determinism. The judgment about determinism and its indemonstrability is not made at all by the speaker. Consequently, the subordinate clause of his utterance can no more express this judgment than the main clause can.

From another standpoint, it is likewise easy to see how little these and similar dependent sentences with "that" really have to do with judgment. They remain intelligible even when what they are attached to is not a sentence at all, but just a word, and a word that itself cannot possibly be regarded as a judgmental sign. The words, "the idea that truth could be suppressed by force" are thoroughly intelligible, but they obviously set the understanding a task that is not essentially different from that set by words like "the most important discovery of the nineteenth century." There is no more judging done in the one case than in the other; so that if the speaker has revealed something of his views, this must be in the subjunctive "could"—which is in no wise indispensable, however. Also, many relative clauses rank as fully analogous to the example just considered. One who speaks of the little tree "that wanted different leaves" is certainly not involving himself in an affirmation of the existence of this little tree, and no one would want to take the relative clause in question for the expression of a negation, either.

At this point it probably requires no special proof, that what has been set forth above about independent sentences of the interrogative and other conative [Begehrungs-] types, regarding their relation to the judgment, can be carried over to those subordinate clauses that follow main clauses of the form "I ask, beg," etc., when these latter clauses appear as secondary means of expression for the desires [Begehrungen] in question, replacing the primary ones discussed above. However, we must still mention certain declarations in sentence form to which the notion of a "dependent clause" does not afford a quite adequate angle of approach, so that the grammarian, too, prefers to speak of "nonsimple"[h] sentences of a separate form. I have in mind the expressions for the much discussed hypothetical and disjunctive judgments, as they are called. With regard to the former in particular, it has surely been emphasized frequently enough that neither the antecedent nor the consequent needs to be actually judged and that, indeed, the gist of the hypothetical judgment can remain intact even for one who regards the antecedent and the consequent as out-and-out false. In the above-mentioned use of the subjunctive we can even see a quite common sign for this state of affairs: "If the weather were good, we could take an excursion today," one says in rainy weather. As for the so-called disjunctive judgment, it probably requires no argument to show that it too belongs in the scope of the present investigation. One who says, "Either the air cools off or the rainy weather will continue," surely no more affirms the one than he does the other.

We know how closely hypothetical judgments of the nature just now discussed are connected with inferences that one draws solely in accordance with their form, as it were, without in any way committing oneself as to the correctness of the "matter." Even in the purely formal pattern, "A is B, B is C, hence A is C," I apprehend the correctness of the syllogism in accordance with the mood Barbara, without in any way involving myself more closely with A, B, and C. And what I experience at that moment will surely find fairly adequate expression also in the hypothetical judgment, "If A is B and B is C, then A is also C."[23] With that, there can be no question about the three sentences by which the above syllogism was expressed; they, too, in no wise express judgments.

§7
Understanding in the Case of Word and Sentence

As one can see, we are confronted with an imposing series of facts. They quite clearly forbid any flat ascription to sentences of the function of expressing the judgment of the one who utters these expressions, as though they had this task once and for all. But if we do not wish to believe in purposeless arrangements in language, then this negative result involves the question as to what it is, then, that really does gain expression in sentences like the ones just examined. We find ourselves led to an altogether analogous question, if we now consider sentences from the standpoint of the listener rather than from the standpoint of the speaker. Language, after all, becomes a means of understanding not only through the fact that something is expressed, but likewise by the fact that what is expressed, or the discourse expressing it, is understood.

If we attempt first of all to get clear about the nature of such "understanding," then nothing seems more reasonable than to take our basis in the interpretation of words as signs mentioned at the beginning of this chapter. If a sign, as we have seen above,[24] is a state of affairs capable of functioning as an epistemic ground, then since it is both justifiable and natural to speak of something as the "understanding" of the sign, this understanding will consist in the experience of the relevant epistemic act. A person who understands the sign is one who, from its presence, actually makes the inference to what is designated. If words are thus signs of mental occurrences in the speaker, then the listener will understand a piece of discourse to the extent that, on the basis of what is heard, he takes note of the mental occurrences that have found expression in language. For the sentence in particular, as far as it expresses a judgment, this means that the listener's understanding consists in arriving at a conviction that the speaker is judging and a conviction as to what his judgment concerns.

And sometimes it does happen that when X expresses an opinion in the presence of Y, the latter thereupon judges, "X is of the opinion that..."—or more precisely, "There is a judgment of the subject X here, with an object of such and such a nature." But the conceiving of these thoughts—above all, the sufficiently clear envisagement and judgment of X's mental state of affairs with respect to act and object—is still far too difficult a task for us to expect that its performance could become an easily masterable everyday accomplishment for someone unskilled in psychology. It is also strikingly apparent how much the person of the speaker tends to recede into the background when one accepts pieces of information understandingly, a phenomenon that occurs even when one is not at all yet inclined to "believe" what is heard. The phenomenon is even more apparent where, from the very beginning, the person of the speaker does not play any part in the situation, or at least does not do so prima facie. So it is, as a rule, with the author of a printed work, especially a work that is supposed to function primarily as a work of art—say a novel or a read dramatic work. The question as to how the understanding of a spoken dramatic work takes place is inevitably connected with this.

From facts of this sort, we see that even where the question is one of understanding, it will still not do to flatly subsume the job of language under the general concept of sign functioning. As far as I can see, this subsumption is unobjectionable only where language is serving to express emotional events. If the speaker expresses feelings or conations, then understanding really does consist in no more than treating his utterance as a sign, i.e., discovering from it, if we may put it that way, what the speaker is expressing. The same thing *can* happen in the intellectual sphere, so far as a word or sentence that the listener hears enables him to discover that the speaker has realized this representation or that judgment; but it *need* not happen, and for intellectual understanding (as we may call it) it is not even the rule. Rather, what appears to have some claim to being the rule here is a general correlation consisting in the word or word-complex awakening in the listener the mental state of affairs that it expresses. As far as there was this correlation, there would be a parallel to the position considered in the preceding section, that it pertains to a sentence by its very nature to express a judgment; accompanying this position, there would now be the equally natural thesis that in understanding a sentence, a listener himself makes the judgment that is expressed in that sentence.

This position, too, has many an experience favorable to it. When I am provided with some account, the way I normally react is to believe what I am told, i.e., to make the judgment, or more precisely the judgments, that have found expression in that account. But the parallel position naturally falls down with the position it parallels. We have met with sentences that express no judgment at all, and it is simply in conformity with the general correlation just appealed to, that a person should have no need of a judgment in order to understand such sentences. And it is of course obvious what we may conclude from this: The very same problem that arose earlier, regarding what sentences really express in such cases, has now cropped up again as a problem about the way in which a person reacts to such a sentence, as far as he understands it.

Meanwhile, there is an appreciable broadening in the range of considerations that have to be brought to this question, as soon as one becomes aware of the following point about the general correlation in question. While this correlation does generally hold between single words and representations, it rather frequently breaks down in the case of sentences, even where the latter really have the job of expressing judgments. I can understand a report given to me in good faith by a notoriously credulous or superstitious person, even if I cannot allow myself to be convinced in the slightest by what he says. One also understands news-stories in the papers, although it is only in the rarest cases that one would be willing to personally guarantee their reliability. This example has another value, incidentally. Understanding, as initially discussed above, was a judging about the judgment of the speaker. Here the possibility of there being such a judging is turned into an exceedingly remote one by the fact that it would presumably be a judgment about the judgment of a newspaper reporter. On the whole, then, it appears that the question as to how the sentence actually functions for someone who understands it is even more in need of a reasonably convincing answer than is the question of its function for the speaker.

No whit closer to solution, of course, is the task of defining the relation between speech and thought in a way that is general enough to be satisfactory, supposing that we cannot accomplish this by subsuming that relation under the very general concept of a sign. This concept, as we saw, fails us chiefly in the intellectual sphere. This is the very sphere in which such a great majority of the functions of language lie that it is notoriously easy to overlook the nonintellectual functions altogether. Mightn't this shortcoming of the sign concept stem from the fact that the relevant concept of "signification" has not yet been made truly serviceable for the solution of the problem in question? I mean that concept of signification which, above, we had to carefully distinguish from "signification" in the sense of the correlate of "sign" and which we had to contrast especially with the "expression."[25] Admittedly, this concept at first seems to exhibit too narrow a range of application. Certainly, we found "signification" in this sense where words were concerned; yet it seems to be missing in the case of sentences, the very things that should be of especial consequence to us, according to the foregoing. But what if it turned out, upon closer inspection, that "signification" could belong to sentences, too, as well as to words? The following investigations will as a matter of course lead to the answering of this question.

III

The Objective

Judged Objectives

We saw that significations are objects. The interest in the former thus leads to an investigation of the latter, and in this way we are led to a science whose special character and justification as a "theory of objects" I have explained elsewhere.[1] Here I shall present my views on certain objects which for the most part have been rather neglected by previous research. In approaching this presentation, however, it will be in accord with the essentially psychological intentions of the present work if I take my start with the experiences that apprehend these objects, at least the recognized and well-known experiences.

Therefore, let us consider a quite ordinary case of negative knowing, so as to appreciate the peculiarity of a fact to which I would like to call attention. If someone says, e.g., in regard to a parliamentary election that was preceded by intense public excitement, that no disturbance of the peace took place, then in the first place no one will deny that "something" is known by means of the judgment in question—assuming that it is quite correct. Yet one might at the outset suppose that this "something" is nothing but the object thought of by the one who meaningfully expresses that judgment—or in other words, the object "disturbance of the peace." And in the absence of any better means of expression, a theorist might even want to say just that. But would a person speaking naturally say that a disturbance of the peace has become known, when it is precisely a case of knowledge of the fact that *no* such disturbance has occurred? And yet even the person speaking naturally has a "something" he can indicate as being known; or strictly speaking, he can do this in a more natural way than the theorist. And in doing this he has in view not something judged *about* but rather, if we may put it this way, something judged *forth,* which in its own way has the character of factuality, despite the negative quality of the judgment in question. As soon as one attempts to give a closer account of this "something," it becomes evident that under ordinary conditions, if we want to avoid artificial constructions, a single word is not readily at

[37]

our disposal for this purpose; yet, a sentence with "that" offers itself as an entirely natural means of expression. In the case of our example, what I know is simply "that no disturbances of the peace have occurred." Admittedly, this is not some piece of actuality that an affirmative existential cognition would by nature be suited to apprehend, but it is still something that can be the object of an affirmative judgment. Surely I am justified in saying, "It is a fact that no disturbance of the peace occurred," or again—though less idiomatically—"It is the case that no disturbance of the peace occurred." And that would seem to imply that the "something" known by means of our negative judgment is nothing other than an object; except that it cannot well be termed the object of that same judgment, as long as by the object of a judgment is meant, as has hitherto been the rule, the thing judged about in the judgment in question.

Thus there arises the need to extend the sense of the term "object of judgment," at least enough to include objects of the type just considered.[2] Yet, there is also a need to give these latter objects a special name, in order to distinguish them from what was formerly looked on as the sole object of judgment, i.e., the object that representation presents to judgment for a sort of working over—that is, the representational object. It seemed most appropriate for me to use the name "objectives"[3] for the new class of judgmental objects characterized by the above remarks. It also seemed appropriate to follow the example of Rudolf Ameseder[4] and use the name "objecta" for the contrasting objects, the ones that might be said to require a roundabout way through representation in order to arrive at the forum of judgment.[5] Although this latter name is nothing more than the Latin translation of the word "object" ["Gegenstand"], by means of an explicit convention[6] it may be understood in the present, restricted sense. From the standpoint of judgment, it is natural and often quite advantageous to express the matter so: Besides an object *of* which something is judged, or an object which is judged *about*,[7] our example contains an object that is "*what* is judged" [*der "ge*urteilt wird"], if it is allowable for us to make anything out of that uncustomary locution. Accordingly, one says, "I know something of (or about) the disturbance of the peace," which is simply that it hasn't taken place. Here, then, the objectum coincides with what is judged about, and the objective with what is judged. So to that extent the judgment has not one but two objects, each of which would have every claim to being called an "object of judgment." Yet, one might prefer to call something an object of judgment in the first instance only if it is proper to judgment in the way that the object of representation is proper to representation; and on many occasions this is advisable. In that case, "object of judgment" may be taken as meaning just the objective.[8]

It should be made clear at this point that the property of having an objective does not exclusively belong to the negative aspect of knowing. If I look at the snow-covered street and say, "There is snow outside," then "snow" is the representational object, the objectum of this instance of knowing. But also, "that there is snow" is its objective, even though the latter does not have that inherent opposition to the objectum that made the objective so easily notice-able in the instance of negative knowing. In the case of affirmation, much more than in the case of negation, it may at first glance seem possible that we are injecting something superfluous by expressly setting the objective over against the objectum. Perhaps the opinion in regard to this apparent super-fluity will soon change, as our discussions proceed. For the present, let me emphasize only the *possibility* of extending the distinction to affirmative knowledge. That possibility is guaranteed as long as the notion of "snow" and the notion "that there is snow" need not necessarily be taken as simply identi-cal. Indeed, they are not identical; and so we can generalize and say that affir-mative as well as negative knowledge has not just an objectum, but an objec-tive as well.

If, therefore, there is no knowledge—no true affirmation and also no true negation—which lacks an objective, then it is easy to see that in this respect the situation is no different in the case of false judgments. For a person who be-lieved once upon a time that there was a philosopher's stone and, as the case may be, that he had found it, the belief consisted in judgments that had these objecta: whatever he conceived this stone and the finding of it to be. And the judgments had these objectives: the existence of the stone and that he had found it. Neither judgment lacks an objective just because its objective is not factual; no more so than the representing lacks an object because in this case what is represented does not exist.[9] And along with the affirmative type of error, which our example mainly illustrates, goes the negative type; this is no different from the former as regards the indispensability of an objective. Gen-eralizing, then, we may say that there can no more be a judgment without an objective than there can be a representation without an objectum. Further on,[10] we shall be led to a point of view from which the connection between an objective and a judgment can be seen as even more intimate than that between an objectum and a representation.

The present situation regarding judgment can also be described in the fol-lowing way. A judgment is always a dependent experience, insofar as an object has to be presented to it by another experience. As one might say, the judg-ment approaches this object in order to work on it—or to think on it. As inci-dentally mentioned above,[11] the presenting experience is not always a represen-tation; nevertheless, it is often enough a representation that our initial consid-erations can start from this case as the typical one. So then the presented object is an objectum which, because of the judgment's concern with it, becomes an object of judgment as well. In a certain sense, it even becomes the judgment's main object, insofar as the judgment might be said to have been looking to it in the first instance, as the thing with which it had to come to terms. The fre-quently employed designation "intentional object," which is not entirely with-out its dangers, could not be applied in a judgmental context more effortlessly than when it is applied to a judgment's objectum. And yet this object has been offered to the judgment merely from the outside, and to that extent it does not belong to the judgment in the way that the objectum does; the judgment is inherently turned to the objective, as the representation is to the objectum. Basically, the judgment apprehends the objectum through the objective; so that in the objective we have the true judgmental object, despite the objectum's obviously commanding position in our interests. It might be thought appropriate to speak of just *the* judgmental object, since one may also speak confidently of *the* representational object. Then as previously mentioned, only the objective may be considered as such, and not that which until now has generally been called the object of a judgment. Later we shall have occasion to return to the analogy between the judgment's relation to the objective and the representation's relation to the objectum.

It might seem strange that we are now claiming two objects for every judgment. For according to the testimony of everyday experience, judgmental thinking is always concerned with just one object and it never exhibits any duality. But one must first of all realize that we do not mean a duality in the sense of an independent or separate, side-by-side existence. The objective does not stand separately alongside the objectum; as something apprehended by the judgment, the objectum always stands *in* an objective. It forms a kind of integral part of the objective. But the judgment really has "to do" with the objectum alone, insofar as natural interest is directed to the latter in order to apprehend it in the objective that belongs to it. Thus, despite its indispensability, the judged is everywhere thrust into the background by the judged-*about,* and for the most part it emerges from this background only when it attains its own position as something judged about.

§9

Judged-about Objectives

The fact that there are such things became apparent to us even in connection with the example that constituted our first appraoch to the nature of objectives. Returning to this fact expressly has, above all, the value of an additional confirmation of what has just been maintained about objectives. To me, certainly, it seems that a direct consideration of the facts about judgment will yield something that is parallel to the object-directedness of a representation and which is quite clearly a characteristic factor in a judgment; so that unless this factor, as embodied in the objective, should be further reducible, we shall have to accept it as being as much of an ultimate given as the representational object. On the other hand, it is hard to ignore the position of someone newly confronted with the demand to acknowledge what is, at least in appearance, a wholly new side to the old and familiar fact of judgment. The situation before such a person is not suited in every respect to influence him in favor of the new thesis. In particular, the form of expression we singled out in trying to familiarize ourselves with the objective must seem strange to him. If someone makes the judgment, "What is harmonically correct can be melodically incorrect," and I maintain that this judgment has an objective, namely the fact "that what is harmonically correct can be melodically incorrect," then surely it does not take much ill will to suppose that my statement is no more than a tautology, utterly empty, and the objective, the thing claimed to be something special, is just the judgment once over again, as it were. Moreover, such a preconception receives support from an etymological consideration. To my knowledge, linguists are in agreement that our conjunction "that" is in its origins nothing but a demonstrative pronoun. Thus, etymologically at least, someone who says, "I believe that what is harmonically correct can be melodically incorrect," basically is saying nothing but, "I believe this: what is harmonically correct can be melodically incorrect." With that, all of the distinctive character of the "that"-clause seems to be removed. It is a sentence like any other, and whatever it may convey—this is at most a judgment and not something that deserves special consideration under the name of "objective."

Under such circumstances, another fact should be able to carry some weight, especially with one who receives my acknowledgment of the foregoing facts with justifiable caution. Namely, there are judgments that cannot be attributed any clear sense in their relation to objects without our calling in objectives. How ought one to understand such an everyday judgment as, "It is certain that the case is not closed"? It is asserted thereby that something is certain— but what? Obviously, what the dependent sentence means. In this particular instance, at least, it can be taken for the expression of a judgment—we have already seen that it is not always that.[12] Is the judgment the thing that "is certain" ["feststeht"], then? As it happens, this interpretation is not exactly senseless in the present case. Still, it will suffice to appeal to the testimony of direct observation to determine whether the one judging is thinking of the judgment—instead of thinking quite exclusively of the case and its being closed. Without doubt, the latter is what he is doing. Accordingly, with a view to precising what "is certain," we find our attention drawn to the objectum or objecta of the judgment expressed in the "that"-clause. As mentioned, it is a question about the closing of the case. But that very closing is anything but certain, in the opinion of the person who is judging; indeed, he maintains the very contrary. Thus, we find our attention immediately drawn to the objective as "what is certain," and I cannot imagine what sort of path would enable one to avoid it here and in all analogous cases. Had "what is certain" been expressed in our example by means of an affirmative clause rather than a negative one, then perhaps the above consideration would not have turned out to be so obvious—in that one might then have been more inclined to take the grammatical subject of the "that"-clause for "what is certain." But for one thing, the sense contained in the standing-firm [Feststehen] figure would prove to be totally inapplicable to the object "closing of the case"—as long as there was not another objective hidden in there. The main thing, though, is that it might not be very good to interpret the affirmative "that"-clause altogether differently from the negative, other things being equal.

Let us see what we now have in the way of additional evidence in favor of the contention that every judgment has an objective, a contention that was supported above merely by reference to direct observation. This can perhaps be set forth most clearly in a formal example, one that may be taken as a schema for the simplest type of situation in question here. If the judgment "*A* does not exist" holds true, then as already mentioned above, I may also judge: "It is the case that *A* does not exist." "That *A* does not exist" is doubtless what "is the case" here—or in other words, the object that is affirmed by means of the supervening judgment. With that, a particularly obvious misunderstanding must be expressly precluded. The object for which the "that"-clause thus stands is surely not the initial judgment, "*A* does not exist"—I mean the judgmental experience that usually finds its natural expression in this sentence. Direct consideration of the accompanying situation precludes any doubt on that matter. And while the present-tense "it is the case" certainly might create the impression that it is, at any rate, a question of the time in which the judging is done, not even that is correct. Or should the person judging normally suppose that things would stand otherwise with *A* if he did not now judge? For all the redundancy, one need only alter the example so that it is a question of a negation rather than an affirmation in the main clause. If I say, "It is not the case that *A* does not exist," then the non-existing thing most certainly cannot be the judgmental experience that finds expression in this same negative sentence. But we can go still further and maintain that not even the *A* of our examples constitutes the object of the judgment expressed in the main clause. For, apart from the fact that *A* 's investiture in the "that"-clause would at least have to be termed groundless, we know that there is really no judgment that *A* exists, but rather a judgment to the contrary. The "that"-clause therefore has its own special sense in relation to objects.

If it may be taken as proved, then, that objectives not only can be judged but can also have judgments made about them,[13] then this judgment-about merits our special interest with regard to its psychological prerequisites. As was just previously recalled,[14] nothing that is not presented to judgment can be judged about. The presenting experience is often a representation. According to fairly widespread opinion, it in fact always is; but it has already been pointed out that the judged-about experience itself can at the same time function as presenting. The presenting experience naturally cannot be absent in the case of judged-about objectives, either. And on this point there arises the question, fundamentally important to this work's investigations, about the nature of this experience.

Of the two possible cases just recalled to our attention, the representing of the thing judged about and the experiencing of that very thing, the second drops out of consideration right away. Experiences are always objecta, never objectives; and for that reason an objective can never present itself for a judgment about it. Accordingly, only representing remains. But can one represent an objective? The answer to this question follows immediately from a preliminary investigation already completed in the first chapter.[15] Possibly the relation of what we spoke of as *negativa* to the objective is still somewhat unclear to one who has not taken cognizance of the objective until the present discussions.[16] But surely no one could fail on that account to observe that there are *negativa* among objectives, too; for it was precisely in *negativa* that the peculiar character of objectives was first set forth in the foregoing. Thus, if we find an objective of the form "*A* is not *B*" judged about—as when one says, "It is true that Schiller was never in Switzerland"—then while *A* and *B* may indeed be presented via representation, the objective "that *A* is not *B*" certainly cannot be presented that way. But if that is the case, then we can only expect something analogous with respect to the presentation of positive but otherwise quite analogously constituted objectives of the form "*A* is" or "*A* is *B*," which we are now surely able to distinguish clearly from the objecta *A* and *B* contained in them. In particular, we can reject the conjunction of the notion of founding and the notion of the production of representations by exactly the same means that we rejected this conjunction earlier, with regard to negation. We have thereby proved[17] that the second of the two possibilities of presentation just now considered for the objective breaks down, too.

The above remarks on judged-about objectives readily suggest a third possibility for such presentation; at the same time it is evident that this possibility had to elude attention as long as attention was not directed to the objective itself. Just as it is a natural characteristic of every representation to represent an objectum, so too we found it to be in the nature of every judgment to judge an objective. So, if the function of presenting an objectum to a judgment belongs to the representation, then it will be permissible to regard the judgment as the presenting experience with regard to the objective. Of course, this will never be the judgment to which the objective is presented and which thereupon judges about the objective. This is, in fact, excellently proven by experience. If a person says, "I find that the weather today already has a spring-like quality," he is making a judgment about the objective indicated, in that he states that he "finds" it. But in order to do this, he must first really find or have found just that, and the finding naturally consists in his judging the objective. And so while making a judgment about that same objective is certainly not a more important step in thought, at least one can have no doubt about its being a second one and having the judgment of the objective as its prerequisite, in the way that judging about a color, a musical tone, or some other objectum has the representation of this objectum as its prerequisite.

Thus, there is scarcely any room for doubt that an objective can be presented to one judgment by another. It is an entirely different question, though, as to whether every judged-about objective requires a presenting judgment or whether the presentation can also be effected by experiences other than judgment. The latter possibility is so little to be rejected *a limine,* that it has, on the contrary, furnished the principal motive for dealing with objectives in this work. Yet, let us not enter into this possibility in the present connection. Instead (probably not without one-sidedness, for this same reason), let us regard the judgment simply as *the* experience that presents the objective for judgment about it, and let us before all else try to delineate the peculiar complication of judgments and objectives that such presentation entails.

Let us again start from a schematic example of the form "*A* is." If a judgment is expressed thereby, then we know that the judgment's main object is the "judged-about" *A*; but we also know that the "judged" objective "that *A* is" is more intimately connected with the judgment itself. With this in mind, we may call the objective the immediate object of the judgment expressed in the above sentence, while the objectum *A,* despite its commanding position, would be called the mediate object. Naturally, this holds for any given objectum O; nor can the situation alter, if a judgment is now made about an objective O', rather than an objectum O. But this time it is not just the immediate object of a judgment-about that is an objective; its mediate object is an objective, too. So a mediate objective may be assigned to this judgment, along with its immediate one. In accordance with the supposition just made, this mediate objective is presented to the judgment about it by another judgment, and it is the immediate objective of that other judgment. If O'_1 is the presented and judged-about objective and J_1 the judgment presenting it, then the judgment-about from which we started can be called J_2 and its immediate objective O'_2. J_2 then has two objectives, the immediate one O'_2 and the mediate one O'_1. So too, conversely, two judgments belong to the objective O'_1; J_1 can be called the immediate judgement, and J_2 the mediate. And if O'_2's own immediate judgment J_2 presented it to a further judgment J_3, a judgment about O_2, this would be the mediate judgment for the objective O'_2. And, theoretically speaking, nothing would stand in the way of our setting judgment on judgment time and again in this manner and thus apprehending objectives which clearly revealed themselves as objectives of ever higher order. Practically speaking, our interest as well as our intellectual capacity would soon enough declare a limit to such an advance.[18]

§10
The Objective and Language

We already had occasion to mention that objectives are never experiences. As the foregoing of itself showed, the objective has close as well as solid relations to language; yet these relations can nowise be based on language's expressing the objective. An objective is as little expressible as a triangle or an earthquake, or an experience that takes place in someone other than the speaker. But language may express an experience that has one of these things as its object, and in that sense any of these things can figure in language. We know such objects as significations, and right away a conjecture suggests itself: Just as the property of signifying objects normally belongs to words, there will be linguistic forms that have objectives as their significations. Let us first of all try to determine the nature of the linguistic forms that exhibit an especially close connection with objectives, so that on the basis of these determinations we can then answer the question about signification.

In our discussions up to this point, the sentence has been quite able to prove its own value as the most natural means of securing agreement about objectives. In the case of judged objectives, it was the independent sentence; in the case of judged-about objectives, it was the dependent sentence, especially the "that"-clause. Relative clauses also can be of service in this regard; no further proof of this is required. What must still be given special consideration is whether in the linguistic expression mere words, instead of sentences, may stand opposite the objective. This amounts to the question as to whether, in the recently enumerated occasions for the use of the "that"-clause, there are equivalent expressions in other than sentential form.

If one therefore makes a sort of attempt to divest "that"-clauses of their sentential form, the first mode of transformation to suggest itself will be one that cannot be said to result in an out-and-out failure in every case. Instead of "I surmise that there has been a mishap," I can quite well say, "I surmise a mishap." Instead of "I remember that he was present," "I remember his presence." Instead of "I reported that he was rescued," "I reported his rescue." Instead of "I know that he has faults," "I know of his faults." And so forth. While even here one may not always be quite certain about the full adequacy of the results of the transformation, a statement about "belief" is noticeably more difficult to treat in this way. To be sure, it is still quite natural to say, "I believe in God (in my right)" and the like, instead of "I believe that God exists (that I do have a right)," etc. Yet, no one would say, "I believe in the table in the room" instead of "I believe that there is a table in the room"; and it is at least very questionable as to whether the fault lies with a shift in the sense of the word "believe." The occurrence of a "that"-eliminating transformation is possibly even more forced in such locutions as "I judge (think, maintain, say) that . . ." and the like. For example, if during the conducting of psychological weight experiments the subject says, "I judge that the weight I lifted first is heavier," then a statement of the form "I judge as to the weight I first lifted being heavier" or suchlike cannot be used as a replacement without a change in meaning.[19]

It is true that this manner of speaking will probably always allow for a more or less inexact designation of the thing judged about. But even if it enables one to determine exactly what it is, concerning which something is "thought," "judged," etc., there is still no information as to whether the judgment in question is to be taken affirmatively or negatively. Quite naturally, the information cannot be lacking in a sentence with "that"; as against this, the information cannot be embodied in the results of the "that"-eliminating transformation. In retrospect, it might also strike one that even in the case of the transformations enumerated above as allowable, the indeterminacy of the judgmental quality is done away with only through a kind of arbitrary limitation. For if all that the locution "I surmise a mishap" means is that the mishap is the object of my surmise, then such an expression is actually devoid of any real information as to whether the surmise has an affirmative character or a negative character; and strictly speaking, it may be considered to be no more than conventional that everyone immediately understands the surmise as being affirmative.

But what thereby turns out to be virtually unworkable, is for the present no more than the attempt to simply ignore the objective in favor of the objectum —or more generally, to ignore the immediate object of the expressed judgment for the sake of its mediate object. It is a quite different question, though, as to whether the objective can come into play linguistically in some other way than through the sentence; and as far as I can see, it is a question that within certain limits very well admits of an affirmative answer. Let us start again with the schema I used at the beginning of the above remarks, the schema of existential statement form. If instead of "It is the case that A exists," I say, "The existence of A is the case," then admittedly the latter means no more than the former, but it also means no less. And instead of "I deny (doubt, maintain) that there is a vacuum," I can also say, "I deny (doubt, maintain) the existence of empty space." In contrast, take the case where the immediate judgment of the objective makes its appearance in categorical statement form, i.e., where it appears in the form "that A is B." In many such cases, the form "A's being B" offers a quite satisfactory substitute. Instead of "I don't deny that the railroad train is arriving," "... that the board is black," or "... that yellow is different from green," we can say unhesitantly, "I don't deny the arrival of the railroad train," "... the board's being black (its blackness)," or "... the differentness of yellow and green." I admit that there is hardly much of a distinction between the verbal substantives that are so useful here and the infinitive. But on the whole neither the distinctiveness nor the serviceableness of these ways of designating objectives is to be disputed at the present juncture. If I have given no consideration to them in my discussions up until now, this is because they appear to be utilizable as equivalents of "that"-clauses only under special provisions and there must first be a more exact statement of the nature of these provisions. "That frosty weather prevails," I can find true,[20] obvious, evident, and so on; not "the prevalence of frosty weather," however. Given a more thorough investigation into the nature and conditions of the use-restrictions that appear in the case of these equivalents, it is to be presumed that insight into the nature of the objective will be fostered in no inconsiderable degree. However, in the present context we shall have to forego the pursuit of these investigations.

Expressions like these, where the sentential form is abandoned, provide especially useful information for the theory of objectives in that they enable objectives to show themselves outwardly being treated on the same footing as objecta. And what is above all worth noticing here is that with this treatment the contrast between the objectum and the objective, at first sight well demarcated, quite surprisingly threatens to become effaced. True, the gap between "table" and "existence of the table" still presents itself as quite unbridgeable. But how do "being different" and differentness or "being black" and blackness really differ from each other? Aren't differentness and blackness assuredly representational objects, the former a founded object [Fundierungsgegenstand] and the latter an object of experience?[21] But in the event that they weren't representational objects, wouldn't it then follow that we are really confronted with objectives in all relations, and indeed, in all the attributes expressible by means of the so-called abstract substantives of grammar?

First and foremost among the things we must notice here, and certainly not unimportant in the present connection, is the fact that "blackness," strictly speaking, surely cannot mean anything but "being black" and that "differentness," likewise, cannot mean anything but "being different." "Blackness" is really something other than "black," though; and analogously, "differentness" is something other than "different"—although as a noun form the latter expression can scarcely be a current one. And if one further asks how "blackness" differs from "black," then it can only be answered that "blackness" in a sense means more than "black." To wit, it means not just the property, but also the position which the property has in something black—or in other words, the property's position in the object which it determines as something black. If black is the property, then blackness is what Ernst Mally has called the "determination."[22] But determining is the private business of the objective, as one might say; something black is just something involved in being black [das Schwarzseiende]. Since it is of the nature of a property to be a property of something, it is not surprising that in the formation of a word that usually has the special designation of "abstract substantive" in grammar, language in a sense adds the property's determining function to the property. But given the lack of acquaintance with the objective, it is just as understandable that people failed to spot the objective in these "abstract substantives" and thus supposed themselves to be dealing with the bare property, an objectum. Naturally, this also holds of terms which signify relations. Later on,[23] we shall have to return expressly to the objective's significance for such terms.

But, of course, no one will be able to provide a guarantee that someone who makes use of one of these "abstract substantives" will never mean the pure property, in the sense of the one which is objectiveless. However, this is an uncertainty that generally cannot be avoided in the interpretation of word-significations, when they are far from being apprehended in their full sharpness in everyday life. But apart from that, the facts just set forth above in no wise tell us that objecta and objectives merge into each other in these substantival and adjectival expressions; they tell us just that the domain of objectives extends considerably further than one might think, if one considered just "that"-clauses.

But regarding the relation between words and sentences, we can see at any event that the matter is not as simple as it might appear at first glance. For we cannot simply say that one must always be dealing with objecta in the case of words and word-complexes (leaving out sentences) and with objectives in the case of sentences. The signification of a word does not always consist in an objectum; often enough it consists in an objective. But if, further, words in the latter case make their appearance as the equivalents of sentences—as we have seen them do—then in the event that such a word has signification, the equivalent sentence can scarcely be denied signification; and thus we come back to the theme of sentential signification put aside at the end of the preceding chapter. Sentences, too, we can now say, have signification in the narrower sense that we precised on the relevant occasion;[24] moreover, these sentential significations are objectives.

But have we thereby also found the answer to the question we raised in the preceding chapter, concerning the factor that places sentences in a distinctive position vis-à-vis other word-complexes? That is, can we simply say that sentences are word-complexes characterized by the fact that they signify objectives? But that would not be conformable to the strict concept of signification just now brought back into consideration. True, we said that insofar as an experience presents its object to thought, signification belongs to the expression of that experience—the object then constituting the signification. Now, however, we know that this in no wise holds true of every sentence. There is indeed an objective over against every sentence, but from what we have so far seen of the facts, the objective is a presented one only when it is judged about, and not when it is simply judged. The "that"-clause typifies the former situation. It is a sentence grammatically dependent on the expression of a judgment, and the judgment has the objective in question as its mediate object. With independent sentences, however, this is not normally the case; and so to that extent such sentences actually have no proper signification in the strict sense. However, the whole situation may make one want to broaden the concept of signification in such a way that an independent sentence can be accorded an objective as its quasi-signification. Then no meaningfully uttered sentence would fail to have an objective as its signification. But even then we could not look to the objective for the characterization of a sentence; for as mentioned, words themselves can have objectives as significations—and what is more, significations in the strict sense of the term.

§11
General Remarks on the Nature of the Objective

The concept of the pseudo-existence of objects was formed on another occasion[25] in response to the custom, subserving brevity more than theoretical rigor, of speaking of an object that exists "in my thought of it" ["in meiner Vorstellung"]—or again, "in my judgment," and so forth. The applicability of this concept to objectives follows from the mere fact that they can be judged about—or for that matter, just from the fact that they can be judged. And taking together all that has been said of objectives, we can now say that our concern with objectives has been exclusively from the standpoint of pseudo-existence. That is, what we have been concerned with so far are various mental facts insofar as they "have" objectives. But if we did not accompany the foregoing psychological treatment of objectives with an apsychological one,[26] however fragmentary, it would mean giving cause for misunderstandings in this matter, a matter that even today has not yet received anything like adequate recognition and consideration. And so it might not be out of place here, if we made the objective, its properties, and its main kinds the subject of some statements belonging in essence to the theory of objects. These statements will take us beyond the sphere of the real intentions of the present work; and that fact may provide some justification if I seem to proceed in a way that is overly dogmatic by my usual standards, merely putting together what other inquiries[27] have yielded—or as it may well be, what I will have to justify more thoroughly in discussions newly on the horizon.

Under such circumstances, it deserves to be explicitly emphasized above all that the objective, like any other object, generally admits of the apsychological approach and therefore demands it. More precisely, this emphasis is directed against what appear to me to be two thoroughly erroneous views. First and foremost, it is directed against the opinion, in conformity with the "prejudice in favor of the actual,"[28] that our knowing or at least our interest can only have to do with what is actual. Thus, if the objective does not belong to actuality, then it would be at most the experience apprehending it that could concern science. But the emphasis is also directed against the relativistic interpretation of the concept of an object which, appealing not without etymological support to the "ob-jecting," won't hear of any object except an "object for the subject." This interpretation strips the objective of that independence vis-à-vis the apprehending experience which, in my belief, belongs to the objective no less essentially than to any bit of actuality "outside of us." A point we shall have to bring up for separate discussion in just a moment is that neither existence nor being in any sense whatsoever is ascribable to an objective on the basis of that independence.

So without any consideration given to an apprehending subject and his experiences, it may be stated that every object has a general and a specific nature. In accordance with this natural constitution, objects divide into the two big groups of objecta and objectives. The possibility of establishing differences within each group is consistent with there being differences between the two classes themselves (or the members of same as such) which considerably exceed the differences within each of the classes. At present we are not in a position to make it rationally evident that the disjunction of all objects into objecta and objectives is a complete one.

No one could in fairness demand a definitional "reduction" of such ultimate things to ones which are more prior, as it were. Yet, the indirect approach taken by Rudolf Ameseder serves excellently for a precise description of the state of affairs given in the objectum and the objective. Using that approach one could put the matter as follows. Every object has being (or non-being). But there are objects that not only have being (in this broadest sense) but also are being, and these objects are the objectives; while that which has being, without being being is thereby established as an objectum in character. To someone who thinks that he can define being, the possibility of a definitional determination of the objective might be suggested by the present situation, where every objective is being (in the broadest sense of the word) and conversely every instance of being is an objective. A definition of being is in fact attempted in the following statement.[29] "Since we apprehend being or existing only in and by an (acknowledging) judging whose correctness is manifest to us, the concept of that which is cannot be obtained except through reflection on such a judging. We characterize as being and existing...that which allows of correct acknowledgment."[a] But such a definition is no better off than if one had wanted to define "green" as the color that one can experience when light between the E and F lines of the solar spectrum affects the eye. As little as the nature of color consists in physical or psychophysical processes or their combination, just as little does the nature of being consist in acknowledged-ness or acknowledgeability. The inadequacy of such a definition is especially conspicuous in the acknowledgeability-version, which in the last analysis would have all being resolved into possibility—a thought that has admittedly often been brought into play with regard to "outer existence" but whose untenability[30] as applied to being-in-general becomes only the more clearly apparent. As with color, so with being; in the former case it all ultimately comes down to *what* one experiences, and in the latter case it all comes down to *what* one judges.[31]

A characteristic that the objective shares with the objectum is that of having being (including non-being). Along with this characteristic goes a fact that is already familiar to us on its psychological side. This is the fact that to every objective there belong infinitely many objectives of higher order, namely all those that can be immediately apprehended through judgments[32] that mediately apprehend[b] the starting objective. Yet one naturally cannot put it the other way round, saying that whenever a judgment judges an objective, as it must, it must also judge about an objective. What is judged about can just as well be an objectum. Accordingly, one cannot maintain that every objective must likewise have objectives of lower order under it, as well as objectives of higher order over it. Certainly it must have an object "under itself," in the sense just indicated, but this object can also be an objectum. But if one starts with a given objective and proceeds "downwards" in the sense just mentioned, one can sometimes meet with a longer series of objectives of progressively lower order, sometimes with a shorter series; but in any case the series to be traversed that way will end with an objectum, supposing that one stays within the limits of the possible. So to that extent every objective occupies the position of an object of higher order.[33] Borrowing a term proposed elsewhere[34] for use in connection with the judgment, one might designate the object or objects on which an objective is positioned as the material of the objective.

In their place within the opposition of existence and subsistence,[35] which comprehends all that is, objectives are analogous to the objects of higher order hitherto considered—not all of them, but the ones most frequently considered. "That A exists," or again, "that it does not exist," is something that "subsists" if the judgment immediately apprehending it might have been correctly made; but it does not exist once over, as it were. And needless to say, much the same thing would have to be asserted of any objective that had subsistents as its own material: "that 3 is greater than 2," or again, "that crooked is not straight"—this likewise can subsist, but not exist. Similarly, of course, the thing to be negated in the case of objectives of false judgments is always subsistence and never in the first instance existence. Admittedly, a negation of subsistence always entails the right to an existential negation; yet it is a right to one that is empty, insofar as the negation holds of everything which, just because it is an ideal object, can at most subsist and cannot exist. It would merely be a counterpart to something like the statement that sameness does not exist between 2 and 3. That is correct, no doubt, but it is by the same token quite devoid of special significance. For not even differentness exists between 2 and 3, and sameness does not "exist" between 2 and 2;[36] the one and the other relation can only subsist.

One thing is striking about the determination that the foregoing gives us. The differentness that subsists between green and yellow subsists necessarily; the sameness that does not subsist between green and yellow necessarily does not subsist; and it is without exception the same elsewhere in the domain of the ideal. But can I similarly say, "That the sun is shining now (that it is not raining now) is necessary"? I cannot; here there can be no doubt.[37] But what follows from this is simply the fact that while cases of subsistence or non-subsistence are often cases of necessity too, they are by no means always such. As we shall have to show, necessity is a property that, strictly speaking, is only in objectives; and, as mentioned a moment ago, it has already become clear in an earlier connection that sameness and differentness are in a certain sense, objectives, too. But necessity does not inhere in all objectives; instead, objectives leave room for the opposite of necessity, i.e., contingency, without our being thereby less justified in claiming that cases of the latter sort are cases of subsistence or non-subsistence.

Among the other ways in which subsistences differ from existences is by their not being tied to any determinations of time, and in this sense being eternal—or rather, timeless. Naturally this holds for the objective too. My desk is a thing existing at a certain time; but *that* it exists at this time is something which subsists now as well as in all the past and future, although it was inaccessible to knowledge in past times and it will have disappeared from knowledge in future times. It is just as timeless, say, as that the right angle is greater than the vertex. Nevertheless, there is no lack of idiomatic locutions to obscure this state of affairs, not to say to throw it into question. One is speaking quite naturally in saying, "The thundering has stopped," or again, "Our quiet being together came to an end." Yet the thundering [das Donnern] and the being together [das Beisammensein] are objectives, and they are being treated as past things. In especially emphatic speech one even says, "That we associated with each other as friends, that is over and done." Still, the choice of words in the last example is certainly incorrect, taken in the strict sense; for the normal instance hardly allows us to speak of a past in which the friendship was already past. In the other two examples, the verbal substantives might afford opportunities for inexact usage, although there is no doubt that like infinitival expressions,^{c} they still primarily signify objectives, as just now acknowledged. Thus, in considering the sense of the abstract substantives "differentness" and "blackness," mentioned in the preceding section, we are not accustomed to distinguish very clearly in thought between the respective cases of "being different" and "different," "being black," and "black"; so too, by *"Donnern"* and *"Beisammensein"* one might easily mean just "thunder" and "a gathering"—and hence, objecta. To these, of course, time-determinations readily attach.

What right at all do we have to find such locutions in need of a more precise account? Shouldn't there instead be a correction of the above assertion of the timelessness of the objective? This assertion has, in fact, been countered with some specious considerations, plausible to the point of obviousness.[38] "When things change, the truth about them cannot remain the same," and surely truths must be objectives; so that the latter turn out to be tied to certain times. But let us consider the situation further in an arbitrarily chosen simple example. One Sunday evening I forgot, say, to wind up my pocket watch; during the course of that Sunday I could still justifiably say, "My watch is running today," or again, "It is the case that my watch is running today." But had I still thought the same thing on Monday, then I should have been in error. Rather, what might have been asserted with reason on that day is, "It is not the case that my watch is running today." Thus, the same objective would have had subsistence on Sunday and would no longer have had it on Monday. Certain it is, that on each of the two days the same words could have been used; but is it just as certain that the objective is the same on each occasion? It is easy to note that on Sunday the "today" imports something different from what it imports on Monday. The word "today," of course, belongs to the type of expression, not in the least infrequently encountered, whose signification is by no means independent of the circumstances under which it is used. With regard to such circumstances, the two objectives that our example actually contains may exhibit agreements; but by the same token there remain two objectives. So it cannot, strictly speaking, be asserted that the same objective had subsistence on one day but not on another. On Monday, too, it would have been unassailably correct that the watch was going on Sunday; or on Sunday, that the watch was not going on Monday. And as far as I can see, this example can serve as a paradigm for all apparently changeable truths. Such truths are always formulated in a way that ties them to the time in which they are thought or expressed. This is not merely a matter of words; as we shall soon have occasion to point out,[39] even the notion of existence suffers from this tie. Be that as it may, the circumstances under which one apprehends or discusses objectives have nothing to do with the objectives themselves; and their truth or falsity, along with their subsistence or non-subsistence, must also be independent of these circumstances. Generalizing, we may say this: The semblance of changeable truth can arise on the part of objectives through the fact that the material of the one and the material of the other exhibit different time-determinations, while the objectives are nevertheless regarded as being identical. They are so regarded because each of these different time-determinations stands in the same relation to an apprehending subject at the time in question. Of the two objectives, incorrectly taken to be identical, the one may easily be factual or true, the other unfactual or false. Strictly speaking, there are no changeable truths; and what have been customarily distinguished by the expression "eternal truths" are merely truths whose objecta are not affected by the succession of times.

Against my foregoing desk example it has been objected that the semblance of changelessness in it occurs precisely through the impermissible neglect of differences of time. For, from the standpoint of one and the same now, "the existence of the desk *subsists* now as something present, *subsisted* a hundred years ago as something future, and *will subsist* in a hundred years as something past. Or in other words, it was true that the desk . . . will exist, it is . . . true that it now exists, and it will be true that it existed at this time. Thus, also, it is true of the desk itself that it is now . . . a thing of the present, and at the time of Caesar that it was a thing of the future, and in the year A.D. 2500 that it will be a thing of the past."[40] There would accordingly be two kinds of temporal changes to be considered: The existence of the desk subsists, certainly, but it subsists as something future, as something present, and as something past; and this subsistence itself is respectively past, present, or future. But, above all, is it really permissible to treat the existence of the desk as being on a par with the desk, as has been expressly done in the place cited? If it is, then the following consequence cannot well be rejected. Someone who said of the desk that it once existed "as something future" would really be expressing himself rather inexactly, and it would at all events be more correct to say that the desk does not exist at all at the time in question; and an existence "as something past" would be in no better situation. In terms of existence itself, the implication would be that this, too, subsisted neither in the past nor the future. But that contradicts the facts; for the objective that there were Roman Caesars subsists and is true, although at present neither Augustus nor Tiberius nor any other Caesar exists. The existence that subsisted a hundred years ago was not exactly a future existence; strictly speaking, it was only the existence of something future. What makes this particularly worthwhile noting is that we are here dealing with an existence that "subsisted" and which on the strength of that could be considered just as much past as a desk that once existed. The fact that a verb has a "tense"—i.e., that, as a rule, determinations of time show up in the verb, whether adverbially or through the verb's inflectional forms—this fact admittedly makes it appear somewhat as though the time-determination belonged to the objective. But if only one will first take the trouble to think out the thought of the objective into fairly distinct form, then, it seems to me, it will also be clearly evident that dates are all of the nature of objecta, not objectives; so that by their very nature, they can never be assigned to objectives. Moreover, there are also adverbs with a spatial signification, and yet hardly anyone will be of two minds about the fact that existence or subsistence can never have a place. This insight has special additional value for our question, insofar as one can idiomatically say not only, "It was in the year 1648 that the Peace of Westphalia was concluded," but also, "It was in England that the parliamentary system first led to significant political results." If one does not want to call in the testimony of linguistic usage in favor of the spatiality of objectives here, then analogous constructions will not be able to provide arguments for their temporality, either.

But one who has followed my interpretation thus far must not give way to any illusion that he is coming into conflict with linguistic expression once again. Suppose that in line with the foregoing one grants me that we really should not say that the "subsistent" in our example is the future, present, or past existence of the desk, but that it is rather the (timeless) existence of the future, present, or past desk. Though that is his judgment, he finds himself confronted anew with the appearance of temporally determined objectives by the verbs "subsisted," "subsists," and "will subsist" used above. And while in respect of existence it would be easy to point out that the time-determination belonging grammatically to "to exist" is to be credited to the objectum table, in the present case the objective is lacking an immediate objectum; that is, the objective "subsisted" has only an objective immediately under itself, namely existence. If it is the existence that "subsisted," "subsists," or "will subsist," then one may reasonably ask where the time-determination really should go, if neither existence nor subsistence will tolerate it. It will have to be borne in mind, however, that language knows no finite verb without tense[41] and that it has only formed a quite imperfect substitute for such verbs in something like a timeless present tense (e.g., "There are years with 366 days," "There are human beings without faults"). On the other hand, there is no lack of a perfectly natural way to connect an objective to some time-determination or another without detriment to the objective's timelessness. This has been done as soon as one speaks of the objective as something that is in any way apprehended. We shall soon have to come back[42] to how frequently this is the case and how, to take a special case, it lends the concept of truth its special character. Now, it is certainly not a momentous step in thought to substitute "it was true" and "it will be true" for the "subsisted" and "will subsist" in our example—i.e., to understand even the foregoing modes of expression as a reference to the time of a correct judgment. But in that case, the change in tense naturally has nothing to do with the objective in and by itself, nor with its timelessness.

It should also be mentioned that the two time changes claimed against me in my desk example do not have to be charged to the objective. The reason for this is simply that it is only the temporal position of the judging subject that makes itself felt in the thoughts of pastness, presentness, and futurity—as in the case of the pocket-watch, above. Admittedly, from that alone all that could be gathered would be the unchangedness of the relevant objective, an attribute which it is certainly correct to distinguish[43] from its timelessness. But the principle, "What we think of as being, we think of as temporal,"[44] if it has reference to thoughts that are correct, seems to me to be refuted in an evident manner precisely by the timeless nature of the objective—and of all subsistents, for that matter, a point to which we shall have to return.[45]

An objective that subsists is also called a "fact." Without artificiality of expression, my desk, just now under consideration, can hardly be called a fact; but that it stands before me, that is a fact. Again, someone who called it a fact that 2 is smaller than 3 would not be expressing himself incorrectly. But he would come into conflict with a tendency that undoubtedly does carry some weight, namely the tendency to limit the range of application of the word "factuality" ["Tatsächlichkeit"] exclusively or at least primarily to the empirically knowable. This tendency is so strong that on occasion it even jumps the gap between objective and objectum, permitting us to call something like muscular contraction a physical fact and willing a mental fact. It is advisable, in the interests of the usefulness of the term "factuality" in the theory of objects, to preclude such a trenching on the domain of objecta, employing a convention, if necessary.[46] But on the other hand, it is advisable not to confine one's self to the narrower sense of "factual" any longer, the sense in which the factual is equated with the "assertoric," to the exclusion of the "apodeictic." For when all is said and done, it is going to be unnatural even from the standpoint of linguistic usage to deny that such things as we learn in geometry are factual. But more important than the domain of application of the term, naturally, is the sense that fixes this domain. And with reference to this sense, one can easily see that the determination of it that now appeared before us as something perfectly obvious, "An objective is factual so far as it subsists," or more generally, so far as it "is," represents something quite inadequate. For if O' is our objective, then an objective of higher order of the form "O' is the case"—or more briefly O'', as we shall call it—can guarantee the factuality of O' only when it is itself factual. If it were not, i.e., if "that O' is the case" were not a fact, the O' would not be a fact, either. But what we are saying now with regard to the factuality of O' further applies to O'' itself. The factuality of O'' can be ensured by means of an objective O''' of the form "O'' is the case" only if this O''' is factual, and so on *in infinitum*. In general, then, one can say that if the factuality of an objective *consisted* in the being of this objective, then since this being would itself have to be factual, etc., one would always be confronted with an open-ended series in which any later, as yet unconsidered member would serve to show that the antecedent members formed an illusory totality. Such a series, one that is forever incomplete in this way, cannot add up to factuality.

Even if one succeeded in overcoming the open-endedness difficulty, using an abstract version of the series like "A factual objective is one that has only subsisting objectives over itself,"[47] in the end one would still have gained nothing thereby. Suppose that O', whose factuality is in question, is "that 2 is greater than 5." Then without doubt the objective "It is the case (or subsists) that 2 is greater than 5" (not *only* it, of course, but certainly it *too*) can be superordinated to O' as O''. And to this O'' one could superordinate an O''', expressible in the sentence, "It is the case that O'' is the case"; and so on. So we certainly do not lack an infinite series of objectives of being, superordinated to our starting objective in the way just required; and yet no one would think to take 2 to be in fact greater than 5. None of the members of this infinite series has any factuality. However many objectives go up, one over the other, they still come no whit closer to factuality.

No objective *becomes* factual through superordinate objectives or *is* factual by virtue of them. An objective must bear factuality in itself; and as far as I can see, its factuality is a basic property for which there is no definition and, at least for the time being, also no description. This property is in a sense complete by itself, whatever objective it may appear in; not only that, but however many positive objectives of being may be superordinated to this property, it encompasses the factuality of all those objectives. If A is in fact B, then the being of this objective is factual, likewise the being of this being, and so on to infinity. By virtue of its factuality, the starting objective constitutes not only the *inferius* for the objectives of higher order, but also the basis for their factuality; this makes for an even closer parallel between it and ideal objecta of higher order. Immediately obvious here and probably still in need of explanation is a certain contrast with unfactual being or being and nothing else; as we saw, such being seems to have a certain dependence on completion by superordinate being. I cannot attempt to consider this matter more closely here. But the question as to how we arrive at knowledge of the basic property of factuality cannot entirely be exempted from an apsychologically intended explanation, either. We shall return to this presently, below.[48]

But I see that the present statements on the theme "factuality," however sketchy they may be, have already taken us outside the question set for the present section, as to what is, in general, true of objectives; for to those objectives, at least, which serve as the (mediate) object of a justified negation of being, factuality cannot be ascribed. The objective "that there is a perpetual motion machine" is simply not a fact. It will be advisable now to go a few steps further into specifics, following the path we have, in fact, already entered upon in the foregoing.

§12

On the Kinds of Objectives

For someone who knows in general what an objectum is and who finds himself faced with the question as to what kinds of objecta there are and just how these objects are constituted, all the variety that one finds in things in this area might easily serve to discourage any attempt at enumeration. In the case of objectives, the analogous question is equally permissible, and the relatively high degree of uniformity of what is involved in this case makes it, at all events, easier to answer the question. In this uniformity, a point that was only now mentioned shows itself again—the objective's characteristic affinity with such objects of higher order as are already known to us.

If every objective may be called being, in the broadest sense of the word, then the totality of objectives divides up according to three pairs of opposites: being in the narrower sense and so-being, positivity and negativity, existence and subsistence. The first of these pairs is sufficiently characterized by means of formal paradigms like "*A* is" for being and "*A* is *B*" for so-being.[49] The attempt to "reduce" the one to the other miscarries in every form, as far as I can see. One can be mistaken about that, if he takes merely equivalent objectives to be identical. As for the fact that there is no third thing beyond being and so-being, the corresponding judgmental evidence is curiously as little accessible a priori as that in favor of the division of all objects into objecta and objectives.

With regard to the opposition of positive and negative, the paradigm itself is dispensable. But in view of the custom, especially in logic, of treating this opposition as a matter of the "quality of judgment," it is worth emphasizing that while the opposition of objectives is undoubtedly paralleled by an opposition of the apprehending judgments, one must not thereby let one's self be led away from granting unto the objective the things that are the objective's. It will make it easier to distinguish between the judgment and the objective if we make a terminological separation of the two parallel oppositions, at least as concerns their respective first members. With reasonable care in expression, one will hardly feel tempted to call a judgment positive or an objective affirmative. Given the occasion, only the judgment is affirmative, and only the objective positive. Admittedly, there is no word other than "negative" at our disposal for the second members.[50]

As against the foregoing, the opposition of existence and subsistence still involves many things that are in need of clarification. Here we can furnish only a quite fragmentary contribution to the treatment of these things. Years ago,[51] I tried to characterize the basic fact of the matter this way: "Even according to linguistic usage, while sameness can subsist between 3 and 3 and differentness can subsist between red and green, they cannot exist in the manner of a house or a tree."

This has given rise to the reproach[52] that I let myself be led astray by a caprice of linguistic usage. As proof of this, I find[53] only the reference to the following dilemma. What I distinguish from each other as existence and subsistence can be different only in the experiences or the objecta. Differences of the latter sort do not have to do with the objective; but differences of the former sort are not detectable. It is so simple, that there is supposed to be "no escaping" for me on this point.[54] First of all, I want to make no secret of the fact that I had hitherto never in any walk of life contemplated "escaping" as an expedient. But as regards the matter itself, I deny the completeness of the disjunction claimed in the above dilemma. Surely the sense of my assertion is precisely that aside from the objectum and the experience there is a third something, and that it is precisely this that exhibits the differences in question—which is to say, the objective. But perhaps the objection merely means that this difference is not knowable without allied differences in the apprehending experiences. I could only agree with that, but I must at the same time deny that such differences are lacking. I must also deny that from these differences those in the objectives are first disclosed. Even someone who is supposed to be able to distinguish blue from yellow requires, for this purpose, two representations that are (in content) different from each other. But distinguishing between blue and yellow does not take place in such a way that first one recognizes the difference in the representations and from this infers that of the colors. The colors are the more immediately apprehensible, and we are far more likely to infer the difference in the means of apprehension from the difference in what is apprehended, than to make the converse inference. So too in the case of the difference between existence and subsistence: in examples of the above sort one apprehends it as immediately as the difference between blue and yellow;[55] but so far as judgments are requisite for the apprehending of objectives, it will be permissible to conclude from the recognition of this difference that there must be something different about the apprehending judgments. Below, I shall return briefly to the factor in which the difference might be sought.[56]

It is always advisable, however, to accompany the appeal to the evidentness of the immediately given with something in the way of mediate verification, especially where the former procedure meets with doubts. Above all, it would easily succeed in precluding the suspicion that we might only be dealing with differences of objecta here. True, existence is doubtless connected with a certain characteristic of objecta, in such a way that objecta that lack this characteristic cannot exist at all. In this characteristic we have that for which, in my opinion, it is most practical to reserve the term "reality."[57] Over against real objecta such as a table and a chair—or for that matter, representation or desire —stand ideal objects, ones whose being can be none other than subsistence, if they do have any being. This class includes numbers, shapes, relations of ground and consequent, and much else, including all the objectives. But what can exist must, as it were, first of all subsist. And if one fixes one's thoughts on something existing at a time t—today, say the dirigible airship—and then assigns a different point in time to it, say a sufficiently past t', then in a simple manner one has apprehended an object whose existence can be denied, but not its subsistence. If A designates the object in question, apart from the time-determination, then we have in the objectum $A\ t$ an existing object and in objectum $A\ t'$ a merely subsisting one. Now, neither subsistence nor existence has its character from the particular nature of a time-determination; so that any suspicion that the transition from existence to subsistence might *consist* in a transition from *t* to *t'* is precluded. So our example rules out any prospect of reducing the difference in question, that of the objectives, to a difference of their objecta.

A deeper insight into the essential difference of the two kinds of being under discussion seems to be provided at present by a basis of comparison that was already under discussion above,[58] in its application to the objective. What exists must exist at a certain time; existence is attached to time. So little is that the case with subsistence, that the sort of thing that by nature can only subsist and cannot exist—something ideal, in other words—tolerates no time-determinations whatsoever. To grant to differentness a time between red and green would have hardly more sense than calling a musical tone white or black. Differentness and likewise just "different"[59] are timeless. Timeless as well are all other objects that subsist without having anything to do with actuality. As "pure subsistences," these could be contrasted to "mixed subsistences"; connected with dates of actuality in a way that we shall directly mention, the latter subsistences might at first seem also to participate in the time-determinations of these dates. However, if one expresses the results of this in the following way, "Existences are temporal, pure subsistences timeless," then one appears to be falling into conflict with the previously advocated principle of the timelessness of objectives; for existence, too, is an objective. However, this appearance is due merely to the inexactness of the above manner of expression, one that is nevertheless fairly customary.[d] What we just designated as existences and pure subsistences would have been better called the existent and the purely subsistent. However, of existence and pure subsistence in the exact sense of the terms, it may be said that the former can be factual only with temporal material, the latter only with timeless material, though existence itself is as timeless as subsistence.

Let us dedicate a few more remarks to the elucidation of the contrast between existence as temporal and subsistence as timeless. It is evident how closely connected are timelessness and the nature of a thing as subsistent, among other ways from the quite remarkable fact that there is no causal investigation in the domain of subsistence, such investigation being inseparable from existence. Through linguistic usage, moreover, the timelessness of the subsistent is often hidden, even when it is an objective. Here we have to do with those "mixed subsistences" of which we were just speaking. Of people who practise the same profession or live together for a long time, it is rightly said that they become more like [ännlicher] each other. Here similarity [Ähnlichkeit] and its degrees seem quite directly related time periods, even though similarity is an ideal object. Yet as one can easily see, the things involved in this particular case are by no means just ideal things; there are also actualities that change and thereby realize the *fundamenta* of different relations. It is not the ideal relation of similarity that is in time, here; what is in time are the real *fund-*

amenta, whose existence can at most impart a sort of quasi-temporality to similarity, which subsists between them without any respect to existence and time.

On the other hand, as regards the time element that is present in existing things and which typifies all existence, it is worth emphasizing that the factor that is so conspicuous in our verbs as tense does not qualify as this element. Of course, it is obvious in the first instance that all existence belongs either to the past, the present, or the future: it was, it is, or it will be. And this point is so crucial to the notion of existence that one is compelled to speak more precisely and say: in the strict sense, only a thing of the present exists, and what was or will be, strictly speaking, does not exist at all. But this would be to make the objective "existence" dependent on subjective determinations, in the first instance those having to do with apprehension. Certainly, the nature of such determinations is of the greatest significance for the psychology of our representation of time, but strictly speaking they have no more to do with the objective itself than, say, a certain individual's visual or auditory proficiency with colors or tones has to do with the colors or tones. Presentness does not really attach to existence or the existent taken by itself; rather, it betokens merely that the apprehended and the apprehending coincide in time, and *mutatis mutandis,* the matter is no different with past and future. For example, for a given astronomical constellation it certainly does not matter whether someone apprehends it and whether this happens contemporaneously with the constellation, or before, or afterwards. How is it, one might ask, that in going from existence into non-existence the constellation is apprehended once at the time of its existence and once again at another time? Certainly it exists at a certain time *t,* and at another time, *t',* it does not exist. But there is nothing of the present and nothing of the past or future about these times; rather, the one is simply *t* and the other *t',* however easy or difficult it may be for us to apprehend them in their own absolute determinateness. Otherwise expressed: grammatical *tempus* actually has no place at all in the notion of existence. And if it is not quite permissible, linguistically, for us to adopt a convention that would divest the term "existence" of a signification which to some extent has always been proper to it, then for the purpose of a special precisive step in the theory of objects the use of a modified expression is advisable. For many years now,[60] the term "persistence" has proved its value to me in private use (and in lectures), and I propose it for present use as a means of designating an existence that is in a sense purified of the subjectivity of the one who apprehends it—of course, only for use in applications where this subjectivity would prove troublesome. It actually does prove so, as we saw,[61] where the grammatical tense threatens to obscure the character of timelessness in objectives. My desk persists at the absolute, objective time *t,* but this persistence remains immutable, from whatever standpoint in time it may be considered.

Returning for a few more words about the fundamental differentness of existence and subsistence, there is perhaps no point of view from which this differentness shows up more strikingly than in the modes of knowing naturally associated with these two types of being. Here it is a question of no less radical an opposition that that between the empirical and the rational, the a posteriori and the a priori—incidentally, we shall have to get right back to this opposition in the following. Existence is known empirically; in principle, subsistence is known a priori. I admit that it is sometimes possible to gain a sort of a priori hold on existence, albeit only so far as the existence is negative; and the guarantee of a subsistence can also be established empirically in light of the existence of the object in question. Add to this what is called the application of the rationally known to actuality, a methodology we cannot now attempt to characterize more precisely. But none of this can overshadow the natural affinity for a certain kind of knowing which makes existence the domain of knowledge naturally adequated to empirical apprehending and subsistence the domain naturally adequated to a priori apprehending. I daresay we can regard the notion of the "caprices" of language as sufficiently ruled out by the fact that the most far-reaching contrasts of epistemology extend into the present context.

One can therefore be sure of agreement with the facts, in placing subsistence in juxtaposition with existence; yet it does not seem possible at present to attain such a conclusive outcome with regard to the completeness of the resulting disjunction. It is perhaps easiest to sense the difficulty in question when so-being is brought into the sphere of consideration and one tries to determine the extent to which so-being always presupposes a being. What then comes out is a certain principle of the independence of so-being from being, formulated by Ernst Mally. I have followed out this principle into some of its consequences elsewhere.[62] It has been sharply attacked,[63] primarily because of the advocacy it has received from me. But without going into the details of the question, which would take us out of our way, it might suffice for our immediate purposes if we can point out some judgment of being, namely a correct one of negative quality, to make clear what is presently at issue.

If someone judges, e.g., "A perpetual motion machine does not exist," it is doubtless clear that the object whose existence is denied must have properties, namely those in terms of which it can be characterized, and that without these properties, the conviction of non-existence could have neither sense nor justification.[64] To have properties, of course, is tantamount to "being thus and so" ["sosein"]. But this so-being [Sosein] does not have existence as its necessary condition, for existence is precisely what is being denied—and correctly denied, moreover. Analogous things could be pointed out in instances of the knowledge of subsistence. In connection with knowing or wanting to know, it often proves useful to make a general distinction between two successive ways[65] in which the object in question is apprehended: there is one's fastening upon[e] an object, and there is the making of a judgment about it. With that, it is immediately obvious that we may say: one fastens upon objects in their so-being; and what is then judged and perhaps known is either the being of what one has fastened upon in its so-being, or else some further so-being of it. One can fasten upon this so-being, and through it the thing which is thus and so, without restrictions as to being, as the possibility of negative knowledge shows. Insofar as that is the case, our fastening-upon finds something already there or given [etwas vorgegeben] in the realm of objects, regardless of how the question as to being or non-being is decided. In this sense, "there are" ["es gibt"] also objects that do not exist or subsist [die nicht sind], and I have designated this fact as the "absistence of the pure object" [das "Aussersein des reinen Gegenstandes"][66]—a somewhat barbaric word-formation, I fear, but one which is hard to improve.[f]

The term arose in connection with the interpretation of that strange "there is" [es gibt] that seems impossible to detach even from objects furthest from being. The effort was to get by without recourse to a new, third kind of being besides existence and subsistence. I have since then more than once had the distinct feeling, however, that this effort cannot overcome the peculiar positivity[67] that seems to lie in the prior thereness or givenness [in der Vorgegebenheit] of everything that can be fastened upon, i.e., (in principle) every object. In consideration of this, I must expressly mention the possibility that beyond existing and subsisting there might be a third something to which no one extends the term being, but which would ultimately have to be characterized as something being-like—though only in an especially broad sense. What must be decided is simply whether absistence itself constitutes a being-determination or merely the lack of such a determination. We are forced to adhere to the latter alternative not only by the law of parsimony, but even more by the fact that in principle there is no *negativum* for the presumed *positivum,* a situation which is altogether unparalleled. There is something else that might point in the same direction. Ignoring certain harmless inaccuracies, one can also characterize the opposition of empirical and rational knowing in the following way. Whereas a posteriori and from existence [Dasein] (naturally of something thus and so) one knows so-being or a further existence, a priori and from so-being one knows a being or a futher so-being. Might not the analogy to existence which so-being enters into, in certain circumstances, account for some of that puzzling "there is" that we observe in connection with things which are not?

In view of the paucity of what I can presently set straight in such an important matter as this, the word "absistence" seems to me to afford an advantage, by virtue of its natural indefinitness; it is at least a suitable means for keeping the question open for further inquiry in the theory of objects. In at least this sense it will be advisable to set absistence alongside existence and subsistence as a third something.

§13
The Modal Properties of Objectives

Turning next to a brief consideration of some particularly important properties of objectives, I can begin most naturally with the fact of secondary expression of judgment, a fact now familiar to us from the second chapter. Consider the circumstance already evident in many earlier examples, that this secondary expression receives a more precise determination through specification of its objective (in a "that"-clause, usually). If I can correctly say, "I affirm (deny, doubt) that..." and the like, then I can just as correctly say, "It is evident to me that..." with the main clause position of the whole judgment now in a certain sense being occupied by a property of the judgment. Of course, this can be said also with regard to a person other than the speaker; again, it can be said without reference to any person. Thus: "It is evident to him that..." or simply "It is evident that..." An impersonal form like this serves to call attention to a fact that actually might have been noticed beforehand, in each of the personal formulations. This is the fact that something which in the first instance presents itself as the property of a judgment now appears precisely as an attribute of the objective figuring in the "that"-clause. Evidence^g is surely as much a matter of the judgment as, say, certainty is; nevertheless, it is more natural—if not for a theorist, then certainly for a layman, at least—to say, "It is evident that 3 is greater than 2" rather than, e.g., "The judgment on this matter is evident." This becomes clearer still in the opposed terms "true" and "false." As we know, these terms cannot be said to exhibit any special resistance to employment in a figurative sense. "True friend," "false teeth," "true words," and "false idea" are simply textbook examples of ambiguity. If one designates a judgment true or false, then somehow one no longer has the feeling of a downright figurative employment of a word. Yet it seems to me that upon further consideration it is impossible to doubt for a moment that the locution "It is true that *A* exists" or "It is false that..." is a far more natural manner of speaking, and in the last analysis the only really natural one. It is harder to call a judgment "probable" than it is to call it "true," and it is still harder to call it "possible," "necessary" or "contingent"; whereas each of these adjectives can be used quite effortlessly as an attribute of the objective. Locutions like "It is probable (possible, contingent, necessary) that..." surely use these adjectives in the way which really befits them.

Our procedure in the following may at first strike one as somewhat superficial: a group of properties is treated as homogeneous out of consideration of the fact that some uncertainty has been felt as to whether the properties should not rather be understood as being properties of judgments. But there is a good tradition for their homogeneity, one based in the concept of the "modality" of judgment; so that in the absence of a better alternative, it would be quite intelligible if the properties in question were to be called *modal properties* of objectives. The tradition admittedly knows nothing of objectives, at least as far as the name goes. But at the very least, in many cases it remains more than doubtful as to how far someone who said or says "judgment" did or does not already mean "objective" by that.[68] As for the list of properties of objectives which are to be called modal in this sense, it will consist almost entirely of the examples just adduced. If one takes the Kantian triad, "problematic, assertoric, apodeictic," as a basis, then one finds one's self led to possibility and factuality (although in the first instance this is factuality in the particularly narrow sense mentioned above),[69h] along with their respective opposites. Truth and probability with their opposites can then doubtlessly be added; and perhaps we shall also not want to do without certainty and evidence, although we cannot vouch for the natural completeness of the resulting enumeration. The great importance of these properties, or at least some of them, is beyond all doubt. And since in the end it is really the significance of the objective which is being felt in the importance of its properties, one or two remarks on this subject will hardly be inopportune. My concern is mainly with the justification for a certain approach to modal properties, an approach that might almost be said to have become popular and which I myself have followed in introducing these properties. I mean the definition of modal properties from the side of judgment. The question as to how we really apprehend these properties is admittedly more psychological than might seem suited to this section, which is still intended primarily from the standpoint of the theory of objects. But of course, our knowledge of the nature of an object is fairly often codetermined by our knowledge of the manner in which it is apprehended.

What I have just called the definition of modal properties "from the side of judgment" is in itself nothing remarkable. It was previously mentioned that the "object" already carries within itself, etymologically, the reference to an apprehending which stands over against it in a certain way, and that the object must first be theoretically freed from this reference. Also, among objecta specifically, there are objects that are determined in such a way that they cannot be freed from this relation at all. This is evidenced by the concept of an appearance; that concept cannot be gotten through any characterization of the appearing objectum by itself.

The reference to an apprehending is likewise natural in connection with the specific case of objectives. First of all, this is where the objective is found tied to a specified apprehending experience. And then the reference is natural where no actual experience is under consideration, but the characterization of the nature of the experience would carry over to the nature of the object, if the experience were under consideration. Actually, when someone maintains today that it is certain that one can fly from France to England, something is doubtless being said about the matter in question, although neither certainty nor the uncertainty that can be imagined at some other time in any way concerns the objective. And if one wishes further to have some account of what it really is that is being said of the objective, one finds oneself left simply with the relation to the certainty of a possible or admissable apprehending. It is just that the object is so constituted that it can be justifiably apprehended by means of a judgment that is certain. Something similar could be pointed out with regard to evidence. Nor has the situation been conceived any differently as regards necessity and possibility, among other things.[70] And it was really this same manner of definition that we previously had to reject in connection with the concept of being.[71] It is appropriate to mention this again here, for the simple reason that the "being" or "existence" that is defined in this way coincides with something which, under the name of factuality (this time in the broadest sense of the word), I number among the modal properties of objectives.

But another reason for my appealing to that rejection as a sort of precedent is that the unnaturalness of the characterization in terms of "reflection" on judgment has long since made itself palpable to me in connection with the remaining modal properties, and I hope that by now I have found a way to dispense with this characterization. Before briefly presenting my attempt in this regard, I shall formulate its theme in the following assertion. It would be in contradiction to the clear-cut testimony of experience, if the roundabout way through judgment—which for lack of anything better I myself have usually taken—were essential to the notions of factuality, necessity, and so on; through experience I become aware of notions of modality that are entirely positive and which is no way recur to judging. Yet if I see the matter aright, in these notions we are dealing at least in part with data that are quite as ultimate as those we have met with in existence or so-being, etc.; so that what we are after is not some sort of reductive definition, but an indication of the occasions in which—or rather, by means of which—these ultimate data come into our awareness. My opinion, then, is not that it would be impermissible to form concepts of the modal properties of objectives in the roundabout way through the properties of the judgment. On the contrary, this can be done in a quite correct and also quite useful way. But it seems important to me that we are not always dependent on this roundabout way and that in the present connection, too, ultimate and basic factors in objectives stand open to our apprehending.

The presentation will work out most simply if I begin with the concept of factuality; but as just indicated, this will not be factuality in the narrowest sense, the sense which we are accustomed to correlate with the "assertoric judgment."[i] It will be the sense in which earlier[72] we found factuality to be fundamentally involved in all knowing.[73] The characterization by way of judgment undoubtedly shows us our next step. An objective is factual when under favorable enough circumstances it can be apprehended with evidence[74] and—which for the time being some may consider to be obvious anyway—with certainty. The question is then whether, as often as we think of the factuality of an objective, we must also think of the evidence and certainty of an apprehending judgment. Experience compels us to answer in the negative, I think. Yet it is difficult to make up one's mind to accept the testimony of experience as long as we cannot envisage any other means of familiarizing ourselves with this occasional property of objectives, a property that is so fundamentally important for our cognitive intentions. I am primarily concerned with showing such a means here.

To this end, I refer back[75] to a contrast already mentioned more than once in this work. It is now some years since I established this contrast; I did so primarily with regard to representational experiences, in the attempt to bring out a factor in these experiences that was like a side specially turned to their objects. This factor was called the "representational content." The designation of "representational act" was to be reserved for the whole of what remained in the representational experience.[76] Accordingly, there is not only a difference of object between the sensing of a musical tone and the sensing of a color; just because of this difference, there is also a difference of content. On the other hand, it is not only an object that the sensing of a musical tone has in common with the reproductive representation of that same tone; just because the sensing does have the object in common with the latter experience, it also has the content in common, although with respect to the act it still differs from the reproductive representation. As soon as it was established that judgments, and not just representations, have objects, it could not have been difficult to see that just as there are generally[77] different representational contents facing different objecta, so too must there be different judgmental contents facing different objectives, though the judgmental act in the latter case, like the representational act in the former case, can still perfectly well be the same.[78] On one occasion we judge being, and on another occasion we judge non-being; on one occasion subsistence, and so-being on another. In order for us to do that, there must be judgments with different contents; differences in the act do not seem to play any generally significant role here.[79] And just as one might be said to have given sufficient proof of intellectual ownership of an objectum when one can appeal to the ownership of a representation with the appropriate content, so too we have provided everything necessary regarding our acquaintance with ultimate data in the way of objectives when we are equipped with judgmental experiences having the appropriate content. I apprehend what existence and subsistence are, and what positive and negative being are, through the affirmative or negative judgments in question; moreover, I do so as directly as I apprehend a color by color-sensation. The former cases no more involve a "reflection" upon judgment than the latter case involves a reflection upon sensation. But then, the same thing might be claimed with respect to factuality, if one could identify some judgmental content-factor that was coordinated with factuality as its natural means of apprehension.

A demand like that would not seem at all easy to satisfy, if we may form our opinion about it by another analogy to representation. The representations of green and red are certainly different in content, but as I have explained else-where,[80] it is rather difficult to set the two contents over against the objecta that we know so well. In a certain sense, we have a more favorable situation in the case of factuality. Here we can easily specify factors in the judgment that go hand in hand with the factuality of the judged objective. These are, of course, the same factors we were led to just previously, when the characterization of factuality took the roundabout way via the judgment: evidence and certainty. But a quite different difficulty makes its appearance at this point. Can it be permissible to take evidence and certainty as determinations of the judgmental content, when at first glance it seems so much more natural to ascribe them to the judgmental act?

And in the case of certainty, first of all, there is no doubt that the latter approach really is the correct one. It is surely natural to suppose that a factor in an intellectual experience lies outside the content, and that it therefore appertains to the act, when this factor can undergo changes without thereby affecting the nature of the object apprehended. This is in fact the case, where there is a change in the degree of certainty. One person will have a very good recollection of a thing,[81] as they say, while another person will have only a very poor recollection of it. The thing stays the same; and what is judgmentally apprehended with such different degrees of certainty need not have actually ever happened.

In the case of evidence, however, it is a very different situation. This might already be seen in the fact that while there cannot be a judgment without some degree of certainty, judgments without evidence are not only possible but anything but rare; the factor of evidence exhibits a type of mobility that one would sooner expect to find in a content-factor than in an act-factor. Yet it seems that the apprehended objective is no more affected by the presence or absence of evidence than it is by difference in the degrees of certainty. A person may see or realize that every angle in a semicircle is a right angle, or he may just believe it on hearsay or without any thought to the contrary; but whichever is the case, his judgment still apprehends the subsisting of the geometrical relation in question. The matter appears in a somewhat different light, however, as soon as one reflects that it would also be possible for a judgment devoid of evidence to hit on the objective that the angle in a semicircle measures 60 or 100 degrees. Hence, while the evidenceless judgment *can* apprehend something factual, it can just as well apprehend something unfactual. It apprehends the factual *per accidens,* so to speak; whereas the evident judgment is by its own nature oriented towards the factual as the means of apprehension adequated to the factual and in that capacity there is no substitute for the evident judgment.[82]

But, of course, this question can still be asked: Does an evident judgment apprehend something other than what an evidenceless judgment apprehends, or does it just apprehend the same thing in a different way? And our being able to ask this is due to the fact that even when the principle of the size of the angles in a semicircle is seen or realized, one appears to be thinking just of that state of affairs and not also its factuality. Yet it becomes clear that this can only be an appearance, when one passes from the mere judging of the objective to the judging about it. When one says, "It is a fact that the angle in a semicircle is a right angle," factuality as a property of the objective is borne in upon us with such immediacy that there is little room for doubt about when this property was apprehended; it must have been apprehended right at the start, along with the objective. Certainly, a "reflection on the judgment" can also be a factor in such a judgment about the objective. It finds its correct expression in an assertion like, "It is evident that the angle in a semicircle is a right angle." But that is clearly to say something different; it is just something that turns out in practice to be very close to the assertion of factuality, in consequence of the fact that the two assertions are interchangeable without error. And as a further consequence, one can often say "evident" when the thing under consideration is not the experience at all, but just the objective—or in other words, when it is really not evidence at all that one is thinking of, but just factuality.

Thus, evidence does in fact stand over against a factor in the objective, as the means of apprehension adequated to that factor, and in this way evidence constitutes one of the determinations of judgment on the side of content. At present I am unable to explain why evidence does not begin to function explicitly until there is a judgment about an objective, and why it is not already functioning explicitly in our judging the objective—or in the "judgment of" the objective, as one might say in analogy to "judgment about." In areas where one is as close to the ultimates of knowing and the theory of knowledge as we are in matters of evidence, there is no reason at all to be surprised if there is not always the same progress as in other areas. And this being the case, it would be at least easy to understand why one might be inclined to look at evidence in the same way as certainty, as a determination belonging to the judgmental act. The particular fact that has now emerged might be recorded in a proposition like this: Evidence does not function as a content of judgment-of, but it does function as a content of judgment-about. As such, evidence apprehends the factuality of an objective no differently than, say, the affirmative quality of a judgment apprehends the positivity of the objective. But by no means do we then have to seek the nature of factuality in the apprehensibility of an objective by means of an evident judgment.

The present view, which I have been compelled to sketch in a few sparse strokes, is surely much in need of elaboration, but I hope it is also capable of elaboration. Our view receives confirmation from the fact that it can now be applied to the remaining modal properties of the objective. So that I can make this clear as briefly as possible, it should first of all be pointed out[83] that factuality is by its very nature located at the end of a scale of magnitude, a scale whose points can be conceived of as representing every degree of possibility.

The word "possibility" is here understood in the sense in which possibility admits of gradation. In this sense, one objective is called "very possible" and another "hardly possible," and in special circumstances, e.g., such as are afforded by games of chance, numerical determinations of degrees of possibility are undertaken.[84] So let us say that all possibility is reduced factuality. And let us say that we know from experience that under the right conditions an objective's possibility is itself immediately apprehended. Then the following question arises, regarding a judgment that has the certainty of evidence. Can this familiar experience be made to shift over into the apprehending of a possibility, by means of some appropriate modifications? In point of fact, this situation occurs as soon as certainty changes into uncertainty or surmise, even though the evidence-factor is still there. I may be justified by evidence in surmising[85] that a certain result will occur in gambling. Naturally, the factuality of the result does not then stand established; but its possibility does, and as a stronger surmise is justified, the possibility is greater. But in this surmise, one's apprehending of the possibility is no more explicit than our previous apprehending of a factual objective's factuality, when we judged that objective. And as in that case, here too a judgment-about provides what is required. One simply judges so: that it is in such and such a degree possible that the result will occur.

Yet as it stands, this very similarity of attitude involves a further difficulty. Wherein lies the difference between the judgment just now characterized, the judgment as to what is possible, and the judgment that occupied our attention earlier, the judgment as to what is factual? In the first instance, the difference is just that uncertainty has taken the place of certainty in the judgment. Now, if certainty pertains to the judgmental act, then uncertainty and its various degrees will naturally also pertain to the act. But in the foregoing, the factor that we found coordinated with factuality was not certainty, but evidence. Indeed, evidence is not absent even in the present case; but does that mean that it also stands opposite probability, as the content coordinated with this object? Actually, it can, if only there is a difference between evidence appropriate to certainty and evidence appropriate to surmise—and that difference does not consist simply in the fact that the one evident judgment has the character of certainty and the other has the character of a surmise. Such a difference in evidence is scarcely the sort of thing one would infer from direct experience; yet it is something exceedingly probable. I daresay the most reasonable supposition would be that evidence, too, can be arranged on a gradual scale. At any event, it is at least very plausible that there is a series of evidential states, each of which legitimates surmises only up to a certain maximum strength. Any possibility that is to be gotten at by a surmise has a magnitude that is matched by one of these maximum strengths, and therefore by the appropriate evidential state; so that this state can likewise be regarded as the means of apprehension adequated to the possibility in question. This conforms to what was shown above with respect to factuality and the evidential state that was then called just evidence. It has now become obvious why it was incorrect to call it just that, and why it should have immediately been called evidence appropriate to certainty. With that, we have shown how possibilities, too (although a special sort of ultimate data), can come directly to our knowledge, in a way that is not replaceable by any periphrastic definition. In particular, the tradition of making possibility into something negative becomes quite dispensable, in view of the direct way, and it is now all the more easy to see how much this tradition goes against the thoroughly positive character of our notion of possibility, unless what is being accomplished is a case of determination that I shall mention below.[86]

So our treatment of possibility comes down to a direct, albeit not yet fully secured, determination of the evidence-factor to a specific form. The basis for an analogous treatment of necessity is a different determination of this factor, and it is one that is in use even in the realm of extrascientific observation. Or what it amounts to, we are dealing with something that in everyday life is usually referred to just by the word *"Einsicht."*[j] The theoretical use of this word basically represents an extension of everyday usage. To see or realize something [etwas einsehen] and to understand it[87] are the same, outside science. True, despite this it is quite unavoidable that we should speak of evidence in connection with inward perception; and the result is that inward perception precisely represents a case of seeing or realizing [Einsicht] without understanding.[88] But for all that, the case of seeing or realizing with understanding is by itself a clearly characterized epistemic experience. It is the experience that has usually been called a priori knowing. That employment of these words lends itself to misunderstanding, and it is in fact rather often misunderstood;[89] but one can hardly get along without it anymore at the present time. In the foregoing we saw fit to claim without further qualification that evidence appropriate to certainty was a content-factor in a judgment; now we can naturally make such a claim about evidence taken specifically as a priori or rational. And if the factuality of an objective is what evidence appropriate to certainty apprehends, then necessity is what is similarly coordinated with rational evidence, as the latter's object.[90] An objective is necessary as far as it can be seen or realized a priori. But we are apprised of the nature of necessity by the seeing or realization itself, and not by a reflection on that seeing or realization. Necessity thereby presents itself as something thoroughly positive, so that the traditional definition of necessity as the impossibility of the opposite[91] seems already prohibited by direct observation.

But besides this, it is obviously simpler to view impossibility as a special case of necessity, instead of the other way round—viewing necessity as a special case of impossibility (namely that of a quite different objective, the opposite one). True, the starting objective is also abandoned in the former approach: an objective is impossible as far as it is necessary that it does not subsist. But this

step to the next higher objective of being—the transition from the evidence of
the judgment-of to the evidence of a judgment-about—is a great deal easier to
execute than the step to the contradictorily opposed objective. The latter objective is indeed connected with the starting objective by very important logical
relations, but for the rest it stands over against this objective as something
completely independent of it. I might add that if impossibility is taken as the
necessity of non-subsistence [Nichtsein], in juxtaposition to it there can also be
necessity in the narrower sense of the necessity of subsistence [Sein]. Considered that way, even necessity would bring the next higher objective into consideration.—In precising the notion of impossibility, one can also strictly follow the negative form of the word. Thus, the impossible is that which is not
possible or which stands at the zero-point of the possibility-line. In this sense,
neither impossibility nor possibility is tied to apriority; by way of contrast,
rational impossibility and the rational possibility derived from it by negation
are customarily distinguished as logical impossibility and logical possibility,
respectively. — Objectives that are by their nature inaccessible to the rational
mode of knowledge are customarily opposed to necessary objectives as contingent ones.

Our inclusion of true and false among the modal properties at the beginning
of this section is less in keeping with tradition than with the nature of the
matter. It seems that in any discussion of factuality and necessity there must
also be some consideration of truth, because of some close natural relationship. In connection with factuality, this relationship can appear as complete
correspondence, which leads to the following question: If on one occasion it is
called factual that A is B, and on another occasion it is called true, what distinction is really operating here? Apparently the distinction is this, that while
the reference to an apprehending judgment only appears to play a role in the
case of "factual," this reference has an essential meaning in the case of
"true." But I (along with others) might have been in error when I sought the
meaning of this reference in the nature of the apprehending judgment,[92] when
it might lie in the very fact of something being apprehended. Not all objectives
can be said to be true or false with equal naturalness; such characterizations
seem rather to appear where the objective presents itself as the real or fictive
view or assertion of a definite or indefinite individual or group, so that it can
then be subjected to a type of criticism.[93] But if these are the circumstances
under which one might employ the epithet "truth," what does it mean? It
would be in close accordance with common sense as well as with time-honored
tradition to answer this way: What one asserts is true when it agrees with what
is—or with what is factual, which is the clearer expression, in view of the foregoing. So in its essentials, the situation is one in which an objective somehow
presupposed as pseudo-existing is confronted with the pure objective, as it
were, on the strength of the latter's factuality. The value of the present roundabout way can easily be seen from the fact that one thereby gets rid of the tight

relation to evidence. As we saw, this relation attaches to factuality, yet it is foreign to the needs that one's knowledge is so often intended to serve. The business of life demands of us that in a given situation we know what is and how it is—is in fact, of course. For this to occur, factuality need by no means make a proxy appearance in the apprehending experience, through its subjective correlate, evidence. There may even be something of the nature of excess baggage in evidence, as against which the requirement of truth represents the practical minimum.

The natural *negativum* of "true" is "false." At the simplest, an objective is called false in the event that it is not true. And so it is called false in the event that it does not answer to any factual objective. Or, finally, it is called false in the event that it is not factual. It seems to me that contrasting the false to the true as a second positive something—in the way that a white rose is contrasted to a red rose[94]—lacks any justification; so that all attempts to make a *negativum* positive by employing the concept of falsehood would also be deluded.[95] An analogous view regarding the opposite of factuality would have been a more plausible candidate for discussion, considering how "blind judgment" actually can be said as a substitute for "non-evident judgment." Yet just as being blind consists merely in not being able to see, so too does being unfactual consist merely in "not being factual." Still, I know the danger of explaining away *positiva* from the world by means of negative equivalents. I am also well aware that the law of parsimony is binding for theory, not for observation or its analogue in the theory of objects. So a certain cautiousness in this matter may still be in order.

If what we have just said about true and false is entirely correct, the following consequence results. Strictly speaking, truth by no means constitutes a new and peculiar modal property of the objective—least of all a property having that fundamental epistemological significance that is usually attributed to the factor of truth.[96] But if this assertion is surprising, it is far more a matter of the wording than the point of it. For the concept of truth has arrived at that fundamental position in epistemology only insofar as it has been thought permissible to lay aside the restriction to pseudo-existing objectives, a move that probably just brings one unawares into the domain of a genuinely fundamental modal property, namely factuality.

Probability is to possibility as truth is to factuality, possibility being a sort of lower degree of factuality. Probability is predicated of an objective primarily insofar as a surmise is directed at the objective. And while the epithet "probable" naturally does not connote correspondence to a factual objective, it does connote the possibility of such a correspondence, the chance of being true.[97] That being the case, one could define probability as the possibility of truth. Naturally, we may ask ourselves what purpose there is in setting the possibility of truth alongside simple possibility, as is done in this reemployment of the notion of possibility. The legitimation lies in the function of surmise as a substitute for insufficient certainty; surmise fulfills this function in proportion to its inherent chance of hitting something true or correct. If one subsequently leaves the objective's presupposed pseudo-existence out of account here, as is done in the case of truth, then probability merges together with possibility. But one can still keep it separate from the latter by making use of the "subjective" aspect of possibility in another way. An objective can be called probable with the idea that it constitutes an object of justified surmise, and one can think of the magnitude of the possibility as accompanying the strength of the surmise that is justified. Of course we cannot attribute any descriptive value to these determinations either, once we look at them from the standpoint of the theory of objectives.

After what has been set forth, I daresay it is scarcely necessary any longer for us to mention expressly that certainty and evidence themselves are, strictly speaking, never properties of objectives, and that they are properties only of judgments. To be sure, they are fairly often grammatically predicated of objectives, but the reason for this is probably just that it is easy for certainty and evidence to present themselves to inexact consideration as representatives of factuality or necessity. At all events, it seems that there are not, strictly speaking, any distinctive modal properties in objectives beyond factuality, possibility, necessity, and their opposites.

When the concepts of factuality and truth come up for discussion, the concept of knowledge cannot go entirely unmentioned. For knowledge is really not the business of knowing, but what is known, which is of course always an objective. Knowledge is not plainly and simply and before objective, or a factual objective; it is the objective as something apprehended, or as something apprehended through the activity of knowing. In that sense, the circumstance that characterizes knowledge represents nothing basically distinct from what we considered above. But for the conclusion of our present remarks on the objective, it might be advisable to give at least an indication of the objective's connections with the theory of knowledge. These connections must have already become quite apparent to the reader during our consideration of modal properties, and they can be seen quite clearly in the very concept of knowledge. Even in name, the theory of knowledge is a theory concerned less with the activity of knowing than with knowledge. And knowledge consists of objectives of the nature just now indicated. So the theory of knowledge cannot be other than a theory of such objectives in one of its most important aspects. But in that case, such objectives are admittedly guaranteed a safe place in the theoretical treatment of the activity of knowing, too; for as knowledge, they are determined by their relation to knowing. To be sure, the peculiar character of this state of affairs is not the least reason why it has been so difficult to make clear the relation of the theory of knowledge (or logic) to psychology. Once one has become mindful of how the so-called "logical" laws—whether of judgment or inference—are first and foremost concerned with objectives, then one has already taken up an impregnable position against "psychologism." Still, it may prove useful to this position if the theory of objectives itself can be apprehended in its natural connection with the remaining domains of the science concerned with objects, the theory of objects.[98] Naturally, it would take us beyond our proper limits if we were also to enter into this side of the matter in the present connection.

§14

Concerning the Term "Objective"

Whenever some theoretical exigency forces one into the attempt to coin new terms, it is surely very important to weigh one's procedure very carefully. Nevertheless, the remarks of the present chapter may already constitute an unreasonably long delay in the return to the real subject of this work, and I would not create a further postponement with observations on the word "objective" if it did not seem best to put in a few words of defense, by now unavoidable, in the present place.

As we know, new publications afford two main standpoints for dissenting criticism, both tried and true: either the thing to be rejected is new but not good, or it is good but not new. Now, newness can never be less of an end in itself than it is in science. So I can speak with some personal satisfaction, when I say that scarcely any objections of consequence appear to have been raised against the material correctness of the remarks that I made about the objective in the first edition of this work. However, the historical antecedents of these statements—and not only these—have become the object of a many-sided interest; hardly a purely historical interest, I might add. The interest has led onto (1) Bolzano's "proposition in itself," (2) Stumpf's "state of affairs," and above all (3) Brentano's and Marty's "content of judgment."[99] Now since it would be merely a matter of faith to understand the reference to these in an exclusively impersonal way, I see myself compelled to counter it with an explanation. The reader who is justifiably interested only in the primary subject matter will hopefully excuse me for this explanation, on account of the special position in which the previously mentioned reference has placed me.

At the time the first edition of this book was written, Bolzano's theory of the "proposition in itself" was as little known to me as to most of my colleagues. Moreover, I cannot remember attending any lectures of Brentano that ever dealt with "the objective" otherwise than in the way that was always inevitable in logic and psychology. Marty's series of articles, "Über subjektlose Sätze," etc., now so much cited by him, began in the year 1884; hence, so far as it was known to me and taken into consideration, it might just as well have disappeared from my memory around 1900. Finally, in a journal article on the psychology of feeling, Stumpf occasionally uses "state of affairs" in the sense of "objective"; but this came quite fortuitously to my attention on the occasion of investigations in the psychology of feeling in 1905.[100] I was first able to gather the technical intention of this usage from a publication of Stumpf's of the year 1907.[101]

So at all events, my statements about the objective are the result of *my* investigative work, and I might mention that this work was by no means effortless. To that extent, then, the reviewer who spoke of the discovery of the objective by me[102] is justified in doing so, despite Marty's displeasure about it.[103] It is not for me to determine whether this judgment will really carry its point some day before the tribunal of the history of philosophy. If that tribunal finds it important enough, it will at any event be able to record the following coincidence. As soon as the first edition of this book had given the objective its first thorough investigations, the literarily manifest interest in "states of affairs" and (within a narrower circle also) "contents of judgment" took a hardly mistakable upswing. To verify this, one need only consult, say, the index to Anton Marty's *Untersuchungen* where twenty-five references are given under the catchword "Urteilsinhalt." Aside from passing references, there are certainly less than half a dozen occasions in which "contents of judgment" are mentioned in "Über subjektlose Sätze," the articles from which I am supposed to have been able to take everything worth knowing on this matter.

For my part, of course, there is no reason to take the possibility that others before me might have thought as I do in any other way than as a welcome enhancement of my confidence of being on the right path. But to the extent that it is more appropriate in this matter to dwell upon what unites rather than what separates, the more the question to which I have to address myself in view of the present state of opinions about the objective assumes a primarily terminological character for me. The question can be formulated approximately as follows: What has been investigated by me, and now also by others, under the name of the objective—this, or approximately this, has, under other names, occupied still others. Does one of these names deserve to be given preference over the name "objective," which I chose for lack of a better one? A few brief observations can now be devoted to this question.

Concerning Bolzano's "proposition in itself," it seems, on the whole, beyond doubt that this above all approximates the objective very closely, if it is not out-and-out identical with the objective.[104] That is corroborated in the latest accounts of Bolzano's theory.[105] Had he received the share of attention and recognition that he so deserved, then there could have arisen a tradition in favor of the word "proposition" for what I mean by "objective," in which case I should be among those not wishing to oppose this tradition. Such recognition, however, seems only just now on the point of breaking through. This has at least one advantage, since there is now nothing yet that would tie us to the expression "proposition," which has customarily been used with reference to linguistic matters.[106] This usage has been so unequivocal that a reinterpretation of this expression in a "sense" independent of speech as well as of thought would have to soon lead to subjectivization of this sense in some cases, and even to nominalistic superficialization of it in other cases. There is only a limited area in which the corresponding tradition has been prepared long in advance and in which this tradition, too, might be preserved. It is certainly most natural to speak of the "principle" ["Satz"] of contradiction, of Carnot's "principle," and of innumerable other "principles" and "theorems" [Grund- und Lehr-"Sätze"]. Without exception, these are obviously all objectives, but with a necessary difference. Customarily we require of them that they be factual; but since it is more natural to call them "true" than "factual," this leads—if the sense of the word "true" was correctly precised above[107]—to the following determination, here primarily a characterizing one: A "proposition" is an objective that is apprehended and perhaps also expressed; it is at least present and formulated in words, as we might say. This factor is even more important than truth or factuality—propositions can also be false. On this interpretation, according to which we are dealing with the formulated objective, the theory of objectives might quite well avail itself of the term "proposition" in its extralinguistic employment, as is indeed done in science and everyday life.

In connection with the word "proposition," it should at least be mentioned that immeasurably often the word "judgment" has been and is employed for "objective," and by no means just by those who have no eye for the separate nature of objectives. Terminological admixtures like "logical" judgments as opposed to the "psychological" call attention to this from time to time. If the danger of superficialization develops naturally here, as in the case of "proposition," the danger of an undue internalization, in the sense of subjectivization, is all the greater. Perhaps through no other verbal usage has more help been afforded illicit psychologism than through this one.

Elsewhere,[108] I have already acknowledged a certain advantage that the term "state of affairs" has over "objective." The former term did not appear to me to be suitable as a substitute, because its natural domain of application is too narrow. It is difficult enough even to call this a state of affairs, that it is not snowing now; but the applicability of the term to unfactual objectives seems to break down altogether. One can hardly call it a state of affairs that the diagonals in a square are unequal or that sharks are mammals. Nevertheless, I do not think that anything absolutely prevents our adopting a convention to disregard this shortcoming; thus, I should by no means want to call the term unserviceable.[109] But I think that when there is now, in "objective," an expression already in employment without opposition from any other usage, I should stay with this expression. But possibly there would be an advantage in bringing the term "state of affairs" into use for the important special case of factual objectives.

The foregoing was already written when, in the next to the most recent treatment of the doctrines of Bolzano,[110] I came across some remarks that oppose the "proposition in itself" to the "state of affairs" and which are thereby so instructive in the very matters discussed here that I believe I ought to reproduce them *in extenso*. "So far as we conceptually apprehend the mental form corresponding to a judgment," it says, "we call it a 'state of affairs' (Stumpf). On the basis of this descriptive psychological analysis, it would then mean a *hysteron proteron* if one thought that he could separate *realiter* the state of affairs or the 'proposition in itself' based on it from the underlying act of judgment." In the note the remarks then continue: "Allow me to make the following brief observations on the distinction between the concepts 'proposition in itself' and 'state of affairs'. A state of affairs seldom appears in consciousness pure; it almost always appears there modified in a certain manner. That is, psychologically speaking, the judgment becomes actual only as intertwined with the most diverse other mental functions—for example, with the functions of comparing, relating, abstracting, apperceiving, and perhaps also with emotional acts, acts of will, acts of stressing, of wishing, of desiring, etc. All of these acts exert an influence on the way and manner in which the state of affairs is experienced in consciousness, they modify the sense of what is experienced, and they thereby make possible the formation of the most diverse propositions-in-themselves for one and the same state of affairs. To take a simple example, if I say, 'I am going to the theatre this evening,' then the state of affairs of this sentence is simply the fact that I am going to the theatre this evening. Yet the sense of the sentence can still be a quite different one. It alters, for example, as often as I emphasize one of the words contained in it instead of some other. In this way I can obtain five propositions-in-themselves for the same state of affairs. But aside from the function of stressing (not to mention the function of synthetic unity and the other intellectual functions), a wishing can be involved, or an act of pleasure. Again the sense of the sentence alters.

In short, even this simple example shows how many propositions-in-themselves can underlie the same state of affairs."

Above all, one can see that Bolzano's "proposition in itself" and Stumpf's "state of affairs" nowise coincide with each other, according to this account. The former is more subjective—though even the latter would already be subjective enough, as a "mental form." As concerns the interpretation of Bolzano found here, I am certainly not unaware of the risk of opposing an author who has shown such confidence-inspiring knowledge of the subject through his publication. But I must admit that I am still unable to bring this interpretation into accord either with the preceding part of Gotthardt's account or with what I myself have gotten from my reading of Bolzano. And in any case, this much seems to me to be certain: If Gotthardt is right, then Bolzano's "proposition in itself" is absolutely not what I mean by "objective."

But also, even Stumpf's "state of affairs" would now be something other than my objective, despite the above statements of mine. This presupposes that our author has not interpreted Stumpf erroneously; but this is as good as precluded by the origin of the publication.[111] States of affairs are, as we heard, "mental forms"; as against this, the objective is no more mental than it is physical. No psychology, not even the "descriptive" kind is able to impart "authentic information"[112] about it, though at present one sometimes hears descriptive psychology set off as something quite special. Thus, our present author sets descriptive psychology in a somewhat strange opposition to "general psychology," rather than to something like explanatory psychology. It is as though the whole matter were something more than the fact that of the two tasks traditionally formulated as describing and explaining, psychology like every science prefers the former to the degree that the latter is less fulfillable. What I mean by an "objective," then, does not belong in psychology, and there will be even less reason to give up the name "objective" in favor of "state of affairs" or "proposition in itself," if I cannot be sure that I would not also have to reinterpret these latter terms in order to give them the signification that seems to me to be demanded by the facts.

If the justification of a thing was directly proportionate to the size of the claims that were made for it, then the last of the terms to be discussed, the expression "content of judgment," would straightway be guaranteed the ascendancy. At first I was simply charged with inventing the new name "objective" for what "was formerly" called a content of judgment.[113] As support[114] for this "was formerly," Anton Marty later cited, apart from himself and Brentano's lectures, five authors, or alternatively four reference sources.[115] What he induces from this, however, is nothing more than "that the name which is unheard of, as Meinong would have it, was and is known in the widest circles."[116] The being "unheard of" I never have maintained.[117] As for the being "known," namely of the word "content," I am little inclined to dispute that. On the contrary, I must appeal precisely to the smoothly familiar quality and the associated unclarity of the metaphor contained in the word "content" as proof that such occasional uses of the term "content of judgment" as Marty had "directly at hand" serve to disclose neither a technical verbal usage nor a conception of the objective which is in any degree worked out. In any case, after the claim about being "known," the announcement that Marty bases on it is surprising, viz., that he is "unable to see any valid reason why one should depart from *this* name (or the synonymous name of "state of affairs" which, e.g., Stumpf uses)."[118] One might perhaps ask why "objective" should be so objectionable, when "state of affairs" can be tolerated ever and again.

But more important than this question of usage, naturally, is whether the thing for which Marty has so zealously propagated the term "content of judgment" really is the objective. At times I have my doubts about it. "As early" as one of the articles "Über subjectlose Sätze," etc.,[119] we have: "Then too, it must be admitted that we can also say of the content of the judgment that it is an acknowledgment or a rejection." Naturally, I could by no means allow that to hold true of the objective in the above, constantly presupposed sense of the word. But in the *Untersuchungen* the name "content of judgment" is praised for being "especially appropriate and striking, as against an 'apsychologism' which wants to ignore the fact that the notion of the 'objective' is not possible without that of a judging."[120] It would surely be gross obduracy on the part of "apsychologism" if it even "*wanted* to ignore" something. So maybe the "content of judgment" is indeed something that is tied to judging in the sense just mentioned,[121] but for that very reason it is not the objective, which we know does not have such a dependency. Also, I would never be able to grant that the objective in my sense is an object only under certain conditions.[122] As for the rest, it is naturally not my task to interpret Marty; at this point, I shall content myself just with a brief additional statement as to why I consider the term "content of judgment" eminently unsuited for expressing what the notion of an objective essentially is, according to my view.

The fault lies primarily in the word "content," supposing that on the appropriate occasion[123] I succeeded at all in defining its sense in a materially and linguistically appropriate way. The question here is, in the main, one of the relation between content and object. Admittedly, I may have overestimated the transparency of that relation on the occasion in question. The many misunderstandings that I found it subject to in the interim have awakened in me a need to go into greater detail on it some day soon. But in the present place this would take us far beyond our limits; so for the present I must content myself with adding only a few more observations to what is already involved in the preceding statements.

Understandably, there can be different interpretations of the metaphor that underlies our custom of speaking of content in the case of mental experiences. It would seem quite unnatural to me, however, to take such advantage of this latitude as to want to regard a piece of reality [Wirklichkeit], say one as imposing as the sun, or alternatively an altogether unreal thing like the round quadrangle, as something "contained" in an experience because it is apprehended by means of an experience. What is apprehended is rather the object of the apprehending experience. If we are to bring the "content" of the experience as near as possible to what is apprehended, this can only be by understanding the content to be the factor in the apprehending experience which is most closely coordinated with alterations in what is apprehended, i.e., in the object. With this interpretation, the presenting experience of course moves directly into the foreground as the thing whose object-related alterations are to be characterized as alterations of content. In connection with the presenting experience we have always thought first and foremost of representations, and usually exclusively of them; so that it is to representations (in the broadest sense) that we can most easily apply the notion of content just now delineated.[124] But if one further finds that judgments, regardless of other functions that they may have, likewise exhibit the function of presenting objects, namely objectives, then that right away makes it plain that we should speak of judgmental contents as well as representational contents. And as a matter of fact, this approach has been employed and perhaps even confirmed in the foregoing. In that case, however, it is clear how singularly inappropriate it would be to say that the objects apprehended in instances of judgment were themselves contents of judgment. Objectives cannot be called contents of judgment, because they cannot be called contents.

By way of anticipation, I might add that on the present basis there is also a special reason why we may not call objectives contents of *judgment*. For I have brought objectives into my discussions in this work only because I want to argue that besides being apprehensible through judgmental contents, objectives also can be apprehended through the contents of those same experiences whose investigation constitutes the real concern of this book. In the following chapter, we shall again be concerned wholly with these experiences, now that we have completed the most important preliminary statements.

IV

The Most Obvious Cases of Assumptions

Explicit Assumptions

From the realization that there are assumptions, there has arisen the question as to where we are to look for them in the mind's activities. We have recognized it as obvious that this question should first of all be answered by attending to whatever relevant facts suggest themselves most readily to psychological observation. The term "explicit assumptions" is not exactly what I would recommend as a technical expression for such facts as I can assemble in the present section; yet there can scarcely be any doubt as to what I have in mind, in setting this term at the head of the section. It is simply a fact that there are assumptions that have their characters written on their faces, as it were—and which may even be quite expressly declared to be assumptions by the assuming subject. As such, these assumptions constitute one extreme of a series. At the other end there are cases in which, as will become apparent later, it requires very careful analysis and perhaps even complicated investigative procedures for us to show that assumptions are involved.

Above,[1] we already encountered examples of such "overt" assumptions— as they could also quite well be called, in contrast to the cases of more or less "covert" assumptions just mentioned. At the beginning, we naturally had to select cases that were especially suited for directing the observer's attention to the distinctive characteristics of the new genus of facts to be investigated. In the present connection, let us just ask ourselves two questions. First, in what linguistic garb are assumptions of this sort ordinarily encountered? And then, what are they intended to accomplish, under normal circumstances?

To begin with the first question, it is readily understandable that an assumption will never be easier to recognize as such than in instances where the subject advertises his experience as being an assumption. This naturally happens where the given assumption shows up secondarily expressed—or in other words, in assertions such as "I assume that..." and the like. The primary expression of the relevant assumption then naturally appears in the form of a dependent sentence. A contrast then develops between such cases and cases where assumptions have an exclusively primary expression, in independent sentences that are not infrequently characterized by a subjunctive mood.[a] The locution, "Let there be a right triangle, one of whose sides is half the length of the other," is one that can only be understood as the expression of an assumption. Finally, assumptions can also be expressed in independent sentences without being specially signalized by means of the subjunctive; we shall get back to this right away. Yet in such cases one might feel a lack of the particularly clear-cut, obtrusive quality that will remain our criterion for classification in this first group.

Our right to the second of the two questions posed above is actually not at all immediately evident. We are asking for information about the end to which a subject engages in assumptions, and it could very well be that such a thing takes place without any ulterior purpose; so that the justification for it—if indeed there should have to be any justification—would lie simply in the fact that the subject finds it natural to engage in assumptions and perhaps pleasant to do so. And it can in fact be pleasant. Building castles in the air and the like is certainly a quite enjoyable occupation sometimes, and much of what will presently have to be mentioned under the headings "play" and "art" could easily be brought in for discussion at this very point. But it is likewise worth noting at this point that assuming is evidently rather often enlisted in the service of intellectual functions that are by no means disposed, not even in the last instance, to let matters rest with mere assumptions, functions that are instead unquestionably directed at the gaining of judgments.

The reader of the above example of the right triangle has surely already thought of how frequently mathematical explanations make use of similar locutions, only then to attach affirmations that no longer partake of the nature of "mere assumptions." Thus, regarding the object of the assumption in question, the right triangle with the sides standing in a ratio of $1:2$ to each other, one need not merely assume something about the relative length of the hypotenuse, or something about the size of the two acute angles. Such things and many others can be affirmed with the certainty that under normal circumstances affords such a favorable distinction to mathematical knowledge. The frequent use of the phraseology in question assures us for the present that in such cases it must be at least quite natural to start out from an assumption. One writer[2] has justly pointed out that it has always been a part of the tradition of a formally correct Euclidean proof to "arrange it this way: 'assumption, assertion, proof' (upon which discussion, determination of the concept, and the like then follow)." And as for recency, it is noted that even "Bolzman in his *Mechanik* (1897) has placed seven 'assumptions' at the head of the work, albeit in a superficial way, and he comments at some length on the method that is thereby made possible, a method which is deductive but which nevertheless measures up to experience." The "hypothetical discussion of concepts," as it has been called in the area of philosophical inquiry especially, is a matter "of testing an assumption introduced for the solution of a problem, testing it by developing its consequences and by comparing the consequences with what is given or acknowledged."[3] It is only one step from here to what is usually comprehended under the term "hypothesis." With regard to someone who is occupied with such a hypothesis and who is perhaps undertaking to verify it in reality, I admit that it will not always be easy to specify the exact point where he makes the transition from the state of assuming to the state of surmising. Yet it is clear right away that there is an apprehending and following out of hypotheses that precedes the formation of any opinion and which is free of any bias. Here even judgment in the sense of surmise stays out of it, and only the assumption can operate. In cases where one speaks of "fiction" instead of hypothesis, the factor of assumption shows up with a certain intensification, since in such cases factual verification is already renounced in principle. The employment of fictions in the areas of science and teaching is illustrated by the float from the standpoint of which one estimates the direction of the magnetic needle's deflection by the galvanic current, using the well-known Amperian rule. Their employment in the areas of law and human action is illustrated by the legal individual, with his rights and duties.

The investigations of the first chapter have opened up the possibility of an even more direct insight into the indispensability of assumptions, in the special case where someone begins with a negative datum, e.g., where he proposes to concern himself with right triangles whose sides do *not* have a ratio expressible by means of a whole number, or with something of that sort. I shall attempt later on to explain[4] why and to what extent assumptions are indispensable to the attainment of knowledge in other cases too, i.e., in cases where it is not a question of *negativa*. For the present, the role assumptions have in the service of knowledge will perhaps become more clearly apparent from the use of explicit assumptions in a less strict and maybe even exclusively practical thinking about things. "Put yourself in my position, and consider how you would then have to act"—not infrequently one expects that compliance with this summons will lead to a personal understanding with someone.

So, everything considered, we see that in functions of rather different kinds, assumptions evidence a kind of logical dignity. The assessment of this dignity cannot be attempted solely in light of these most obtrusive cases of assumption; nevertheless, as soon as we are really able to make such an assessment, it could help us to become acquainted with a characteristic feature of the fact of assumption.

§16
Assumptions in Play and Art

My present concern naturally cannot be to get at the nature of these peculiar and significant expressions of the mind's activities. The only thing that is to be attempted here, and the thing that seems to me to be executable without any difficulty, is the proof that we are justified in claiming that assumptions are determining and possibly even constitutive factors throughout these two areas.

I. It is customary to subsume the intellectual attitude of the child at play under the word "fantasy" ["Phantasie"]. The child is primarily the one I have in mind in the following. And if this word is understood in a sense that I shall advocate further on,[5] then I also have no objection whatsoever to such a use of the term in question. But until now, it has mostly been considered a matter of course to speak of the activities of the imagination [Phantasie] just as functions that involve no transcendence of representation. Then in supposing as much, the customary interpretation makes the intellectual attitude of the one at play to be just the representational function, and we can raise the question as to whether such a characterization really corresponds to the facts.

Beforehand, though, there ought to be at least some mention of the interpretation that stands in extreme opposition to this one, although at the time of the first publication of these remarks[6] I was of the opinion that no one who had any sort of eye for the facts would be inclined to spend any time with it. I have in mind the attempt to make out that the child at play really is in a state of delusion during its play, i.e., that a chair which it has harnessed to the table as a horse to a wagon really is taken by the child to be a horse and that the table really is taken to be a wagon. Every adult has retained enough recollection of his childhood to be able to see immediately the unnaturalness of such an interpretation. Moreover, any person who has had the opportunity to observe children is far more likely to have had occasion to wonder at the sureness with which children even at an early age know how to distinguish between play and earnest, than to find them confusing such situations. Of course, occurrences of the following sort are anything but rare: the child that is supposed to put away its playthings explains that this is not feasible at the present time, since the doll is sleeping or the horses are too tired, or something of the sort. And the parents who are willing to put up with such an answer are liable to receive it innumerable times henceforth, with the most incredible variations. But no one would really want to regard this as more than a contribution to the almost inexhaustible chapter on children's subterfuges. It doesn't mean that one can safely deny the possibility of rare exceptions. To the contrary, I shall have to content myself with giving just this assurance: that I myself have never encountered an exceptional case of this sort and that no credible report of such an event has ever come to my attention, either. This might well suffice to prove that the characteristic thing about the intellectual state of the child at play cannot be the presence of a judgment, or more precisely, that it cannot be a delusion of the one who is playing. Beyond that, the delusion would be quite incomprehensible as to its causes.

As against this, the aforementioned customary appeal to the "imagination" ["Einbildungskraft"] of the child is doubtless far and away the more natural one, even when one thereby supposes that he has simply thrust the matter over into the domain of representations. Yet one cannot really get by with representations; and in this matter as in so many others, negations provide testimony that is particularly unambiguous, despite the externality of it. Thus, one would have to maintain that in the case of play negations never enter the picture in the respect which concerns us here. But in view of the facts, there is little chance that we shall have to reckon with such a denial. The boy who is playing that he is Siegfried and who is pretending to be invulnerable—perhaps also invisible, if he is using the magic helmet—such a boy certainly does not have to wait to be invented by a theorist. Thus, play presents us with experiences that are at all events quite similar to those by which we were first able to persuade ourselves of the existence of assumptions. And so these experiences would in the first instance show that assumptions do in fact occur in play. But then consider this further point: that when the intellectual attitude of a child at play exhibits a negative character, that negative character is the only thing about the child's attitude that sets it apart from an affirmative attitude. If that may be asserted, then I daresay the following general assertion is very strongly suggested. The intellectual attitude of the child at play is less than judgment, but it is more than representation; which is to say, it is an attitude of assuming.

And this is exceedingly well verified by direct observation.[7] The verification is so clear that one can hardly go wrong in surmising that the only reason we have previously been so willing to put up with the "representation view" was that the unworkability of the "judgment view" was always forcibly apparent and there seemed to be just these two views at our disposal, and no third one. But now there *is* a third one at our disposal, the "assumption view." And with this possibility now before us, no one will find it difficult to recall how often he has in effect borne witness to such a view with remarks to the effect that the child at play "feigns" properties, situations, and so forth with regard to himself and others, but that as long as the playing lasts the child often acts as if he believed in the fiction, even though such a belief is furthest from his mind. The practical importance—I mean the importance in terms of action—which assumptions show here forms at the same time a natural counterpart to the logical importance already mentioned above. The logical importance is not lacking in play, either; in that context, consistency and reasonableness are at least regarded as quite sensible requirements, even though their accord with the ways of children is not without its limits.

With this, we move quite naturally from the play activities of children to various play activities of more or less adult people and to playlike activities that are of an altogether "serious" nature, insofar as they are intended as training for a "time of emergency," a training which allows one to "feign" this emergency. From the war-games of military school and the practice drills of town fire departments on Sunday to the great maneuvers of whole armies, there is a series of more or less complicated and systematically devised happenings which, though they cannot be reckoned as play activities, are like the latter in that each of them is based on a more or less complicated system of assumptions.

II. The fact that art cannot be devoid of all connections and affinities with play is already evident in an admittedly quite superficial level, for there exists an artistic practice that is called simply "playing." It must be admitted that in the artistic sense of "playing," language probably points to the instrumentalist's activity just as clearly as it does to the actor's, and our present interest is in the first instance mainly centered on the actor's. But then, in the actor's playing, the effective presence of assuming stands forth in an altogether unmistakable way.

It is true that the situation in which the actor finds himself regarding his part at first seems to admit of two interpretations. One of them is in conformity with the rationalistic tendency that is always so natural to the naive outlook, a tendency that continually attaches the highest importance to the role of deliberateness. Here one surmises, perhaps because it appears to be the most natural thing, that the task of the actor consists in copying the external aspects of the behavior of the person to be portrayed. By experience, the actor must be sufficiently well-acquainted with these external aspects to copy them in premeditated deliberateness. In doing so, he creates the outward appearance of inner events whose occurrence in him are no more real than his identity with the personality being portrayed. It may actually be that there is no histrionic accomplishment in which this or that detail is not acquired by deliberate learning. But to the extent that what is picked up in this way predominates, one usually gets a sense of mere routine, and this is not really allowed to pass as true histrionic art. Respecting this art, it has always been thought—and upon consultation, the greatest actors have borne evidence to it—that it is above all requisite that the actor "put himself in the position of the one being portrayed."[8] This requirement lies at the basis of the second of the two interpretations of histrionic activity that I just indicated as being at our disposal. If the one who is doing the portraying is able to "imagine" ["sich einbilden"][9],[b] that he is the person being portrayed,[10] and he finds himself in the context of events that is given to him through the action of the play, then—sufficient aptitude being presupposed, of course—he will also behave outwardly in the way that the one to be portrayed presumably would have to behave. And the aims of acting are naturally and harmoniously fulfilled as natural instincts replace the much too scanty empirical data, not to say the theory, of expressive movements. Naturally, I do not suppose that the whole secret of the histrionic art is summed up in this very simple prescription; for our purpose, it suffices that we have been led onto this "imagining" or "putting one's self into the position of the other" as something that is at all events a fundamentally important and characteristic factor in the attitude of the interpreting artist, and that we now have a motive for raising the question as to the psychological nature of this "putting one's self in the position of."

The answer requires no long reflection, if one recalls that the type of attitude in question fully coincides with what children do when they play soldiers or equestrians or something of the sort. So we needn't offer another, special proof that assumptions have a quite fundamental position in the mental processes of the actor practising his profession. The matter does not come to an end with the purely intellectual attitude; on the contrary, assumptions then serve also to bring the emotional side of the assuming subject into a high degree of sympathy. Here again we have evidence of the significance of assumptions, a significance that goes far beyond the intellectual domain. As to whether the feelings and desires that emerge as a consequence of assumptions are just the ordinary ones, as it were, or whether facts of feeling and desire of a special kind make their appearance in such cases, we shall have to come back to that again in a later connection.[11]

It is easy to move from the actor's art, which is predominately discursive but in any case reproductive, to the essentially discursive but productive art of the writer of poetry or fiction or drama. And with that, it becomes obvious that in the writing of his drama, the dramatist will inevitably be confronted with the task of "placing" himself in not just one but, by turns, almost all the roles of the drama. In the case of the epic writer, too, aside from whether he is discoursing in verse or prose, it is only by way of exception that the stories he has to tell will be true ones. Similarly, the feelings and moods that the lyric poet expresses never, or at least hardly ever, coincide with what he actually feels at the given moment. To an appreciable degree, the "fiction" comes into its own in all these cases; but then, fiction is just assumption.

The role of assumptions in the remaining arts is more complex, and for that reason it would be best not to discuss it in the present remarks, which are merely suggestive in their intent. One fact, though, might be readily appreciable in its own right. To the extent that these arts, too, strive and reach beyond what is given sensually by them—or in other words, to the extent that the plastic artist or musician also becomes a poet or imitative of a poet—to that extent, at the very least, the assumption will enter into its own as a distinctive factor in the attitude of the artist in these other arts.

§17
The Lie

There is an understandable reluctance to be overcome before we can bring ourselves to make an investigation of the lie in immediate connection with our statements directed at art. By adopting that sequence, we are according recognition to a certain affinity between a human activity that stands very high and one that stands very low. But it is just a part of the mysteriousness of human nature that the high and the low in it can dwell together in such close proximity. Anyway, facts are facts, and we are not free to shut our eyes to this or that fact at our own discretion. In the present connection, this would have been wholly impracticable, for the predominant feature of the related subject is precisely what makes it lie in the sphere of facts that interests us right now.

The affinity in question is a thing quite well-known to everyone, anyway. It has been pointed out often enough—perhaps more frequently and emphatically than fairly—that the line between the innocent activity of the child's "imagination" and mendacious behavior in children can by no means always be easily and sharply drawn. With adults who are fond of telling stories because they are good at it, the situation may not be much different. As concerns wordless lies, everyone also knows, of course, that in the business of daily life acting talents by no means always constitute a perfectly innocuous endowment.

Next, the factor that characterizes the attitude of the liar as opposed to the attitude in art and play is not at all difficult to specify *in abstracto*. It is, of course, the attempt to deceive. It goes without saying that this is of the utmost ethical import. Psychologically, however, it is in the first instance just a newly added component of a complex state of affairs, a component that might help us to make a correct judgment as to the remaining components of this complex. And it actually is of such help, in the line of thought that interests us here. A person who wants to deceive another surely does not himself succumb to the deception in question. Of course, it may be that he is himself deceived; hence, in the belief that he is deceiving, he may be saying something true despite himself. So it would be more exact to maintain just this: A person who wants to deceive has, at any event, a different opinion than the one he pretends to have, and he consequently does not himself make the judgment that he wants to bring about in the other person. In the case of play and art, there is indeed very good justification for surmising a discrepancy between what is believed and what is apparently believed, but there is more than one occasion on which we are unable to make fully certain of it. In the case of the lie, the matter is settled from the start: The liar does not himself believe what he assumes the appearance of believing. And so this confronts us rather sharply with the question as to how the liar actually does apprehend what he wants to make the other person believe.

In this matter, we should not allow ourselves to be misled by the language of daily life, where it is often said that the liar says something other than what he thinks. All that one is really justified in asserting is that the liar says something other than what he believes. This modification is important, because of the well-known fact that much can be thought which is not believed. Thus, the question as to what the liar really thinks remains very much an open question. On the other hand, there can be no doubt about the response that this latest question requires. What the liar utters is not merely empty, i.e., subjectively meaningless, words. That is, while he does not believe in what he says, he does think of it—without believing in it. But this is exactly what we have already encountered above, in play and art, even though the total attitude receives an entirely different character from the intention present in the mind of the liar. If this is the case, then all the essential theses of the preceding sections can be carried over *mutatis mutandis* into the present case.

Nevertheless, the very fact that the liar does something deliberately provides an angle of approach for a different, considerably more complicated way of looking at the matter. If someone proposes to influence the conviction of another in a definite way, his attitude to what he proposes to do will presumably have to be the same as that of any other conative subject,[c] or less generally, any other person who wants something. That is, he will presumably have to apprehend what he wants. In our case, what is to be produced is a particular conviction in another, and one who wants to bring that conviction about must apprehend exactly that, a conviction. And of course, this is not just the object "the other's judgment," apprehended in the abstract; it is the very judgment in question, distinct from other judgments in respect to act and content. Now if one takes it as obvious that such an apprehending ultimately must be nothing but representation, it might begin to appear as though one had gotten round the need to appeal to assumptions by bringing the conative goal into consideration. And as far as it is a question of negative judgments, here too it would appear unnecessary to call in the assistance of assumptions, since it really shouldn't be any harder to represent a negative judgment than to represent an affirmative one.

This interpretation could be delineated in a formal example somewhat as follows. If someone wants to make X believe that *A* is not *B,* then he need only represent "X's judgment that *A* is not *B*"; and in the end, couching his lie in words, he need not do anything at all beyond making clear, to the X whom he is about to deceive, what the judgment involves. But first of all, one may ask whether it is so easy to represent "X's judgment." Many a thing in the investigations of the preceding chapters might have aroused doubt about this.[12] But the confrontation with this question is not especially characteristic of the case of the lie. One has occasion to bring another's state of understanding into the sphere of one's intentions not just when one wants to deceive him, but also when one wants to inform him about something. Hence, it would be more natural to wait until later on before attending to this matter.[13] And in the present connection, we shall be able to reach a decision without consideration of it. It suffices to ask oneself a simple question. Am I at all able to think of X's judgment that *A* is not *B,* if I do not in the first place somehow think that *A* is not *B*? If need be, I can certainly bring the determination "X's judgment" into connection with the thought of *A* and *B,* but I can never form the thought "that *A* is not *B*" as a determination of the thought of X's judgment in a way that would obviate the explicit inclusion of the objective that *A* is not *B*. (The only possibility we might have to allow for is that of quite artificial roundabout paths.) Therefore, quite apart from the fact of experience that X and his judgment are far from being thought of on each occasion, it is still the case that the liar, if he wants to apprehend his goal precisely, must have already conceived the thought of the *A* which is not *B,* the very thought which in the foregoing was seen to be incapable of realization without an assumption.

And as it turns out, the results of direct observation are in perfect agreement with this consequence. The agreement is most prominent where it is a question not of an isolated mendacious assertion but of a tissue of lies which, say, the need of the moment forces a person to develop further, perhaps in a quite unforeseen way. For the simplest guideline in this case will be the same incomparably simple one that we saw in the case of "playing" in the broadest sense: as far as possible, one will put himself in the position of a person who really believes what he is saying, or what he is in some other way making the other person believe. And this "putting one's self in the position" is the state of affairs that has been familiar to us for quite some time as the assumption.

Specifically as concerns the rejection of the roundabout way through another's judgment, there is an additional and separate verification for what we have been saying in the frequently observed fact that a person who wants to deceive others can easily end up deceiving himself, ultimately believing his own lie. Suppose that it was characteristic of the intellectual state of someone who wants to deceive that he dwells upon the other's judgment (which is represented, let us say). Presumably he would have to apprehend this judgment by its specific content, not by its specific object. And then it would remain wholly incomprehensible why his intellectual state should ever pass over into a judgment that does not even have an object in common with that state: To revert to our formal example, this judgment of his own would concern "*A*'s not being *B,*" whereas previously the thing under consideration was the object "the other's conviction." By contrast, the similarity between an assumption and a judgment with the same object is so great that one would have to find the transition of the one into the other (along with the transition's being unnoticed) already quite comprehensible in itself, even if it were not excellently verified by experiences of a quite different kind. I am thinking particularly of our experiences of the transition of a hypothesis into a surmise and strict assertion. So we shall not go wrong in regarding any sort of mendacious activity as proof of the presence of one or more assumptions.

§18
Assumptions in Questions and in Other Desires

At first glance, it may seem strange that one should simply assign questions to the domain of desires,[d] as has already been done in the second[e] chapter. But there is actually no more behind it than the remarking of something obvious. We can set aside the so-called rhetorical questions. These are not questions at all, strictly speaking. They are close to the sphere of our present remarks, however, in that someone asking a rhetorical question might easily find himself in the position of "feigning" the state of a real questioner. Rhetorical questions aside, then, it is undoubtedly true that a person who asks a question wants to receive an answer. We can also leave out of account the easily overlooked complications that arise in the special case of the various didactic questions and questions related to them, as well as in the case of other things loosely termed questions. Then it is clear that a person who asks a question wants to know something, and that by means of his question he is giving notice of what it is that the desired knowledge is supposed to concern. The sentences that language provides for this purpose are ones that have already found a place in our list of cases where sentences can express other things besides judgments. It seems simply obvious that in a matter where one feels one's self unable to judge, and where one consequently wants to attain to the ability to make a judgment, one will not go ahead and make a judgment anyway.[14] But there must be a restriction as to the domain of validity of this approach, an approach already employed above. There are still questions that have a judgment as their essential presupposition and which thereby indirectly express a judgment, even though they do not directly express one. When someone asks me what times the railroad trains stop in the vicinity of the house I live in, he is maintaining, albeit only "*implicite,*" that I live in the vicinity of a train stop. When someone asks who owns the lake-fishery, he is presupposing by his question that there is a fishery on the lake that he has in mind. And so on. Questions of this sort proceed from a knowledge that is merely on certain points not yet sufficiently determinate. They aim at the filling in of the relevant gap in knowledge; hence, they can aptly be called completion-questions[15]—or perhaps determination-questions. There is a strikingly sharp contrast of an admittedly external sort between these questions and ones that cannot be answered in a proper way except by "yes" or "no." In view of this feature, they have been called confirmation-questions.[16] But strictly speaking, this name for them takes into account only one of the two possible answers, namely the affirmative one; to that extent, it might be preferable to call these questions "decision-questions."[17] At any event, the decision-questions are the ones to which we shall have to give our entire attention, in view of the theme of the present investigations.

To get clear about the mental state of someone who asks a question, it would be advisable for us to determine first of all what such a person wants to attain by means of his question. Without doubt, the goal in this case is just as much an extension or enrichment of his knowledge as it is in the case of a determination-question. But the interest of the person asking a decision-question is not in getting at something additional on the side of the object; this becomes clear from the nature of the two proper answers, neither of which is able to alter the situation on this side. All that such an answer can do is to enable the person asking the question, in the event that he trusts the one asked, to take a position regarding the object given in advance by him, by making an affirmative or negative judgment regarding it. This means that the questioner as such does not yet make a judgment in the matter that his question really concerns, that the purpose of the question is to enable him to make a judgment in a matter in which, for whatever reason, he is unable to judge at the time of the question. So in brief, a person asking a question—and it is always the decision-question that we have in mind—as a questioner is not making a judgment. What is he doing, then?

The answer that one most readily thinks of, or at any rate the answer most in accord with tradition, is the following. The one asking a question is in a sense presenting the one asked with an object for a judgment that has to be pronounced; the asker is himself representing this object, and he is at the same time ready to attach an affirmative or negative judgment to this object, according to what the answer turns out to be. But now, a look at the commonest of the relevant interrogative sentences tells us that these sentences always have an affirmative or negative form of their own. The object of the decision-question is never just an objectum or complex of objecta, but always an objective—which naturally must be either positive or negative. The fact that the answer desired by the one asking the question can in principle be "yes" as well as "no" can make it appear—and has made it appear[18]—as though the question itself were neither affirmative nor negative, but some third thing apart from these. True, the answer is allowed a choice between affirmation and negation, so to speak; but it is not for this choice to determine whether the objective of the question is to be positive or negative, but to determine whether it is factual. What the answer provides is a judgment about [Beurteilung] the objective of the question, concerning its factuality. When the verdict of this judgment-about is unfavorable, this can very well have the effect of the questioner turning to the contradictorily opposed objective and dropping the objective that he has in a sense been contemplating by means of the question. But as concerns this question-objective, it is in no wise the business of the answer to create a place there for the opposition of yes and no. On the contrary, this opposition is already present in the mental attitude of the one asking the question; and if the investigations we have so far carried out have in the main hit on the right thing, then something more than mere representation must have occurred on the part of the person asking the question.

The reader may already have found it easy to guess the conclusion we are driving at; but before we draw this conclusion, we must consider another possibility, one that in a number of cases undoubtedly shows up as a well-attested reality. Could not the decision-question be interpreted in the following way? The person asking the question presents the one asked not only with object-material but, at the same time, a surmise about it; what he wants this person to do is just to transform the surmise into at least a practically adequate certitude, whether it corresponds to the surmise itself or to the contradictory of the surmise. This characterization of the situation actually has been claimed to be one that is obvious without special proof.[19] And it does seem plausible in itself that a person is not going to ask whether something is so when he expects to hear that it is not so; and vice versa. Furthermore, as I said, experience is by no means consistently opposed to the characterization in question; and the requirement that one refrain from any surmise with respect to a given objective may be a demand that is not easy to fulfill in utter strictness. At the same time, the aspect of this matter which I just now called intrinsically plausible receives a curious elucidation from the fact that the negative decision-question not infrequently carries a contrary suggestive force. We are quite familiar with this in experience; it is a suggestive force in the direction of the opposite decision-question. For the negative decision-question often reveals, on the part of the questioner, a prior opinion that is opposed to the negation and which is therefore affirmative. It is most natural for someone to ask, "Aren't we approaching the goal of our hike?" when he thinks he already perceives that goal and he wishes to hear his surmise corroborated. We cannot here enter into a more detailed investigation of this curious fact, and at any event it suffices for our immediate purposes to point out that there are fairly many decision-questions in whose formulation—which is by the nature of the case usually affirmative— a prior opinion plays no part whatsoever. An opinion may be present in the asking of a decision-question, but very frequently it is nowhere near strong enough to count as a practical consideration. Determination-questions also have negative formulations that are motivated emotionally rather than intellectually and which can be understood sometimes as an expression of a wish, sometimes as the expression of a reluctance. So for a good many of the decision-questions that are to be met with in reality—indeed, for the truly normal cases of such questions, and in the first instance for their differentiation into affirmative and negative—there remains no other interpretation than the reference to assumptions, a reference that provides the easiest and most natural solution to otherwise forbidding difficulties. A person who asks a decision-question is making an assumption with regard to a given objective, an assumption that is affirmative or negative according to the circumstances, and the desire expressed in the question is a desire to attain to the corresponding judgment, or to its qualitative opposite.

At the same time, this result makes it natural to ask whether the decision-question constitutes the only instance of desire in which assumptions are involved. Undoubtedly, questions occupy a special status in relation to other desires. Maybe the first thing one should attribute to this status is the fact that, in dealing with a question, one customarily pays attention to anything but its conative character. As concerns the object of the question, the special status of questions shows up in the fact that the interrogative object cannot at the same time be the object of the interrogative desire, if I may put it that way; for what is desired in the asking of a question is, after all, some knowledge. Again, the special status shows up in the fact that in the asking of a question, the knowledge that is desired by no means stands out as clearly in the character of conative objectum as is usually the case with such objecta. A person who asks a question surely thinks of the interrogative object, but the fact that he also thinks of the knowledge of this object is so far from standing out clearly that one might have one's doubts about the conative character of the question.[20] One thinks immediately of a somewhat analogous situation in the case of feelings. Aside from "feelings of knowledgeworthiness,"[21] feelings are addressed to knowledge not as value-feelings, but in a special form that I have called knowledge-feelings.[22] For such feelings, it seems that the object of the relevant knowing or judgment can only constitute a quasi-object; yet the object, which is so evident in the case of value-feelings, cannot quite be pinned down empirically. Or might this situation originate simply in the fact that the object in the case of knowledge-feelings has to be a mental object? Then the same thing would presumably hold in the case of knowledge-desires, which are represented for us here by the question. The objectum—an affective one in the former case and a conative one in the present case—must be mental, and in the apprehending of what is mental, the mental can easily be obscured by its own object.

However this may be, the fact remains that a question is not just another instance of desiring, if we may put it that way. This fact comes out in the linguistic expression, too: what the interrogative sentence exhibits in the way of an object is not the object of a desire, as is ordinarily the case in conative sentences. And in the secondary expression of one's asking, the sentence that is dependent on the declaration of the asking is most naturally attached to this declaration with a "whether"—whereas a "that" usually serves for the secondary expression of desires of the more ordinary sort. Over against the sentence, "I ask (should like to know) whether the weather will stay settled," we have the alternative locution, "I desire [wünsche] that it stay settled." At the same time, one can see that in this case a dependent sentence with "whether" can be regarded as the more natural expression for the assumption that a question involves. Despite other differences between the two types of dependent sentences, it might even now be immediately apparent that in the connection which primarily interests us a "whether"-clause of this sort is closely analogous to the "that"-clauses which appear in connection with other desires. "Mere representation" does not suffice, if one is to desire that something occur or not occur; and this is just because of the opposition of yes and no that figures in this as well as other types of experience. Therefore, assumptions must be called on for assistance. But we shall not go into this matter in the present place, since later investigations[23] will make it considerably easier to form a conclusive judgment about the situation.

§19

Assumptions Evoked by Suggestion

Until now, we have been considering play, art, questions, etc., exclusively from the standpoint of a subject who is primarily active in these things, and we have been seeking out assumptions in the attitude of such a subject. Now, however, we are concerned with operations which—some of them frequently, others without exception—reach beyond the subject who is primarily active in them and which in a certain way encroach upon other subjects. It is to be expected that the subjects who have been caught up in the assumptions we acknowledged in the foregoing will be determined by these assumptions, in the sense that further assumptions will be elicited in these subjects. Or as we can say, if the word "suggestion" is understood in its broadest sense, free of any pathological connotation, assumptions will be evoked by suggestion in these subjects.

And so it is in fact. In the first place, we know how often there are playmates in children's play; fairly often they are a quite indispensable prerequisite of the game in question, and usually it is of primary importance in the attitude of these playmates that when assumptions are "communicated" to them they react to these with assumptions about the same object. Then there can be a continuation of the game, by the drawing of practical or logical consequences and perhaps even by the more or less arbitrary addition of new assumptions. In like manner, the creative as well as the reproductive artist has in his presence, as a more or less indispensable complement, the "public" that receives his efforts. And in the attitude that constitutes this "receiving," assumptions evoked by suggestion again play a fundamental role. This time too, of course, the role of assumptions is most prominent in the case of the discursive arts—as concerns which, there is most likely nothing in the distinction between hearing and reading that would be essential to the line of thought that we are pursuing. These arts confront us simply as one more case where the perplexity in which we find ourselves, short of an appeal to assumptions, comes to light in an especially obvious manner.

To persuade ourselves of this, we need only ask a question in connection with, say, one of the simplest and best-known folktales: What position is one really taking in respect to it, as one apprehends it? The situation of one who simply believes the "wondrous story" may be set aside here as an exceptional case which is as uncommon as it is psychologically uninteresting. But also, in view of the fact that in such a tale positive and negative things are all jumbled up together, we needn't go back to the idea that what we have here is "mere representation." Yet mightn't there be a way to bring in judgment, even though as just mentioned, the listener does not believe what is related to him? In the time when assumptions were unknown to me, I tried two ways of mastering the difficulty. For one thing, one might imagine that the listener represents someone, say himself—or the narrator or someone else—who really be-lieves what is related. The other expedient would consist in the conjecture that, at the time of hearing, the listener believes, i.e., judges in accordance with the narration, but then immediately takes back the judgments that come about in that way, so that the listening does not introduce any undue changes in the state of his knowledge. Neither of these two hypotheses will present itself as especially attractive to the natural epistemic sense of one who hears of them for the first time; and so I can be brief in my substantiation of the judgment that rejects both of them, a judgment that I, too, pronounce at the present time.

Expecting representations of judgments of someone who has the story of the Seven Swabians or of Sleeping Beauty told to him has no support in direct observation, and it also seems to be wholly unnatural in the face of all else that we know. With that, the first hypothesis is rejected, quite apart from the fact that for reasons already known to us—primarily on account of negations, whose appearance is doubtless always inevitable—we still mightn't be able to avoid the introduction of assumptions on this hypothesis. The second hypothe-sis would perhaps be easier to keep free of this last-mentioned deficiency. And because we are considering this second hypothesis in relation to the folktale, its *prima facie* impressiveness is not as great as it might very well be in other cir-cumstances. The "educated person," at least, will submit only very unwillingly to the demand that he believe a folktale, or even believe it in passing. But, he generally doesn't take a novel that he is reading to be a "true story," either; and yet he will perhaps concede without any special reluctance that during the reading of it he does maintain an attitude to the action and the individual per-sons which is very much as though they were real. Thus, the notion that in the reading of the novel something more than mere representation is going on will have impressed many a person as something obvious, and many a one will then find that it does not require too great a step to conjecture, further, that what he is reading is something that he believes, i.e., judges—not lastingly, to be sure, but during the reading and before he takes time to reflect on it. But even in this case, it is at most by way of exception that closer examination will en-able us to find the situation correctly characterized. On the whole, this second hypothesis stands in no less decided contradiction than the first hypothesis to what inner observation says to us about our attitude. Moreover, the sudden change of opinion claimed by the second hypothesis would in any case be a matter of my arbitrary power. It is customary in other cases to regard convic-tion as something relatively independent of volition. What sort of indepen-dence would it be, if it were at every moment in my power to evoke this or that conviction in myself by suggestion, however much it might go against my other views, and then in the next moment dispel it by suggestion? Add to this that such a sudden change in conviction—aside from the fact that it, too, would be something unparalleled—would be far less able to escape attentive recollection and self-observation than the process that the first hypothesis tried to bring in,[24] which process was, after all, in a certain sense less tangible.

Standing in most favorable contrast to such artificialities at this point is the thesis that the listener need perform no other task than assuming that which, as we saw, the narrator himself assumes in narrating. On the part of the hearer, too, a certain logical working up of what is assumed is by no means excluded; after what has gone before, there is no longer any need for expressly emphasizing this either. At the same time, the mental attitude with respect to the simple tale is paradigmatic for the mental attitude with respect to fictive works of any degree of complexity, whether their type be that of the novel or that of the drama. And then the many aesthetic difficulties concerning artistic deceptions, deceptions in which it is normally the case that nobody is really deceived, are cleared away in a manner that is as simple as it is in conformity with experience.

Besides this, drama itself teaches us that it is not only with the aid of words that assumptions can be evoked by suggestion. There are also dramatic presentations without words, after all; and even if the artistic value of such presentations is not deserving of too high an estimate, the position in which they place the onlooker, with respect to his intellectual attitude, is undoubtedly quite similar to the position in which the listener to a fictional narration finds himself. Accordingly, these presentations enable us to see that ordinary drama, the drama that is based on words but with respect to which it is nonetheless a custom to speak of spectators, not listeners, provides its spectators with assumptions not only by means of words, but also by means of concrete representations from the domain of sight. With that, we have achieved the transition from the discursive to the plastic arts, and it is proved that even in relation to these latter arts an observer will be dependent on assumptions in pretty nearly every case where what is concretely set forth in the work of art has some claim to "significance." But even the intelligent listener's attitude to a musical artwork[25] alerts us that the role of assumptions again extends beyond the sphere of direct "portrayal." At the very least, everything seems to indicate that the place of assumptions in this attitude is no less important than the place we might have assigned them in the artistic experience of the creative musician.[26]

But now we must go back again to our paradigm-case of the narrated folktale, since another important fact about it has to be noted. We started out by supposing that what the narrator himself is expressing in his narrative is just assumptions. But that is a supposition that in many cases cannot be verified at all, since the narrator might adopt the very same outward manner even if he were narrating things which he didn't just assume, but really took to be true. In such cases, of course, the subjective effect on the listener is frequently the same as if the narrator were expressing mere assumptions. And from this observation, a fact already mentioned in the second chapter becomes newly apparent: In order to be understood, the expression of a mental state of affairs needn't at all evoke the same state of affairs in the one who understands the expression. But in particular, we see from the above observation that when a speaker expresses convictions, the listener's understanding by no means depends on his having these convictions evoked in him by suggestion. Who could remember, say, having adopted the opinion of a theoretical opponent even temporarily, when it was a question of checking his proof? Moreover, wouldn't that procedure normally entail losing the main motive for checking through the proof? In positing such a procedure, one is undeniably moving unawares into the province of the hypothesis of arbitrary change of conviction, a hypothesis already considered above in reference to our attitude in the case of narratives and rejected for good reasons. So in the present case, too, only assumptions are available as the way in which the listener will react to the words, primarily the sentences, of the speaker. Therefore, all cases where the hearer wants to or has to leave his view *in suspenso,* regarding a judgment communicated to him, are also cases of assumptions.

With these brief suggestions, I want to end my enumeration of the facts of assuming that make themselves quite plain to us in direct observation, without exactly being willing to vouch for the completeness of this enumeration. I think, though, that with these suggestions of mine we are so far from getting through to the most important ways in which assumptions mesh in with the operations of the human intellect, that there has hitherto been no chance to bring up the things which are most fundamental in this regard.

V

The Objective and Assumptions

---

§20
The Apprehending of Objectives

In the preceding chapter I thought I might put together some material as being "the most obvious cases of assumptions." In handling this material, I avoided rather than sought the opportunity for more detailed analysis. I was, after all, anxious to start from facts whose familiarity to us originates in an approach that is pretheoretical and which is therefore in the first instance directed at complexes and not elements. We have thus had no occasion to make more than casual use of the theses of the third chapter; yet the reader can hardly have failed to see how difficult it would have been to separate the matter of assumptions from that of objectives, had the approach been just a bit more detailed—or how in every case where we had occasion to note assumptions, objectives were very intimately involved. Naturally, we also have to say right away what this close connection is based on. An assumption no more lacks an object than a representation or a judgment does; and if it is in the nature of representing that its object is always an objectum, and in the nature of judging that its object is always an objective, then it is unmistakably apparent in the nature of assuming that it, too, has the objective as object. As early as the opening statements about assumptions, we had occasion to insist on their determinacy within the antithesis of yes and no as a characteristic factor, a factor that separates assumptions from representations and connects them with judgments. It is now easy to see that this factor may also be identified by reference to the character of the objectives apprehended by means of assumptions: like judgments, assumptions are affirmative or negative according to whether they apprehend positive or negative objectives.

Naturally, this same fact can then be expressed from the standpoint of the objective: Objectives can be apprehended not only by means of judgments, but also by means of assumptions. Above, in the third chapter's discussions, just the first of these two possibilities was taken into consideration; this was actually a one-sidedness in the treatment—a one-sidedness that was noted in pass-

[98]

ing, by the way. But hopefully there was enough reason for this in our endeavor to keep the matter of objectives as independent as possible of that of assumptions, in the initial theses concerning objectives. Now, quite to the contrary, the thing to do is to consider the two domains of facts—that of assumptions and that of objectives, each domain sufficiently secured in its own right—in the connection that belongs to them by nature. In doing so, we shall not go wrong in regarding the analogy between the judgment and the assumption as holding also with respect to the matter of immediacy or mediacy[a] of apprehension that confronted us earlier[1] as the contrast between judged and judged-about [beurteilte] objectives. The difficulty is that there is no way to form analogous terms from the word "assume" without doing some further violence to language, even though it will scarcely be a fundamentally false verbal construction to set "assumed-about" [beannahmte] objectives alongside "assumed" objectives. But if need be, it will suffice to speak of immediate as opposed to mediate assuming of an objective. There may be occasions when it is the business of immediate assuming to present an objective to mediate assuming.

Perhaps it will foster clarity of insight into the facts if I contrast the above delineation of them with Bertrand Russell's view.[2] As far as words go, Russell indeed shares the position expounded here, that objectives can be apprehended by means of assumptions; but as far as the fact of the matter is concerned, he contests this position. For he also believes that assumptions themselves are nothing but representations and that their special character consists only in the fact that they are representations of objectives.[3] Naturally, this would mean that there are no assumptions at all in my sense and that by the very same token assumptions in my sense are entirely out of the question as means of apprehending objectives. Along with that, this view might seem suited to force us back more or less to the standpoint prior to the investigations set down in chapters 1 and 3. But it is to be hoped, on the contrary, that the contact with empirical data gained by means of these investigations has already become sure enough that in the face of Russell's position we need do no more than to become somewhat clearer as to where the peculiar character of assumptions, of which we are often so directly aware, really does have its seat.

To that end, all that is presently necessary is for us to keep an eye on the judgment's relation to the objective, or more precisely, to the objective judged by it. If A and B are representational objecta, then we can surely say the following: If someone believes at one time that A is,[b] or that A is B, and at another time believes that A is not, or that A is not B, then with this change nothing has changed in the representational objects, and therefore presumably nothing in the representations, either. If one follows Russell's way of thinking, one might at first want to contest this, since presumably even the opposition of "is" and "is not" could be included among the things represented. Since I do not believe that this view will be shared by many, I suppose I may conduct the counterargument in a way that is a little *ad personam*. Russell himself makes a distinction between what we have called the opposition of positive and negative and the opposition that we find between the affirmative and negative;[4] he distinguishes the determinations in the objective from those in the judgment.[5] Further, positive and negative objectives are presumably apprehended by means of affirmative and negative belief, even according to Russell's view. Well then, in the many cases with which we are already acquainted, experience shows us that positive and negative objectives can also be apprehended without belief, or in other words, without judgment; but we shall hardly attempt to describe this as though representation were suddenly brought into play for the apprehending of these positive and negative objectives. If in the case of belief, it was rather by means of the judgment that this opposition was apprehended, then something sufficiently like a judgment is needed when belief is lacking; and this something is just the assumption, in the sense with which we are already so well acquainted. Naturally, one can go ahead and include this judgmentlike something in the domain of application of the term "representation," if one employs a definition for that purpose; this procedure is just as easy as the alternative of defining an "assumption" as that which is not a judgment but which nevertheless apprehends an objective. But in the end, it will still be a matter of classifying what is immediately at hand; and in the entire domain of representational objecta, there is no dichotomy like that of the positive and the negative. Hence, the means of apprehension that are associated above all with the members of this dichotomy can scarcely themselves be assigned to the class of representations.

So without modifying the sense in which we have hitherto used the word "assumption," and in particular, without simply *ex definitione* according assumptions the property of apprehending objectives, we can maintain that objectives are most certainly accessible to assumptions, and not just to judgments. But now a further question suggests itself, namely whether objectives might not be apprehensible by means of other intellectual experiences as well. The theses of Russell's just now considered have already directed our attention to representations. And in point of fact, according to everything else we know in psychology, representations are the only other candidates. But they most emphatically are candidates. For over the years, we have become accustomed to regard representation as the means of apprehending anything in the way of an object that we confront intellectually, whatever sort of thing it may be, and at the same time to acknowledge representation as the indispensable foundation of all intellectual operations.

Thus, a quite respectable tradition apparently accords two very different properties to representations. And we ought not by any means to overlook the fact[6] that the second of these properties does not enter into the province of our present problem at all. Let us illustrate this at once by looking at the kind of case that concerns us most at this point. On the relevant occasion it was pointed out[7] that it is impossible for any objective not to be positioned on some object-material. This material may in the first instance be another objective, but there cannot be another objective again and again without end. At the beginning of any series formed by increasingly higher-order objectives, there must be at least one objectum. Let A be the symbol for this objectum. Every possible objective is subject to the condition of an objective of the form "A is" or "A is B"; which is simply to say that no objective can subsist without an objectum. Further, would I even be able to think of an instance of being without thinking of something that is? In general, then, can I apprehend an objective without apprehending an objectum A along with it? One can readily see how this is related to the question as to whether one can think of red without thinking of extension, and whether, say, one can think of color without thinking of a determinate color. The course of psychological research has taught us in recent years to be at least more cautious than we once were in answering this question, and it will not be so easy for us to have a round no ready for the analogous question in the matter of objectives. But even supposing that we could answer that way—and here lies the decisive thing for us—nothing in the slightest would be settled thereby as to how we apprehend the extra element by which, somewhat summarily expressed, the object A differs from the object "A is" or "A being." Thus, even if I must without fail represent an A in order to apprehend an objective, that is certainly no reason why I should have to apprehend the object "being" once again by means of representation (which would of course have to be another representing than that of A), and there is always the question as to whether I could apprehend it by means of representation at all. But that is precisely the question to which an answer must now be sought.

And as far as I can see, this answer cannot turn out other than negatively. To regard representation as a sort of universal means of apprehension, which no apprehensible object could ever elude—that might have the appearance of obviousness in its favor, as long as one was not sufficiently attentive to objectives in their difference from objecta. But if one juxtaposes the objects "mountain" and "existence of the mountain" as well as can be done, then unless I am mistaken, along with the fundamental differentness of these two objects, the differentness of the ways in which they are apprehended will also make itself quite directly apparent. If apprehending the mountain is (*cum grano salis*) representing, then it seems that the apprehending of its existence has to be something other than representing. And in any case it will be permissible to ask how one really knows that representing is capable of leaping across the gap between A and "A being." A few moments ago, we employed certain considerations to establish, against Russell, that assumptions were suited to the apprehending of objectives; essentially the same considerations now serve to show that we cannot expect such a function to be performed by experiences that lack the "polarity" which is so familiar in judgments (in feelings and desires too, for that matter) and which seems indispensable for the apprehending of the opposition of the positive and the negative in objects.

But for the present, what we have said holds true only by the presence of a tacit reservation which, for all its naturalness, must now be expressly identified. The previous considerations have been employed only against a sort of direct apprehension of objectives, comparable to the apprehension of objecta in cases such as the sensing of a color or the reproduction of this sensation. But I can also indirectly represent[8] a color, e.g., a certain green, by thinking something like "color in the region of the E-line of the spectrum," or less precisely, "hue between yellow and blue" or suchlike.[9] So too, I can apprehend an objective indirectly; and it has been hoped that through the roundabout path thus opened up, one might be able to bring objectives themselves within representation's sphere of power, as it were. In the first instance, it would be *negativa,* e.g., with nonred thing meaning something "of which it is false that it is red."[10] As to how frequently, or rather how seldom, observation provides testimony to the occurrence of the thought of true and false in the instance of such a *negativum*—this is immaterial in the present place, where we are primarily concerned with the passableness of the roundabout way. It is therefore more important that, as we saw, the thought "falsity" evidently cannot be formed without the employment of a negation.[11] If that is the case, then a negative character belongs to the seeming positive, to the thing that was supposed to take the place of an apprehended negative in order to help avoid the difficulty of *negativa.* Thus, falsity itself is faced with the inadequacy of representational apprehending that was established above. In the opening chapter of this book[12] it has already been shown that the result one arrives at is no more favorable when one tries to make sense of the so-called negative representation in another way. Now it is easy to see that the thing which proved inaccessible via mere representation was simply the objective, ineluctably drawn in by negation.

But by means of a somewhat more general definition, couldn't we realize a roundabout way that would better lead to the goal, and which would furthermore take in not just negative objectives, but positive ones as well? Above,[13] mention was made of the attempt, by means of "reflection on judgment," to establish the nature of the objective as the "content of judgment," so that "being" would be definable as "allowing of correct acknowledgment."[c] Here too, as we had occasion to emphasize above, it is immaterial that by direct apprehending we can get closer to being than this; for our present question is not whether objectives can be apprehended in yet another way than by representation, but whether one can at least apprehend objectives by means of representations, however else one may be able to apprehend them. Accordingly, another thing becomes more important: the "allowing of correct affirmation," or however else one might formulate it, is surely itself an objective. Doubt as to whether objectives can be represented cannot be dispelled by replacing many objectives with few, or even with a single one. In the latter case, it would still be at the very least undecided as to whether this single objective was, for its part, apprehensible by means of representation or not.

Nevertheless, the notion that concerns us here can be given a new twist, and one might hope by that means to get round this residual objective, if we may put it that way. If something allows of a correct affirmation or negation, then to that extent it stands in a certain relation to affirmative or negative judgment. Without entering upon a closer determination of its nature, let us call it just the relation X. Surely relations can be represented: If a certain J were the judgment in question, then the determination "in relation X to J" wouldn't have to be any more difficult to represent than, say, "humanlike," "as an angle," and so forth. By means of the determination "in relation X to J" our objective might therefore be apprehended in a purely representational manner. Right away one will conceive the instinctive suspicion that there must be some jugglery in such a simple solution to a problem that looked so difficult just a moment ago. Yet even if we assume for the present that this suspicion is on the whole unfounded,[14] there is one feature of this reformulation that sticks out by itself, as it were; and though this feature is somewhat remote from the context of our present interests, it cannot altogether be ignored. If the reference to negation is to be allowed to stand as a way of representing objectives, then it must in the first instance be possible to represent the negative judgment itself. But are there representations of judgments?

Elsewhere,[15] as already mentioned, I have sought to show that in the case of inward perception, the representing of experiences that are present to the perceiver—and hence, in particular, judgments that are present to him—would be a theoretical complication without any support in observation. One may instead grant inner experiences the ability to present themselves to inward perception. Connected with this is the fact that in the case especially concerning us now, i.e., the case of judgments, it is less appropriate to interpret the recollection of experiences now past as a representation of judgments than it is to interpret that recollection as the extroversion of present assumptions. The latter idea is applicable also to the apprehending of judgment-experiences other than one's own as well as to the apprehending of judgment-experiences "*in abstracto.*" At the present juncture we cannot yet argue that this approach (aided by the concept of imaginative experiences, not to be expounded until later[16]) takes in not just judgments, but all apprehensible mental occurrences; but this comprehensiveness will be well suited to lend a firmer footing to the thesis we are concerned with here—that to be apprehended, judgments require no representations presenting them. Specifically as regards inward perception, I have been confronted with the question[17] as to whether my interpretation is also adequate for the "apperception" of what is inwardly experienced, as well as for the "perception" of it. Or since I should like to put it in the most general terms right away, the question is whether, in the absence of a special sort of representing, there could arise the different intellectual operations of abstracting, comparing, etc., which ordinarily seize upon representational contents. And the same point of view obviously underlies the objection made against me from another side,[18] that it is "not possible to make a plurality of pain-feelings conscious in a single, present pain by holding the former to a certain characteristic. There are no 'general' pain-feelings." Questions of this sort are doubtless well worth considering;[19] but as far as I can see at present, the answering of them presents no insurmountable difficulty. If the perceived experience presents itself to judgment, then why shouldn't other mental operations have a sort of access to that experience? Thus, to take a more specific case: If in relation to judgment an emotional experience can sometimes function in the way that a representational content does, then why shouldn't it also do that in relation to the concept-forming operations? Only in the event that there were no imaginative experiences[20] would it follow that "revivals" of experiences had to be representations of them, if they weren't repetitions of them.[21]

So if I am right in maintaining that everything mental is in the strict sense unrepresentable, then no one who apprehends an objective by means of "reflection on judgment" can remain within the bounds of representation in doing so. The reason is just that if it is the normal situation, and one does not make the very judgment which is to be brought in, then the judgment is apprehended by means of an (extroverted) assumption. As it happens, our perspective opens up on a broad domain of application for assumptions at this point, but we cannot go into the further details of it now. In many cases where judgment-experiences enter into the sphere of our intellectual activity, and these experiences are not presently our own or are others'—or they are indefinite as to their subject—they will be able to be given to us only by means of assumptions intellectually processed in a certain way.

But let us return to the question concerning the indirect representing of objectives. It is now clear that if this representing is to be brought about by means of "reflection on judgment," then at least in the case where the judgment becomes an object to be handled in a certain way intellectually, the range of representation is thereby exceeded. Even if the relation should be representable, the judgment can be apprehended only by means of a judgment or, failing this, an assumption. Might there be other ways to get at an objective indirectly? The multiplicity of these ways may be hard to exhaust, theoretically; practically, this multiplicity might well be left out of consideration here, especially as the eighth chapter will have the task of showing how little even the "representing" of relations could be confined to mere representation. The above claim, that the objective cannot be apprehended by representation even indirectly, is now perhaps sufficiently secured by what has been set forth, at least for the range of possibilities that have any sort of empirical likelihood.

Let us now make brief mention of two more points. As regards these points, it has been asserted that I have not been able to maintain consistency in the view just set forth.[22] The one point concerns the contrast between "A exists" and "*A* is existing." For a reason that is presently unimportant, I thought that under certain circumstances I ought to attach a special significance to this contrast. In the latter sentence, "*A* is existing," the predicate "existing" ["existierend"] can only be represented, it was said, and not judged or assumed, "as Meinong, if he were able to remain consistent with himself, would have to profess."[23] I hope that my ability to be consistent has been underestimated, at least in this particular case. The case—interesting in itself, but again rather remote from the present connection—seems to me to be characterizable at its simplest in the following way. As we know, instead of "The paper is white," I can say, "The paper is white-being [weiss-seiend]"—not very meaningfully, but doubtless correctly.[d] And if I have reason to believe that, although I can represent "white," I cannot represent "that something is white," then I shall not expect to be able to represent "being white" ["Weiss-sein"], or even "white-being." Naturally, this is not to deny that in these different wordings there appear signs of very specific intellectual processings of the starting data that make for our original awareness of an objective. What holds for the objective of so-being now holds *cum grano salis* for the objective of being. It holds *cum grano salis*, because "being existing" ["Existierend-sein"] is a rather inadequate equivalent for "existing" ["Existieren"]: "Being existing" can in a certain sense be granted even of the object "existing golden mountain," say, and even of the object "existing round quadrangle," whereas "existence" will no more belong to the one than it does the other. But what matters is not the paradoxes and difficulties (reducible, anyway, by means of some caution and tolerance with respect to the terms). I have never flattered myself that I was able to remove these paradoxes and difficulties completely.[24] What matters is the question of why representing should be considered more of an essential prerequisite for the apprehending of the objective "existing" ["existierend"] than it is for the apprehending of the objective "white-being" ["weiss-seiend"]. I deny the essential role of representation in either case, on the grounds specified above; yet even if I am mistaken in this denial, I do not know what it has to do with my "consistency."

A fact already well-known to us is brought up as a second, "still more interesting case." This is the fact that objectives can not only be judged, but can also be judged about. We are supposed to be unable to make clear how "*A* is" and "it is true that *A* is" are distinct from each other without drawing on a *representation* of an objective.[25] I hope that I may summon the reader of chapter 3 of the present book as witness to the contrary. If we leave out of account the superfluous complication caused by bringing in the truth factor, then the distinction consists simply in the fact that in the one case it is a question of the being of *A* and in the other a question of the being of the being of *A*. As far as I can understand,[26] the question as to the means by which the one and the other object are apprehended does not come into consideration at all in this distinction.

To be sure, if the question is raised as to "how, though . . . the two judgments are intertwined with each other, or how the one is built on the other,''[27] then there is nothing of substance that I can answer at present; but I doubt that this provides the basis for a reasonable objection to my interpretation. Yet in order also that no unreasonable offense be taken at there being something judged-about which is not represented, it must by all means be recalled again that this needn't at all be a case where there is judging without any representing. If the object "that A exists" is given to us by means of a judgment, this is simply the judgment that concerns A; so in that A is represented, this judgment was by no means one that occurred without a representation as its psychological prerequisite. But where merely the object A was "given" by means of representation, there is now also an object "that A exists" available for further intellectual treatment, and the present interpretation is just that this is a sort of outcome of judgment, an outcome in which representation does not again participate. The objective is thus always positioned on an objectum, and the latter cannot under any circumstance be denied the content appertaining to it as the firm basis for its representation.

Another thing seems to me to be still more important, however. If in view of the facts, we must decide to admit that every knowing, no matter whether it is affirmative or negative, knows "something," that every judgment judges "something," which is not an objectum but which does stand over against the judgment in question in the way that the objectum stands over against its representation—if we admit this, then the ability to apprehend this "something" has therewith already been granted the judgment. It is the business of each judgment to secure its immediate objective on its own authority, as it were.[28] If so, then one is really at a loss to see why the help of a representation should be necessary in order for the judged objective to become the object of the ensuing judgment about it, especially as the judgments-about that ensue here are anything but independent of the judgment initially laid down for them. If I am entitled to the judgment, "A exists," then in view of this judgment I am entitled to a second judgment concerning the objective of the first one, viz., "It is the case that A exists." I am so certainly entitled to this second judgment, that to the philosophically naive it does not seem to differ at all from the first.

So I can summarize my present knowledge of this matter[29] in the following proposition. Objectives can doubtless be apprehended by means of assumptions, too, as well as by means of judgments; but not also by means of representations, and for the apprehension of objectives there are no further means available to us. And from this there results a heuristic principle that is especially fruitful for the further progress of research into assumptions, a principle that at the same time more than adequately justifies our bringing objectives into the sphere of investigation of the present work. What follows immediately from the proposition we have just formulated is namely this: Anywhere in the course of our mental activities that we encounter an objective that is demonstrably inapprehensible by means of judgment, there an assumption is indicated. In retrospect, one can now easily see that this principle already came into use implicitly in the investigations of the preceding chapter. For such heterogeneous cases of assumption as concerned us there to be recognized as cases of assumption, it was always necessary for us to make sure that in each relevant situation, distinctly albeit superficially characterized, the objective that made its appearance was not apprehended by means of a judgment. But the explicit acquaintance with the principle that we have now gotten puts us in a position to discover assumptions even where the situation, as I called it, doesn't obtain or doesn't as clearly obtain, and where it might not even be adequately characterizable until assumptions have made their appearance. From the more complex states of affairs mainly considered up until now, the investigations therewith turn to more elementary states of affairs, hopefully with some chance of preparing the way for the demands of a future detailed treatment, possibly even an experimental one.

§21
Approached Objectives. The Interpretation of
Secondary Expressions of Judgment

Intellectual as well as emotional activities afford opportunity for investigations of the sort just indicated. What was previously called the "encountering" of an objective in our mental activities naturally goes back to the fact that mental experiences accost an objective, as it were, and that objectives are in a sense drawn into the sphere of our experience. And this can happen by means of intellectual as well as emotional types of activity or attitude. For the intellectual types, the expression "to apprehend" is doubtless sufficiently familiar to us. It may appear questionable even as to whether this expression suffices for the intellectual domain under all circumstances. However that may be, it is not to be carried over to the emotional domain. I certainly do not find any term readily available that would be colorless enough to encompass with equal naturalness the intellectual and emotional aspects of the question. Since the need for a sufficiently comprehensive term does make itself felt here, I shall attempt to accommodate this need by calling this mental accosting of objectives the approaching of them. On this basis, I can speak of intellectually as well as emotionally approached objectives. Apprehending is consequently intellectual approaching; and if we are to go by the present state of our psychological knowledge, it seems beyond doubt that objectives as well as objecta are reached by emotional approaching only if there is an intellectual mediation. In other words, objectives that are to be approached affectively or conatively [durch Fühlen oder Begehren] must first of all be apprehended. But there is also intellectual approaching that presupposes that its objects have been apprehended. With respect to objectives, all judgment-about presupposes judgment-of; we called the former "mediate" precisely because it proved to be grounded on the latter as on something immediate. And in line with that, of course, we can then speak of everything that is emotionally approached as being mediately approached. With this, we have reached a standpoint that will permit a simple characterization of the normal function of the "that"-clauses we have been encountering so frequently, and which will allow us to perceive the special significance of these clauses for the theory of the objective. "That"-clauses are simply the natural designation for objectives that are approached mediately (intellectually or emotionally, it doesn't matter).

One can see right away that these mediately approached objectives are the ones to which the heuristic principle formulated above applies most naturally. If the nature of the approaching in question entails that the objective cannot be immediately apprehended by means of judgment, then this objective—whose apprehension is indispensable under the given circumstances—must be apprehended by means of an assumption. An assumption must present it to mediate approach, or to the experience constituting this approach.

Having marked out the anticipated situation in this way, I shall now start by looking into its occurrence in the intellectual domain. Our first concern is therefore with judgments-about that rule out the possibility that the objectives in question are presented by means of judgments, or which make it look unlikely that the objectives are presented in that way. As to whether the objectives in such cases show up in linguistic attire and what this attire is, that in itself is naturally a matter of incidental concern. Yet in the present case, too, expressed things are the ones that are more tangible from the standpoint of investigation. It is likewise inessential whether we have to do with primary or secondary expression when something is expressed. But in cases that are closely connected with our present interest, peculiar difficulties are found to stand in the way of a correct explanation of secondary expression, and on account of these difficulties we shall have to stay on a bit longer here, before we proceed to the main investigation.

To be precise, it is a question of cases where the speaker expresses the fact of his judging by enunciating a judgment about this judgment. Sentences such as "I judge (am convinced, believe, think, surmise) that A exists" and the like are surely to be understood in this way, and the accompanying "that"-clause always betrays the reference to an objective. At the same time, any doubt that this objective has the secondary judgment as its immediate judgment seems to be remote.[30] Still, there is an astonishing number of expressions that seem to stand on altogether the same footing with those mentioned, and yet require a different interpretation. These expressions thereby create doubt about the general validity of the above interpretation—indeed, almost doubt as to whether it is valid at all. The fact of secondary expression brings about a peculiar complication, one that can easily lead to confusions if one does not keep it in mind. This complication makes a more detailed investigation of the situation a little difficult. Suppose that I say, "I am convinced that A is"; then in the first place, a judgment is attested by primary expression. On the one hand, this judgment has to do with my conviction, and on the other hand, of course, it has to do with the thing I am convinced of—the objective of this conviction, in other words. This judgment is by no means the primary subject of discussion in the following. On the contrary, the question that is to be raised at this point is whether the relation between the *secondarily* expressed judgment and the objective that figures in the "that"-clause must always be, or even as a rule is, the relation of an immediate judgment to its objective. So it is a question as to whether the "that"-clause objective could not instead serve as an object judged about even for the secondarily expressed judgment. The investigation of this question, an indispensable investigation as concerns clearer insight into our domain of facts, can hardly involve any real difficulties of fact; but as is now easy to see, this investigation is made somewhat difficult by the danger of bringing in what is primarily expressed in the place of what is secondarily expressed.

Let us say, then, that someone uses a sentence of this type: "I deny that *A* exists." Can we in this case still understand the main clause as a secondary expression of the judgment immediate to the objective, in the way which seemed generally obvious to us before? A judgment that has the objective "that *A* exists" as its immediate objective, insofar as it judges this objective, can be linguistically expressed only by means of a sentence which signifies the objective. And so the judgment is characterized by means of the sentence "*A* exists." But with that sentence, nothing would be negated; something would be affirmed. Yet, the negation expressed in our main clause is roughly to the same effect as if one had judged, "It is not the case that *A* exists." As we can see, the negation thus lies in the mediate judgment. So it is with the assertion, "I deny that *A* exists": what the main clause expresses is the judgment that is mediate to the objective. We may take it for granted that sentences such as "I dispute (doubt) that . . ." and the like will be interpretable in like fashion. The same holds for the locution "I don't believe that . . ." Here the only striking thing is that the expression for negation is standing in the wrong place, so to speak. It is as though the point were to negate the believing; whereas ordinarily there will indeed be a belief, but one of negative quality. Then too, sentences like "I deny that *A* does not exist" are not meant in the manner of "I make the negative judgment that *A* does not exist." This becomes clear simply from the fact that a person speaking in the former way is normally not of the opinion that *A* actually does not exist, and that he is rather denying precisely that.

At the same time, it is seen from this that one may not lay down a principle like the following: that if the main and the subordinate clauses exhibit like quality,[31] then the main clause enunciates the judgment that is immediate to the objective—and that when the clauses have opposite qualities, the main clause enunciates the judgment mediate to the objective. Nor may one conclude from an affirmative quality in the main clause that this clause concerns the immediate judgment; for even locutions such as "I confirm (affirm, assure you) that A does not exist" exhibit that opposition of quality in the main and subordinate clauses which, above, provided us with the sign that the main clause must have to do with the mediate judgment. Consequently, all that we have left are cases with affirmative quality in the main clause as well as in the subordinate clause—cases in which the possibility of an interpretation in favor of the immediate judgment ought not to be ruled out, at least not at the outset. But if we want to maintain some measure of uniformity of interpretation in the case of affirmative and negative expressions—or if in other words we want to interpret "I affirm that A is" no differently than "I affirm that A is not"— then all that can be said is this: If the main clause is qualitatively indeterminate,[32] then it relates to the immediate judgment; if it is qualitatively determinate, then it relates to the mediate judgment.

Yet it is not always certain whether or not the judgment secondarily expressed by the main clause is determined in quality by that clause. More precisely, it is not always certain whether we are dealing with indeterminate or affirmative quality. If I say, "I maintain (recollect, surmise)," etc., then it is not thereby certain that I am simply referring to the immediate judgment and that this judgment is just being characterized as an assertion, a recollection or a surmise; the words may instead be intended as an indication of assent to such a judgment, assent by affirmation of the objective, and hence as an indication of the judgment that is mediate to this objective. Likewise for the special case where the main clause and the subordinate clause both exhibit affirmative quality: We cannot offhand reject the possibility that the principle just enunciated might again suffer an exception here and there, in the sense that the main clause had no other function than to characterize the judgment appearing in the subordinate clause—the judgment immediate to the objective, in other words—somewhat pleonastically as an affirmation. At any rate, we can say in general that in the secondary expression of judgment, quite contrary to first appearance, mediate judging occupies a clearly preferential position as compared with immediate judging. Consequently, if one finds a "that"-clause which is dependent on the secondary expression of a judgment, then in by far the greatest number of cases one can be sure that this secondary expression concerns a judgment that is mediate to the objective enunciated in the "that"-clause. Incidentally, it may be expressly emphasized that when the "quality" of the main clause was under consideration above, the thing in question was not the quality of the judgment primarily expressed in the clause, but just the quality of the judgment secondarily expressed in it. With secondary expressions of that sort, after all, it is always obvious that the judgment that has primary expression in them can be nothing but affirmative; an assertion concerning what is *not* going on in me could hardly be regarded as an expression. What has been set forth remains valid in cases where, unlike the cases hitherto considered, the intellectual occurrences in question are not in the speaker, but in individuals other than the speaker. It makes no difference to the relations between the objective and the judgment immediately or mediately appertaining to it whether one says, "I believe (dispute) that..." or instead says, "He believes (disputes) that..." etc. So the relevant assertions will probably have to be interpreted without exception from the standpoint generally formulated above. The fact that the opposition of primary and secondary expression no longer has any application in cases of the type in question needs no separate remark.

From what has been set forth, we see that it can after all occur, though only by way of exception, that a "that"-clause concerns a judged objective rather than a judged-about objective. Our interest lingers no further with these exceptions, since what we are concerned with in the following is simply the way in which an objective is presented to a judgment about it.

§22
Assumptions in the Case of Judgments About Objectives

Since all judgments-about are in the last analysis simply judgments, the contrast of being and so-being applies to them, too. Thus, judgments about objectives are either being-judgments about objectives or so-being judgments about objectives. The former judgments-about conform to the paradigm "This, that A is B, is the case" or the paradigm "This, that A is, is the case." The latter judgments-about conform to the paradigm "This, that A is B, is C" or the paradigm "This, that A is, is C."[e] It is not now difficult to specify forms for the two types in which the presentation of the objectives in question is dependent on assumptions.

First of all, as concerns being-judgments about objectives, it is immediately obvious that in no cases where these judgments-about have a negative quality can the presenting experience be a judgment. If I assert with conviction, "It is not the case that A exists," then I cannot possibly at the same time believe in the existence of A. Consequently, the objective "that A exists" is not judged by me under these circumstances; and so, in accordance with our heuristic principle, it can only be assumed.

By contrast, there is obviously no obstacle either in the nature or in the sense of an affirmative being-judgment about an objective which would rule out the presentation of the objective by means of a judgment. Indeed, it can only be an instance of such a presenting judgment when, for example, someone has a conviction that A exists, and he adds a corroborative "Such is the case" to this conviction. Still, there are enough occasions on which it remains the most natural thing to interpret an affirmative judgment-about analogously to a negative one, i.e., to turn to assumptions rather than judgments as the presenting experiences. Admittedly, this is never demanded by the very nature of the affirmative being-judgment about an objective, but just as little is it precluded.

Such equal treatment of affirmative and negative being-judgments about objectives will be particularly apposite in cases where being-judgments about objectives appear as a kind of intellectual position-taking, as they so often do.

I am thinking of the sort of experiences that occur in their clearest form where a ready-made judgment approaches us from the outside, as it were.[33] We then react to this judgment with our own, and by the latter's agreement with or its opposition to the first judgment, we are brought into a position of concurring or objecting. Then emotional factors can show up in such a close and readily formed connection with this position, that one may feel tempted to regard these accompanying extraintellectual facts as being the truly distinctive element in the situation.

The uses of the words "yes" and "no" afford the simplest examples of this position-taking. First of all, there is the case where the one who is using these words has come upon an opinion or a view in some matter; he, too, has previously formed an opinion or view in this matter, or he forms one right then, and it either agrees or disagrees with the one given. At any event, it is well worth noting that this relational fact of concurring or dissenting is what first of all commands the attention of the people involved. The result is that in the first instance this relational fact is what gets expressed, and the judgment of the speaker, which underlies the relation as an essential term of it, is for the most part left implicit. In considering this situation one can hardly help thinking of the many cases in human affairs where agreeing or contradicting is actually the main concern for the people involved, and the thing on which the agreeing or contradicting bears is altogether a secondary matter. Next, there is a case where the yes and the no function in a somewhat weaker way. In this case what is given in advance is merely a fictive judgment or a trial judgment, as it were. In short, what is given is one of those questions in which the finished judgment usually originates, by means of the "yes" or "no" of the person who is being asked the question. Even this person's judgment is the taking of a position, though in the process he has to do merely with a feigned opponent instead of a real one.

It is by no means solely in the matter of questions that we find ourselves led back to the material of the preceding chapter. The thing with regard to which one is to take a position must first of all be apprehended, of course, and this apprehending is an understanding of what is submitted for the taking of a position. As to how it is submitted and whether the fact of its being submitted is judgmentally understood in its particulars (e.g., in the particular that the matter concerns the enunciated conviction of another person), this is quite immaterial to the circumstance that primarily interests us here. This is, again, the circumstance that at the time the position is being taken the objective cannot yet be given by means of a *judgment,* since a person who already judges cannot be just about to take a position regarding another person's judgment concerning the same object; he must already have taken a position. So in the present case, what the "that"-clause expresses is nothing but an assumption, even when the position taken is one of agreement anyway—i.e., even when the judgment that was nearest to the assumption, in that it apprehended the same objective, would afterwards be wholly in accord with the convictions of the person taking the position.

If we now turn from being-judgments about objectives to so-being judgments about them, what first strikes the eye is that the fundamental difference between being and so-being can become surprisingly blurred, in that some so-being judgments about objectives constitute little more than equivalents of being-judgments about them. It surely does not make much difference whether I say, "It is the case [es ist] that A is B" or "It holds [es gilt] that A is B"; nevertheless, holding [Geltung] is predicated of "that A is B" in the second case, and predications normally concern so-being, not being.^{f} But other locutions, too, such as "It is true that A is B" and "It is certain that A is B," are rather closely related to being-judgments about objectives. Hence, it is not astonishing that even in so-being judgments about objectives, one finds assumptions functioning as presenting experiences in a way that is quite similar to what has been pointed out above, in connection with being-judgments about objectives. In the present case, as regards so-being, the decisively important judgments-about are again the ones that preclude any presenting judgments, this time because of the nature of the predicates. If I find it "contradictory (impossible, unthinkable) that A exists" or suchlike, then by that very fact I cannot be judging the objective in question; it must be an assumption that is presenting this objective. What we have here, essentially, are equivalents of negative being-judgments about objectives. But even as regards the so-being equivalents of affirmative being-judgments about objectives, they too will be seen to manifest the aforesaid taking of an intellectual position. Naturally, then, one can say that even this second equivalence proves effective on behalf of assumptions.

Furthermore, the extremely great variety of things that can appear in objectives of so-being as their material entails that presenting judgments can be precluded in another, quite different way. Here we even find cases that at first glance do not seem to involve judgments about objectives at all, in the sense of the remarks of the preceding section. For what is secondarily expressed in these cases is not the judgment about [Beurteilung] an objective, the objective enunciated in a "that"-clause, but the judgment of [Urteilung] it. Cases of this sort will still come under the heading of so-being judgments about objectives, since the primarily expressed judgment, which was generally left out of account in the preceding section, connects the secondarily expressed judgment with the objective given in the "that"-clause in a way which obviously falls under the heading of so-being judgment about this objective. Yet it is really quite remarkable, in cases of the sort in question, that in a sentence like "I judge that A is," the judgment secondarily expressed in the main clause has to find expression a second time in the subordinate clause, in that the latter clause cannot be expressing anything but a judgment, either. And it is also quite remarkable that in an assertion like "I surmise that A is," the "that"-clause, understood as the expression of a judgment, says too much in comparison with the uncertain main clause. At the very least, all this gives rise to the question whether the interpretation in terms of an assumption might possibly be just as apposite in cases where it would still not be senseless to understand the "that"-clause as the expression of a judgment. Bearing more pointedly on the role of assumptions that interests us here is another state of affairs. In general, it is closely related to the preceding state of affairs, though here there can no longer be any question of a secondarily expressed judgment, since the main clause has precisely the task of expressing the lack of such a judgment. Negations such as "I do not judge that..." or "I am not convinced that A is" admit of no misunderstanding in this regard. By means of a judgment that is emphatically *not* present here, the objective that is just as emphatically present cannot possibly be given. What the "that"-clause expresses under such circumstances naturally *cannot* be anything but an assumption.

Just how great a variety of things can be subsumed under the heading of "so-being judgment about an objective" can be seen again in the fact that even judgments concerning the relations between objectives are ultimately just so-being judgments about objectives. Here, too, assumptions have a position of first-rate importance. However, I want to reserve the next chapter for more detailed comment on this; for unless the investigations which this requires are to be stripped of their natural connections, they will compel us to go beyond the sphere of judgments-about in one quite important respect. It is true that we have hitherto taken only judgment-of and judgment-about into consideration[34] as cases in which an objective is intellectually approached; but it must not be overlooked that one can also approach an objective in such a way that it is included in some intellectual operation that does not constitute a case of judgment. This in fact takes place when, say, we infer from one objective to another, an operation that is so close to the previously mentioned judgments concerning the relations of objectives that it is not always easy to secure one's self against confusions. For this reason, it would be best to make a joint investigation of the role that assumptions play in these two modes of activity, which are so closely connected with each other.

Even if we do provisionally leave out of account what the next chapter will have to ascertain in this regard, the following can still be said at this point, by way of summary. In cases of judgment about objectives, it is certainly out of the question for us to maintain that the act of thought by which an objective is, as it were, put forth for a judgment about it *cannot* ever be a judgment. Yet the nature of the judgment mediately apprehending[g] the objective rather often entails that any judgment immediate to the objective would, as a conviction of the same subject, be incompatible with the former judgment. Moreover, it is frequently the case that the subject who makes a mediate judgment must be in a position to keep himself free of conviction, or does keep himself free of it, as far as concerns a judgment immediate to the objective. On every such occasion, we are dealing with an objective that can be given to the judgment about it only by an assumption.

§23

"Judgments Subject to Recall" "Conscious Self-deception"

There are two standpoints from which one can attempt to weaken the foregoing proof of the role of assumptions in our intellectual activities. Either the ability to present objectives is accorded also to representations, or judgments are enlisted as presenting experiences even in cases where judgments appear to be precluded by the nature of the mental situation. How little unaware I was of the two approaches in question at the time of the writing of the first edition of this book can be seen from the discussions in the preceding chapter that have been carried over into the present edition unchanged in this regard.[35] Still, I have been confronted with the two approaches as if I had never heard of them;[36] and even in the face of my recent rejection of these approaches,[37] they have again been insisted on. Because of that, the possibility of representing objectives was taken into consideration once again, in the foregoing.[38] Here, somewhat as in an appendix, we must again consider the other possibility, viz., that judgments might be present even in those cases where they appear to be precluded.

It is none of my doing, if the author who again adopts the position rejected by me coins the unattractive catchword "judgments subject to recall" for it. By this he means "a judging or believing... but not one of those autocratic ones 'that succeeds in the full and lasting nullification of the critical judgments opposed to it'—a belief or judgment, therefore, that does not get to make its weight felt fully in every direction, especially not in the practical direction."[39] Thus, aside from the absent logical or practical consequences, we apprehend the novel as we would a credible account, and we apprehend the drama as we would an actual event happening before our eyes. At work in this is the influence of our feeling and desire on our judging, and we are always free to reinhibit this influence, as it were, and in that way return to the state of conviction determined by our environment and our past.

The interpretation thus outlined is not intended to apply to all cases of assumption; and it is even quite explicit in its exception, for example, of assumptions made for the purpose of conducting a mathematical proof.[40] I would say that its immediate domain of application is rather intended to be that of art. To that extent, the preceding chapter would have been the more suitable place for an opinion on this interpretation. But on the other hand, the present context, which is already serving intentions of a more theoretical kind, will actually better accommodate the psychological position that is fundamental to our examination of the view in question. It is also worthwhile observing right away that the elementary cases set apart for consideration in the preceding section are scarcely going to be open to reinterpretation in accordance with the view in question.

So let us consult with experience regarding these "judgments subject to recall" connected with the drama or the novel. We may of course immediately dismiss those cases where a reader takes his novel to be a credible factual report or where a spectator does not know, or has forgotten, that he is seated in the theater. However frequently or seldom they may occur, there are cases where the judging is not "subject to recall" and is at most subject to the possibility of being set right. So here we have a judging that is admittedly erroneous, but which is in other respects no different from ordinary judging. But now, when I try to characterize the normal state of affairs in accordance with my own experiences, which I have no reason to think abnormal, then the result is simply the following. During the time I have paid any attention at all to such things, I have never directly perceived myself believing, i.e., judging, and I also have never been able to recollect doing that. In particular, this holds for occasions where, right as I was addressing myself to a product of "discursive" art, I attempted to give an account of the nature of what I had experienced in the moment immediately preceding, either in response to someone else's query or by reason of some reflective pause, whatever the occasion for it might have been. I might mention in passing that while the attempt has certainly prejudiced the impression of the thing that was just then presented, it has not prejudiced the intellectual understanding of that thing. On no such occasions could I observe anything of those reactions of value-feeling and desire that would have infallibly made their appearance in the face of something believed, not to say something also taken to be present. It would seem that I may or must adhere to my own experiences, as long as there is an absence of more exact analytical and statistical investigations in this matter—or better still, investigations of an experimental sort. If so, then in the first instance the following question develops out of these experiences. Where does one really get the right to speak of judgments at all, in the domain in question, and to mitigate the resulting conflict with experience by ascribing the strange attribute "subject to recall" to the judgments? It does indeed seem that this mitigating tendency, naturally not a conscious one, has already asserted itself in the description of these "judgments," a description that I have reproduced above. For in view of the facts, it is at least putting it rather leniently, to say that these judgments just lack the aptitude for "full and lasting nullification" of critical opposition, and also to say that they lack no more than the capacity to make their weight felt "fully in every respect," particularly in the practical respect.

Still, we should not neglect to raise this question: Does it really make such a great difference in one's mental attitude, if one reads the political or local news-stories in a paper, or if one instead reads the novel-installment or the literary page? On the whole, I think I have a distinct sense of the movement preparatory to a new orientation, when there is a change from the one sort of reading to the other. The sense is especially distinct when one has been taking a news-story to be factual, but the things that it contains at last make one realize that the whole thing might just be a fabrication. But there are two factors by which the difference in what I now called the orientation is somewhat hidden from attention. The one factor is that a person is by no means always in a believing, i.e., judging, stance with regard to newspaper stories, apart from his judgment that this or that very item is in the newspaper. Here we have understanding with suspended conviction; and that by itself is assuming. In this case, as one might expect, there cannot be any markedly different reactions to what is in the news section and what is in the literary and entertainment section. The other factor, however, lies in the circumstance that while fabrications command our interest in a different way than reported things do, it can very well be in a stronger way, too. What is so extraordinarily decisive here, as we know, is the manner in which something is presented to us. Thus, if someone should happen to think that what is judged must in any case be superior in interest to what is not judged, then he can easily be led by this indirect path into acknowledging the presence of judgments when in fact there aren't any judgments.

So as far as the domain of facts that it is supposed to elucidate is concerned, not only does the appeal to "judgments subject to recall" lack the character of a description of observed events, but the hypothesis is so foreign to experience that one may reasonably doubt whether it fulfills even what is customarily required of a *"vera causa."* The deficiency is supposed to be remedied, on the one hand, by appeal to the wavering nature of many judgments; on the other hand, the appeal is to the openness of our convictions to determination by emotional factors. There would be scant profit in it, if this remedy should result in an unassailability of the sort that can ultimately be traced back to the special obscurity of other matters; and without doubt, the two points just mentioned are among the least clarified ones in psychology. But at least this much can easily be seen, it seems to me: that from this side no support worth mentioning accrues to the business of "judgments subject to recall."

First of all, as regards wavering convictions, there doubtless are such convictions. Notably this is where the available reasons are sufficient only for surmises and, in disregard of that, the judgment makes a sort of rash ascent to the height of full certainty. In this case, judgmental motives entering into play through reflection or in some other way can lead to a scarcely less rash veering round into the opposite. The veering round may indeed happen quite often, in cases where reasons or simply just judgmental motives pro and con enter into conflict with each other. But what does this or any other kind of wavering of our opinions have to do with experiences in connection with the novel or drama? Either one fails to recognize the true situation and believes in what one reads or hears, in which case one may soon be set right by the environing reality or in some other way; or, which is usually the case, from the very beginning one does not believe, and in that case there is naturally not the slightest occasion for any wavering.[41]

Now, we are supposed to be dealing with waverings that are traceable to emotional influences. It is unnecessarily circumstantial to call in old and new voluntarism as witness to such influences; they are, after all, attested to by the most significant, most historically noteworthy events in the religious and ethical sphere, and likewise by thousands of minor data of daily life. But there is a peculiar irrationality about all these facts, as I believe I am allowed to say concerning such experiences, given the lack of sufficient clearness. The irrationality is not incompatibility in the logical sense, of course, but it is somewhat similar to the latter. Its true character has yet to be determined; but even in its presently unanalyzed state this irrationality can hardly escape an attentive person. Yet one is unable to discover any such irrationality whatsoever in our attitude to the discursive or any other art. But aside from that, one is at a loss to explain the possible origin of the emotions that are supposed to exert their influence in the artistic context. No doubt we are referred to aesthetic feelings;[42] but such feelings can assert themselves only as a reaction to the effects of the work of art, and therefore not before one has read for a while in the novel or has followed the action of the play for a while. The necessary receptivity has to be brought in by the reader, of course, even for such a beginning; and by experience we know that this receptivity is normally established right away, as soon as one takes the book in hand or sees the curtain go up. But what is experienced then, in a sort of emotionless beginning stage, can scarcely consist in "judgments subject to recall"; it must either consist in ordinary judgments or consist not in judgments at all but in assumptions. And as far as I know, nothing in experience tells us of this beginning stage ever being followed by a stage involving a significantly different attitude.

We may add that such things as "judgments subject to recall" are not even likely to be encountered in those cases where one can normally expect to find some emotional influences on intellectual activities. So my assertion that these things would surely have to be judgments of a quite unusual nature[43] will presumably still stand. Despite everything, it may be "antecedently" difficult for many a person to decide which is the more probable—such strange judgments, or affirmations and negations that have the character not of judgments but of assumptions.[44] But the decision is made easy by the fact that there are also assumptions in cases where even Marty, as mentioned, does not think himself obliged to appeal to "judgments subject to recall";[45] whereas these "judgments," if what has been set forth is correct, are nowhere empirically verified. Yet as hypotheses, they could find confirmation only in the fact that they were capable of replacing assumptions in some, though by no means all, cases.

Nevertheless, in concluding these remarks dedicated to defensive criticism, I do not want to leave it unmentioned that there is an interpretation of art to which considerable attention has been justly accorded during the past few years, and that the notion of "judgments subject to recall" could expect to find especially favorable points of connection with this interpretation. I mean Konrad Lange's theory of "conscious self-deception." The name of the theory is the least important thing here; it does seem clearly enough to imply judgment, but as its originator quite well knows,[46] taken literally it really means something quite impossible. But in the juxtaposition of "illusion-provoking elements" and "illusion-disrupting elements,"[47] as well as in the accompanying possibility of turning now to the former and now to the latter, we seem to have a combination of factors that would, to a surprising extent, favor the change of conviction just mentioned. Of course, Konrad Lange himself scarcely seems to conceive the matter in the manner of "judgments subject to recall"; at least, he occasionally stresses quite emphatically "that not only a real deception, but even the attempt at it or the approximation to it, is unwarranted in art."[48] But it would surely be unfair to demand more from the psychological exactitude of the art historian than he thinks it advisable to credit to the "philosopher's" technical understanding of art,[49] and so I cannot consider myself exempt from the duty of briefly establishing why I cannot grant the appeal to "judgments subject to recall" even in the face of the facts brought in by Lange.

Of the two main reasons that determine this rejection, the one is in a way directed against the author of the illusion theory himself, despite what I have said. To wit, I do not believe in the necessary two-sidedness of the art-experience; so little do I believe in it that I regard all thoughts of whether the artist has done his work well or poorly, and as to what means he has employed thereto, etc., as altogether extraneous to art. This avowal may be taken quite personally; I know that Lange does not exactly hold this standpoint in high esteem, regarding it as that of the layman[50] and perhaps even that of the "pedantic scholar" or "solid bourgeois."[51] But I also know that the highest that art has offered me in my life was free of that double-sidedness. Also, there is an art to whose theory and practice I hope I stand close enough to be able to enter imaginatively into the position of the creative artist in both respects. And on the strength of that, I believe I may affirm quite confidently that as an artist I would never feel myself so betrayed and forsaken as I would in the face of the artistic understanding [Kunstverstand] contained in a critique that is merely knowledgeable in artistic matters [kunst-verständig]. This, too, is intended in an entirely subjective way; and in view of the authorities that Lange is able to call in for support, there may not be much place for it in our discussion. But it is a fact, and to that extent free of any subjectivity, that with many of those who enjoy art a work of art normally elicits just the one type of attitude, be it that of the layman or not; and upon our reference to this, all that has already been said about against "judgments subject to recall" immediately becomes effective.

Now, the same thing holds—and this is my second ground of objection—even on suppositions that are as favorable as can be imagined to the two-sidedness postulated by Lange. Even then it remains simply a fact of experience "that in the normal case of artistic enjoyment one does not at any moment really allow himself to be deceived."[52] And in that case, the attitude that we take to "illusion-disrupting" reality actually provides a quite favorable opportunity for one to realize, by means of the contrast between it and the other attitude, how one feels in the judgmental apprehending of objectives and how one feels in the nonjudgmental apprehending of them; and in the last instance, this nonjudgmental apprehending will simply have to be an assumptive apprehending. It has already been pointed out from another quarter[53] that such an interpretation could not but prove helpful to the lucidity and conciseness of the Langean position.

§24
Emotionally Approached Objectives

Thus far, it is only in the intellectual domain that we have investigated the role of assumptions in the apprehending of objectives. Yet assumptions play an eminently important part in our emotional life, too—and again as the means of apprehending objectives. In the present chapter, we must briefly enter into this other side of assuming. But in order to do so, we must fill out, in at least makeshift fashion, an omission that could not be avoided in the third chapter. Our investigations in that chapter were at first directed at the objective as pseudo-existent,[54] i.e., at the apprehended objective as such; and for that very reason, since apprehending is after all primarily an intellectual operation, it was easy for us not to go beyond the intellectual sphere in these first investigations. Now we want also to pursue the assumption into the emotional domain a bit, and so we must first of all make up for what has been neglected above, at least by taking a few cursory glances to persuade ourselves of the importance of the role that belongs to the objective over against affective and conative experience [Fühlen und Begehren]. Here, too, it is particularly cases of secondary expression that render us good service.

As concerns feelings, first of all, one need not look very long in the area of their secondary expressions to find "that"-clauses which reveal the objective. Admittedly, one will not expect to encounter any objectives in the case of sensory feelings; with aesthetic feelings, though, we are already in the opposite case, and objectives are quite frequently encountered. With regard to the first part of Bjoernsen's *Beyond Our Power,* let us say, it is quite natural for a person to remark, "It displeases me that Pastor Sang at first had no reaction to the tragic end of his wife except naive astonishment at a kind of misunderstanding." Similarly, locutions such as "I am pleased (elated, feel better) that..." and the like are thoroughly apposite. To illustrate this further by quotations is quite unnecessary when the foregoing has already contained much discussion of art-experiences. Until now, admittedly, these experiences entered into consideration only on their intellectual side; but the things that were intellectually apprehensible objects in the situations I discussed now present themselves to us also as objects of our emotional attitude to art. It is hardly of importance to the present connection whether, in that case, the objectives in question[55] are to be looked upon as "aesthetic objects" and whether they are also to be regarded as special "aesthetic elementary objects" in the strict sense of the term coined by Stephan Witasek.[56] Further on,[57] we shall return briefly to the same question. But in any case, even Witasek has not denied the significance of objectives in the domain of aesthetic experiences; on the contrary, he has expressly emphasized it, and it is, after all, only this significance that is in question in the present connection. Next, judgment-feelings[58] are turned towards objectives, and in an unmistakably direct manner. Indeed, even knowledge-feelings are to a certain extent turned towards objectives. Thus, someone who is getting his first glimpse into the modern theory of microorganisms may easily find it interests him that the perfection of our optical devices is an indispensable prerequisite to the present state of our knowledge and skill in this matter. But it is value-feelings, especially, that command our attention in this connection. Such feelings, of course, find their most natural expression in locutions like "I am glad (sad, afraid, hopeful) that..." etc. Here it will simply have to be affirmed that a relation to an objective always attaches to the very nature of valuing, the state of affairs fundamental to all value-feelings. Value-feelings are existence-feelings:[59] Already implicit here is the proposition that value-feelings are in the first instance oriented not toward a certain thing, but toward the existence[60] of this thing. This state of affairs comes out quite unmistakably in the fact that instead of the existence of the thing in question, it can be the non-existence of it on which a value is set. Yet "that"-clauses are by no means always used in the expression of valuings, and we must not allow this to throw us off the foregoing insight. I can easily say, "I set value on this book," where it would be more exact to say, "I set value on the fact that I have this book."[h] And as in a number of previously mentioned[61] cases from the epistemic domain, it mightn't even be inexactness in the former case. For it could well be that the objective in turn establishes a relation between its objectum and the value-feeling and that in lieu of any finer differentiation of what is indifferently termed "value-object" [Wertobjekt], it is sometimes the objective and sometimes its objectum [Objekt] that is signified by this term.[62] In other cases, it is not even necessary to keep this possibility in view, since in these cases the "that"-clause is merely replaced by expressions that are already familiar to us as equivalents of "that"-clauses. Instead of "I place the highest value on this, that my students think independently," I can indeed say, "I place the highest value on my students' thinking independently" —or on their "independence" or suchlike. But what is brought into play in such ways of speaking are just those verbal substantives and abstract nouns whose signification we already managed to make clear to ourselves earlier.[63] It might be worth mentioning that the case is otherwise with such locutions as "I love (revere, respect, esteem) him" and suchlike, where "that"-constructions obviously could not be put in without violence. Value-feelings are doubtless also at the root of the mental experiences that find expression in these locutions; but the previously mentioned peculiarity of expression will have to be regarded as a sign that it is not *only* a matter of value-feelings in this case.

What has just been set forth about value-feelings applies, if at all, in an even more obvious way to desires,[i] and as far as I can see, it applies to all desires. The often striking analogy between judgment and desire shows up also in the circumstance that every desire as well as every judgment has its objective. Just as one cannot judge without judging as to something, so too one cannot desire without desiring something, and in the present instance this means more precisely desiring that the something in question exist or that it not exist, that it be in such and such a condition or that it not be in such a condition.[64] And here, too, there are forms of expression which lack the "that"-clause—the child wants the apple, the adult longs for happiness, and so forth. But again, the interpretations verified several times in the foregoing are apposite. First of all, it can again happen rather frequently that the "that"-clause is merely replaced by one of those verbal substantives or abstract nouns that are already familiar to us as equivalents of such clauses, to say nothing of infinitival constructions like "I do not want to leave the interests of the whole community out of consideration."[65] If such an interpretation is precluded, as in the above examples of the child and of the adult, this is still nowise to be interpreted as though we had found desires that had no objectives. It is easiest to persuade oneself of this by considering that a desiring which had only the representational object apple or happiness before it would, for practical purposes, be just as indeterminate as a desiring with regard to which we had yet to decide whether it was a matter of desire or reluctance [Widerstreben]—or to take a special case, a matter of *velle* or *nolle,* "wanting to" or "not wanting to," as the inexact usage for the contrary goes. I am assuredly not of the opinion that every instance of reluctance is to be interpreted as the wanting of a non-existence.[66] Reluctance is as qualitatively distinct vis-à-vis endeavor [Streben] or desire, i.e., as much opposed and qualitatively original, as displeasure is vis-à-vis pleasure, or negation vis-à-vis affirmation. Yet if all that the assertion "I desire X" is supposed to express is a desiring that bears on X as its object,[67] then while this assertion can mean that what is important to the desirer is the existence of X, it can just as well mean that what is important to him is the non-existence of X.[68] In either instance, desire bears on X as its object; but in one instance we should be confronted with a state of affairs that was identical in its practical significance, albeit not in its psychological nature, with a reluctance that likewise bore on X as its object. In short, if the locution "I desire X" is generally not misleading, we can mainly credit that just to a special linguistic usage. In the strict sense, it would always have to be made quite definite as to whether desire was directed to the existence of X or directed to its non-existence, just as it must be settled whether desire has a positive or a negative sign, as it were.

Naturally, in the case of feelings and desires, as in the case of judgments, there is no lack of attributes that are related to the experiences but which are in the first instance to be accorded to the objectives in question. "It is nice (pleasing, regrettable, annoying, interesting, of great value, important) that..." etc. "It is advisable (requested, optional, imperative) that..." etc. It hardly need be added that the first of the two groups of expressions just adduced belongs to the affective domain, and the second belongs to the conative domain.^{j} In the latter domain, the relevant attributes or adjectives seem generally less easy to discover. Besides attributes, we may also expect to find relations. This is already guaranteed by the fact that, like my conviction, my pleasure or sadness and likewise my resolution may "have as its reason...." I shall have to forego any further detailed consideration of this matter at present.

§25
Assumptions in the Case of Feelings and Desires

Perhaps what has just been set forth has made it reasonably clear how deeply objectives penetrate into our emotional life, if we may put it that way. Then at this point all that remains to be asked in regard to emotional experiences is how far assumptions are requisite for approaching the objectives of these experiences, which is like what we asked above in regard to intellectual experiences. As far as is presently known, feelings and desires lack the capacity to approach objects immediately, no matter whether these objects are objecta or objectives. Hence, whenever an objective is accosted by an emotional experience—or more briefly, whenever an objective is emotionally approached—this at the same time signalizes an intellectual approach. Thus, we again stand before the dilemma that is already so familiar to us: either a judgment or an assumption. And again the idea is that where the psychological situation precludes a judgment, the presence of an assumption is proven beyond doubt.

As for *desires,* the task can be handled in a very simple way. I suppose that the observations of the preceding chapter have shown that what I desire, strictly speaking, is not in the first instance *A,* but only that *A* be or that it be "thus." If so, then we can see right away that a judgment cannot be the means by which such an objective is given to the one who desires. This can be seen from the obvious fact that no one can desire something which, in his own opinion, has already come true. Thus, if I judge that A is or is not, there cannot then be any desire directed towards this objective. If, on the contrary, there really is desire, then the objective cannot possibly be thought by means of a judgment, and there remains nothing but the assumption. Of course, this is nowise affected by the fact that someone can very well desire, with regard to a thing which presently exists, that it should also exist in the future. "That A is" is simply a different objective than "that in the future A will be." A person who desires the latter can also be convinced of the former, but only for the reason that the conviction as to a present existence does not yet by any means include the conviction as to a future one.

The situation is not quite as clear in the case of reluctancies. Analogously to what has just been set forth for desires, it now turns out that a person who showed resistance to the occurrence of an event A could not possibly be convinced that A will not take place at all. But by this fact, nothing at all is predetermined with regard to the act of thought that gives the objective underlying the reluctance. For if the objective to which someone is reluctant is "that A occurs," then the judgment that is precluded by the reluctance has the objective "that A does not occur," i.e., the contrary of the objective to which the person is reluctant. Still, we may add that for the person who is unshakably convinced that A will occur, it will be normal or "reasonable" to subdue his reluctance to the unalterable.[69] So on the one hand, we may not go so far as to maintain that a reluctance to "that A is" precludes one's being convinced of it —or in other words, precludes a judgment with the objective "that A is." On the other hand, it is at least the more natural thing for the reluctant person not to regard what he is against as being inevitable; so for such cases as these, it is established that the objective of the reluctancy in question is given not by a judgment, but by an assumption. Thus, the assumption is an indispensable psychological prerequisite for all desires with a positive quality, and for desires with a negative quality it is at least far and away the normal thing.

I shall refrain from any detailed consideration of the cases where an objective is imputed properties that are taken from a conative experience directed toward this objective. Obviously, such cases are not especially characteristic of the matter of assumptions. Moreover, many of the relevant predicates are of the same type as objective-predicates traceable to *feelings* pertaining to the objective in question. Consequently, we had best turn to these feelings now, and in particular to aesthetic feelings and value-feelings. On both sides, the matter at first glance appears to be so simple as to suggest that it would be reasonable to turn aside from more detailed observation.

In the case of *aesthetic* feelings, first of all, the objective is not always— indeed, is not even normally—yielded by a judgment of the feeling subject. This, we saw,[70] was certain to the extent that one can take it for granted that being convinced of the actuality of the "aesthetic object" is by no means necessary for the appropriate attitude to that object. This has been acknowledged in the assertion that the aesthetic attitude is essentially based on representation, on "appearance," and from this I myself have drawn the consequence that aesthetic feelings may be essentially defined as representation-feelings.[71] Recently Stephan Witasek, too, has formulated the main result of his aesthetic investigations in this proposition: "the aesthetic state of the subject is in the main a feeling (of pleasure or displeasure) together with an intuitive representing, the two being together in such a way that the representing constitutes the psychological prerequisite of the feeling. Aesthetic feelings are representation-feelings."[72] But this result is of so little immediate use to the case for assumptions, that the formulation of it occasions Witasek to turn polemically[73] against my assertion[74] that the objectives of the aesthetic domain that were mentioned in the preceding sections "are given not by means of judgments but by means of assumptions and that there is reason to give up speaking of representation-feelings and to speak instead of assumption-feelings." However, what Witasek is disputing here is merely that these "assumption-feelings"[75] (which are also recognized by him) are aesthetic feelings; by no means does he dispute the fact that the objectives normally entering into consideration in art are not believed and, hence, that they must at any event be assumed. Naturally, this latter point of view has application not only where it is a question of our attitude to works of art already at hand, but likewise where an objective is accorded or, as it may be, denied an aesthetic predicate. With this, there is also revealed to our understanding an essential part of the prominent role assumptions play in art, a role that in the preceding chapter became forcibly apparent to us simply out of the direct observation of the facts and without any particularly detailed psychological analysis.

It seems just as easy now to determine the significance of *value*-feelings for assumptions, except that the result in this case has the opposite sign, as it were. If value-feelings are by nature judgment-feelings, then it is indeed clear that assumptions have no application in their regard. Yet it seems to me that a closer investigation of our attitudes to value-objecta will show that assumptions have a very important role in these attitudes, and a role that is very important for the correct apprehension of the facts of value-theory. But this matter cannot well be explained without our going into detail on some things that are rather remote from the remaining context of these remarks. I shall therefore devote a special chapter to these investigations.[k] This probably will be made all the easier to do by the fact that in the foregoing there has been no mention of an aspect of desires that is, it seems to me, very important for our knowledge of these experiences; the consideration of assumptions is an effective means of explaining this aspect. More precisely, we shall be involved in questions pertaining to the motivation of desires, and answering these questions will also be important for the correct apprehension of the facts concerning value. It is advisable, then, to have the relevant investigations precede those that concern our attitude to value-objects.

However, before we pursue assumptions into this somewhat more narrowly circumscribed area of our emotional life in this way, let us return for a while to the sphere of intellectual activities. Our first concern is with relations between objectives and with operations on objectives. These two matters were mentioned only in passing at the end of section 22, and we want to take a somewhat closer look at them, because of the assumptions that are involved. But another important as well as extensive role of assumptions in intellectual operations also has to be shown; there are many objectives to which this role is antecedent, as it were, in that it chiefly concerns their material—the material being constituted in the first instance by objecta, though admittedly sometimes by objectives. Here we are concerned with experiences that as a rule precede the real intellectual treatment of an object, as the normal condition of this treatment. In these experiences the mere presentation of the object in question provides at best only a part of what is requisite; the remainder of the contribution devolves on assumptions, so far as the latter do not already have to enter into the presentation itself, as ancillary to it. So these things are essentially matters of intellectual psychology, and the next three chapters are to be devoted to them.

VI

Assumptions in Operations on Objectives

---

§26
Immediate and Mediate Evidence

Here we shall be primarily concerned with a domain of facts that has long been among the most intensively treated parts of the theory of human knowing. As "formal logic" it has even seemed to many people to take in practically everything that can claim the attention of the theory of knowing. Today the one-sidedness of such a view is clear to anyone at all discriminating; but we have never quite been able to get over one of the most serious consequences of such one-sidedness. It is a consequence that surprisingly and yet characteristically affects our knowledge of the very same epistemic activities that have always provided the favorite and quite expressly preferred theme of investigations in formal logic. I mean the derivation of judgments from judgments—deducing or proving. It is not just that the multiplicity of moods and figures actually encountered here, or perhaps constructed first, has completely diverted attention from those facts that do not freely accommodate themselves to arrangement under these "forms." Besides this, present-day epistemological research has inherited a question that is still open in its essentials and yet contains one of the most fundamental problems that epistemology is called upon to approach. This is the question—to all appearances a much more primitive one —concerning what sort of facts we are really confronted with in all of these inferential procedures. Under such circumstances, it is naturally going to be somewhat risky to throw even the most modest attempt at answering that question into the middle of an exposition that is devoted to an entirely different matter. But for one thing, the answer that I think I can give is really an extraordinarily modest contribution, even if it is correct, since at bottom it offers little more than a reference to direct observation. Certainly, there is no way to avoid this reference; but by that very fact, it is not something that should be claimed as a special theoretical accomplishment. But the main thing is this: that what I have to say in this book regarding characteristic cases of assumptions has such a close connection with the way I believe I must interpret proof and inference, that I cannot at this point let my interpretation go entirely without exposition. For the rest, though, I also hope that the unconstrained agreement between the two sides, which I think I can point out, will be of service not just to the conception of assumptions, which must by all means be legitimated in this book, but also to what I shall allege concerning the nature of inference.

The peculiar high standing in virtue of which certain judgments, as against others, are regarded as cognitions is in the last instance always traceable to the fact of evidence.[a] And since this fact is itself something ultimate, it can rightly be conceded the rank of the basic or central fact of all epistemology.[1] All evidence is dependent on judgment, of course, and it has long been customary to juxtapose immediately evident judgments, judgments that stand in their own right, with judgments of merely mediate evidence. Mediate evidence is called that because it has its origin in the evidence of other judgments and ultimately, of course, in the immediate evidence of other judgments. From such a contrast there naturally arises the question as to whether the difference between the two types of evidence concerns just their origin or whether it also concerns their nature. Otherwise expressed, the question is whether a mediately evident judgment is not at bottom just as evident as an immediately evident one, or whether mediate evidence might at the same time also represent a sort of less perfect evidence, something like a lower order of evidence.

Prior to any consideration of experience, the question could also be formulated in the opposite direction, as it were, namely by asking whether mediate evidence might not somehow signify a more perfect order of evidence. But if that possibility struck someone as being worth discussion, it could only be someone totally naive in epistemology, someone for whom nothing but what is proved can stand as fully certain—despite the fact that every proof must ultimately be grounded on something unproven. As against this, the notion that mediate insight might be of slight epistemic value finds good empirical support in the strikingly different cognitive attitudes that we take with regard to a geometrical axiom, say, and then again with regard to a theorem of this science, when it rests on a line of proof that is no more than moderately complicated. Actually, even the older epistemology placed "intuitive" knowledge ahead of the "demonstrative." And if one remembers the complaint, so often repeated since Schopenhauer, concerning how Euclidean geometry just forces its propositions upon our conviction, as it were, without leading one to a proper insight[b] into the demonstrated state of affairs, then one must straightway ask whether the instances of "mediate evidence" obtained in this way can still have any claim to be regarded as instances of evidence. And then that raises the question as to how such "mediate evidence," which would then strictly speaking not be evidence at all, is supposed to be capable of giving a judgment an epistemic standing like that which is given it by "immediate" evidence—more precisely, just plain evidence—which by this account such judgments simply do not have.

§27
The Nature of Mediation of Conviction

Evidence attaches to judgment, as we mentioned; and however mediation of evidence may have to be interpreted, it is in each instance a special case of the mediation of conviction. If we regard mediation of conviction from the side of objects, then under favorable conditions it is called "proof"; but under other conditions, e.g., if the presuppositions are erroneous, mediation of conviction can still very well take place, notwithstanding the fact that the conviction so obtained has no claim to be regarded as being really legitimated. Perhaps it will make the answering of the above question easier if we first of all try to gain an insight into the general nature of the mediation of conviction.

Accordingly, the question is simply as follows: I am convinced that *A* is *B*; from that I infer that *C* is *D*. What really is going on when I infer? When I do so, it is quite unnecessary for me to speak explicitly of "inferring." It is often inferring that is expressed when I say simply: *C* should or must be *D*, *because A* is *B*. Still, this same word sometimes connects members of a causal sequence, as when one says of a ball that it is moving "because" it has been struck by another ball. And if this is not right away passed over as one of the many cases of ambiguity,[2] one can immediately find an indication of the most obvious answer to our question—an answer, moreover, which is obvious even without reference to the linguistic factor. What could this "because" more naturally signify than that the second judgment has arisen from the first, from the judgment to which one does after all appeal—or that the first judgment has given rise to the second? Moreover, there can hardly be any doubt that the first judgment constitutes a partial cause of the appearance of the second judgment, even if it is not the total cause.

However, against such an appeal to the causal relation, it has been rightly said[3] that two judgments can very well stand in a causal connection without our thereby being able to speak of the one as inferred from the other. Take the case of a person who expects thunder as soon as he has seen the lightning. His conviction about the imminence of the noise is certainly due to his perceptual judgment about the lightning. But what is happening in no wise need be the same as what finds expression in the sentence, "There was a flash of lightning; consequently there will be thunder." One *can* generally make such an inference when conditions of the given sort are present; but on such occasions the distinct character of the situation when one does so becomes all the more plain in contrast to the situation when one doesn't.

Another argument against the interpretation under consideration may be more conclusive; in any case, it has greater essential significance for the present matter. If the causal connection between the two judgments were the decisive thing regarding their relation, then one would never be in a position to know by direct perception whether and from what one has inferred something, since the causal connection between a partial cause and the relevant effect can never be perceived. An inferential state of affairs would thus be recognizable in an individual case only on the basis of those occasionally rather extensive operations of thought that are elsewhere required in order to ascertain the causal connection of inner and outer events. But this most assuredly contradicts our experiences of the immediacy with which one is normally able to give an account as to whether and from what a given judgment is inferred. Naturally, this unperceivability of the causal relation also prohibits one from emending the above attempt at a definition so that the second judgment is said to be inferred when one perceives the causal connection with the first judgment; for this perception never does occur.[4] But it is true at this juncture that the relation essential to the inferring must be one that is accessible to direct perception and one which furthermore does not preclude the causal connection.

A closer look into the nature of this relation can be obtained most easily by attending to a feature that is peculiar to a priori judgment; it will not then be difficult to find something analogous to this feature in the case that concerns us. What with the distinctive dependence of the a priori judgment on the nature of its judged-about material,[5] it is understandable that the one who is judging must in the first instance turn his attention to that—the nature of the material. Where it is a question of something quite easily knowable, such as the differentness of black and white, the direction of attention may not be very conspicuous; but it will reveal itself quite clearly in the case of a judgment where the differentness in question is fairly close to the threshold region. So in general one can say this: that a priori judgments are made in view of the character of the judgmental material, whereas in an a posteriori judgment the character of the material has no such significance. Suppose, now, that by reason of the conviction that A is B and B is C someone arrives at the further conviction that A is C. Then it is obvious that in order to arrive at this result he must, as it were, dwell upon A, B, and C—or the material of the premises. Not only upon this material, it must be admitted; understandably, a great deal hinges on whether A is or isn't B, and whether B is or isn't C. Thus, what the person that is inferring must dwell upon is not just the material contained in the premises; rather, it is the objectives that appear in the premises, inclusive of the material. The essential role of objectives is something that one could already gather directly from the linguistic expressions customary in such cases. Thus, one says, "From this, that A is B and B is C, it follows that A is C." Or occasionally one puts it more briefly, as mentioned above: "Because A is B and B is C, A is C" or "...A must be C." These objectives, then, are the decisive thing in the mediation of conviction—supposing, of course, that they are judged, i.e., believed. Let us not inquire as to whether the believing suffices by itself for the obtaining of the mediated conviction or whether one must also take the very fact of believing explicitly into consideration by means of a special judgment. Nor can we attempt to go into the other peculiarities of the operation presently in view, an operation that is familiar to everyone from inward experience. For the time being, we may have enough with the characterization by the aid of the long-familiar analogy with the a priori judgment, an analogy to which, as we all know, the designation of said judgment as "a priori" already refers us. In accordance with this analogy, we may now say that someone makes an inference when, drawing upon a conviction already present, he forms a new conviction *in view* of the former one.[6] The experience to which one refers in using words of this sort seems to me to be typical enough to do without a further description.

If I am not mistaken, there are still quite a few cases in which neglected observations, or at least ones not as yet carried on methodically, will lead to facts that have previously been unnoticed and which are irreducible from the standpoint of the present state of analysis. In the present case, therefore, I do not hesitate to assert that the obtaining of one judgment from another, the mediation of conviction or judgment, is essentially characterized by a peculiar real relation of the mediated judgment to the mediating judgment or judgments. An analogue for this relation can be found in the domain of desires,[7] a domain that is in many other respects constituted analogously to the facts of judgment. This analogue has a name long in use. To wit, just as in view of one conviction I can arrive at another, so in view of one desire (e.g., the desire for an end) I can arrive at another desire (such as the desire for the means). Here it is said that the one desire has the other as its "motive." The state of affairs in the domain of judgment is striking enough in its similarity to justify carrying over this term into the intellectual domain. I shall accept Hillebrand's terminology,[8] therefore, despite my original scruples in this matter.[9] I would think it further advisable only that where necessary, facts of the sort in question, as instances of motivation of judgment, should be contrasted to instances of the motivation of desire. With regard to the judgments standing in this special motivational relation to each other—and analogously in the case of desires, for that matter—it will satisfy various needs if we contrast the "motive" or "motives" to the "motivated," so that the relation of motivation can also be defined as the relation between the motive and the motivated.

In making these remarks, I have implicitly taken a position opposed to the interpretation of inference that I advocated[10] years ago, though this interpretation has actually already been explicitly abandoned by me.[11] According to this interpretation, it would be as though an inference were at bottom nothing but a hypothetical judgment in which the dependence of the motivated on the motive is expressed. I do not think that I have to dwell upon this position here, especially since it is devoid of *prima facie* plausibility as long as correctness and evidence are left wholly out of consideration. Still, in this position I can now see the unsuccessful expression of a need that was perfectly legitimate in itself. And as we shall see, I believe that through the recourse to assumptions I can give due recognition to this need. We shall later have occasion to return to the aforesaid hypothetical judgment.

§28

The Mediation of Evidence. Seeming Difficulties Here

We now turn to a special case that is fundamental to the theory of knowledge. This is the case where there is not just the mediation of one conviction by another, but also the mediation of one instance of evidence by another—not just the obtaining of a new judgment, but the obtaining of a judgment that is justified. Suppose that it pertained to the hypothetical judgment just mentioned to be a mediation of conviction and that in light of this, that judgment deserved to be spoken of as the real "inferential judgment," as I once wanted to call it.[c] Then one might look to the evidence of this judgment for the state of affairs constituting the so-called mediate evidence.[12] But as already admitted, the *Schlussgesetz,*[d] as Sigwart aptly called it,[13] is not the *Schluss* itself. Or more precisely, the insight into the holding of that law [Gesetz] is neither the inferential [Schluss-] operation nor the result of this operation. On the contrary, the result—actually this is clear as it stands—cannot be anything but the insight of the *conclusio.* And as a matter of fact, this is the only thing that accords with what was determined above, with respect to the mediation of conviction; along with "conviction in view of" there is now "evidence in view of," somewhat like a special case of the former. It is basically such a simple matter that there could be no doubt about it whatsoever, if it were not for the apparent difficulty in something already mentioned at the beginning of this chapter—the evidencelessness of so many conclusions about whose correctness and validity no one is uncertain. We must now take a somewhat closer look at the relevant facts of the matter.

It will be appropriate to ask ourselves, first of all, whether the difficulty in question might be inherent in *all* cases of the mediation of evidence. Certainly, it is furthest from anyone's mind that a judgment should attain to evidence by means of a reference to another judgment which itself lacks evidence. But though a judgment may remain inaccessible to the insight of the judging subject as long as he does not proceed beyond the judgment's object-material, isn't it often the case, at least under favorable circumstances, that such a judgment receives evidence [Evidenz] in "view" of another judgment that is evident [einleuchtend] to the subject? And doesn't this newly acquired evidence, apart from its origin, perfectly exhibit the character of insight obtained by the direct path? It is perhaps easiest to satisfy oneself that something of the sort really does happen by considering the theorems of geometry that are relatively easy to prove, but which may not become evident [einleuchten] in advance of the proof. For example, the intuitive[e] representation of a triangle does not by itself give precise enough information as to what the sum of the angles of a triangle is, or in particular, whether it is greater or less than 180°. Yet, the well-known construction that we use here permits us to see at a glance that the resulting trisected angle is a straight angle and that the three angles into which it divides are equal in size to the angles of the triangle.[14] And so in this case we really are dealing with a roundabout way that leads to insight. The inferred judgment is not evident in any other way than the premises are; the only thing that is different is the manner in which this evidence comes about—the foundation on which it is established.

Something quite similar can be found in the case of other judgments, ones which in other aspects of their epistemological character can exhibit the utmost dissimilarity to the examples just adduced. A person does not know which is the older, his friend X or his friend Y. He knows that X has completed his forty-seventh year; and now he learns from a reliable source that Y is just forty-six years old. With that, of course, he now also knows that Y is the younger; and the extent to which he can see or realize this, i.e., the evidence of it for him, is as great as one would normally ever want for such matters of fact. The same situation that emerged in the a priori domain of knowledge now emerges in a domain that is wholly or at least partly empirical: Mediated evidence is different from the unmediated only in its provenance, and for the rest, the one is as much evidence as the other. At the same time, this situation agrees so naturally with the contrast expressed in the terms "mediate" and "immediate" that it is hard not to suppose that we have found the genuine paradigm-case for all mediation of evidence.

Be that as it may, circumstances are not as a rule as favorable as in the examples just adduced. Even in daily life, not to mention science, proofs and the giving of reasons are for the most part much more complicated. On the one hand, the factor of complication shows up in the number of premises that have to be kept together, and on the other hand it shows up in the premises' constitution with respect to objects. Consequently, the inferring subject is for the most part not in a position to apprehend the premises with that intuitiveness that so often forms the indispensable prerequisite for immediate evidence. And even if someone can muster up enough conscientiousness, attentiveness, and time to judge all the premises one after another, with the evidence due them, he normally cannot keep hold of this diversity of judgments, not to say each of the judgments' evidence, up to the point where the conclusion is settled. Yet such a thing would have to be accomplished, since the "view" that is characteristic of the motivational relation can bear only on judgments present to the mind. Moreover, as mentioned, genuine evidence cannot be obtained from situations that are evidenceless or which are inferior in respect of their evidence, as it were. And so we have now reached the point where the conclusion's "mediate evidence," which makes its appearance despite these conditions, seems to confront our theoretical interest with the real problem about such evidence.

It may be, though, that the difficulty is easier to overcome than one might at first expect. First of all, we must be clear about what sort of evidential state the premises actually *can* be in, under the given circumstances. Suppose, therefore, that someone has to adduce a theorem of congruence in order to carry an argument through to its conclusion. Or just suppose that he has to make use of the theorem discussed above, the one concerning the sum of the angles in a triangle. In carrying out his argument, he cannot expressly go back into the reasoning behind the theorem. What about the evidence now? Will the judgment now be made in a wholly evidenceless manner? This doubtless can happen—but must it? And can it be affirmed, even for the majority of cases, that one who employs such premises in his deliberations stands in the same relation to these premises as he would if they were just opinions pulled quite arbitrarily out of the air? One who constructs or calculates will certainly employ many mathematical formulas and theorems of whose proof he is not thinking, perhaps even many whose proof he would not be capable of furnishing right away; but he will not employ a single one he does not believe to be correct. But how does he come by this opinion? Usually, I should think, through the fact that he *recalls* once having gone over the proof of the correctness of the theorem or formula. But if such is the case, then can one in all strictness maintain that as he now judges in accordance with that theorem or formula, his judgment does not have *any* evidence? The a priori evidence that constitutes the peculiar advantage of mathematical cognition over the rest of knowledge—this admittedly has been lost. But is the recollection of having gained insight into this or that theorem, or indeed even of having been justifiably convinced of its correctness, poorer than the recollection of an experiment, a recollection that one confidently takes as a basis for the induction of some lawlike regularity? Or is it poorer than the recollection of an encounter with this or that personage, which in everyday life is confidently taken as the starting point for certain practical entailments? So as certain as it is that memory has its own share in evidence,[15] just as certain is it that the formulas and theorems employed without accompanying consideration of their derivation are themselves not matters of evidenceless judgment. It is just that there is an evidence of lower epistemic standing in place of an evidence of higher standing. Something could have been judged with evidence appropriate to certainty; now it can only put in its appearance with evidence appropriate to uncertainty, even though the uncertainty may be one of those that are confidently taken as certainties in the practical business of knowing and acting.

For the rest, the premises in question by no means always have to be of an a priori nature. In thinking things over, a person may rely on generalizations from experiences of which he has no individual recollection. This can easily happen in the course of considerations pertaining to the domain of theoretical mechanics or some other chapter of physics—or in considerations from any other given scientific or extrascientific domain of facts, for that matter. It may indeed be that it is an original right of ours to make various judgments of an inductive character without any express recollection of the instances from which they have been drawn. But even disregarding that, once a person has inductively inferred something in accordance with all the rules, he can make use of the inductive results on another occasion, when he recollects that he established this or that. Entering into consideration along with this is the confidence in what others have established, the recollection that one had good reason for such confidence, and various other things. Among these other things, perhaps we would find the various kinds of surmise-evidence. These, like the various kinds of memory, have yet to win through to recognition in epistemology. However, the detailed discussion of them at the present place would take us beyond our proper limits. From what has been set forth so far, probably only this much can now be asserted with any claim to general validity: If someone, on whatever circumstantial grounds, does not make a judgment with full evidence—or more precisely, with the highest-standing evidence that he or the judgment would be capable of—he will still not normally and conscientiously make the judgment without any evidence at all. Thus, while a loss of evidence is suffered, it is not like a total annihilation; rather, it is merely a sort of reduction in evidence, with an evidence of lower epistemic standing taking the place of an evidence of higher standing.

From this it results that the difficulty supposedly consisting in the *conclusio* having an evidence the premises wholly or partly lacked is only a seeming difficulty. Even under the unfavorable circumstances that we considered in broaching this matter, the premises normally do not wholly lose their evidence; rather, this evidence merely undergoes a reduction. In view of these premises, one can confidently grant the *conclusio* an evidence that is not of higher standing than their reduced evidence. The only remaining possibility, then, would be that under certain circumstances the *conclusio* could be found by experience to have too high a degree of evidence in relation to the premises. But there is no danger of that at all; this is already indicated by the oft-cited fact that as a rule one cannot be quite as sure of what has been proved as he is of the grounds of the proof. At bottom this is nothing essentially different from what is manifest in the previously mentioned hostility of Schopenhauer to the Euclidean conduct of geometry. Here, of course, we disregard the fact that the blade of this hostility is really directed against the advantages in exactness of precision-objects[16] and of the conceptual thinking directed at them, advantages that Schopenhauer did not sufficiently appreciate.

Our comments on inferences from a priori premises have shown that on the occasion of a reduction of evidence there is apt to be a transformation of the epistemological character of the judgment in question. Or more precisely, it has been shown that something that would by nature be capable of being known a priori now strictly speaking only shows up as a posteriori knowledge. This too is in accord with experience, insofar as by "insight" one customarily means a priori insight in particular, i.e., the insight that is obtained from the nature of the objects—or in other words, that which has the advantage of being insight with understanding.[17] A person who does mean this is then of course apt to find an inference from apparent a priori premises devoid of that "insight" that he customarily looks for under this name; and to that extent he will agree in his own way, not unjustifiably, with a reproach to the effect that some of the Euclidean proofs produce conviction but no insight.

But now, what if the inferring subject, contrary to the supposition made above, introduces his premises entirely without evidence—in which case, of course, true ones as well as false ones can slip in? And what if only correct ones are employed, and in that way a useful *conclusio* is reached? In this case, of course, the element of usefulness will not alter the fact that the *conclusio* is as surely lacking in evidence in any genuine sense as the relevant premises are. It is true, as we shall soon see,[18] that such situations by no means have to forego all share in evidence on that account; but in principle they still shouldn't be incorporated in the problem of mediate evidence, since they do not present us with any sort of evidence in the ordinary sense, immediate or mediate.

All that remains to be taken into consideration now is the second of the points mentioned above, the great number of things that may have to be united in one thought. One can see right away that this circumstance no longer stands to alter anything important in the interpretation of the mediation of evidence that we have made good on other points. Actually, it now seems necessary to take just two more things into account. For one thing, the capacity of normal intelligence in this regard oughtn't to be given too little credit. For another, it will have to be taken into consideration that aids of the most diverse sorts partly reduce and partly lighten the work of thinking. Such aids include symbols, formulas, and operations on same; they include auxiliary and mediating notions which on occasion enable us to at least indirectly bring in judgments that no longer have been able to remain present to the mind. An inference of the form "A is B, B is C, C is D..., M is N; hence A is N" might represent an example of the simplest sort; here certainly not all of the premises can remain present to the mind at the same time. As long as the subject in this case keeps the object A well enough in mind to know at every step that the newly supervening predicate must also hold of A, then from this together with the judgment of memory as to the origin of what has thus far been obtained, a judgment which is in its own way evident, there certainly results a new evidence. Admittedly, this is again an evidence that stands epistemically lower than that of the premises, perhaps also lower than that which one may subsequently be able to obtain by means of reflection on the rank of the premises and their relation to the *conclusio*; but in the end it is still just another instance of evidence. Naturally, it might take us beyond our proper limits, were the attempt made here to look into the multiplicity of relevant facts, though we might add that their preciser determination could set a wealth of worthwhile tasks for the psychology of knowing. For the immediate purposes of the present investigation, what has been set forth probably suffices to substantiate our general thesis. This is that mediate evidence actually differs from immediate evidence only by its origin, but that it will as a rule carry traces of this provenance in the form of a loss of epistemic standing as compared with some, many, or all the premises. But what has just been spoken of as a characteristic origin consists primarily in nothing more than the relation between the motive and the motivated. It is the judging "in view" of a conviction already given, in the form in which we first encountered it in the case of evidenceless judgments and in which it can be simply carried over into the case of the judging and inferring which are equipped with evidence.

§29

Evidence from Premises Judged Without Evidence

In the foregoing, we have crossed over from the mediation of conviction to the special case of the mediation of evident conviction by means of evident premises. But as everyday experience tells us, it is by no means necessary that evidence should belong also to the motivating judgments, if the mediation of conviction is to put in an appearance. The most erroneous or at least groundless opinions notoriously can function as premises. Naturally, it is still precluded that a motivated judgment as such[19] should have a higher epistemic standing than its motives, and for that reason it is also obvious that a *conclusio* drawn from evidenceless premises cannot, as such, have any sort of evidence in the ordinary sense. It must appear all the more remarkable that normally there does already inhere in every motivated judgment—or in other words, every judgment made in view of other judgments—something that one cannot, even on the basis of direct observation, deny a certain similarity to evidence. Of even greater weight, perhaps, is the proof of this similarity that human thought in distant and recent times has produced so frequently and so much against its will, in confusing merely mediated convictions with evident judgments and letting the derivation of a judgment from other ones stand as a proof of that judgment. Too, we have often enough marveled at how easily the thirst for the why can be satisfied by the first good "because," when it's just a "because"— i.e., something that does its duty as a judgmental motive. In the last analysis this would be incomprehensible, if the one who judges "in view of" other things were not as a rule already somewhat in the mood for evidence, whether or not evidence belongs to the motives. But if as a rule one is so disposed, it is only as a rule. Just as there are judgments without evidence in the customary sense of the word, so too, we must not fail to recognize, there are cases of judgmental motivation without the evidencelike factor just mentioned, though these cases are presumably much scarcer. If, say, someone takes it into his head to conclude affirmatively in the second figure or universally in the third figure, then we will admit that he probably also judges "in view of" the premises; yet we shall scarcely be able to grant any sort of share in evidence to this motivated judgment.

Given what was just said to be the rule, now comes the question as to what we really have here in this evidencelike factor. Do we have a right to speak simply of evidence in this case, and to broaden the concept of evidence accordingly? In the first edition of this book,[20] rather than actually answering the question myself, I was content to expose the question to the possibility of a more detailed investigation, and I coined the provisional term "relative evidence." From the practical standpoint, this term seemed to gain some recommendation for itself from the fact that under favorable circumstances "relative evidence" appears together with evidence in the ordinary sense—or just plain evidence, if you will—and that it then seems to serve as a sort of prerequisite of the latter. From the theoretical standpoint, however, this fact might raise the question as to whether the evidencelike quality mightn't ultimately be just an appearance that is created by our dealing with conclusions which, for their own part, stand in the suggested close relation to evidence in the strict sense. This interpretation is somewhat reminiscent of approaches that have readily been termed "empiricist" in psychology. It would not be the first time, if the "empiricist" thing did not come close to qualifying as the eminently empirical thing, i.e., the thing that is in conformity with experience. At any event, the testimony of inward perception does not for the present seem to be exactly favorable to such an interpretation.

However, perhaps we shall be able to attain to some clarity in these matters if we turn away from the undeniably rather strange case at hand, where evidence results from evidenceless judgments, to some cases which are in a certain sense even harder to accept. These are cases in which evidence, besides not being traceable back to evidence, is not even traceable back to judgment. Here it will become immediately apparent that the provisionally formulated concept of "relative evidence" can be replaced by a concept that does better justice to the facts.

§30
Evidence from Unjudged Premises

For the rest, the matters involved here are quite ordinary ones. Even at the beginning of this chapter, we had occasion to mention the fact that the doctrine of inference is customarily worked out in a way that is in the first instance formalistic, in that practically nothing appears of any attention to the concrete experiences of the person who infers. One's primary interest is merely in what the premises and conclusion stand for objectively—which is incidentally very indicative as to the way in which the tenor of the theory of objects naturally predominates in the doctrine of inference—and one is interested in matters apart from objects only so far as these matters have to do with the requirement of evidence. But this evidence is far from being dependent on the evidence of the premises or the *conclusio,* or indeed even on their holding true; it has such an independent position in this regard that we have long been accustomed to deal with the "formal correctness" of an inference quite without regard to the "material truth" of the judgments making their appearance therein. Indeed, in identifying the regularities that are associated with inferring, it is apparently not considered at all important to operate with what is really judged, as premises and conclusions. In feigned judgments, one can gain insight into everything requisite; and unless one is somehow quite convinced of the "material" falsehood of these judgments, their correctness can be left *in suspenso* without any ensuing difficulties. And without doubt these facts deserve the attention of anyone who wants to attain to sufficient clarity about the mediation of judgment and evidence. But if one looks at them in light of the real object of the present remarks, these facts appear as the immediate reason why a sort of digression into the question of mediate evidence had to be undertaken in the foregoing. It is hoped it will turn out presently that such a digression was indispensable to the acquisition of a relatively secure foundation for the following. But it is hoped, too, it will turn out that the following itself has a claim to a place in an investigation concerning "assumptions."

And so what happens when, to follow the more concise and less exact way of speaking, I infer a conclusion from some premises and my conviction with regard to both, i.e., the conclusion quite as much as the premises, is left *in suspenso*—unless I am somehow convinced that neither the conclusion nor its presuppositions hold true? It seems clear that there isn't actually any inferring. But as to the evidence which is undoubtedly present here, one might try to relate that to a judgment concerning a certain inferential state of affairs, a state of affairs that has proven its importance in actual inferring and which receives attention in the present case only out of regard for the possibility of a future actual inferring. Or more precisely: We find certain *prima facie* points of agreement in inferences, actual inferences, of course; we distinguish them as "form," something that can be filled out with any given matter, meaning thereby merely that if the premises held true one would be justified in asserting the conclusion. Accordingly, in the quasi-inference presently under consideration there would really be nothing at all to see or realize [einzusehen] except that this quasi-inference exhibits a "form" that has in fact already proven itself in successful inferential operations, i.e., ones leading to instances of insight [Einsichten]. Of course, it really is beyond doubt that our knowledge about "forms of thought" arises in the first instance out of our experiences in living thought. But in order to see or realize the validity of the mood Barbara or Celarent, are we really dependent on induction from a series of conclusions drawn from experiments or at least taken from memory? Concerning this, I cannot doubt for a moment that for the securing of all the evidence that is necessary in this case, indeed the evidence that is in the first instance characteristic of this case, the quasi-inference suffices all by itself, even if its components do not hold true or are undecided. If that is so, then it proves that the "correct form" must have some significance other than the one we just tentatively considered.

Recourse to the previously mentioned ["Schlussgesetz" =] universal-hypothetical major regulating the inference might promise better results in this connection. Actually, the whole theory of inference has hitherto been much inclined to dwell upon this "law" ["Gesetz"], and for that matter, direct experience informs us that behind such a "law" there lies a state of affairs that is accessible to evidence in a particularly striking manner. In view of what has been said, of course, there can no longer be any thought of looking for the nature of an "actual" inference in the *Schlussgesetz*; but that isn't at all what we are now considering. Rather, the present question is whether the insight into the "formal correctness" of an inferential operation cannot at least be described as the evidence of a hypothetical judgment.

It is considered obvious—how justly, we want to try to determine further on[21]—that what is really affirmed in a hypothetical judgment is to be sought neither in the antecedent nor in the consequent, but in what lies in between the two, so to speak, i.e., the relation which brings them together. More precisely, it is manifest that a connection is being affirmed—but a connection between what sort of parts? In the special case at hand, this question has an obvious answer, although it might remain to be seen just how far this answer admits of extension to the whole domain of hypothetical judgments. To wit, one can suppose the following: that the things between which the connection is claimed are the premises on the one side and the *conclusio* on the other—judgments, then—and that in the cases of suspended or even contrary conviction with which we are mainly concerned just now, these judgments are not made but just represented.[22] Thus, I represent to myself that I judge the premises,f and I then arrive at the evidence that these judgments are compatible only with a third judgment, the one given in the *conclusio*—or in other words, that if the former hold, the latter also must, or however else one may care to express it.

However, I do not think that I need to go further into the determining remarks that this interpretation will bear in its specifics; since even without regard to these finishing touches, the untenability of the main idea is sufficiently clear when one compares it with experience. For experience shows us clearly that in seeing or realizing the validity of the oft-cited mood Barbara, say, I think of neither myself nor my judging, but merely of the subjects and predicates in question and what concerns them. Hence, it is a wholly unempirical and therefore unserviceable expedient, in the case of the mere apprehending of the forms of inference, to assign to *represented* judging the role which, in actual inference, falls to *actual* judging.

Here I have returned to possibilities whose consideration might have already been rendered superfluous by the investigations in the earlier chapters of this book; I have done so primarily in order that I might thereby expressly oppose my own older theses. Once one has learned to pay attention to the objective, one can always tell just by the look of a hypothetical judgment, as it were, that it is concerned with the objectives that come into play in the signification of the antecedent and the consequent, respectively. With this we have arrived at a point where the investigation into assumptions may be allowed to dwell upon a type of thing that is important for the emergence of assumptions, quite without regard for the questions concerning us at the moment. It is true that the antecedent objective and the consequent objective,[g] as we can both briefly and intelligibly put it, are each of them always treated in logic as a sort of judgment, one whose "quality" and "quantity" are allowed to be variable, for instance, just as in any other judgment. But as is so often the case, "judgment" here means nothing more than "objective," strictly speaking. For there is actually no question at all of believing the antecedent, or the antecedent and the consequent, at least not as a matter of necessity. And according to our oft-tested principle, an objective that is apprehended and not judged must be an assumed one. We can therefore say quite generally that on the above suppositions, what we have in the antecedent and consequent of the hypothetical judgment is the expression of assumptions.

If we now reapproach inferences with suspended premises from this angle, at first it does not appear unfavorable to a definition of such inferences as hypothetical judgments. For it is obvious that suspended premises too, which must themselves be objectives, by supposition cannot be judged and that these premises therefore can only be assumed. However, the hypothetical judgment and the inference with suspended premises no longer appear to coincide, when one asks what relation between the antecedent objective and the consequent objective is claimed in the judgment and when one then looks into this relation in the case of the inferences presently under consideration. The relation by which the hypothetical judgment is governed, as it were, can be quite superficially but clearly enough characterized as an if-relation, as far as there is a desire to prejudge this relation as little as possible in regard to its nature. The person inferring—and this seems an indisputable fact of experience—normally does not think of this if-relation at all. And if he should think of it, this thinking does not constitute the inferring—no more so than thinking of a since-relation constitutes the inferring in the case of ordinary inference, i.e., inference from believed premises.

What the recourse to the hypothetical judgment (in its traditional interpretation) is thus unable to accomplish—this might appear to be obtainable by a consideration of the aforesaid assumptive character of suspended premises, together with the question as to whether this character also has to be assigned to the conclusion, as may seem obvious at first sight. This question is suggested by a very striking peculiarity of linguistic expression. To wit, in order to express such an inference, one might begin thus: "Let A be B, and further let B be C." In these subjunctives,[h] it becomes especially obvious that we are dealing with assumptions. But now, one can hardly continue, "Therefore, let A also be C." Only the indicative "therefore A is C"—or better, "then A is C" —appears natural here.[23] Thus, language does not allow us to treat the conclusion the same way as the premises. What this indicative seems to call to our attention is just this: The conclusion in the inference from suspended premises could not, after all, itself be suspended. It couldn't merely be assumed; it had to be judged?

Admittedly, at first glance this looks like sheer absurdity. If I expressly leave it undecided as to whether A is B and B is C, how am I supposed to then be able to maintain something about A and C? But in using the aforementioned indicative mood, we have such a feeling of confidence that one may well ask whether the expression "then A is C" mightn't be understandable in some such way that a judgment could be looked upon as well-justified. There is such an interpretation, as a matter of fact, and it has been broached fairly often in the theoretical treatment of the syllogism. If, for the sake of simplicity, we stick to the formal paradigm that is already in use here, the one for the mood Barbara, then we can of course speak as follows. There is by no means any lack of an object A to which the predicate C can be justifiably accorded. This object is the A which has the predicate B—and not simply the predicate B, but the B to which the predicate C belongs.[24] Of A, thus determined, C can be confidently predicated. There can be no guarantee, of course, that this A exists, or even that it subsists; but this is in thorough conformity with the epistemic situation befitting the fact of suspended premises, i.e., objectives that are merely assumed and not believed. The conclusion holds in the limited sense just specified, on the supposition that the objects constituting its material are independent of existence and possibly even of subsistence. This accords quite well with the premise-objectives' independence of subsistence, which was supposed in order for these objectives to be brought into the sphere of consideration of the person making the inference.

What has been stated here in the mood Barbara could of course be set forth *mutatis mutandis* in any other mood of categorical inference, likewise in forms of inference lying beyond the range of these moods. Cases of this latter sort can be illustrated by means of the *modus ponendo ponens* of hypothetical inference, which for our purposes could be brought into a formal schema like the following. "Grant that this relation hold: if A is, then B is. Further, grant that A be. Then B is." In this case, one might say the following: If A is, then the B that is if A is—this B is, too. Here, however, the place of the resulting categorical judgment in the preceding formal example is taken by a hypothetical judgment, one that cannot be eliminated, as far as I can see. It is also very distinctly noticeable here that the evidence of such a judgment originates in its tautological nature.

But in this very same tautology, which is so clearly reminiscent of the "analytical judgment" in the strict Kantian sense, we can see the element of likeness with the preceding case: the determining limitation of B is again what is essential for the judgment in question to hold true. And here, as in the former case, the judgment takes place "in view" of something that is not judged but assumed. But both these cases differ essentially from what we met with above under the name of "view," in connection with mediate judgmental evidence; for in the two present cases, what is "viewed" shows up incorporated in the material of the judgment. Only in appearance, then, does the "view" extend beyond the judgment; the latter is in truth an a priori judgment of a quite ordinary nature. It has no premises at all, in the strict sense. A closer look shows that the assumptions preceding the judgment do not really serve for the apprehending of premises. Rather, they ready the a priori judgment; in a certain way, they fasten upon its objects and submit them to judgment. In the course of later investigations we shall come to recognize an essential function of assumptions in the way that they do this.[25]

In the objective of this judgment, then, we always have a *conclusion* that has been so far restricted as to have an exclusively formal meaning. This judgment necessarily holds true when the above-mentioned hypothetical judgment holds true, and conversely. After what has been discussed, this fact is just an obvious as the fact that the two judgments are fundamentally different—which is placed beyond doubt by considering the objectives that are judged in each case. But then can we look upon this latest judgment as being the essential thing in an inferential operation that merely develops the formal aspect—and therefore also look upon the evidence of this judgment as being the peculiar evidence which under favorable circumstances goes with the "inference from suspended premises"?

Not even this is the case; the reason is simply that in the inference from suspended premises it is not the restricted conclusion but the full one that shows up. What we get is not that A with certain determining qualifications is C, but simply that A is C. That this result shows up bound to certain conditions, e.g., with respect to B—this is an essentially different notion, however closely correlated with the aforementioned restriction this conditioning may be, as regards its holding true.

We may therefore sum up the matter simply: In the inferences with which we are concerned—the inferences from premises that are not judged and which are therefore merely assumed—the movement is neither towards the [Schlussgesetz =] universal-hypothetical major regulating the inference nor to the restricted conclusion, whether categorical or hypothetical, Instead—as we may add, changing from negation to affirmation—the movement is to the full conclusion, but as assumed rather than judged. The analogy to inferences in the strict sense, inferences from judged premises, is obvious: As the latter lead from the judging of the premises to the judging of the conclusion, so the inferences with which we are concerned lead from the assuming of the premises to the assuming of the conclusion. In view of this finding, which is certainly quite plausible in itself, one can only ask the following. Since we were able to maintain, on the basis of such easily accessible experiences, that something like evidence attaches even to inferences from assumed premises, what are we to make of the fact? As far as I can see, in the presence of this fact as well as in light of the failure of our attempts to identify any judgments as the prerequisite bearers of this evidence, the only lesson that can be learned is that assumptions, too, can have evidence, not just judgments. The analogy to ordinary inferences then becomes an even more radical one: It is clear that in both cases of inferences we must be dealing with the evidence "in view of" that we met with above in so-called mediate evidence. True, it will not strike everyone as an unobjectionable consequence, that not only judgments, but assumptions, too, can be evident. And perhaps the same is true of the consequence that assumption-evidence partakes of the nature of mediate evidence, when no cases of immediate evidence in assumptions seem to be empirically ascertainable. It will be better, nevertheless, to return to these matters in another connection.[26]

Even now, however, it would be best if we pointed out a problem that might come closer to solution, given that there are assumptions which are evident in the way just indicated. This is a problem about evidence that we came across in connection with inferences from premises judged without evidence.[27] We found a certain insightfulness in such inferences. It stands in somewhat surprising contrast to the lack of evidence in the premises; actually more surprising is the contrast with the lack of evidence in the *conclusio,* which in the last analysis is always an obvious and quite natural lack. Yet it hardly serves to advance our comprehension of the facts to any considerable extent when we say, in line with the first edition of this book, that this *conclusio* lacks absolute evidence but does in return have a relative evidence of its own. On the other hand, it is a fact that we have met with evidence even in the case of assumptions —namely an evidence "in view of" assumptions, when one would be unable to give any reason whatsoever for according the latter any advantage of evidence. So it might not be amiss to conjecture as follows: What at first presented itself to us as a kind of judgment-evidence from judgments without evidence must be viewed as an assumption-evidence accompanying a conclusion-judgment that is in itself without evidence. It must be admitted that this would hold true only on the basis of a supposition that we shall likewise have to return to, further on,[28] and which can nowise be regarded as obvious, considering the present state of our knowledge. This is the supposition that every judgment involves, *a poteriori* as it were, an assumption of the same objective, somewhat in the way that a shorter straight line is contained in a longer one—in a word, the way that the part is contained in the whole. Then, of course, to go with an experience that was without evidence as a judgment, there could still very well be an evidence that concerned just the assumption contained in the judgment. From this point of view, a special concept of "relative evidence" in the case of judgments becomes superfluous; however, it could keep on in its previous role of fixing a problem, so far as the view just set forth still might not have done justice to the facts.

As to the main result of the investigations of the present, chapter, however, we can now formulate it in the following way. There are not only inferential operations that lead from judgments to judgments, but also ones that lead from assumptions to assumptions. The latter operations can appropriately be called assumption-inferences and opposed to the former taken as judgment-inferences. Assumption-inferences can quite well occur by themselves; but in addition, they are always implicit in judgment-inferences. This is clear from the fact that the "form" of assumption-inferences, too, can be viewed from the standpoint of correctness and incorrectness, or of evidence and nonevidence. Naturally, evident judgments are inferred only from evident premises. Yet despite the deficiency in evidence of judgments that are inferred from premises without evidence, these judgments, too, exhibit a share in evidence. It coincides with the evidence of the assumptions that are implicit in these judgments, and it is so little dependent on the premises being judged, that this share in evidence can also occur without any judging at all, just as soon as the relevant premises are apprehended by means of assumptions.

The solution to our problem which I have presented here seems to me to have no mean advantage in the fact that, in this solution, the affinity of inferences in the loose sense with inferences in the strict sense is preserved in the point which is essential to inferring, notwithstanding the differentness of the situation, on the one side and on the other. On the present suppositions, one can well understand why the operation with which we are now concerned, an operation on suspended or even rejected premises, is straightway called "inferring" ["Schliessen"] even though there is no conclusion [Schluss] at all here, in the customary sense—and in that sense no concluding being done [geschlossen]. The latitude of this usage would be incomprehensible if there were as much of a difference between such apprehending of the "pure form" and inferring as that which we have to recognize between the making of a relational judgment and the obtaining of evidence for a judgment from other judgments. However, the obtaining of the evidence for an assumption from other assumptions is a process constituted quite analogously to that of inferring in the strict sense; hence, given this analogy, it is quite understandable that the differences, in themselves certainly not inconsiderable, should recede into the background, thus enabling the use of the word "inferring."

§31

The Nature of Hypothetical Judgment

The investigations of the preceding sections have led us repeatedly onto the subject of what is customarily called a hypothetical judgment, in the tradition of logic. It seems to me that we are required to go expressly into the nature of such judgments at this point, for one thing by the fact that there is a quite characteristic role for assumptions here, too. For another thing, in the first edition of this book I attempted to formulate this role in such a way that hypothetical judgments would themselves be nothing but assumption-inferences. That would be roughly the counterpart to the attempt, combated above, to make an inference into a sort of hypothetical judgment. So this seems to me to be the correct place to yield expressly to the opposition that my thesis has encountered and to concede that this opposition is warranted. But in addition, it seems to be the correct place to set forth why, nevertheless, I do not think I can fall back on one of the interpretations of the hypothetical judgment which have prevailed up till now.

Supposing, then, that someone utters the sentence, "If a perpendicular is dropped from the apex of an isosceles triangle to its base, the latter will be bisected," what would normally be occurring in the speaker's mind? In particular, let us first of all ask whether anything is to be seen of a judgment concerning a connection. If one approaches the facts from the standpoint of this question, then whatever else may be the case, it seems beyond question that these facts enable us to observe surprisingly little of any thought of a connection or kindred relation. Here and there such a thought may quite well play a part, I admit; but should that entitle one to characterize the complete experience that is expressed in the hypothetical period as the judgment as to a connection? And here we may go still further and ask: Does the locution "If... then..." really even have the task of expressing a judgment? It would actually be rather strange if for that task one used a sentence-complex of the form "If A is, then B is," where in the first instance the antecedent and the consequent, considered by themselves, function in the same way that sentences normally do, but the judgment as to a connection did not figure in any sentence of its own, nor did the relation of connection, ostensibly the most important thing, figure in any subject-word or predicate-word.

This consideration is confirmed by the fact that if the "If... then..." locution were at all suited to express a judgment, then most strangely this judgment could only be an affirmative one. For there are no negative hypothetical judgments. The fact that the antecedent and the consequent each can be negative has nothing to do with this question, of course. We are far more likely to feel tempted to claim the status of counter-instance for assertions like the following: "If the sun is shining, it need not on that account be hot" or "... does not have to be hot," etc. Even clearer than this example, in which one might not always be sure about the conditional relation between what is meant by the antecedent and the consequent, would be an affirmation such as, "If a quadrangle is equilateral, it still does not have to be a square." But on closer inspection, the consequent in such cases is seen not to deal with heat or squares, but primarily with having to be [Müssen].[29] Hence, between the antecedent and the actual consequent the situation is quite the same as always. I admit, consideration is quite explicitly being given to the connection in this case, and I am not thinking of denying that under certain circumstances such a connection can quite well be affirmed or negated. But from the linguistic attire in which such affirmations or negations usually make their appearance it becomes only the more clear that what shows up expressed in hypothetical sentence form is never likely to be a judgment as to a connection.[30]

One might get better results, if one tried to orient oneself by an analogy with compound sentences that are constructed much as the hypothetical ones are and which are in other ways closely related to the hypothetical. "Where there is much freedom, there is also much error." "As soon as [sobald] it begins to get dark, the gas lamps will be lit." In the latter example, the *sobald* could be replaced with the word *wenn* in the purely temporal sense, the word that one occasionally still attempts to treat specifically as *wann* in opposition to the conditional *wenn*—with the attempt fairly often leading to a rather distinct awareness of how difficult it is to separate the one *wenn* from the other in individual cases. Well, what is signified by such a construction, one with local or temporal conjunctions? If I say something like "Where *A* is, there *B* is," that may very well express a judgment. But is it a judgment that stands next to or, as it were, behind the two sentences, "*A* is" and "*B* is," at most apprehending their objectives in a special relation? Plainly not at all. In the first instance, the expression of judgment lies simply in the consequent, and the antecedent merely furnishes another determination for the material of the consequent. Our compound formal sentence simply asserts something about where *B* is, in that *B*'s place is made more precise by means of the place of *A*. Which is to say, *B* is in the same place as *A*. A temporal example could be handled in quite the same way, of course. Mightn't we be able to learn something from these examples for the case of conditional constructions?

First of all, let us go back again to the example of the isosceles triangle. We want to observe that this example, too, can be expressed in a form other than the hypothetical without undue alteration of the sense. One need only say something such as that the base of an isosceles triangle is bisected by a perpendicular dropped from the apex. If there has really not been any substantial alteration of sense here, then even as it stands our hypothetical judgment does not deal with a connection or a dependency between the antecedent objective and the consequent objective but with the bisection of the base of an isosceles triangle. Thus, the objective of the consequent is judged with a certain limitation that is more precisely determined in the antecedent. As we see, this is quite analogous to the result obtained in the case of temporal and local clauses. And what is judged is very much the same sort of thing as the restricted conclusions treated above in the case of purely formal inferences.[31] This latter correspondence is obviously not an accidental one; since after all, every formally valid inference—and so in the first instance, as we ascertained, every assumption-inference—can also be expressed as a hypothetical judgment. If I say, hypothetically, "If all human beings have their weaknesses, then even Goethe was not free of weaknesses," it is surely obvious that there is at the same time an inference *ad subalternatum* with suspended *subalternans* here, and through this inference the justification for judging the restricted conclusion is straight-way guaranteed. That leads one to suspect that what is judged in the hypothetical judgment is the consequent restricted by the antecedent. This is undoubtedly more in accord with the way that the hypothetical judgment looks to the uninitiated than is the interpretation of this judgment as the judgment as to a connection. And then too, this latter interpretation seems hard to reconcile with direct experience, especially in that it involves treating both the antecedent and the consequent in the same way, as the *fundamenta* of a relation of connection. And if I understand correctly, the thesis of the restricted consequent has quite recently found another theoretical representative.[32]

This interpretation of the hypothetical judgment, which today seems to me to be the one that affords the most natural adjustment to the facts,[33] in some cases has linguistic expression standing in *prima facie* opposition to it. It might be opportune to comment specially on this here, if only because in the foregoing it was linguistic expression which, in the instance of the applicability of the indicative mood in the expression of conclusions, first called our attention to restricted propositions [Sätze].[i] If we stop again for a moment with inference, we find that the indicative fails to work as soon as inferring from suspended premises passes over into something that is harder to take, as it were. This is the case of (formally correct) inference from false premises—that is, from premises taken to be false by the person who is inferring. Here inference encounters no obstacle in the fact that the person inferring also takes the conclusion yielded in this way to be false. Every indirect proof affords a relevant illustration of this sort of inference. In such proofs, the subjunctive can again be used in connection with the premises: "Supposing that A were B, and supposing further that B were C." But it cannot continue, "then A *is* also C," but only "then A *would* also be C," although the restricted conclusion doubtless still holds and, hence, could always gain expression by means of a sentence in the indicative. All that is easily enough translated into the language of the hypothetical judgment, of course. It is likewise easy to think of things that are not immediately amenable to the form of an inference. Thus, in the poem, the little tree says that if it "could wish as it chose" it "would wish for leaves of purest gold" and do such and such—here we find a uniform use of the subjunctive throughout, the mood that we have long known to be the sign of an assumption. Ought we to go on speaking of the judgment of the restricted consequent-objective, in this case? A demonstration of the restricted-consequent thesis on the basis of the subjunctive is naturally out of the question. It will be enough if one can show that the subjunctive does not in every way rule out a judgment. And this seems possible for me to accomplish. It is true that in considering a triangle of unequal sides I can say quite correctly, "An isosceles triangle would have the angles at the base equal"; but I am far from merely assuming the equality of angles in the case of the isosceles triangle. Here the subjunctive and with it the assumption bear just on the actuality of the equal angles, and we shall be well justified if we interpret the subjunctive in the consequent of hypothetical judgments in the same way.

However, it might be that another difficulty cannot be completely cleared away to everybody's satisfaction. It concerns the case already cited above, seemingly the simplest, which is represented formally by the expression "If [wenn] A is, then B is," understanding this expression not temporally, but conditionally. Here the impression is as if the very simplicity of this situation entails that there can be no working point for an appropriate restriction of the consequent. With a somewhat more definite example, the matter immediately appears more favorable, even with as colorless an example as the favorite one of the grammar teachers: "If there are gods, then there are also works of the gods."[34] This we can reformulate approximately so: Works of existing gods themselves exist. Still, these same existential sentences seem to present an insurmountable obstacle. All restricted conclusions and consequents are to be taken independently of existence;[35] this must already be obvious. Yet how can an existential sentence hold true independently of existence? Perhaps Franz Brentano's transformation of sentences into negative form, which Anton Marty[36] has so insistently held up to my eyes, promises a way out. One actually could with justice say, "A does not exist without B" in the example, "There are no gods without works." Above,[37] I have already set this controversy aside for another occasion, and I cannot enter any further into what is relevant to it. Yet I think I shall have to forego taking something as negative when it is so clearly affirmative as the examples in question. This is quite apart from the fact that such a transformation seems far more likely to result in a restricted antecedent than a restricted consequent. Moreover, one should not have to depend at all on such a relinquishment of affirmative quality; for, strange as it may seem, there really are existential affirmations that are independent of existence. As a matter of fact, these affirmations belong to a domain of judgments whose affinity for restricted propositions [Sätze] has already brought itself to our attention, namely the domain of analytic judgments. To use a paradigm that I have already employed elsewhere,[38] it is indisputable that an existing golden mountain (or even an existing round quadrangle) exists. And yet no golden mountain (or round quadrangle) exists. Thus, a proposition of the former sort holds true independently of existence. From there, we immediately come closer to our above hypothetical judgment-formula if we temporarily put B in the antecedent in the place of A, which gives us "If B exists, then B exists"; for a proposition like "An existing B exists" is hardly very different from this. And if I take A back into the antecedent, the tautological character disappears again; but aside from that, the situation stays the same as it was in the restriction-proposition "B, in the case of an existing A, itself exists." Here there can be no more objection to a determination that restricts by means of "in the case of" than to one that restricts by means of "without," as in the aforesaid "A without B does not exist." There is naturally as little against the existence of the works of existing gods as there is against that of the existing golden mountain, if in each case one takes "existence" in the special sense I indicated under the provisional heading of "existential predication."[39] I hope that in the meantime I have taken another step forwards in the clarification of this matter; yet the matter remains obscure enough that it would not seem incomprehensible, if someone were to stumble at the present explanation of the hypothetical judgment—an explanation that most likely couldn't be carried through consistently without the inclusion of this "existential predication." But for my own part, I should be at a loss for anything that was at all comparable to this interpretation, in respect of naturalness. And so I shall formulate it in this assertion: There really is a judgment present in the hypothetical judgment, and what is judged therein is the consequent restricted by the antecedent.

As one can see, the position thereby taken is one that fits into the group of interpretations of the hypothetical judgment that Benno Erdmann has called "consequent-theories."[40] All the same, I hope that in the foregoing the "consequent-theory" has been worked out into a form in which it is not exposed to Erdmann's objections. One point in particular has surely not been left out of consideration in the foregoing, namely that the hypothetical judgment can hold true when not just the antecedent, but also the consequent, fails to hold true.[41] This point makes no difference here, since what it accounts as the consequent of a hypothetical judgment is just the nonrestricted consequent, which can quite well be false, even when the restricted one is entirely correct. Yet, it cannot be denied that the consequent-theory is not adapted to a distinction between affirmative and negative hypothetical judgments.[42] But there is scarcely any harm in that, if I was justified above in my assertion[43] that such distinctions are no more present in the quality of hypothetical judgments than they are in the modality. Nevertheless, bringing in the standpoint of quality also serves to advance our present claims. For from this standpoint one may ask: If, as might be taken for self-evident on the basis of what has been said up to now, the hypothetical judgment is the restricted judgment of the consequent and nothing else, then why not at least call hypothetical judgments affirmative whenever this consequent is affirmative, and negative whenever it is negative? So our characterization of the hypothetical judgment must at least be an incomplete one, and we have to look around with a view to its proper completion.

It seems to me to be especially favorable to such a project, that one can easily pair off hypothetical and ordinary "categorical" sentences that say surprisingly similar things, despite their difference in form. It certainly makes no great difference whether I say something such as "A triangle that is equilateral is also equiangular" or I say "A triangle, if it is equilateral, is also equiangular." Benno Erdmann speaks here of "hybrids,"[44] but hardly with justice; certainly only the second of these two assertions is hypothetical. I do not want to neglect calling attention, incidentally, to how clearly this similarity speaks for a "consequent-theory" and to how difficult it would be to reconcile this similarity with a different interpretation, especially with the theory used as a point of departure above—the connection-theory, if we may call it that.

The main question, however, is now this: Can we specify the factor that distinguishes the second of these two very similar judgments from the first—and thus presumably constitutes or contains the characteristic element of the "hypothetical judgment"? Apparently it is essential that the determining restriction of the subject-concept "triangle," present in both cases, occur through a conditional clause in the second case, and not through a relative clause. What is the significance of this? It is apparent that not every determination suited for expression by means of a relative clause is also expressible by means of a conditional clause. Thus, one could say without hesitation, "A triangle that is inscribed in a circle and has equal sides also has equal angles"; whereas the assertion, "If a triangle is inscribed in a circle and has equal sides, it also has equal angles," would be noticeably less correct. And the reason for the latter situation is obviously that the circumscribed circle does not matter for the equality of angles, whereas equality of sides is precisely the property that makes the equality of angles credible to the one judging—indeed, accessible to his insight. The judging is done "in view of" this equality of sides,^{j} whether it be the relative or the conditional clause that is used in the linguistic expression; however, the conditional clause at the same time expresses what is viewed. It is by no means indispensable that on every occasion evidence should result from this "view," as it will in the present example, given a favorable instance; even evidenceless conviction is enough. Even less requisite, as it were, is the development of a special consciousness of the view by reflection on the operations essential to it. And just as little is an essential role played by an apprehending of the relation between the restricting objective of the antecedent and the restricted objective of the consequent, the objectives on the basis of which the view could lead to evidence.

So in general, we can say this: It is only in the case where a judgment is made "in view" of a restricting objective that we are dealing with a "hypothetical judgment"; but also, the term is used only in cases when there is an expression of this view, too, as well as the judgment itself. From that, we can now understand why there are no negative judgments among the "hypothetical judgments"—and strictly speaking, no affirmative ones, either. The "hypothetical judgment" as a whole is in fact not a judgment, but an operation that involves a judgment. This operation can take place or not take place, but it cannot take place now affirmatively and now negatively.

In consideration of what has been set forth, it is for the present certainly more correct to speak of a "hypothetical sentence [Satz]" or a "hypothetical period" in the grammatical sense than to speak in a psychological sense of a "hypothetical judgment." Yet in their use, the expressions "hypothetical proposition [Satz]" and "hypothetical judgment" have more or less outgrown the subjectivity of a linguistic expression and an experienced operation; the situation here is the same as in the case of "judgment" and "proposition" without further qualification, when these words have reference to objectives. How is this situation reconcilable with our remark about the grammatical sense? I can, after all, speak of true or false hypothetical judgments, no less correctly than I can say in particular, "It is true that if one ignites oxyhydrogen gas it explodes." And it is not as though it were a rare exception for someone to think something like that when he utters a sentence of the hypothetical form. In the use of a "hypothetical" sentence, it is no more one's intention to state something as to what is going on in one's mind than it is one's intention, in using a "categorical" sentence, to communicate what this sentence expresses, i.e., the judgment-experience with its more or less fine determinations. As here, so too in the former case: The signification is something far different from the experience that shows up expressed. What is more surprising is that in the hypothetical judgment there comes to light a signification that by no means coincides with the restricted consequent-objective under consideration in our above analysis. Thus, the investigation is now confronted with a two-fold problem, first to ascertain the type of this additional signification, and then to show the relationship in which it stands with the experiences described above.

So the question is first and foremost this: What is the thing that can be true or false here? Naturally, it can only be an objective; but how does this work out more precisely? Perhaps it is indicative of the nature of the situation that the answer to this question has to be pretty much the same as the answer we had available above,[45] where what we had to do was get acquainted with the objective of the categorical sentence or judgment. If someone says, "*A* is *B*," then the objective forming the signification of the sentence is really nothing except that *A* is *B*. And if someone says, "If *A* is *B*, then *C* is *D*," then here, too, the objective can be most naturally described by saying that it consists in this: that if *A* is *B*, then also *C* is *D*. However, if one cannot rest content with this somewhat tautological information, then the next thing will be to indicate the subsistence of the if-relation between the antecedent objective and the consequent objective as the real "sense" ["Sinn"] of the assertion in question; but perhaps not with the feeling that one has become fully versed in the matter. One may then try to establish an understanding of the nature of this if-relation by identifying it with the one objective's fittedness for restricting the other in an appropriate manner and, under favorable circumstances (which include, above all, the repeatedly mentioned "view") for making this other objective evident. But again it will be impossible to close one's eyes to the fact we already had occasion to mention above, that in the "making" of a hypothetical judgment there is under normal circumstances nothing observable in the way of explicit thoughts of the if-relation and absolutely nothing observable of a crystallization of these thoughts in the way just attempted.

And with that, we arrive at the second question. Under such circumstances, how does a "hypothetical judgment" come by its signification? We know[46] that signifying is always tied to an apprehending experience. No such apprehending experience was seen in the results of the above analysis of what primarily goes on in our minds in the case of a hypothetical judgment. Where are we to look for such an apprehending experience, then? I want to confess right away that I can give only a very inadequate answer to this question. This much appears to me to be certain to begin with: that one can experience the hypothetical judgment, an operation composed of assuming and judging, without going beyond the judging and assuming—and therefore, also without apprehending the signification in question. Next, it seems to me that this same operation serves also for the apprehending of its signification, just as soon as one employs it in the required way. As we shall still see,[47] not even a representation is sufficient all by itself for the apprehending of an objectum; even the representation needs to be correctly employed. The distinctive element in the situation with which we are presently concerned is this, however: Here a more complex operation seems to take the place of the representation, or actually (since it is now a question of an objective) the place of a judgment or assumption. We might seek another analogue for this operation in the domain of representation: the production of representations, along with its parallel on the side of objects, founding.[48] So far, we know the latter only as objectum-founding, i.e., as the founding *of* objecta *by* objecta. Mightn't there also be an objective-founding, the thought here being chiefly of just a founding *by* objectives? Or to put it more precisely, mightn't the above-described operation on the antecedent objective and the consequent objective be the producing activity that yields a new representational or conceptual entity, something apprehending a *superius* whose *inferiora* are objectives, as would be true in the case of a collective of objectives?

I should not mention such unfinished conceptions at all, if I dared not credit them with a future. But this would not be the place to dwell upon them; for the time being it must suffice if we characterize the situation in a manner as external and, by the same token, as free of theory as possible. To this end, maybe we can speak as follows. It is as if the above-described operation on the antecedent objective and the consequent objective were the very operation by which we apprehended the peculiar complex state of affairs whose *inferiora* are formed by these two objectives. I call this situation the "quasi-extroversion" of complex intellectual operations—a terminological choice whose provisional character is so obvious that what it reflects must certainly not be a theory, but just the need for theoretical elucidation. Nevertheless, this very makeshift permits one to bear in mind that it is not just in the operation of hypothetical judging that we meet with quasi-extroversion. The assumption-inference, too, signifies something that under favorable circumstances can be a truth. These favorable circumstances are what one calls the "formal correctness" of an inference. It can also be a judgment-inference, as far as that is concerned.

From a practical standpoint, the signification of the operation of inference is so close to that of the hypothetical judgment as to suggest the attempt to take the two as identical. Furthermore, the little saying about the person "that invented the If and the But" may remind us how signification—secondary signification, of course, in the sense defined above[49]—is attained not only by the if-operation, but also by the but-operation and likewise by many another operation that attains expression in a conjunction. The operations of agreeing to and rejecting something, operations that we express by means of "yes" and "no," have already been mentioned in this way, too.

Particularly in the area of the hypothetical judgment, our approach to a new interpretation comes in useful for the problem of the epistemic ground. What causes especial difficulty here is the subjective aspect that shows up even in the name, the reference to knowledge—a subjective aspect which is, however, combined with the sort of transcendence of the domain of mere subjectivity which allows one to simply call a given objective the epistemic ground of some other objective. The relation of epistemic ground to epistemic consequent can hardly differ very much from what we have hitherto been calling the "if-relation." But what was attempted above—the reduction of this relation to one objective's fittedness for restricting another and for motivating an evident judgment of [Urteilung] the restricted objective—certainly does not reproduce the notion of an epistemic ground.[k] Reflection on our experience is just as foreign to this notion as it is, say, to the notion of necessity. It is clear right away that such scruples disappear in connection with quasi-extroversion. What this enables one to apprehend is scarcely in the first instance a relation, but it is a complex of objectives which, being in this relation, permit the relation to be abstracted. It is also understandable that under such circumstances there is especial danger of slipping into an unduly subjective vein. The operation itself is naturally something experienced, and the words for it are in the first instance expressions of experiences. Now if there is another (secondary) signification for these experiences, in virtue of their quasi-extroversion, then it will not be cause for amazement if the nature of this latter signification threatens to be more or less obscured by the seeping in of experiential data.

Retrospectively, one realizes now that while the so-called hypothetical judgment is like a normal judgment in exhibiting two sides, an experiential side and a significative side, these sides are quite different from those of the normal judgment. The experiential side does not consist simply in a judgment; it is a more complex mental operation. Of course, there is a judgment present in this operation, namely the judgment of the restricted consequent. As for the significative side, there we find a peculiar complex of objectives, a complex that need not be apprehended by the person who "judges hypothetically," but can be—with the help of the operation constituting the hypothetical judgment. There is still lacking an analytical description of this apprehending experience; but it, too, naturally contains a judgment, and it is due to this judgment that one can so often feel oneself tempted to regard the hypothetical judgment itself as a judgment as to an if-relation. The fact that the operation of inference has a signification in like manner, and as a matter of fact has a closely related signification,[50] has afforded the main reason for seeing the inference itself as consisting in the apprehending of the [Schlussgesetz =] universal-hypothetical major regulating the inference.

But as concerns the apprehending of the if-relation, it has resulted above all that what is really judgment in the "hypothetical judgment" is not in the first instance focused on this relation and that one can therefore judge hypothetically without making a judgment as to the connection of the antecedent objective and the consequent objective. No doubt the operation constituting the "hypothetical judgment" can help apprehend the if-relation in a somewhat more mediate manner, via "quasi-extroversion." But then this is still a quite different way than it would be if, for the apprehending of this relation, one took the roundabout way of "reflection" on the experiences concerned. With its complicatedness, this way would remain far from the business of thinking, at least extratheoretical thinking.

Should I have succeeded in the foregoing in getting closer to the facts than I did in the relevant remarks in the first edition of this book,[51] then I have the objections of Gustav Spengler[52] to thank for this. For me, these objections became the occasion for a particularly intensive review of my statements. The results of this review go beyond Spengler's opposition, insofar as this writer, in agreement with my position in the first edition, is inclined to let the so-called hypothetical judgments—not all of them or even most of them, but a good many of them—stand as assumption-inferences; whereas today it strikes me as being more appropriate to make a quite general denial of this, as far as normal cases are concerned. I agree that the examples cited by Spengler do not put great obstacles in the way of the transformation into assumption-inferences, if one does not mistake the sphere of intellectual motivation for that of emotional motivation and if one raises no objection to the subintellection of premises.[53] But it seems to me that it cannot but be decisive for the description of the nature of hypothetical judgment, that a special transformation is required first, and that without this transformation our thought in the instance of a hypothetical judgment leaves off at the restriction of the consequent, so to speak. But since there is usually no immediately ensuing judgment as to the "connection" here, my agreement with Spengler's opposition to an "assumption-inference view" does not mean that I am reverting[54] to the "connection-theory"[55] espoused by Spengler. On the contrary, I am in full agreement with Benno Erdmann[56] in rejecting this theory.

Yet, might not my "consequent-theory" compel me to reject the last-named inquirer's "following-theory" ["Konsequenztheorie"] of the hypothetical judgment?[57] What Erdmann calls a "copula" I should naturally, in line with earlier remarks,[58] have to relate to that factor in the objective which has confronted us in its two main species as being and so-being. Besides these two species, a third would have to be posited, i.e., "following." Among the things characteristic of it would be the fact that by its very nature it constituted an objective of higher order, always presupposing other objectives as its material. As one can see, that wouldn't exactly be difficult to incorporate in my interpretation of the objective. It is just that I have so far not succeeded in verifying on the basis of the facts that "there is" really such a third species of objective. But couldn't sharper discernment in the theory of objects persuade us to adopt just such an opinion in the future? In this event, of course, the fact of judgments concerning restricted consequent-objectives, to which we have been led by the above investigations, would still stand.

As for the interpretation itself, the interpretation of hypothetical judgments that we have advocated above, a reasonable assessment of it ought not to overlook the somewhat wavering character that attaches to it in virtue of the underlying statement of the problem. This statement was tied to linguistic expression, to the range of employment of syntactical expressions like "If...," then..." and the like. Naturally, no one will be willing to swear that in all cases where such expressions are employed, thought will come to a halt with the judgment of the restricted consequent, without taking the additional step to the assumption-inference that is so closely related to that judgment. This would be as unlikely as the converse: that a complex of sentences connected in the manner of an inference should afford a guarantee against our occasionally settling for a judgment of the restricted conclusion. Just as little will we be able to estimate with any exactness how often a judgment as to the relation between the objectives comprehended in the operation may supervene on judgment and inference (inclusive of assumption-inference). So it can only be a quite summary calculation that led me to think that I must decide in favor of the judging of the restricted consequent. In the end, what is more important for the present state of our knowledge is the question whether the relevant experiences, at the points where they actually arise, answer to the description attempted here— and the question whether still other experiences, hitherto ignored, mightn't arise in the given circumstances.

§32

Operations On and Relations Between Objectives

In light of the real object of the present investigation, it would be appropriate to summarize the results obtained in the last sections in the following way. The apprehension of the "formal" strictness of an inferential procedure presents a problem that turns out to be accessible to solution only when one takes into account that an inferential procedure in respect of suspended or even rejected premises is quite possible, too. It is possible as soon as the place of judgments is taken by those judgmentlike facts that we have called assumptions. Though the expression "inferences from suspended premises" at first glance seemed to have something of "wooden iron" about it, more closely regarded, it is a quite appropriate expression; for along with judgment-inferences, which are usually the only inferences taken into consideration, there are also assumption-inferences.

Yet, however close in various ways a hypothetical judgment may be to an inferential procedure used merely with a view to formal strictness, the hypothetical judgment has its basis in a judgment whose objective consists in the restrictedly understood consequent. As to the evidence that results, in favorable instances of this basic judgment, the role of the restricting antecedent is particularly apparent in the linguistic expression. Only in the antecedent is it mandatory that assumptions be involved. Here all that assuming serves to bring about is one's fastening upon an object that will determine the consequent in such a way as to guarantee its holding true.

Let us follow the tradition of taking up the disjunctive judgment immediately after the hypothetical; and let us do so without inquiring into the legitimacy of this tradition, insofar as what has to be pointed out is just that in the case of disjunctive judgment, too, there are circumstances where assuming will be quite indispensable. Assuming will not always have to take place. The formula "A is either B or C or..." can no doubt be understood in the sense that A is something or is the subject of something that constitutes an element in a collective "B and C and..." formed for whatever reason. But such a notion is not free from artificiality; as a rule it will be more natural to think, "Either A is B, or A is C, or..." where it is not the objecta B, C, ... that come in alongside each other, but the entire objectives. Also, the collective itself can be one already formed from objectives; so it is when one judges, say, "Either A is B, or C is D, or E is F, or..." In each of these cases, the mutual exclusion of the terms of the disjunction, together with the absence of a decision in favor of one of the available possibilities, entails that the relevant objectives cannot be apprehended by means of judgments and that they can therefore only be apprehended by means of assumptions. So not only is judging just as much involved in the disjunctive judgment as the hypothetical, but the disjunctive judgment is also like the hypothetical in that it will normally be made only on the basis of assumptions.[59]

The intellectual experiences that have been occupying us in the present chapter, the inference and the hypothetical and disjunctive judgments, can quite well be taken together under their common aspect, the operation on an objective, if only one does not take the word "on" as indicating an alteration or some other real influencing. To undergo that would obviously be impossible for objects like objectives, which are ideal in nature. In line with this, nevertheless, one might regard even the mere business of approaching, and specifically the apprehending with which the preceding chapter was concerned, as being an operation on objectives. But if only for the need of the moment, let us limit the sense of the word "operation" to activities that already presuppose an approach. Then we can say the following about the operations on objectives considered in the foregoing: Apart from inferences in the strict sense, namely judgment-inferences, all these operations stand in need of assumptions, sometimes in greater degree, sometimes in lesser. It is now easy to show that this holds true of yet another group of operations on objectives. In certain forms, these operations have such a close connection with assumption-inferences and hypothetical judgments that there has often been an attempt to reduce both assumption-inference and hypothetical judgment to them, with the result that we ourselves had to refer to these operations more than once in the investigations of the preceding sections. I mean the apprehending of relations between objectives, to which we must now return briefly, with an eye to the role assumptions have in that apprehending.

First of all, it is readily understandable that objectives, no less than objecta, enter into relations and complexions; they can even themselves be relations and complexions. The law of association and Weber's Law are two such objectives; hence, together, they make up a binary complex^l quite as truly as do red and green, and like these colors, they stand in a relation of difference. With regard to certain objectives, it is readily apparent that the combining of them into a complex might well amount to a protracted repetition of the operation that confronted us a moment ago in the form of the disjunctive judgment. Closer to what was considered in the preceding sections, though, are certain relations that are seen to be by nature dependent on objectives for their terms. To this group belongs, above all, the oft-mentioned if-relation, to which we can right away add a since-relation. We cannot attempt here to see how each of these relations stands with regard to connection in the foregoing sense [Zusammenhang], necessary connection [notwendige Verknüpfung], incompatibility, compatibility, and coexistence, along with ground and consequent, according to the various meanings of these words. It takes little effort to see that in all of this it is primarily a matter of relations between objectives and that relations between objecta enter into the matter at most only through a certain mediation by objectives.

Again, as we know, there are many relations between objecta that subsist quite apart from whether the objecta exist or not. Congruent triangles have their respective angles and sides equal, although such triangles do not exist. Hence, relations of this sort might be termed independent of existence with regard to the objecta constituting their terms. Similarly, notwithstanding their actual subsistence, they might be called independent of subsistence with regard to the objectives that may possibly constitute their terms. That Newton discovered America is certainly something other than that Goethe was born in Leipzig. And so this otherness, this differentness, is therefore undoubtedly a fact, although neither of the two terms of this relation of difference is factual. Naturally, we can also notice the same thing in relations that can subsist only between objectives; in the foregoing, we met with a sufficient number of if-relations whose obtaining could have been justifiably asserted, no matter whether the relevant objectives do or do not subsist.

It is right away apparent what these facts should mean for someone who wants to know about the circumstances in which assumptions make their appearance. Allow that there are, between objectives, relations whose subsistence is independent of the subsistence of the objectives. And allow that we can know the subsistence of such relations as experience shows. Then the relevant unfactual objectives, and likewise the objectives about whose factuality nothing is known, must be presented by means of something other than judgments; for judgments, apart from cases of error, are not available to us at all. In line with the principle so often employed, we may therefore say in general: Whatever the range is, over which the subsistence of relations and complexions of objectives can be seen or realized independently of the subsistence of the *inferiora,* that is also the range of employment of the assumptions that constitute the indispensable basis for such insight.

VII

Assumptions in the Apprehending of What is Presented. Intending.

§33
Preliminary Note

From problems that remain to some extent a precinct of formal logic, let us now pass on to the evaluation of a fact that all mental activity shares in, as something fundamental to itself—even though epistemology can in a certain sense claim a prior right to deal with this fact. There are hardly any mental events without objects,[1] and there is certainly no representation without an object. Now, if I see the matter aright, it will not be hard to satisfy ourselves that in what is called "the representing of an object"—nay, in any sort of apprehension of an object—a quite regular function devolves upon the assumption. Thus, in virtue of this function of assumptions, their range of occurrence cannot be regarded as narrower than that of apprehension itself. But as was more than once the case earlier, here too the explanation of the state of affairs in question makes it inevitable that we inquire into some of its conditions, and that for the moment we appear to digress again from our true subject. This time it is the nature of objectivity that we must enter into with a few considerations.

It is natural to regard the objectivity of a representation as fully actual only when an object to which the representation can be directed is actually there. At the outside, subsistence of the object could be allowed to pass as the equivalent of existence, as in the case of the objecta of geometry. This point of view was in fact decisive for my relevant disucssions in the first edition of this book. Since that time, I have been enabled, in particular by increasing habituation to the approach that is characteristic of the theory of objects, to perceive such a mandatory reference to being (factual being, of course) as a manifestation of the very presupposition which in the intervening time and in another place[2] I opposed as the "prejudice in favor of the actual." But at present it may still be that the overcoming of the earlier approach is not secure enough for me to suppress this approach entirely here, simply replacing it with the one that now seems appropriate to me. In the following, therefore, the discussions in question will be reproduced from the first edition with only inessential changes. The reader will be kept aware of the provisional character of the discussions only by the fact that, for reasons to be given later, the sections containing these discussions are always explicitly entitled "the being view." It will then be easy, by means of a few rectifications, to arrive at the approach that seems to me at present to be unobjectionable.

§34

The Being View: (a) Concerning the Judged-about Object

What I have just called the being view takes its start most naturally from the judgment; more precisely, it takes its start from that property of the judgment which, from the epistemological standpoint, might fairly be called both the basic property of the judgment and the fundamental fact of epistemology. If I am justified in judging that I feel pain, that I have this or that wish, or suchlike, then it is an obvious fact of a quite trivial sort that the pain or the wish really does exist. The same holds true of houses that I see, carriages whose rattle I hear, the struggles and negotiations in and for China of which I am thinking, and so on. There may be need of an examination as to whether I have a justification for judging affirmatively with regard to the existence of these things; but if I have the justification—or which in the end amounts to the same thing, if the evidence requisite to the relevant affirmative judgments can be mustered up—then there can be no doubt that these things actually do exist. This is not intended to predetermine anything whatsoever regarding the area within which affirmations of this sort are available to us. It is just that in view of inward perception, even the most thoroughgoing idealism will hardly be inclined to deny that there are such cognitions. But if this is conceded, then it is necessary only to recall the position that a person finds himself in, when he is convinced of a certain state of affairs, in order for us to realize, first of all, that it would be absurd to expect someone who is convinced to doubt the actuality [Tatsächlichkeit] of the state of affairs in which he does after all believe. We shall also realize that it would be no less absurd to grant that the conviction was justified and also grant that the doubt was justified.

Now, this is such an obvious matter that only a hypercritical affectation would get one involved in the fruitless attempt to interrupt the normal functioning of common sense in the present regard. Yet there is still something in this cognitive apprehending of an actuality [Wirklichkeit] that might be called the miracle of epistemology, to vary a well-known saying of Schopenhauer, or the basic fact of all knowing, as it undoubtedly better could be called. For this fact there is neither description nor explanation; there is just acceptance, the attitude that in the end we are always thrown back upon, in the face of ultimate facts. I suppose I should not avoid the customary word "transcendence"[3] in designating this fact; following this usage, the aforementioned basic property of a justified existential affirmation can also be spoken of as that judgment's transcending toward an actuality. Let us add, although for the immediate purposes of these remarks it might perhaps be dispensed with, that with the appearance of affirmations of subsistence alongside existential affirmations, a new domain opens up. It is true that in this new domain, justified affirmations do not have transcendence in the strict sense; but they do have something akin to it, something for which the designation "quasi-transcendence" seems appropriate to me. The identity that a theorem of congruence affirms is not an actuality in its own right, but the relevant judgment occupies a position with regard to "subsistence" that is quite analogous to the position of inward perception with regard to the mental actuality that it apprehends.

The reference to the fact of transcendence in a justified affirmative judgment of being serves above all to establish unequivocally what the object[4] of such a cognition is. If the object of a being-cognition consists in the thing whose being is cognized by means of the relevant judgment, then in our present case the object cannot really be anything but the actuality toward which the judgment in question transcends. In our above example, consequently, the feeling or wish, or whatever it is that is affirmed with justification, constitutes the object of the affirmative judgment in question. Then something analogous might be said of the affirmative judgments to which quasi-transcendence pertains: congruence is an object of the cognition of subsistence mentioned above. Nevertheless, this observation might already contain a sort of broadening of the notion of an object, a notion that in its original simplicity was perhaps based exclusively on transcendence in the primary sense. But in any case, the broadenings that this notion receives through its extension to unjustified affirmative judgments as well as to negative judgments are substantially more important broadenings. In these extensions, too, the connection with what we have before us in true affirmations' transcendence is unmistakable.

With regard to a false affirmative judgment, first of all, in what sense can we speak of an object—not of a cognition, of course, but of a judgment, nevertheless? No doubt a person who is judging is equally serious in his conviction, whether or not he is also justified with regard to that conviction. But if he isn't justified, then transcendence would have to be basically out of the question. If we still assign an object to his judgment in that case, then as far as I can see, this object can only be the product of a sort of fiction, the motivation for which may lie in the fact that a person who is in error does in very many respects feel just like a cognizing subject. If I am in error in judging that A exists, then it is only through the fiction that I am justified in so judging that one can get to an object like that which belongs to an affirmative cognition. But the fiction of being justified can be avoided by a broadening of the notion of an object. All that is required is that what a judgment would transcend toward, if it were justified, also be called an object of a judgment. On this interpretation, there will naturally always be an object even for a false affirmative judgment.

As for the object of a negative judgment, the path there is not hard to find from where we are now. Admittedly, a justified negative judgment in the first instance differs quite strikingly from a justified affirmative judgment through the very fact that the former constitutes a sort of diametrical opposite to the affirmative judgment's transcendence. But the fictive manner of dealing with the situation, tried out successfully in the case of false affirmations just now, can also be applied without difficulty in the present case. In the case of a false affirmation, one feigns the truth of it; so too, in the case of a true negation one can feign that not it, but a true affirmation, is present. And if one replaces the fiction with the modification of the notion of an object in this case, too, then even the definition adopted above for the false affirmative judgment can be carried over pretty much unchanged. For I can also assign something to the negative judgment as its object, namely what it would transcend toward if it were a justified affirmation instead of a negation.

It is unnecessary to give special consideration also to the case of the false negative judgment here. For it is immediately obvious by this time that not just a true negative judgment but every false one, too, is susceptible to the fiction or broadening just urged. Indeed, it is understandable how one might even be inclined to regard the move involved in the broadening as still less forced in the case of a false negation than in the case of a true one. Along with this, then, one sees how the broadened or modified notion of an object is applicable to judgments of any given character, no matter whether they be affirmative or negative, true or false; and one sees how at this point we now have before us the sense in which an object is the business of any judgment without exception. This sense is taken from affirmative cognition, but it is so little tied to affirmative quality or to a cognitive standing, these factors being rudely thrust aside by the aforementioned fiction, that we can scarcely proceed further without raising two questions. What does it really mean, to ascribe objectivity to a judgment—a negative one, say—if we understand objectivity to be a property that the judgment would have under certain conditions that are in fact unfulfilled in the given case—conditions that are, indeed, unfulfillable on account of the very nature of the judgment in question? Further, what does it mean to say of a judgment that it *has* the object in question when at best (with false judgments) this object exists merely *per accidens* and at worst (with true negative judgments) it does not exist at all?

§35
The Being View: (b) Actual and Potential Objectivity

The first of these questions obliges us to determine more precisely who or rather what really *"has"* the object. If someone has not learned to do gymnastics, then I cannot say that he can do gymnastics, even if I know that he could do them if he learned gymnastics. And the assertion would be more foolish if I knew that he was quite incapable of learning gymnastics, short of becoming another person, as it were. But this latter, stronger case is that of the judgment in our above deliberations. The object that the negative or false judgment would have if this judgment were affirmative and true—this object it simply does *not* have. Or, expressed more precisely: If, despite everything, that judgment can in some sense be assigned an object, objectivity cannot attach to the judgment itself. Rather, objectivity has to be the property of something that is connected with the judgmental state of affairs but is not affected by the quality and correctness of the judgment. And as a matter of fact, there actually is such a thing in every judgment: it is the representation. This is something without which there could really be no question of a judgment[5] but which, at least in principle, can serve as the "psychological prerequisite"[6] for an affirmative judgment as well as a negative one, and a true judgment as well as a false one. A representation being by nature indifferent, as it were, it is much more natural to ascribe to it, as its property, something that would come into play in the event that a justified conviction of affirmative quality could be established upon this representation. It is essentially the same as when I attribute a good memory or physical agility to someone at a time when he manifests neither the one nor the other. It must be admitted, however, that there are representations where a justified affirmation is precluded, if not by the nature of the representation, then at least by its external circumstances. And in consideration of such representations, the attempt to deny them objects has actually more than once been made. It will become apparent soon enough why such an attempt must be rejected. At all events, it is by now clear that objectivity is a property which, although originally conceived with reference to cognition, by its very nature deserves to be termed a business of representation. If objectivity is nonetheless assigned to a judgment, too, without regard to the particular nature of the judgment, strictly speaking this is done only in the roundabout way, via the representation on which the judgment in question is based.

But we still have to answer the second question. Even if it is primarily representations that "have" objects, what sort of "having" is it, really, when that which the representation in question "has" can just as well not exist? With the help of the earlier comparison with the case of memory, one can take in the situation at a glance. Who could with any exactness say that I "have" the date and the tune that I can recall by dint of memory? Thus, strictly speaking, "the representation has an object" is at all events a rather unusual form of expression. No attempt will be made to supersede it, since it seems to be so generally in use; it would be well, however, to keep in mind that what can be legitimately meant in that usage might come out better in the expression "objectivity"—of which we have made passing use in the foregoing, anyway. By this expression, as with the word "memory," a kind of ability of the representation is designated; like any other ability, it comes to light only under certain circumstances, i.e., the favorable ones.

The notion of an object, or more precisely, the notion of objectivity is consequently a kind of dispositional notion or notion of an ability. What the disposition inheres in is strictly speaking the representation, and only by mediation of the representation is it the judgment. That to which the disposition disposes—or in other words, what I have called the correlate of the disposition,[7] though recently it has been more descriptively designated as the yield of the disposition[8]—this correlate or yield is the cognition of a certain actuality (or quasi-actuality). It is the cognition which under otherwise sufficiently favorable circumstances is attainable with the help of this representation as psychological prerequisite. But what I have called the basis of the disposition[9] is given in the content, the factor in virtue of which a certain representation is precisely that representation, i.e., is the representation of precisely that object.

Actually, it seems to me that this interpretation satisfies the requirements of truth in all but one important point. Doubtless even abilities are facts, but they are never facts of perception. If it is not the object, but the objectivity, that is the truly factual element in the representation, and if this objectivity is an ability and nothing but that, then it is precluded that I should ever be able to perceive this objectivity. And yet everyone thinks he knows by experience—and by the most commonplace experience, at that—that his representing is "directed" at objects. And many a person will regard it as obvious that this directedness even constitutes another essential element of the objectivity. Aren't we at this point confronted with claims that are perfectly irreconcilable with what has been set forth up to now?

We are not running into any trouble here, at least not in connection with the last-mentioned point, for that point can easily be accommodated through a specific determination of the concept of objectivity. The concept so far expounded may be appropriately designated as that of mere *potential* objectivity, and over against this potential objectivity we can set an *actual* objectivity. By the latter is meant not the mere ability-to-be-directed, but the actual directedness. The question as to what one is to understand by this actual "directedness" seems to be a far more difficult one to settle, however. As has just become clear, it must be a matter of something inwardly perceivable. In light of this, one might try to work the matter out for himself this way: What we inwardly perceive is merely the content that happens to be present and to this perception we then add an interpretation to the effect that this content, as the presumptive means of cognition, is coordinated with certain objects apprehensible by means of it. For a time, I actually attempted to make do with such an expedient,[10] but the artificiality of it can remain only very imperfectly hidden to an impartial eye. And so it seems to me to be no slight advantage that ways and means to cope with even this difficulty can be found by adverting to the fact of assumptions.

§36
The Being View: (c) The Role of Assumptions

In the first place, it is clear that the difficulty in question exists only in connection with the objectivity of *representations* and *negative* judgments and not where we are concerned with affirmative judgments. Whether the latter are true or false, we can tell just by looking at them, as it were, that if an object is not apprehended by means of them, at all events one is supposed to be. That stands to reason, at least as far as it is certain that by the "apprehending" of an object, or however else one may express it more or less figuratively, one can understand nothing whatsoever except affirmative cognition. Suppose, therefore, that in some case I perceive that I have an affirmative cognition—which is scarcely possible otherwise than by my perceiving the evidence of a judgment that I am making, in addition to the fact that I am making it. In such a case, the perception says as much as anything is able to say to the effect that I apprehend a piece of actuality or quasi-actuality. If, however, I affirm without evidence or even erroneously, then this cannot change anything in the slightest in what inward perception *can* catch sight of with regard to the objectivity of the judgment in question. For if someone is really convinced, then he is simply convinced, whether or not he be justified in his conviction.

However, the representation that is as yet free of judgment—the negative judgment will be under consideration presently—this representation does not yet contain anything at all in the way of a reference or directedness to an object. In itself, it is just potentially objective,[a] not actually. If we do nevertheless know of such reference through the testimony of inward perception, in the end this can only be understood as meaning that something other than "mere representation" is present in the case of such a representation. This something cannot be a judgment; we are after all expressly speaking of representations without judgment. What it can very well be, however, is an assumption, an affirmative one, naturally. And as a matter of fact, if someone can see the objectivity of a representation accompanied by a judgment just by looking at the representation, then in the same way he will be able to see the striving or tendency toward object-apprehension in a representation that is accompanied by a judgmentlike state of affairs—i.e., by an assumption of the same quality as the judgment. And one will have to admit that it is an entirely natural approach to represent an object to one's self in the manner of someone "acting as if it were real." But the conjecture or assertion that we then make, that all actually objective representing is accompanied by affirmative assumptions, is remarkable enough to require some special consideration.

First of all, it should be recognized that by this thesis I am nowise asserting that there are never any representations without assumptions, let alone asserting that there can never be any. Objectivity in one sense is the ability to serve, under favorable conditions, as the psychological prerequisite of a judgment of affirmative quality—though as we shall see, it might be better to say an assumption of affirmative quality. Such objectivity, which is to say potential objectivity, is obviously wholly independent of whether an assumption is actually connected with the representation or not. It belongs to all representations. It is another question, however, as to whether one may assert that all representations are directed to objects in an equally explicit manner, or in other words, that they are all actually objective. The weighing of this question might have to wait on a careful consultation of experience. If I see the matter aright, the case where one gives himself up to representation altogether passively, without "making anything of it," i.e., just as a person does in allowing himself to undergo a feeling, may not be exactly frequent in the instance of a normal, grown person, but it is still quite well enough authenticated. Where this is the situation, naturally the assumption is lacking. Even then the representation is objective, but it could not really be said that on the part of the representing subject there is anything present like an intention to represent the object.

Further, it must now be pointed out that apart from the previously mentioned testimony of inward perception, the introduction of the assumption also has the value of eliminating the difficulty already touched on above, a difficulty that otherwise still attaches to the very notion of objectivity. It remains somehow awkward that a representation like that of the round quadrangle, despite the contradiction that it involves, should be credited with an ability to serve as the basis for an affirmative cognition. It is more awkward, however, to do as has indeed oftener been done and to refuse any object to the representation of the round quadrangle on the strength of the foregoing, when one normally can perceive the "directedness" to an object in this representation quite as well as in any other. It is true, as said, that this representation is altogether lacking in the fittedness for being affirmed with evidence;[11] however, it is by no means lacking in the fittedness for serving as the psychological prerequisite of an affirmative assumption. The assumption, after all, is in no wise bound by the principle of contradiction.[12] For that reason, it is advisable to base the idea of objectivity on the assumption instead of on the judgment. This can be done both as regards objectivity understood merely as potential and as regards the actual "directedness" to an object. Objectivity is accordingly defined as the ability of the representation to provide the basis for an affirmative assumption; but a representation is accordingly said to be directed toward an object when its content is made the content of an affirmative assumption. This definition doubtless somewhat weakens the notion of an object. After all, the notion takes its meaning from its connection with transcendence or quasi-transcendence; for the assumption is able to replace the judgment only on account of its similarity to judgment. But in return, these definitions have the advantage of wholly unrestricted applicability to representations, however the representations may be in respect of content.

In passing, it may be pointed out that this view is also suited for bringing somewhat closer to our feeling for language an opposition, or rather one member of it, that at present creates a rather strange impression, given a bit of etymological reflection. There is no doubt at all as to what is meant by the contrast of "immanent" and "transcendent" object [Objekt],[b] and we are so accustomed to the use of these expressions that one does not as a rule have occasion to wonder about the participial form of the word "transcendent." But once one does so, it proves rather difficult to justify this form as long as one thinks only of what is apprehended or apprehensible by means of an affirmative judgment as being as "object" ["Gegenstand"]. For it is not the table or the chair that "transcends," but the judgment: the latter in its own way takes hold of an actuality, in a certain manner reaching beyond itself and "going beyond" the limits of subjectivity. The case is otherwise, when by "object" ["Objekt"] we understand the assumed as such, to put it more concisely than clearly, and when on principle we assign it its natural place inside the limits just mentioned, following the older linguistic usage in doing so. It is then a quite comprehensible figure of speech to say that it remains inside these limits and is thus "immanent," as long as nothing more than the assumption is present, potentially or actually. Then we may add that when a justified affirmative judgment comes to its assistance, the object goes out beyond these limits to meet a piece of actuality, as it were, and even reaches it in the sense of identity with it. In this sense, then, it transcends. Naturally, this assistance, too, can be conceived either as potential or as actual; accordingly, one may speak of a transcendent object [Objekt] even in the case of mere representations or solely in the case of judgments—justified affirmative ones, naturally.[13]

§37

The Being View: (d) Objectivity in the Case of Negative Judgments
and Assumptions

Returning to the fact of "directedness to an object," we find that express consideration of another case is still pending, a case that makes the indispensability of our recourse to assumptions stand out again quite clearly. We have seen the sense in which affirmative cognitions can be said to be directed toward objects, and the sense in which this can be said of representations. But for the case of negative judgments, the analogous question has not as yet been answered. And any doubt that the question has to be raised here is removed by experience, which suggests an object in the case of negative judgments quite as clearly as in any case where we meet with objects. But as already mentioned once, it is especially difficult for us to make reference to an affirmative judgment where the opposite of such a judgment, namely a negative one, actually is given. At this point it is easy to see how the whole difficulty disappears immediately upon the recourse to assumptions; but what is primarily important is that experience also provides rather direct testimony that affirmative assumptions are in fact involved in cases of negative judgments.

We know that the peculiar position of negation with regard to affirmation has long since commanded the attention of more than one observer.[14] It has been noted that it is of the nature of negative judgment not to "come in at will," as the musicologists say, but to require a sort of affirmative "readying." If A is B, then there is reason enough in this for a possible conferring of B on A in an affirmative judgment. But as for denying that A is, e.g., C, the reason and opportunity for that seem to be present only when the thought of affirming C of A is not too far from the mind of the judging subject. This fact that negation refers back to an affirmation having the same object comes out also in the peculiar way, already mentioned, in which the linguistic expression of negation is distinguished from that of affirmation. If affirmation and negation stood side by side on an entirely equal footing, then to be sure, one would be able to count on having the means of expression for a judgment pure and simple, and then having the trimmings by means of which the judgment would be distinguished as affirmative or negative, as the occasion demanded. Yet language normally offers a definite expression for affirmation *to begin with,* and this expression is changed into the expression of negation only by means of a special addition. A negative statement is formed with the help of the word "not," which is connected to the affirmative statement; the word thus affords a sort of outward proof[15] that negation supervenes on an affirmation already given.

However, it can be seen right away that someone who carries this point as far as to claim that an affirmative *judgment* is a prerequisite for the negative one is most certainly doing violence to the facts. If I negate the existence of a round quadrangle, then something certainly must have given me the occasion to do so; still, there would have to be something odd about the whole thing if I had previously believed in the quadrangle's being round. Also, where a *quaestio facti* has its answer in a negative judgment, the occasion for this answer may very well have been a real question, but by no means can it have been an anticipation of the answer by means of an affirmative judgment. Yet, the reference to the possibility of a question in the present connection quite clearly suggests the idea that, to obviate the excessiveness that we are indicating, the role of prerequisite for the negative judgment be conferred on an affirmative assumption rather than on an affirmative judgment. With that, it is directly understandable how one who may have noticed the affirmative background but has not yet become explicitly aware of the fact of assumptions may find it rather difficult to describe this background more fully; so that in the end he decides on a manner of speaking that is more figurative than exact, and he simply calls this background an affirmative judgment.

In this way, due recognition is also granted to what linguistic expression, as mentioned, seems to reveal about the relation between affirmation and negation. The sentence "*A* is *B*" doubtless expresses an affirmation; but we already know that as a rule this affirmation is a judgmental affirmation only in the case of independent sentences and that with dependent sentences it is an assumptive affirmation instead. So since the expression of a negation is actually formed by means of an addition to the expression of an affirmation, this can be straightway taken as meaning that affirmation constitutes a natural *prius* with regard to negation. Yet the decision as to whether the affirmation is a judgmental affirmation or an assumptive affirmation might reasonably be left hanging. For in cases where we are concerned just with the internal make-up of the negative sentence, not its position with regard to other sentences, the question of whether it is dependent or independent is of no consequence whatsoever. But again, direct experience shows that there normally cannot be any talk of a reversal of conviction when a negative judgment occurs, and so we arrive at the same result: That which readies the negative judgment, as a sort of natural antecedent of it, cannot be anything but an affirmative *assumption.*

On the basis of the foregoing, it might now stand as proven that a negative judgment, by its very nature, always carries an affirmative assumption along with it as antecedent. In that case, there is strong support for something that we emphatically advocated earlier, which was the recourse to assumptions for the definition of an object. It cannot appear strange at all, that a negative judgment is every bit as much directed to an object as an affirmative one is, if an affirmative assumption is an essential state of affairs in this "directedness." For then, of course, this state of affairs is already present in the negative judgment as its prerequisite, whereas the affirmative judgment itself represents merely a sort of redoing of the affirmative assumption.

Our presentation of the facts concerning directedness to an object is incomplete at still another point, though. We now understand how this directedness may be asserted of the great majority of representations and also how it obtains in all judgments, affirmative and negative. But what shall we say of the state of affairs that has in each case made that understanding initially possible for us in these matters? What is the situation in regard to this directedness in the case of assumptions themselves? It stands to reason that one can no more deny the directedness of assumptions than one can deny the directedness of other mental facts. It is likewise readily understandable that a new legitimation of this concession for the case of affirmative assumptions is unnecessary. For if the foregoing is correct, "directedness" and affirmative assuming are basically one and the same fact. But now, there are also negative assumptions as contrasted to affirmative ones. What sort of position do negative assumptions have in regard to the problem of objectivity? If I see the matter aright, this question can be answered on the basis of experience simply in this way: Not only the negative judgment but also the negative assumption requires a preceding affirmation. In this case it is even more obvious that the preceding affirmation can hardly partake of any character but that of the assumption. Even so, affirmative judgments as a starting point are far more of a possibility in the case of negative assumptions than they are in the case of negative judgments. But the affirmative assumption remains a sort of minimum that will always be provided for.

§38

Self-Criticism. The Absistence View

I hardly think any special explanation will be required as to why I thought I could apply the term "being view" to the interpretation that has been formulated in the last four sections, following the first edition of this book. For according to this interpretation, representations would have an object in the really strict sense of the word only when they are directed toward existents or subsistents, or in a word, toward beings. But it seems just as clear to me now that the interpretation starts to detach itself from this point of departure during the course of its prosecution. For there are representations that would be directed to objects with being, if only these objects did have being; and the interpretation must allow these representations, too, to pass as objective. And there are representations that are not even directed to beings, but are merely so constituted that under favorable circumstances they could be thence directed, at least in the fictive sense just specified; and even these representations are potentially objective. In all this, there is more than a mere "weakening"[16] of the initial definition of objectivity. For if objectivity consists in the "having" of an object, and the "had" object must be one that has being, then a representation simply does not have an object in any of the instances of fiction, and at this point one really cannot quite see why objectivity is still ascribed to the representation, despite its dependency on a fiction. At bottom, it is a representation without an object, and those proceeded in a more consistent fashion who flatly termed a representation like that of the golden mountain, not to say the round quadrangle, objectless.

Yet even now this attitude strikes me as being completely in conflict with the facts. Just as clearly now as before, the facts tell me instead that when I think of unclouded human happiness or of the perpetual motion machine, my thoughts are directed to "something," i.e., to an object, just as surely as if it were a matter of the most everyday piece of actuality. And if this is so, then the above interpretation cannot be absolved of the "prejudice in favor of the actual" mentioned at the beginning of this chapter, or at least a prejudice in favor of beings. If the object as such is absistent[17] and we recognize this, then right there we have an object-apprehension that is unconfined by the limits of being. With the detachment of the notion of an object from factuality, there is no longer any compulsion to accord a central position in our considerations to knowledge and to the many less natural things[18] without which the association of knowledge with this center could not well be established. And instead of bringing out objectivity as a property of the representation only at the end of the investigation,[19] one can now begin the exposition with a reference to those facts, which are quite obvious in advance of any more detailed investigation.

In the first place, it is perhaps clear that our intellectual relation to objects does not consist simply in the fact that we know the objects, or as would in many cases be more correct to say, that we know something about the objects —or better still, of the objects. If so, then it might be better if a word less colorful than "knowing" were to stand for this intellectual relation to objects. The term "apprehending," already much employed in the foregoing, might recommend itself as such a word. We can then quite significantly speak of the beginning of this apprehending as a "fastening upon"[c] and in this sense we can assert that if one is to make anything intellectually of a certain object, it is first and foremost necessary that one fasten upon it intellectually—which is not to say that this fastening upon must always temporally precede the rest of the intellectual work on an object. Experiences, then, have an object or are objective simply insofar as they serve for the apprehending of the relevant object, and the main question now is what the nature of experiences of this kind really is.

No one would hesitate to identify representations as these experiences. Since factuality does not enter in as a matter of principle here, all that really seems necessary is to represent the object. We do not in the first instance ask whether representations are in fact always indispensable; we ask whether in the many cases in which they are indisputably present, they suffice by themselves for the apprehending of the object. A quite simple consideration actually suffices to prove the opposite. Apprehension is in any case an action. Representation, taken entirely apart from everything that might be mentally realized on the basis of representation, is just as much a passive condition as feeling.[20] So when an object is apprehended, another experience must have added itself to the representing.

Yet it would mean rather little for us to skeletonize a purely passive representational experience in this way, which is really just definitional, if we were unable to exhibit the actual occurrence of this experience in the processes of the mind, and to verify right then and there that the apprehending of an object is in fact out of the question in such an occurrence. In a certain sense, representation that does not go beyond passivity may indeed be regarded as an exception; yet it is a far less infrequent exception than one might believe at first sight. Thus, it is true that every sensation is adapted to the apprehension of its object, one that has been aptly called the sense-object;[21] but how far this apprehension is from actually taking place all the time is shown by the abundance of what is imaged on the periphery of the retina under normal circumstances—and to that extent indirectly seen—without the relevant objects, which are actually causing our sensation, in any way making their presence felt in our mental processes as objects. The noises around us, and much of what the so-called lower senses offer us, are experienced in quite the same way.[22] One's doubts as to whether anything at all is sensed under such circumstances rather often meet with explicit firsthand knowledge about the effects of such experiences, e.g., about the disturbing influence of so-called side-representations in the activity of comparing.[23] Moreover, these effects are frequently familiar, even expected. For example, we rather often understand spoken discourse without the very things that are heard—the experienced sounds, distinct and indistinct, and what is based on them—entering objectively "into our awareness."[24] And so it is not uncommon, even immediately afterwards, for someone to be fully cognizant of the sense but by no means fully cognizant of the words that were used. And in the case of words that one reads, it often enough turns out the same way. For the accomplished musician, note-symbols usually recede wholly into the background, and so on. In a word, a good many sensations, under the special circumstances in which they occur, do not serve for the apprehending of their objects, not even when our attention is turned to them as in the case of listening and reading—which is admittedly in a quite special way.[25] Something similar is to be observed also in reproductive representations,[d] especially in the case of part-representations that are neglected for the formation of *abstracta*. And so direct experience shows that mere representation, as a special case of which sensation was brought in here, is insufficient for the apprehending of objects.

Less direct, but no less cogent, is another proof of the same point. We had occasion to point out how in every representation the representational act, which is something relatively invariable, stands opposed to the content, a factor that varies along with the object, or more precisely, along with the objectum.[26] This implies a certain correlation between contents and objecta. For our present question, it is important that this is not a correlation that is undisturbed under all circumstances. I mean that the same object can quite well belong to different contents, and different objects to identical contents. The important thing here is this second case. It is exhibited most strikingly in the difference between the results of the extroversion and introversion of the same representation.[27] In virtue of this extroversion and introversion, what is apprehended as the object is on one occasion something physical, e.g., a mountain, and on another occasion something mental such as the representation of the mountain in question or even the content of this representation. No less important are the different degrees of precision with which one and the same content can be employed for the apprehending of objects. It seems possible that in the extreme case the difference between these objects comprehends even the opposition of phenomenal and noumenal objects.[28]

It is clear, naturally, that these differences in what is accomplished in the way of apprehension cannot be charged to the account of the representational content, which has undergone no change; thus, something else besides representation must be involved in the accomplishment.

This additional factor certainly hasn't escaped prescientific psychology; for there is a term for it in daily life, a term that has been overlooked for a remarkably long time in theoretical usage. A word that has not been understood, or an unclear turn of expression, can easily give one occasion to make clear what is thereby "intended" ["gemeint"].*e* Also in regard to a gesture or sign of some other sort, one can inquire as to the "intention"; and a person who addresses A and receives an answer from B may have occasion to state that he "meant" A when he spoke [den A "gemeint" habe]. With locutions of this sort, we are doubtless always dealing with a directedness to an object. Hence, it is at least a quite permissible transference of meaning, if we turn to those representations by means of which an object is in fact apprehended and we say that one intends something by those representations. The note of deliberateness that certainly attaches to many a use of the expression "intend" need not be carried over, inasmuch as it does obtain just in a number of cases. For the same reason, we needn't let ourselves be influenced by another, essentially different sense of the expression, in which *Meinen* and *Meinung* are compared with judging and believing and the like as something less perfect than these. Supposing all this, then to begin with it is at least a quite apposite way of speaking that we have gotten, when we say that the only representations that really and actually apprehend an object are those where, or by which, something is intended; and that one can accord only potential objectivity to representations where this intending does not occur. At the same time, we find ourselves faced with a question that can be quite simply formulated: What kind of experience do we now have before us under the name of intending?

One thing is clear immediately: We are certainly not dealing with passivity here, but with activity. But what kind of activity is it? Of course, it is not at all obvious that we must be able to give a better answer to this question than the answer we would have had for such questions as what representation is, what judgment is, and what assuming is. Intending might simply amount to a *sui generis* mental experience. But as is always the case, it would be a theoretical advantage here if we could manage to get through to ultimate facts with what is already known. And I shall attempt in the following to show that this actually can be accomplished in the case of intending.

The business of knowing will lead us to that point, if I am not mistaken, and we may entrust ourselves to this guide even though it had to be emphasized, just previously, that while in regard to nonactual objects there is no knowing (at least if this reservation can be taken *cum grano salis*), there can well be an apprehending—an intending, in other words. In the case of knowing, as we repeatedly had occasion to mention, one prefers to think of the apprehending of actuality; and so the natural question is whether we could say what my experience consists in when, for instance, I "intend" my friend X in words or thoughts. As a matter of fact, it is simple to give an answer here. For the fastening upon something actual is typically accomplished by our knowledge of the actuality of something, or in the absence of conditions favorable enough for knowing in the strict sense, at least a correct judgment as to the actuality of something. So the important thing in the case of the "intending" of the friend will be just my conviction, justified or at least in conformity with the truth, that the friend exists—my judgment that he exists. It will be similar to the cases in which I fasten upon or intend actual things by means of perceptual judgments, which are likewise nothing more than existential judgments. What has to be avoided here is just the confusion of existential judgments with the judgmental adding-on of a quasi-attribute "existence," i.e., confusion with the "existential predication" that we had occasion to mention above as being a most imperfect substitute for a real existential judgment.[29] So I intend the friend by bearing in mind the fact that he exists.

Next, what happens when, for example, I fasten upon the object "right triangle" to address myself to certain properties of it, perhaps for the purpose of ascertaining some geometrical truths? This time it is not a question of something existing, no more so than in the rest of geometry. It is a question of something subsisting, though. Accordingly, intending a subsisting thing as such can hardly consist in anything but the making of an evident or at least true judgment of subsistence (and perhaps the dispositional facts that result from doing so).

At this point, what has been set forth can also be expounded in a somewhat different manner, one in which the matter of objects moves farther into the foreground. What one can say is: I apprehend the objectum friend or triangle *in* and so to speak *by means of* an objective of being that is itself apprehended by means of a judgment. Regarding this objective, it is immediately noticeable that in order to apprehend it we do not require yet another intending. What the representation does not bring about all by itself, the judgment directly accomplishes: It apprehends its object, namely the objective; and it is not customary to call that another "intending." I "intend" the friend, but normally not also his existence. Now, as has already been remarked earlier, the position of representation with regard to the objectum is somewhat analogous to judgment's position with regard to the objective. Judgment immediately apprehends an objective. So, too, representation immediately apprehends an objectum; but it does so in an incomplete way, as it were. Representation needs, as something indispensable, the help of an apprehension that is mediate, one going through the objective. It is evident that this mediate apprehension must supervene on "mere representation," if the latter is to be made into the intending of the objectum in question. In turning to the very objective deemed indispensable for our intending, we see right away how little intending is restricted to the case of representing or to objecta. As remarked, this objective itself *need* not be intended; but it *can* very well be intended. By way of an objective of higher order, an objective, too, can be mediately apprehended. When I assert that the existence of my friend is a fact, I really no longer intend my friend; I intend his existence.

In all the cases we have taken into consideration so far, it has been a factual objective that mediated the apprehending of an objectum. What if such an objective is not at one's disposal? If the person apprehending is in error on that score, it can scarcely mean any important alteration in the main issue. Thus, if someone speaks in good faith of spirits, "astral bodies," and the like, then by having recourse to existential judgments he does "intend" these objecta, which are simply objecta whose objectives are lacking in factuality. But what if someone intended something like "phlogiston," in order to make this judgment about it: that there isn't anything of that sort? Or say that for whatever reason, he "intends" an objectum and thinks about it without therewith giving any consideration at all to the question of its existence or non-existence. In view of the course that our investigations have taken in the earlier chapters, no one would find reason in this to conjecture that in such a case objectives must play less of a part in his intending. Only this much is certain, that under the given circumstances the objectives which, as it were, mediate the intending cannot be immediately apprehended by means of judgments. And thereby, in accordance with a pattern of inference that has oft proven its value by now, we are afforded an insight that is again basically important to the main theme of the present work, namely that aside from representations, assumptions play a quite essential role in the apprehending of objecta in such cases. This is also in thorough accord with the testimony of direct observation. It tallies with our clear-cut experiences in many cases, that in order to give a thing some thought, a person "places himself in the situation in which there is such a thing." Assuredly, there are also less clear-cut cases, but their relatively indefinite character can usually be accounted for rather easily by consideration of the duration and circumstances of the experiences in question.

So we arrive at the following result, concerning the mental action that has to be accomplished on the basis of passive representation, if representation is to apprehend its objecta. This action—intending, in short—is either judging or assuming; more precisely, it is either the judging of being or the assuming of being. Earlier, it struck us as plausible that a verdict of implicit assuming should be returned, *a poteriori,* as it were. And if that is permissible now, then we can say more briefly: All intending is assuming. In this way, as can be seen, we arrive at a result that is quite similar in its essentials to the one we arrived at above, on the basis of what was there called the "being view." But as against this view, the view that has now been brought forward was actually based on the supposition that even in the strict sense the objectivity of representations goes beyond the domain of beings [über den Bereich des Seienden hinausgeht]; hence, we can now speak of an absistence [Aussersein] view as to objectivity. Still, there would be no use in adhering to the *terms* "being view" and "absistence view," once one had decided for the absistence view. It is just in the section headings that I have made use of these terms, and I have done so in order to preclude any misunderstanding about the purpose of reproducing the discussions of the first edition in the four preceding sections, the purpose being mainly that of revision and rectification.

The view being advocated here might be more appropriately characterized as the assumption view, though this would not convey the opposition to the discussions of the first edition. One who is inclined to agree with the present view need not ignore the following. What we maintain about intending, that it is in its essentials tantamount to assuming, cannot as yet be taken to be as firmly established as the theses in the theory of assumptions developed in the earlier chapters of this book. And since, of course, even a treatise on assumptions would not have any cause or right to make the domain over which assumptions extend appear greater than what merely corresponds to the facts, I do not want to leave it unmentioned that I myself have come across at least a *prima facie* basis for seeking the nature of intending in something other than assuming. In doing so, however, one immediately comes into contact with another difficulty, one already set aside above[30] as unresolved. This difficulty is indeed rather natural with an "absistence" view, I might add; I mean the problem of absistence itself. Imagine this problem resolved in such a way that absistence turns out to be a kind of positive being; we did not see fit to reject this view out of hand earlier. Thus, absistence would somehow have to be coordinated with subsistence and existence as a third kind of objective of being. Then the apprehending of absistence would naturally be the business of judgments fitted for this. Their fittedness would be guaranteed by the special nature of their content. In that case, couldn't we try to situate the nature of intending in the judgments that serve for the apprehending of absistence, rather than in assumptions? For there is one respect in which absistence and intending exhibit a most striking agreement. On the relevant occasion, we already emphasized that absistence exhibits the peculiarity, most strange for a kind of being, that as a *positivum* it has no *negativum* opposed to it. Now at all events, it seems to be a fact that all the intending thus far regarded is affirmative in nature;[31] as for negative objectives, whatever type they may be in other respects, they do not mediate any such apprehending. Still, the importance of this coincidence, which naturally gives some pause for thought, is in my estimation more than offset by the obscurity that for the present attaches to absistence and whatever mode of apprehension may appertain to it; and meanwhile, the remaining aspect of the whole matter appears to me to speak entirely in favor of assumptions. So for the present, I think it will be of service to the theory of assumptions, if I look into the questions concerning intending a bit more in the following.

But in the next connection, we must immediately make mention of an imperfection of the assumption view; this is an imperfection that will hopefully disappear as we elaborate on it. As a reason for not crediting the apprehension of objecta just to a passive representation, I had occasion earlier to mention the fact that the same content can serve for the apprehending of different objecta. By way of proof of this, a provisional reference was made[32] to extroversion and introversion as well as to difference in the degrees of precision. One may now reasonably ask whether the recourse to assumptions (or even judgments) enables us to understand such differences. I must admit that at present this is still only to an extremely modest extent the case. The above effort has yielded only this much: that while representation all by itself does not seem to offer any room at all for such variable factors, one can now think of something like different angles from which assuming can seize upon the representational content, and perhaps also of different strengths in which the seizing upon it can take place. It goes without saying that a theoretical effort cannot in the long run remain content with such vague notions.

In the foregoing, almost exclusive priority of consideration has been given to representations as the basis for intending. Yet this can scarcely have given rise to the illusion that only representations can function in this way. For first of all, representations can be introverted, and not only they but also other elementary and complex experiences—specifically, judgments, feelings, and desires. Again, even objectives can be intended, as we already mentioned above. If we are looking for a concept that is in some measure capable of covering such a variety of things, then as far as I can see, the most serviceable thing at hand is the idea that I formulated above,[33] the admittedly quite colorless idea of presentation. Presentation really means nothing but this: that an experience provides intending, i.e., assuming, with an object, in that intending seizes upon this experience as its basis. If an experience has an object of its own (an immediate object), which is an objectum in the case of representation and an objective in the case of judgment, then the experience either presents this object or presents itself. And then there are the special complications that were dealt with briefly by me elsewhere[34] under the title of extroversion of imaginative experiences; but we cannot enter into this in the present place.

Intending has itself already been characterized above as mediate apprehension of an object. We must now add that not every mediate apprehension, or apprehension via an objective, constitutes an instance of intending; it has to be an apprehension through which one fastens upon an object intellectually and by which that object is conceivably held fast. One normally thinks of what one sees, say; one "has that in mind" [das "meint" man]. Notwithstanding that, we know that one needn't believe right away in the actuality of something that is portrayed in a picture. If one hears that it is something actual, and on the strength of that one now believes in the actuality of what is portrayed, then in this supervening belief we certainly have a mediate apprehension of the objects seen—for the sake of simplicity, one may presuppose any desired degree of fidelity to nature in the portrayal of these objects. Yet it will be difficult at this stage to include the temporally supervening belief with the intending. So, too, in the case of a person who has been familiar with the content of a certain legend and who comes to find out, possibly quite contrary to his expectations, that the content is historical: He is now adding on belief, as it were, and if he can do this he must have already intended the content—the legendary events, more precisely—and the belief does not at this stage belong to the intending. So the important thing is the fastening-upon which may nevertheless occur by means of a judgment at the very outset. All this accounts for the fact already mentioned in the foregoing, that intending can never have a negative character. Negation, be it in the sense of mere assuming or even in the sense of judgment, is never a fastening upon something. But if I am to believe that a thing is not, or even assume that, I must have fastened upon that thing. In order, therefore, to judge or assume that it "isn't raining" (that being understood in the sense that at a certain time in a certain place no rain exists), one must in the first place fasten upon the object "rain"—think of it, intend it. An affirmative assumption of being is all that need be present,[35] and it can scarcely be regarded as an unempirical complication. So the proposition that the negation of being in a certain sense presupposes being-affirmation will probably be able to hold up. Below,[36] though, we shall find that it is scarcely compatible with the facts to give so-being the same treatment as being in this connection.

Aren't there in addition cases in which we fasten upon objects without objectives of being having the essential significance that they do in the cases of intending just considered? I remember a certain rose, say, and I thereby "have that in mind" in the way already described. But I do not know whether it was red or white, and I ask myself or someone else about this. But as I do so, I must fasten upon the objects "red" and "white." Must I, to this end, specially assume their being? I can find nothing of this in experience. As we saw on the relevant occasion, the assumption "the rose is white" or, again, "the rose is red" is indispensable for asking the question about the rose. But as far as I can see, this same assumption might suffice for the apprehending of the object "white" or "red," to the extent that such an apprehension is necessary here. Whether one wants to call this fastening-upon "intending," too, is perhaps a matter of terminological convention. In any case, we are again dealing with an apprehension via an objective, and this objective once again ensures that activity will have a role in the form of a judgment or an assumption. The objective is not an objective of being, though, but an objective of so-being, and this suggests the question as to whether so-being mightn't have a special significance even in quite clear-cut cases of intending. In this significance of so-being, a special role of judgments of so-being and assumptions of so-being would be making itself felt. In the next chapter, first of all from the standpoint of a quite different formulation of the question, we shall try to obtain the particulars on this matter.

VIII

Assumptions and Complexes. More on Intending.

Intuitive and Nonintuitive. The Simpler Case

In the preceding chapter we saw that a representation or any other presenting experience requires an assumption, if it is to be actually directed to an object. It can be shown now that assuming also has quite distinct functions reserved for it in the case where that object is a complex—theoretically a special case, but one that in actual practice hardly forms a distinct species. To satisfy ourselves that there are these functions, let us start off with a more precise assessment of a contrast that is still in the class of insufficiently investigated matters, despite its pressing importance in psychology and epistemology. From everyday experience, we all know that there is sometimes an intuitive character to our representing, sometimes a nonintuitive character.[a] And we know that sometimes one actually has the choice as to whether he wants to rest content with a nonintuitive representation or work his way through to the intuitive representing of the same object. We also know that one often finds himself obliged to resign himself to the former mode of representation, supposing that he is not, say, expressly striving for it on account of certain advantages that it too possesses. Such factors of expediency and the weighing of them are remote from our present interest; yet, we might find it useful to raise the question as to what really constitutes the nature of intuitive representation as opposed to the nonintuitive.

Elsewhere[1] I tried to get a characterization of this contrast by considering the following fact. In nonintuitive representing, use is made of object determinations that are strictly speaking incompatible with each other; whereas in intuitive representing only compatible elements appear united in the complex of the intuitively represented object. For example, if someone hears the words "a cross that is red"—for the present we shall keep to as simple a paradigm as possible—then he can react in such a way that he conceives the abstract representations "cross" and "red," and perhaps also a representation, likewise abstract, of the relation of coherence that is supposed to connect these two

[179]

determinations. From this material, he forms a complex in an appropriate manner. Grant that in the process each of the abstract representations requires what I have elsewhere[2] called a concrete substrate. That is, I cannot represent the cross *in abstracto* unless at the same time, even if in a certain sense *per accidens,* I represent it in a definite place, in a definite size, in a definite color, etc.; nor can the red be represented except as there are definite data of place, size, shape, etc., attached to it. Granting as much, then it is easy to see that in the absence of some special precaution the place represented along with the cross will not coincide with that of the red. Nor will the shape incidentally given to the red be the form of a cross, or the color given to the cross be red, let alone this determinate red, etc. In a word: The substrate that is incidentally given with each of the abstract items meeting in a complex will usually agree neither with the other substrates nor with the abstract items that are foreign to this substrate.[3] A complex representation constituted in this way is said to be nonintuitive. This is in contrast to a representation that originates in a direct intuition or is a reproduction of same. In such a representation, the red somehow appears cross-shaped right away, or the cross shape somehow appears red right away; and in respect of inessential determinations, both are tied to identical substrates. In this case, one says that the red cross is intuitively represented.

Even today, I do not think that anything of consequence can be said against the correctness of these results—apart from the fact that solid confidence in the indispensability of the "concrete substrate" has not been able to hold up in the face of the psychological investigations of recent years. Except where this admittedly important circumstance enters into consideration, the question is merely one of a criterion by means of which the intuitive can be distinguished from the nonintuitive as sharply as possible. To that extent, it must at the very least be left undecided as to whether there is likely anything else that one can indicate that would meet this demand equally well. Nevertheless, and this is perfectly compatible with the foregoing, the definition just reproduced affords practically no insight whatsoever into the nature of the contrast under consideration. In this sense, it is no better than information on sound vibration rates: Although such information affords the most precise way of specifying the different absolute pitches, it tells a deaf person very little about the distinctive character of those pitches. The present definition of the contrast of the intuitive and the nonintuitive suffers from such a deficiency. The situation is clear as it stands, but it can also be seen in the fact that a negative characterization of intuitiveness is really all that is brought about by that definition; whereas every unbiased observer will find the essential state of affairs at least just as positive in the case of intuitiveness as in the case of nonintuitiveness. Moreover, it is equally significant that while the characterization is kept object-oriented the object-material thereby brought into consideration is for the most part so inessential to the abstract representation to be characterized that according to a legitimate tradition one does not assign it to the object of this representation at all. Someone may actually be unable to represent a cross otherwise than as colored, or a red color otherwise than as in connection with some extension or other—and to that extent also in a definite shape. Yet even then there is no place in the object of the abstract representation "cross" for anything in the way of color, and no place in the object of the abstract representation "red" for anything in the way of shape. So while a conflict in which the "substrates" play the sole role or at least an essential role can admittedly constitute an important and striking concomitant fact of nonintuitiveness, it can in no case constitute the principle fact to be described.

The preceding reflections naturally give rise to the question whether there is still any prospect of deriving a characterization of the intuitive and the nonintuitive, free of the deficiency just indicated, from the object of the representation in question. We get an answer to this question by considering the fact that I am able to represent the red cross of our example intuitively as well as nonintuitively. Admittedly, it may at first seem natural, precisely in view of what was discussed above, to say the following about the nonintuitive representation of the red cross: that the cross which is represented here is not red and that the red which is represented here is not cruciform. But this seeming paradox is easily disposed of when one recalls how frequently one speaks merely of "representing" in cases where in more precise terms one would have to talk of "representing intuitively." True it is, what is *intuitively* represented in the case of a nonintuitive representation of the red cross is actually a cross of a different color than the one required and a red of a different shape than the one required. Yet such a narrow employment of the word "representing" is naturally nowhere less apposite than where we are supposed to be doing justice to another mode of apprehension in comparing it with the intuitive. If we take it as a point of departure for all further deliberations that there is also a nonintuitive representation of the red cross, besides the intuitive representation of it, then this not merely implicitly but altogether explicitly contains an acknowledgment of the fact that the nonintuitive representation, too, is a representation of the red cross and that it thereby has the latter as an object just as genuinely as the intuitive representation does. But then, if one and the same object can be apprehended in an intuitive representation as well as in a nonintuitive one, it seems beyond doubt that the object cannot be what bears the difference in question. Thus, it seems that the contrast between intuitive and nonintuitive representation must lie elsewhere than in the object.

§40
Composition and Juxtaposition

If the thing resists characterization in terms of objects, it might be more accessible to a description from the side of the contents. To be sure, there is no *prima facie* basis for the supposition that in the case of an intuitive representation of the red cross the part-objects "cross" and "red" would need contents different from those in the nonintuitive. But finding ourselves quite naturally led to part-objects and thereby to part-contents, now we just as naturally find our attention drawn to the way that might stand open to the solution of the difficulty at hand. For it is possible that these same part-contents combine into wholes of different sorts, or more precisely, into different real complexes.[4] And so it is possible that just because they remain the same part-contents, they remain coordinated with the same object. Yet since the real relations existing between these part-contents would not be the same in the one complex as they were in the other, the representations would have to be regarded as different representations, albeit representations of one and the same object.

For the sake of simplicity, we are for the time being considering just the case of direct representation.[5] Then the question as to whether a representation is intuitive or nonintuitive actually can be raised only with respect to complex objects, which of course always indicate complex contents. Even with regard to facts of an altogether different sort, one feels compelled to appeal to the diversity of real relations between contents. I mean the "production of representations," which allows representations of first one *superius* and then another to result from representations of the same *inferiora*. This situation is not likely to come out to be anything but the establishment of different real relations between the founding representations, or more precisely, between their contents.[6] Similarly, one can regard the distinction between intuitive and nonintuitive as being based in the fact that it is possible for the same part-contents to come together into real complexes of two different types, complexes whose signification as a whole is independent of the nature of the contents that make up the constituents. On this supposition, the perceivable *prima facie* difference of these two cases immediately receives its due.

It would naturally be desirable at this point if we could also furnish something in the way of a characterization of these two complexions or relations.[7] Perhaps some contribution in this regard really is promised by the natural significations of the expressions "executed" and "indicated." They very readily suggested themselves to me once, as a means of marking the contrast in question. To be sure, out of fear of offering occasion for misunderstandings, I later thought I should give up these expressions;[8] but then they were taken up again with approval from another side.[9] An "executed" connection is what I had called the connection of part-representations that forms an intuitive representation; the connection constituting a nonintuitive representation I had called a "merely indicated" connection.[10] Actually, it does seem as though one halts before a merely nonintuitive representation of the red cross, as if it were a problem that can be solved only by someone who works through to the intuitive representation of the red cross. But on closer examination we find that behind the apparent descriptive adequacy of such a mode of expression there is just the preference for intuitiveness over nonintuitiveness. This preference was already in evidence in the exclusive use of the word "representation," rejected above. The preference stems from the greater efficiency for the normal requirements of knowledge that characterizes an intuitive representation. It is true that if one thinks of intuitive representations as being the goal toward which all representational activity obviously aims, then the nonintuitive representation of an object signifies a problem as yet unsolved, the analogue of the "merely indicated" arithmetical operation. But of course, this arithmetical comparison no longer contributes anything to the characterization of the situation, once one desists from such a teleological approach, as we might call it.

I know of no other way in which the two complexions of contents to which we have been led could be described, unless possibly by recourse to some new indirect considerations. The comparison employed above, involving pitches and vibration rates, proves useful not only with regard to the merely indirect characterization that can be attained in terms of the vibration rates, but also with regard to the indescribability inherent in the pitches. We know that in spite of this indescribability and the much greater ease of specifying the vibration rate, the fact of a certain vibration rate doesn't entitle us to neglect, much less completely ignore, the fact of a tone-sensation, a tone-representation in the narrower sense. So too, it signifies an increase in knowledge, however modest, if we see the state of affairs characteristic of intuitive and nonintuitive representing as two different ways in which contents can be complicated, even if we should remain incapable of describing these two forms of complexion in greater detail.

What we can still do, however, is to give suitable names to these two forms of complexion. Unless my language-sense deceives me, the German language has two terms readily available for that purpose. We have seen that the contrast of intuitive and nonintuitive is tied to representations of complexes.[11] Conversely, we can also say that every representation of a complex object is determinate in respect of the antithesis of intuitive and nonintuitive—which of course by no means entails that every complex object [Objekt][b] must be both intuitively and nonintuitively representable. If what has just been set forth is correct, the determination within this antithesis takes place according to the connection in which the part-contents occur. Now, this connection presents itself either as a natural one, i.e., one such as is given to us without assistance when we perceive a complex object, or as a relatively artificial one, a connection that under normal circumstances is brought about only by our intellectual activity. We might call the first connection a closer one, as against the second, looser one; and if it is proper in the first case to speak of a *com*position [Zu-sammen*setzung*] of the elements of the content, then in the second case the expression "*juxta*position" ["Zusammen*stellung*"] might not be ill-chosen. With the aid of these terms, the result of the investigations up to this point can be summarized as follows. Representations can combine into more complex representations in two different ways; they can form representational compositions, but they can also form representational juxtapositions. In the first case, the object apprehended by means of the representational complex is intuitively represented, in the second case nonintuitively.

Language has fairly clear-cut means of expression for the designated modes of combination of representations.[12] If the words "red cross" and "cross that is red" are considered in comparison with each other, one will hardly find it difficult to see in the first locution more of an expression of an intuitively represented complex and in the second locution more of an expression of a nonintuitively represented complex—in other words, the expression for a composition in the former case and the expression for a juxtaposition in the latter case. If hardly any doubt arises on this point, the reason is just that a simultaneous apprehending of the part-objects is generally characteristic of an intuitive representation, and a successive apprehending is generally characteristic of nonintuitive representation. The latter sort of apprehending better answers to the unwieldiness of the circumlocution by means of a relative clause. As on all the preceding occasions for calling upon the testimony of language, I must naturally leave it undecided as to how far the history of language verifies the interpretation in question. But a look at the present-day situation will tell anyone this much: that there certainly cannot at this time be any question of a consistent discrimination between the two modes of expression. On the whole, the relative clause may in fact be less frequently employed as an expression for intuitive representation; yet no one hesitates to use the shorter, adjectival expression also for nonintuitive representations. But for all that, the two modes of expression are natural enough to be taken as the basis for a temporary convention in the interest of theoretical discrimination. So in the following, wherever a composition is to be dealt with, I want to employ an adjectival expression on the model of "red cross," and I want to reserve relative clauses on the model of "cross that is red" for the designation of juxtapositions. But since the adjectival form of expression is so frequently employed for this latter purpose, it is advisable to keep open another adjectival way of designating juxtapositions on various occasions. I want to use the locution "red-being cross"[c] as a model for this, though such a usage is still more in the nature of a convention. It is understood, however, that this convention is limited to just those cases where it is a question of composition or juxtaposition as objects of our investigation; in other cases where I employ the one or the other of these means of expression, I am far from wanting to convey anything to the reader as to whether I have employed intuitive or nonintuitive representations in conceiving the sense of my remarks in such and such a place, much less whether I want the reader to conceive it the one way or the other.

§41
The Logical Indifference of Juxtapositions

Like a number of our earlier remarks, the preceding ones may at first sight have given the impression of a digression from the real theme of these investigations, with only the concluding observations allowing one to surmise a certain connection with this theme. I hope that it will serve to dispel any suspicion of an unjustified digression, if we take a closer look at the situation that confronts us in juxtapositions. Among the different factors that serve to distinguish juxtapositions from compositions, we find a fact long familiar to us as fundamentally important to our purposes: determinability in respect of the antithesis of yes and no. Nonintuitively, I can combine the representations "cross" and "red" not only into the representation of the "cross that is red" but also into the representation of the "cross that is not red"; and in this freedom, nonintuitive representation has the advantage over intuitive representation. It is true that intuitively I can easily represent a cross to which one could correctly deny the property of being red, since the cross is, let us say, blue or white. But as for the "not being red" itself, the possibility of apprehending this is not given in any kind of intuition or intuitive representation; it is left exclusively to nonintuitive representation to provide such a possibility.

In view of what has been said earlier, it is now easy to draw the required conclusions from these facts. It is first of all obvious that representation cannot possibly by itself be responsible for the thought of the "cross that is not red"; the negation that is present here is not a matter for representation. But again, the thought in question does not at the outset signify any judgment. And so there can be no doubt that an assumption, obviously one of negative quality, plays a constitutive role in the nonintuitive representation of the "not red-being cross." Now, the representation of the "cross that is red" cannot possibly differ from the representation of the "cross that is not red" merely by the fact that negation is lacking in the former, with everything else in it being as in the latter. For otherwise, in the representation of the "cross that is not red" there would have to be given, along with this cross, also a "cross that is red"— which nobody would want to maintain. From this it follows altogether analogously to earlier results, that just as truly as the representation of the "cross that is not red" requires a negation, an affirmation must be constitutive of the representation of a "cross that is red." But in the former case, no negative judgment is required, just a negative assumption. Just as naturally, an affirmative judgment is not required in the latter case, but an affirmative assumption is required. But this right away carries the consequence that "juxtaposition" is by itself logically indifferent. The juxtaposition of the representations of "cross" and "red" (along with the representation of an appropriate relation, of course) does not yet decide anything as to whether the cross is represented as red or not red, the red cruciform or not cruciform.

This means that juxtaposition by itself does not at all suffice to connect the objects of juxtaposed representations into a complex object. On the contrary, this is brought about only by the assumption that follows on the juxtaposition; and at the same time this assumption, by virtue of its quality of affirmation or denial, stamps the complexion, accomplished only by means of this assumption, with the affirmative or negative character that nonintuitive representations always carry. From this it further follows that wherever one may meet with a nonintuitive representation, an assumption always has a part in the representation, and the latter becomes a "nonintuitive representation" only by means of the assumption; prior to that, we really have no more than a juxtaposition of representations.

In the face of this, there arises the question as to how things stand with regard to assumptions in the case of intuitive representations. We have already seen that such representations lack a certain mobility between yes and no. As long as I unite the elements "red" and "cross" in an intuitive fashion, what comes about is always just a red cross and never the opposite of it. One might now interpret this in such a way that an affirmative assumption always follows on composition, in order to stay as close as possible to the analogy with nonintuitive representations. However, as far as we are concerned just with the affirmative character of intuitive representations, it would also make itself apparent if the composition by its very nature precluded any assumption or judgment except an affirmative one being attached to the composed content. For if a representational complexion were utilizable in an exclusively affirmative manner, then an affirmative character could rightly be ascribed to it even when that utilization was omitted.

Starting from here, however, one might make an attempt to resume the investigation that was brought to a sort of conclusion above, asking whether we mightn't also be able to interpret nonintuitive representations in the same way—thus sparing ourselves the recourse to assumptions even in the case of what is nonintuitive. Grant that the affirmative character of an intuitive representation consists merely in the fact that the form of complexion peculiar to this representation admits of no intellectual handling except on the pattern of affirmation. Then why couldn't the affirmative character of one nonintuitive representation and the negative character of another nonintuitive representation similarly be reduced to the fact that the representational complexion in the first case by its very nature can only be handed as affirmative and the one in the second can only be handed as negative? As we can see right away, the main difference lies in the very fact that a representation can be handled either way, in the sphere of the nonintuitive. Nonintuitively, I can just as well represent a cross that is red as one that is not red. So if the same form of complexion belongs to all nonintuitive representations, the form that was to be designated by the expression "juxtaposition" in the foregoing, then it is precluded from the start that a character even indirectly bearing on the opposition of yes and no should be ascribed to this form, in analogy to composition.

Of course, it is by no means obvious from the start that all nonintuitive representation takes place by the employment of one and the same form of complexion—or more precisely, that the complexion employed in the representing of the cross that is not red is not a different sort than the complexion employed in the representing of the cross that is red. But if I consult with experience on this matter, I find in the first place that in nonintuitive representations I never meet with any difference in the form of complexion that matches the affirmative and negative character of such representations—never any such difference whatsoever. As far as I can observe, I deal with the representations "cross" and "red" in quite the same way, whether the cross I want to represent nonintuitively is a red-being cross or a not red-being cross. And a good indication that the mental situation cannot well exhibit extensive differences can be gotten from the frequency of the confusions to which the nonintuitively represented is exposed in the most ordinary life situations, with respect to the yes or no given in it—whether in the recounting of something not experienced, but only heard about, or in the carrying out of nonintuitively apprehended instructions, or in some other situation. Add to this something that can claim especial cogency, since it is the most obvious of things, namely that one who thinks of the cross that is not red is quite directly aware of the negation involved in this thought. He knows that he is not just framing a thought incapable of being handled in any way except on the pattern of a negation; he knows that the negation is already present in the thought.

Doubtless the situation is less plain in the case of the "cross that is red" and the like. But even here, one might not want to content one's self with the mere possibility of assertion, as regards nonintuitive representations of an affirmative character; for even as regards intuitive representations, one may already find that it accords better with direct experience to claim an actual and not merely optional affirmation. With perceptual representations, this affirmation almost without exception appears in the form of a perceptual judgment; whereas with other intuitive representations, this affirmation might of course be an assumption instead.

§42
The More Complicated Case

The obligatory role of assumptions in the event of intuitiveness would already be guaranteed by the results of the preceding chapter. As for the immediately preceding path of consideration, that can scarcely be called theoretical even in the most modest sense; yet as we now see, a mere step or two along this path was enough to lead us onto a similar role that assumptions have in the simplest case of nonintuitiveness. This is the case that does not go beyond two components. We want to press theoretically deeper, so as to reach a somewhat more satisfactory understanding of the function of assuming in the types of intellectual work presently under consideration. It would be better to attempt this in conjunction with a more complicated case where, besides the two terms of a relation, the relation itself enters into consideration, perhaps as something specified in advance.

Suppose that, for whatever reason, we find ourselves faced with the problem of representing two given objects A and B in a relation R specified in advance, e.g., green and yellow in the relation of differentness. Whatever else, it is immediately clear that in principle this problem, too, can be solved in the two different ways known to us as intuitiveness and nonintuitiveness. The ease with which the second way in particular is realizable can be seen at its simplest in the fact that everyone has already solved the problem as posed, once he understands merely what he is supposed to do. Of course, we could just as well have maintained this above, for the connection of the two objects red and cross. Next, there can be no objection if the previously formed concepts of composition and juxtaposition are applied to the present case. But under no circumstances can we treat the three terms now given, A, B, and R, as being on the same footing. From this fact, one can easily sense how little would be accomplished by the mere reference to the real relations between contents; and the fact compels us to raise the more far-reaching question as to whether the solution of the given problem, however it is to come about, intuitively or nonintuitively, can be managed at all with representing as its sole means.

That is indeed the question that I wanted to raise here. Can I really "represent" to myself that A and B are in the relation R? As soon as we give it any thought, we can see at least that merely representing A, B, and R at the same time certainly does not suffice for compliance with this demand. Say someone thinks about the differentness of two singing voices while his eyes rest on a green meadow with yellow flowers. He certainly represents green, yellow, and differentness all at once; yet he is by no means thinking of the differentness of the flowers and the meadow, or the differentness of yellow and green. And so he certainly does not accomplish what the problem previously set for yellow and green requires. What is needed seems to be just that R be brought close enough to A and B, close enough for one to represent R itself in the correct relation to A, on the one hand, and in the correct relation to B, on the other hand. But as simple as this requirement appears, just as certainly does it lead to a defective infinite series. That is, if R' is this last relation that we introduced, then the means by which A and B are to be represented in relation R is nothing but the fulfillment of exactly the same task as just now had to be accomplished for A and R with regard to R'.[13] Naturally, the problem is thereby only moved back, in that the further question as to how, say, A and R are to be represented in this relation R' points to a further relation R'' between A and R' and so on *in infinitum*. But an infinite series formed in this way would be defective; back along the path presumably covered, each step involves a prerequisite step that would have had to have been realized before there was a right to regard the basis of departure for the whole series as being realized—which naturally means that such a realization cannot take place at all. Thus, our problem of thinking of A and B in the relation R remains insoluble as long as we go at in in no other way than by the mental addition of new relations.

It is then natural to expect that what cannot be accomplished by means of an objective addition to the given representations of A, B, and R—which would, as such, really be an addition to the contents—might be attainable by means of an operation on the contents, an operation through which these contents would be brought into a suitable real relation[14] to each other. It is indeed quite natural to suppose that in order for A and B to be represented in the relation R, it is requisite that the A-representation and the B-representation be in a definite relation to the R-representation. Moreover, this is evidently the point of view that has already come into play to some extent in the above contrast of composition and juxtaposition, in that the conceiving of the members *in* relation is essential to the conceiving of the complex "red cross" or "red-being cross," in accordance with the principle of coincidence.[15] But if we find it hard to deny to complexions and relations of content a certain part in the conceiving of complexions and relations of the coordinate objects, it is just as hard for us to imagine how all requirements on the objective side could be fulfilled in this way. Yet in order to be fully clear how this is the very issue whose theoretical settlement we still have to arrive at, it is necessary to give some closer consideration to the relation between the representation, or more precisely the content, and the object appertaining to it.

§43

The Relation Between Content and Object. Adequation

Our main concern this time is the nature of the characteristic relation between the content and the object appertaining to it. Naturally, we can best expect to get information about the nature of this relation from actual cases of knowing. So these would be cases where an instance of being, whether existence or subsistence, is apprehended by means of a representation with the help of a justified affirmation. Hence, giving existence an unwarranted degree of preference here as elsewhere, it is a question of representations that we have long been accustomed to designate as *adequated* to the actuality that they apprehend. Accordingly, the relation between representation and object that we find in need of more precise characterization could also be called the relation of adequation. And we are not without a sort of traditional preconception as to the nature of this relation, either. For it seems almost self-evident that if someone is to know an actuality, and therefore represent it just as it is, he will approach his goal more closely, the closer his representations are to the actuality to be represented. Accordingly, adequation would be tantamount to an agreement of the representation with the actuality; and we know what part the goal of knowing, so defined, has played in idealistic and nonidealistic epistemology and metaphysics—and still plays, albeit under slogans somewhat modified from time to time.

But now, it is by no means the least estimable benefit of a fundamental distinction between object and content, that it allows us to perceive a misunderstanding in the interpretation of adequation just characterized, a misunderstanding that shows up only where this distinction is neglected. To wit, it is by all means correct to the point of triviality that if I want to apprehend a quadrangular table by my thinking, I should conceive of the table, e.g., neither as round nor as oval, but simply as quadrangular. But does this somehow mean that for this purpose my representation itself, or more precisely its content, would have to be quadrangular? Or is not the requirement limited, rather to this: that my representation, if it is not to lead to any error, must simply be the representation of *something quadrangular,* i.e., of a quadrangular object? On closer inspection, therefore, the agreement required is by no means an agreement between my representation and the actuality in question, but an agreement between the object of my representation and this actuality. At the same time, when we consider that the representation or its content can be neither round nor oval nor quadrangular, and that it can be neither extended nor even physical, but is ineluctably mental in nature—then we have one of the clearest arguments that in the content and object of a representation we usually have to do with *toto genere* different kinds of things.[16] But these reflections at the same time serve to show that the demand for agreement or even similarity between content and object is unfulfillable, at least for all representations of physical objects. And once this is realized, it no longer takes much effort to see that not a trace of legitimation for such a demand can be found in the nature of knowing, to the extent that knowing can be apprehended. As far as a representation can serve as the basis for an evident affirmative judgment, it offers me a means for getting hold of an actuality, as it were, or intellectually apprehending it—which of course might be a quasi-actuality, something "subsisting" rather than "existing." But we cannot then place this known actuality or quasi-actuality back alongside our representation of it, on a par with the representation, so as to compare these two matters of fact for similarity or dissimilarity. A representation is adequated to an actuality or quasi-actuality in the event that there is an evidently certain affirmation that in a sense legitimates the representation. As far as I can see at the present time, there is no basis here for any claim that the content of the representation has any definite similarity or dissimilarity to the actuality that is coordinated with it.

Elsewhere,[17] I have tried to give a somewhat more detailed account of the consequences this thesis has for the interpretation of so-called outward perception. But as has been rightly pointed out in opposition to me,[18] the things I said there[19] regarding inward perception can appear not to corroborate what has been set forth above against similarity as the nature of the relation of adequation, but to throw it into question. Yet it does not really rest with me as to how the facts offer themselves to description. If the content and its object lie qualitatively far asunder when the content, as is inevitable, is mental and the object is physical, then there is nothing that can be done about it. Conversely, due to the self-presentation of inner experiences, at the moment when a quasi-content offers itself to knowing, it does coincide with the object that is to be apprehended. But from that we are to infer not that a content and an object must be similar to each other, but only that the two can be similar unto the limit point of identity. This identity guarantees the constant correlation of object and content as a matter of necessity. It is quite understandable that there should be some advantage of reliability, in that situation. The general property of all knowing, that of a "transcending" beyond itself, is not itself thrown into question by this identity in the present moment; for the knowing-experience is something other than the experience that constitutes the quasi-content. The latter experience furnishes the knowing with its objectum-material, so to speak. The difference becomes especially conspicuous where this material—which is also its presenting (or more precisely, self-presenting) experience—is not anything so dependent in nature as the content of a representation would be, but is, e.g., a feeling or desire.

As to how it happens that the relation of adequation between content and object obtains in a case where there is such great similarity and in another case where there is such great dissimilarity, I admit I can give no answer at present. The natural thing, of course, is to make the differing epistemic situations of introversion and extroversion responsible for the discrepancy and to set one's hopes on being able to obtain an eventual clue to the characterization of introversion and extroversion themselves, from the difference between the relations of adequation in the two cases. I must refrain from going further into these important problems; to the essentially negative result obtained above, I must rather join the question, indispensable for the present investigations, as to whether we might not be able to get round this negation by means of a positive determination concerning the nature of the relation between the content and the object apprehended by means of the content.

It is true that one ought not cherish too far-reaching hopes in respect of a matter that so clearly bears the mark of a basic fact of epistemology, not to say *the* basic fact of epistemology. But in one respect, at the very least, a more specific determination of our relation of adequation seems to me to be acceptable even now without the slightest hesitation. I mean the assignment of this relation to one of the two major classes that make up the entire domain of relations, the classes of ideal relations and real relations. Some quite simple reflections provide us with information on this matter. If the thing that I know is itself real, or more precisely a bit of actuality, then it most assuredly cannot in any way be affected by my knowing; so we can put it, with a degree of precision that is not too great, but which probably suffices for the moment. Moreover, the known doesn't at all have to be something actual; the insight into an identity or a possibility, among other things, has something ideal as its object. The knowing act, along with the content forming its basis, is admittedly always real; but something real can only stand in an ideal relation to what is ideal, never in a real relation to it. Now if the bearing of knowing on the known is independent of the real or ideal nature of the known, then even for a real object of knowledge it results that the knowing can stand only in an ideal relation to it. With that, the "real unaffectedness" we spoke of simply receives a new verification. Finally, a verification of this sort is afforded also by the general aspect of the situation that always confronts us in the case of knowing. If our intellectual activity is to reach some actuality or quasi-actuality, then certain qualitative conditions must be fulfilled, which would in truth suggest itself even to a quite amateurish sort of reflection. For one thing, there must be a fulfillment of such conditions on the part of the experience in question. Again, such conditions must be fulfilled on the part of the relevant actuality or quasi-actuality. In respect of their nature, the two must be suited to each other, as it were. This "suiting" is of course far from having to be similarity, let alone identity; but we shall have even less reason to look for a real relation in it, and we shall scarcely be in error if we see at least a recognition of the ideal nature of "adequation" in the traditional view of this relation as a sort of similarity.

§44
The Objective Significance of Real Relations Between Contents

As already declared above, I have so far taken only the relation of affirmative knowledge to its object into consideration. But we can now say quite generally: The relation between a representation and its object, or more precisely the relation between the content and the coordinate object, is an ideal relation, no matter what the more precise nature of it may be. And for present purposes, this result throws all the light that is necessary on our starting question. This was whether any of the real relations between the A-content and the B-content and R-content might be able to modify the position of these three contents in such a way that instead of the three objects A, B, and R standing over against them, there is just the one object "A and B in relation R," or say "the relation R between A and B."

The question can be easily answered if one gives it a more general form; then as an example of an ideal relation, something that is generally more familiar to us can be substituted for adequation—as we can now quite unqualifiedly call the ideal relation between content and object. Generalized, the question reads something like this: If two or more given objects stand in ideal relations to other objects, can these relations be modified by the fact of the given objects entering into some real relation with each other? To take an example: I think of a color X and a place Y, which latter is by no means to be understood as restricted to a single point. The color naturally has its similarities and dissimilarities with respect to the various other colors; the place, likewise, has its relations of position and distance to other places. Now, if I bring the color X to the place Y, then will something in these relations of the color to colors, or something in these relations of the place to places, or something in each of the two spheres, alter into this or that qualitatively determinate, different situation?

No one will hesitate to answer no. Yet generalized, this means that ideal relations are in no way influenced by the real relations into which their members enter. At bottom, this is obvious enough; for ideal relations attach once and for all and with necessity to terms of determinate character, and consequently these relations cannot be affected by what we might call the outer vicissitudes of their terms.

But now, adequation is an ideal relation, too. The A-content, B-content, and R-content can themselves be regarded as objects[20] exhibiting, among other ideal relations, relations of adequation to the objects A, B, and R, respectively. It is clear that one may do with these contents as he wishes; as long as one does not change their character, i.e., make them into different contents, one cannot change their ideal relations, either. And if they have not already, from the very beginning, stood in the relation of adequation to the object "relation R between A and B," then this relation is not going to be earned, so to speak, through relatively superficial changes in these contents.

With that, we may have proved that a representation of the object "relation R between A and B" or "A and B in relation R" can be reached from the given A-content, B-content, and R-content neither by means of a newly added content nor by the establishment of real relations between these given contents. A third alternative for the contents in question cannot be taken up without going beyond the domain of representing, and so one may reasonably be apprehensive of already having proved too much through the preceding. For it shows that there is no representational content whatsoever that can be coordinated with one of the complex objects named again just now. However, one needn't stumble at this result, if it turns out that what we were first inclined to expect of representations, as their own exclusive accomplishment, can quite well be accomplished if, though only if, judgment or something sufficiently akin to it is brought back into play.

§45
Intending by Way of Being and Intending by Way of So-being

In our attempt to get clearer about the situation described above, we should scarcely succeed if we didn't first hark back to the facts that occupied us in the preceding chapter under the heading of "intending." We found it to be a characteristic of intending that it apprehends objects (in the first instance objecta) by way of an objective in which they stand. In the cases with which we were concerned in the preceding chapter, this objective was an objective of being. In the present connection, the main thing to be established is this: that besides objectives of being, objectives of so-being can very well serve the purpose of intending.

To understand this clearly, let us consider an arbitrarily chosen categorical judgment of the form "M is N," e.g., the sense of the sentence "My desk is quadrangular.'' Then to begin with, in the subject M one immediately recognizes the ''intending'' situation familiar to us from the preceding chapter: In representing M apprehended in an objective of being, one fastens upon^d something about which a judgment is to be made. In the desk example, it is an existential judgment that serves for the apprehension in an objective of being. But now, one easily notices that N, too, can be called upon for the intending of the object in subject-position. Admittedly, a categorical sentence is not the adequate expression for this other intending, as long as it remains an independent sentence. The case is doubtless different when one makes it into a relative clause. If I say, ''The desk of mine that is quadrangular,'' then there can clearly be a fastening upon something (by way of distinguishing it from my round desk, say) in which the determination of so-being now placed in the subordinate clause plays a quite essential role. The fact that N, too, can serve the purpose of intending emerges even more clearly when one takes care that this function is not obscured in the way that it is in the locution ''M that is N.'' If one removes all determinations from M, so that in place of these there is just the room for determinations, as it were—thus, if one says, ''something that is N'' or ''that which is N''—then all determining is provided simply and solely by means of N. In the function of providing the representational basis for intending, the N-representation has now completely taken the place of the M-representation. But as is clearly apparent, it has still not done so in such a way that N would now be directly apprehended in that objective of being in which M previously stood. Rather, N keeps its characteristic position as ''determining object''[21] or ''determinator''[22] in the objective of so-being. It has belonged to this objective from the start, and it is only through the mediation of the objective of so-being that it can be turned to the purpose of intending that M previously served. I suppose we could say that N intends something by way of so-being that still must be intended by way of being, i.e., in the way familiar to us from the preceding chapter. The two cases of intending that thus present themselves to us can therefore quite intelligibly be distinguished from each other as intending by way of being and intending by way of so-being.

Let us complete the characterization of intending by way of so-being by calling attention also to the following fact. To put it more briefly than exactly, not only can the predicate of a given sentence serve the purpose of intending the subject, but conversely the subject can also serve the purpose of intending the predicate. Now effected from the side of the subject, the determining once again becomes clearer when one as it were substitutes an empty place in the form of ''something''—for the predicate N. This substitution first of all yields ''M is something.'' That can now be turned around so: ''something about M'' or ''something that serves as the genus for M'' or in some similar fashion. Then the determining function of M is clear. Clear along with it is the fact that the intending by way of so-being here makes use of M in the manner that it made use of *N,* above; though in all this, the one manner of intending by way of so-being does nevertheless represent a sort of inversion of the other.

If one now looks for examples of intending by way of so-being, in order to become more familiar with it in its applications, then even in turning to ordinary perception one finds oneself confronted with the question as to whether one mightn't already be dealing with cases of obligatory intending by way of so-being. Of course, it is not really the "sense object" black, warm, or some other such thing that we perceive, but rather the black thing, the warm thing, and so forth.[23] And the inner aspect of such experiences makes it indubitable that what we are working with is not a combination of intending by way of being and intending by way of so-being, but a relatively primitive form of intending by way of being, i.e., a form still quite untouched by abstraction. From the fact that the nature of a sensory concept tends toward the elementary, it develops that a color, temperature, auditory tone, or other sense-object constitutes a property abstracted from the genuine concretum; whereas the object of a perceptual representation is this concretum, apprehensible only through intending by way of being, or more precisely, through existential judgment. Thus, concreta are the true domain of pure intending by way of being.

Intending by way of so-being nevertheless comes into its own wherever, as is indeed the rule, we apprehend objects by the mediation of their more or less abstractly represented properties. This is quite explicitly the case in such substantivized adjectives like "the black" and "the cold," by which, clearly, nothing can be conveyed except "something that is black" and "something that is cold." And just how important here is the distinction that obtains between the mere intending of the property and the intending of something bearing the property can be seen most easily from the fact that black, for example, never can be heavy, whereas the black, such as coal, can quite well be heavy. We may take it for granted that the situation will be no different with other objects like a chair or table and a sphere or cube; and so on with all things that we apprehend by the aid of words or their meaning. For what differentiates these word-meanings is primarily the relevant properties; these latter must be referred to the thing that they are supposed to characterize, and this referral cannot take place otherwise than through intending by way of so-being.

Apropos of the coal example, it is perhaps worth noting that even the object "something that is black" does not admit of the predication of heaviness, as long as one comprehends in it no more than just this black something. For in the first instance, "something that is black" and "something that is heavy" are really things of two different sorts; and it is only when, by "something that is black," I intend an object that has or can have other properties besides blackness that the affirmation, "The black is heavy," can be in accord with the truth. Through mere intending by way of so-being the intended object is, as it were, closed to further possible determinations. If in the intending of an object supplementary details are contemplated, even though it be just indeterminately, then and only then does the object appear as an open one, so to speak. So in light of that, we might speak of objects intended open and intended closed, or more briefly, of open and closed objects.

Intending by way of so-being can, incidentally, find application in the apprehending not only of things but also of properties, as far as properties themselves can have properties. And in principle, of course, this is by no means to be ruled out. "Something that is bright (saturated)" or suchlike can quite well be a color, of course, and hence a property.

The case of the above-mentioned inversion is indicated by the meaning of those words where what we have is not a thing designated by means of its properties but, on the contrary, the property designated according to the thing in which it is found. What we find in the human being, the seigneur, or the amateur as their characteristic properties we call human, seignorial, or amateurish.

In the foregoing, intending by way of so-being has almost exclusively been elucidated in cases of how-being. It stands to reason that such intending can be met with in the case of what-being.[24] I shall forego entering into further detail here, as another question is far closer to the main interests of the present investigations. We know well enough that in the intending of objects a quite essential role belongs to the objective of so-being as well as to the objective of being. The objective of so-being is something different from the experience that apprehends it, as is the objective of being; yet these experiences are constitutive of intending in the case of so-being as well as being. And so the question is, in what way are objectives of so-being immediately apprehended in the case of intending by way of so-being?

It is either by means of judgment or by means of assuming. This choice of alternatives no longer requires special justification at the present stage of our investigations. But as for the further matter of the role of judgment in intending by way of so-being, it seems natural to allow this role to be defined in analogy to intending by way of being. Thus, if I intend "the inventor of the typewriter," it may seem rather obvious that since I believe not just in his existence but also in his having invented the typewriter, I am entitled to employ not just a judgment of being in my intending, but also a judgment of so-being. But such an interpretation rather unexpectedly runs into a difficulty right at this point. Once I have apprehended the object in question, I can doubtless justifiably ascribe the determination "inventor of the typewriter" to him, i.e., by means of a judgment-experience. Indeed, such a judgment can have an altogether tautological character in the present case. But if it is a question of initially fastening upon the object, and doing so through a certain objective of so-being, then how could a judgment concerning this so-being precede this apprehending of the object, as the means thereto? In mere intending by way of being, there is no difficulty to the utilization of a judgment on the basis of a representation given in some way or another. Likewise, intending by way of being can be carried out by means of a judgment when this intending is connected with intending by way of so-being. But in our present example, the basis that representation would otherwise provide can only be made available through the apprehending of an objective of so-being, and in this case judgment does seem to come too early for the apprehending.

However, let us not dwell upon this matter, though it doubtless is still very much in need of clarification. For what has been set forth does at least give us this result: We can straightway see how little the objective of so-being can be judged, where the being of what is intended is left uncertain, let alone where it is negated. True, the "mountain that is of gold" is certainly golden, and the lightweight storage battery that we should so like to produce is certainly light, although at the present time the latter exists no more than the former. On the strength of that, one might again conjecture that the respective objectives of so-being, "the mountain is of gold" and "the storage battery is light in weight," are to be apprehended by means of judgments. But this time, as before, we can say without any reservations that the so-being through which I initially fasten upon an object cannot already be adjudged to the object by me. For to do that, I must have already fastened upon the object. Once this has taken place then the fastening-upon objectives, if I may speak this way, apply to the object analytically in the Kantian sense. But before the fastening upon or even during it, I lack contact with the facts. The fastening-upon objectives cannot be judged; they can only be assumed.

The result just obtained finds a verifying application in the theory of definition. The application is verifying in the sense that it might remove the unsatisfactory character of which the theory of definition has hitherto been unable to divest itself. The question as to whether a definition is a judgment or something else has resisted answer from the viewpoints hitherto available. As it really wouldn't do to rank defining simply under the heading of representing, it was thought that one had to keep looking to those judgments, concerning words or things, that one had in view in framing the concepts of nominal and real definition. Now such formulations as those can be quite desirable incidental functions of a definition; yet ultimately we cannot be wrong in thinking that they don't constitute the core of what we have in a definition. As far as I can see, only two functions can be regarded as constituting this core. Theoretically they are very different from each other, though they always coincide in practice. *Either* someone who defines specifies the objective of so-being by means of which he "forms" or "constructs" objects or does whatever else one might metaphorically say he does to them (metaphorically, because objects are not made by us, but can only be chosen out of the infinite abundance of absistents). In other words, he specifies the objective of so-being by means of which one fastens upon the object.[25] *Or* the definition is a specification of the objective of so-being that can claim for itself the tautological validity of an analytical judgment, in that this objective follows what I have just called the fastening-upon objective and gives the characterization of an object already fastened upon or picked out. In this second case, the definition is naturally always a judgment; on the first interpretation, however, it is just as certainly never a judgment, but always an assumption.

So at any event, we can say by way of a final verdict that along with intending by way of being, there is an intending by way of so-being. We were able to characterize intending by way of being as assuming because assuming is contained even in judgments; but outside of the judgmental intending by way of being, a purely assumptive one is perfectly well attested to empirically. In connection with intending by way of so-being, assuming plays an even more commanding role, in that fastening upon an object through a *judgment* of so-being is probably altogether out of the question.

Intending by way of so-being differs from intending by way of being in this further important regard, that while negative intending by way of being could scarcely take place in actuality, there is nothing in the slightest against intending by way of so-being with the aid of negative assumptions. The objects we fasten upon can just as well be characterized negatively as positively. We have already encountered this negative intending by way of so-being in a very general form at an earlier point of the present discussion. The insufficiency of mere representing for the apprehension of various objects first became clear to us in connection with "negative concepts."[26] These concepts now straightway reveal themselves to us as characterized by means of negative objectives of so-being. Here, quite as in the case of the paradigm we drew upon a while ago, "that which is *N*," the significance of these objectives for the distinguishing of what is intended becomes especially clear from the fact that what is intended (negatively, this time) in the first instance lacks further determinations. "Non-*A*" really means nothing other than "something that is not *A*" or again "that which is not *A*." We can now see what a hopeless beginning it really was, to want to use "mere representing" to fasten upon the "*negativum N*," as we called it at the time.[27]

It will not seem strange that objectives of so-being as well as objectives of being play a role in our fastening upon objects, if one is heedful of the fact that it is actually not being but so-being that constitutes the nature of objects. For as mentioned, all intending can be regarded as a sort of selection from the infinitely graded abundance of absistents, a selection made on the basis of initially given determinations. These determinations are in the last instance properties —so-being in other words; and what is more likely to be found remarkable is that a fastening-upon according to mere being, i.e., without explicit employment of so-being, is possible. We can only suppose that even in the data of mere representation, together with the intending by way of being that is grounded on them, objectives of so-being are at least implicated. For example, if I perceive the door of my room, then I doubtless in the first instance experience the fastening upon an object through an intending by way of being. But no one would deny that determinations of so-being like being brown, being rectangular, etc., are implicated. Indeed, no one would deny that the whole object that is being-intended[28] through perception must be resolvable into objectives of so-being like "something that is brown," "something that is rectangular," etc., with the possible exclusion of a remainder that has yet to be given closer scrutiny and which seems to lie concealed in the "something"— which word is perhaps not employed here in the most general fashion. On the other hand, we have seen how intending by way of so-being is connected in the closest way with intending by way of being; so that the whole contrast of what appear in the first instance as cases of intending by way of being and intending by way of so-being can at least frequently be reduced to the contrast of implicit versus explicit intending by way of so-being. Admittedly, in this fact of implicitness a peculiar problem awaits solution.

Be that as it may, the bearing on the correlation of content and object is straightway clear, and since this correlation has already occupied our attention in another regard,[29] we oughtn't to leave it wholly unmentioned that the preceding serves to diminish the closeness of the correlation in altogether new ways. For one thing, it is clear that it must make a difference as to what object one fastens upon, if a content forms the basis for an intending by way of being or if it forms the basis for an intending by way of so-being. Of course, sometimes there will be no great change in the situation either way. For example, if I look out at the early spring landscape in front of my window, then it probably amounts to the same thing, if I say "This exists," or if I say "There exists something that is the bearer of the complex of qualitative and quantitative data seen by me"—i.e., "There exists something that is thus [so]," where the "thus" is used with reference to what is directly in view, just as the "this" was used previously. The case is otherwise, when on one occasion I apprehend the color black through intending by way of being and on another occasion I use the same content to think of "something that is black," or more briefly "something black." It becomes clearly evident how great the difference is between what is intended in the former and the latter cases when, instead of the indeterminate "something black," one calls upon some of the more determinate objects that satisfy such an intending [die durch eine solche Meinung mitgetroffen sind], which would be "a board that is black," "a hat that is black," etc. Any object is affected and thus far intended along with others, as long as it and the objectum that forms the determinator in the relevant intending by way of so-being constitute a so-being objective of the black-being type. Whatever there is in the way of factual objectives of this type—positive ones, naturally— provides the basis for what is known in logic as the "extension." It might be important from the standpoint of the theory of objects, however, that we are not in every sense dependent on this "extension," i.e., that intending can disregard the limits of factuality. For besides the factual objective "Pitch is black,'' there are (in the sense of absistence) also objectives such as "Milk is black.'' If one assumes such an objective, then naturally by "something black'' even milk can be intended. This is an extension of the boundaries of intending that oughtn't to go unmentioned here, on account of the particularly obvious role of assumptions in it. Among the various objects that stand over against the same content in this way, the one that is apprehended through intending by way of being—an object which, given a certain content, in all accuracy must always be just one—occupies an obviously special position in comparison with the rest. We can make room for this fact by calling the object apprehended through intending by way of being the proximate object of the content in question; and we can call the objects apprehehended through intending by way of so-being the more remote objects of this content (or quasi-content, as the case may be).

So on the one hand, very many, possibly infinitely many objects stand over against the same content (such as the black-content). And on the other hand, since a blackboard, for example, is something black as well as something quadrangular, either the content of the representation "black'' or the content of the representation "quadrangular'' can serve for fastening upon one and the same object. Naturally, this does not at all hinder the fact that black and quadrangular are still two different objects; indeed, even "something black'' and "something quadrangular,'' both taken "closed,'' are different. All the same, the objective of so-being "something black is quadrangular'' (where "something black'' must be intended "open'') is factual; and so under favorable circumstances, one and the same object certainly can be intended with the two contents. And it surely would not be natural to call only the blackboard an "object'' and, as against that, "something black'' and "something quadrangular'' contents. Nevertheless, this has happened (e.g., in Husserl's oft-cited example of "the victor of Jena'' and "the vanquished of Waterloo''); and if I see the matter aright, it has created considerable difficulty for a natural discrimination between the terms "content'' and "object,'' as well as for a sufficiently general employment of the latter expression—or the insight into the natural generality of the notion of an object.

§46

Problems in Intending and Their Solution

The discussions of the preceding section aimed at completing the foregoing chapter's theses as to the nature of intending. As sketchy as these discussions may be, they have surely sufficed to preclude any doubt that it was mainly problems in intending that served as the starting point for the investigations of the present chapter. It is indeed one of the most routine things in our intellectual life, that we should find ourselves faced with such problems [Aufgaben]. The perceptual representations that the surrounding reality evokes in a wakeful subject can be approached from this angle, along with whatever else in the way of representations and analogously functioning experiences presents itself to consciousness, from outer or inner causes. A very special place in our considerations belongs to language's intellectual resources of suggestion. In the face of suggestion, the work of understanding probably always constitutes an accomplishment with regard to proper intending. And we are also well enough aware by now that, just as problems in intending can in general be solved in two different manners, namely through intending by way of being and intending by way of so-being, so too, the results of the solution will mainly have to exhibit two characteristic forms, according as the one or the other manner of intending claims the main role in our characterization.

But before we pursue this matter in somewhat greater detail, we must go back to a question that was discussed in the preceding sections. It is the question as to how we are supposed to be able to apprehend *inferiora* in relation or complexion, in view of the ideality of the adequation-relation. It does seem that only two ways to do this could be open. The one way is that of adding the appropriate representation of a *superius* onto the representations of the *inferiora,* and the other way is that of placing the representations of the *inferiora* in a suitable real relation to each other, and perhaps also to the representation of the *superius* in question. We had to recognize both ways as being equally inadequate. But the situation appears in a more favorable light as soon as we take into account that besides representing, a (judging or) assuming always has an essential function here. However obscure the essence of the apprehending of objects must remain for us, at least one thing can easily be believed regarding the contents that constitute the starting point for the operation of fastening upon an object: The real relation these contents have to each other could by no means be indifferent to what in a sense satisfies the operation of fastening-upon. In seeing this, we are still quite far from any genuine insight into the nature of the process, to say nothing of its finer differentiations, and it must be left to future research to show whether we can even hope for an approach to the goal of better comprehension in so fundamental a matter. But considering the difficulties that obtain here, we can surely cite the following result of our recourse to intending or assumptions as a not altogether contemptible gain. The fact of the apprehending of objects of higher order no longer confronts us as a wholly unfathomable paradox.

But if for the present we are still lacking in more precise knowledge of how assuming or judgment begins to accomplish what representation alone is not able to accomplish, then the following can be taken as a very welcome confirmation of the view I have set forth. As Bertrand Russell has justly pointed out,[30] one can arrive at the same result through a simple deliberation conducted exclusively from the standpoint of the theory of objects. It is perhaps just our abbreviated manner of characterizing an object of the form "*A* and *B* in complexion *C*" that prevents us from being aware of the fact that an objective has an altogether obligatory role in this object. This fact comes out linguistically when one says something of the form "*A, which with B constitutes a certain complex,*" or "*the complex that is constituted by A and B,*" or suchlike. And according to the principle of coincidence, we have a complex fact even in the case of the "relation R between A and B." At any event, it may be considered quite analogously to the way we considered the complex: In its unabbreviated expression, the meaning of "relation R between A and B" is again just "*R, which subsists between A and B*" or "*A, which stands in relation R to B*" or suchlike. Generally speaking, then, where there is a complex, there is also an objective as integrating factor in it, and one who wants to apprehend the complex cannot do it otherwise than by apprehending the objective, too. From that, it now becomes directly understandable, in the first place, why representing fails in the presence of complexes in the broader sense just employed —objects of higher order, as one can also say—when these objects cannot somehow be divested of their complex character by means of abstraction. But further, we know that where the point is to apprehend an objective, the means thereto can be found only in a judgment or an assumption. From the considerations developed in the preceding section, we can also see why, in the question we are now concerned with, judgments must be left out of consideration in so many instances. Beyond this, of course, it is only assumptions of so-being that have derived any immediate advantage from our present view of things from the standpoint of the theory of objects; for it was objectives of so-being that we found in complexes. But we have found that objectives of so-being are at least implicated in objectives of being, with the result that evidence for the latter carries evidence for the former along with it; and though many other things may remain obscure in the matter, this fact of implicitness makes it cease to appear completely unintelligible, when in certain circumstances we find the function of assumptions of so-being taken over by assumptions (or judgments) of being.

Let us now turn to the contrast of the intuitive and the nonintuitive, which we discussed as such at the beginning of this chapter. First of all, there is something that is readily understandable and which must surely have made itself apparent by now. It was in connection with the so-called simpler case that we were first led onto the contrast of composition and juxtaposition. Yet even in this connection, the reference to this latter contrast can be of no service in characterizing the former, as long as there is a difficulty created by the ideality of the relation of adequation. The ideality of this relation, recalled some time back, threatens to show that the real relations between the part-contents are of no importance for the nature of the *superius* that is to be apprehended. Even if this difficulty has been removed by our proof of the participation of assumptions in apprehending, one can't fail to see that the contrast of the intuitive and the nonintuitive—as it occurs in the more complicated case, too, not just in the so-called simpler case—receives a more clear-cut characterization from the reference to intending by way of being and intending by way of so-being than from the reference to composition and juxtaposition.

For the present, let us keep to the "simpler case," which was illustrated above by the "red cross" and "the cross that is red." Here one can see right away that intuitiveness goes with intending by way of being, where objectives of so-being are merely implicated, and that nonintuitiveness for its part goes with explicit intending by way of so-being. With the surest intuitiveness, the red cross offers me that very intuition that is characteristic of what we might call pure intending by way of being. The part-contents, whose proximate objects consist in "red" and "cruciform," are in this case "composed" in the pregnant sense of the term. This seems to be the condition under which intending by way of being can get hold of the object, a complex that implicates objectives of so-being. Say that without the help of perception, the mental activity of the subject succeeds in composing the uncomposed part-contents given to it. Then the subject can intuitively apprehend the complex "red cross" without perception. The situation is quite different, of course, in the case of the "cross that is red." Here in the subordinate clause, "that is red," intending by way of so-being is shown altogether out in the open, at least with regard to being red. And of course, it cannot be gathered from the words just how far "something that is cruciform" or the like mightn't with greater exactness be put in place of the objectum "cross," which at first undoubtedly offers itself as something being-intended. So at the very least, the objective of so-being "the cross's being red" is quite certainly involved. The contents "red" and "cross" now occur only in juxtaposition, and this form of complexion seems attainable under all circumstances and quite independently of the nature of the objecta that show up in the objective. For this is simply the way that contents appear in connection with each other when we understand words in the most superficial manner, as we can straightway do with, say, "quadrangle that is round." It can likewise be seen that since the present question is one of explicit objectives of so-being, the positivity of this objective is by no means requisite. I can apprehend "the cross that is not red" quite as well as "the cross that is red," and obviously by essentially the same means. But on the other side, it is equally comprehensible that a mode of apprehension that merely implicates objectives of so-being cannot implicate negative as well as positive objectives. Negative objectives of so-being are in reality excluded from intuitiveness. The contrast with the nonintuitive also shows up in the fact that intuitiveness is far from being attainable with any given part-objects. For "composition" makes definite demands on the object-related or content-type material that is to be connected; the demands are so strict that in the success of the composition, and hence in the realization of intuitiveness, one may see a thoroughly adequate criterion of possibility, while conversely impossibility has often been called incompatibility and has in all seriousness been confused with the failure to get something intuitive.

The more complicated case, as I called it above, is complicated only by the introduction of a third term R, which was reflected in the representation by a special content and which is dispensable in the simpler case. Actually, there is hardly anything special about this case, now; it merely allows somewhat more variation in the way of looking at or designating the thing in question. Suppose that red and green are given in accordance with the example used on the relevant occasion. Suppose, further, that the content of the representation "different" is produced by means of express comparison. Then with that, this content comes into such a position, or more precisely such a real relation, with regard to the red-content or the green-content that what one customarily expresses as "the relation of differentness between red and green" can be apprehended at a glance, as it were—or to put it more correctly, apprehended in an evident judgment of being. That which accordingly "is" can then also be designated as "red and green in the relation of differentness." Less naturally, one may also designate it as "red in the relation of differentness to green" or "green in the relation of differentness to red," according as attention is turned to this or that side of the complex state of affairs. In essence, we are always left with the same thing, namely the intuitive manner of apprehending the two *fundamenta* in relation. To consider the opposed case of nonintuitive apprehending, again from the standpoint of intending by way of so-being, we have only to satisfy ourselves as to the particular nature of the objectives that must be implicitly concerned in the intending by way of being just observed.

It is primarily a question about the special character of the object designated above by R. One usually calls this object a relation, although for reasons given in another place,[31] the designation "relatant" ["Relat"] seems more appropriate now. We shall certainly not succeed in explaining by means of a definition what this relatant is, as exhibited in the object "different,"[32] for example. But it is undoubtedly a most distinctive characteristic of such objects that they constitute the How in certain objectives of how-being,[33] namely the ones whose object of determination[34] or determinand[35] consists of at least two objects and not just one. In the case where red or green constitutes the How, for example, the determinand is essentially just one object. Red appears as a property in the most diverse things, yet in each thing by itself, without requiring a second thing. Yet, neither red nor a red thing can be different all by itself; a second thing has to enter in along with it, and then differentness will belong to these two together in the quite special way that one meets with solely in the case of the relation, or in the case of the relatant. The situation is otherwise with the complex, but akin to the foregoing in the plurality of determinanda. To be a couple naturally belongs neither to the husband by himself nor to the wife by herself, but only to the two of them. We see here, incidentally, that it is a matter of the What, and not as with the relatant a matter of the How. But apart from peculiarities of this sort, the objective "A and B are R" is an objective of so-being like any other. And the apprehension of this objective, too, can appear as intending by way of so-being, except that what is intended in this case is neither A by itself nor B by itself, but A and B together. But along with that, it is natural that there should still be an objective of so-being that connects A alone or B alone with the relatant $R,$ as soon as this last is determined by the respective other member of the relation. I cannot say of red simply that it is different, but I can very well say that it is different from green. Nor is it any less natural to say that green is different from red. Again, objectives of this sort can form the basis of an intending by way of so-being which is once again directed only to A or only to $B.$ Nothing is more ordinary and more significant for the business of knowing than this fastening upon an object via a relation—alongside which, in principle, there is doubtless also a fastening upon via complexion. It is now many years[36] since I first distinguished this mode of apprehending as "indirect representation," in opposition to "direct representation," i.e., to the ordinary way of intending by way of so-being as well as to intending by way of being. It speaks for the importance of the matter as well as for the naturalness of the designation I proposed, that the same word for the same matter now repeatedly makes its appearance on the part of inquirers who surely would have made note in their writings of an influence by me, had such an influence been present.[37]

With this matter cleared up, nothing more stands in the way of our applying the notion of intending by way of so-being also to the nonintuitive apprehending of "A and $B,$ which stand in the relation $R.$" Naturally, no matter what the nature of $A,$ $B,$ and R may be, the requisite objectives of both positive and negative quality are available in this case, too. That is to say, here too, all problems in intending are immediately solvable in nonintuitive modes of apprehension—which is seen in the fact that these problems are straightway understood. And of course, the characteristic nature of the situation doesn't change when the problem in intending shows up in the other possible formulations, say where one speaks of "the relation of differentness between red and green," "red, which is different from green," or suchlike.

With particular regard to the contrast of intuitive and nonintuitive, in whatever connection it is taken, two things have to be pointed out. At the beginning of this chapter, it seemed to emerge that this contrast could in no case concern the object, since under the right conditions the same object can be apprehended both intuitively and nonintuitively. Now that we are acquainted with the distinction between less remote and more remote objects, we know that the same object can quite well be apprehended through different contents when it is their more remote object, although with these contents, different proximate objects naturally must be involved. As for intuitive and nonintuitive apprehending, it has in reality turned out that we do have to speak of a difference in the objects here, insofar as on one occasion objectives of being are typically involved, on another occasion objectives of so-being. Only the notion of the implication of objectives of so-being in an intuitive apprehending's objective of being affords some prospect of toning down the appearance of such great heterogeneity a little. — The other thing can be pointed out here only in passing. In what has been set forth in this chapter, the intent is not to maintain that we speak of intuitive and nonintuitive only in regard to oppositions that appear straightway subsumable under the contrast of intending by way of being and intending by way of so-being. For one who contrasts intuitive representing with thinking in concepts, the lack of an "intuitive substrate," thought to be perceivable in the latter case, may well be the criterion.[38] As already mentioned once, the attitude of present-day psychology toward the possibility of such a lack has become much less negative than the attitude I once thought appropriate.[39] But it would lead us much too far away from the subject of these investigations, if we were to try to look into this side of the problem of intuitiveness at the present point.

The investigations of the last two chapters have had the primary purpose of bringing out the part that assumptions play in the apprehension of objects where it is a question of the intending of the latter. Our main result can now be briefly summarized as follows. The fact that representational contents and other presenting experiences are objective is in the first instance just the fact of potential objectivity, an objectivity that becomes actual only by the advent of an activity through which the relevant object is apprehended as the material of an objective—i.e., is intended. Specifically, every content or every presenting equivalent of a content can be used for fastening upon its proximate object, and this takes place through intending by way of being. But in addition, the relevant content or quasi-content can also be directed to more remote objects, through intending by way of so-being. As the immediate apprehension of an objective, intending by way of being as well as intending by way of so-being is a judgment or an assumption. In the case of intending by way of being as well as intending by way of so-being, judgment is often precluded by the special nature of the situation. Here intending becomes entirely dependent on assuming. However, to the extent that we are justified in regarding every judgment as an experience which, as it were, *a poteriori* implies a situation of assuming, one could also say this: All intending is in the last instance assuming, and assuming can be found everywhere that objects, whether they be proximate or more remote, are intellectually apprehended.

IX

The Psychology of Desire and the Psychology of Value

§47
Preliminary Note

In the fifth chapter we saw that an assumption, in the character of "psychological prerequisite," was just as certainly essential to every conative act [Begehrungsakt] as the act's directedness to an objective—or almost as certainly essential as that, not to leave reluctancies out of account.[a] This holds true in the first instance only of desires [Begehrungen] that are actualized, but it suggests the question of whether an assumption mightn't already be involved in the developing desire. It is not part of our present interest to insist on an utterly strict observance of the contrast between simultaneity and succession, and the expression just now reemployed, "psychological prerequisite," may serve to indicate that. Our purpose in introducing it[1] was precisely to make a certain indeterminacy of approach possible within certain limits. As concerns the relation between representations and feelings, to which I first applied the designation in question, it is in no way counter to the nature of a psychological prerequisite that a representation and a feeling should occur simultaneously. So too, if someone claims the assumption as the psychological prerequisite of a desire, he needn't at all regard it as out of the question that under certain circumstances the objective or the assumption yielding it should enter "into consciousness" at the same time. But at present, our concern is exclusively with cases where the objective is already given prior to the desire that is directed at it and where the act of thought by means of which the objective is given must be regarded as a partial cause of the occurrence of the desire—and in that sense as the motive for the desire. Above, we found that it was proper to claim assumptions for desires already in existence; and it is just about as clear that the act of thought now in question cannot be anything but an assumption. It would be superfluous to dwell separately on this point, if it were not also the point at which the matter of assumptions enters into connection with the much discussed problem of the motivation of desire, and into connection with the more fundamental problem of the nature of desire. In this context, too, we shall be able to see the profit that there is for psychology in knowing that there are assumptions. So if we look into some questions of the psychology of desire and feeling somewhat more closely in the following, it will not be a digression from the main theme, at least not one that is harder to justify than in the investigations of the preceding chapters.

Nevertheless, the impression that we have abandoned the object of the main investigation is a matter of especial concern this time. For what I want to consider a bit more closely through the following presentations is a theoretical problem that usually takes the form of a question about the role of feeling in desires. We want to assess what assumptions are able to contribute in this regard; and we can scarcely do that without giving some consideration to the state of theoretical development that has been attained without recourse to assumptions. Yet I have no intention of actually weighing all the possibilities that arise in this connection. In the main, it will be enough for us to refer to the relevant discussions of Christian von Ehrenfels,[2] which in important points are connected with the critical expositions by means of which, as early as the university lectures of the first half of the eighties,[3] I strove to define my own standpoint at the time. I have for many years professed[4] a negative position in regard to Ehrenfels's attempt at a solution, at least concerning the main ideas in this attempt, and in referring to these discussions of his, I should like to make use of the opportunity that it gives me to substantiate this position.[5] To this end, certainly, we shall on occasion have to refer expressly to assumptions; still, in the interest of the reader who has already convinced himself of the untenability of the "law of the relative enhancement of happiness" and its consequences or who is otherwise disinclined to go into this matter in the present connection, let us note that it is with section 53 that the investigation expressly concerning assumptions is resumed, on the basis of the rejection of such a principle of correlation.

§48
Desire as a "Relatively Felicific" Representation

It is taken as a matter of course in everyday psychology that desire is, in its occurrence, closely connected with feeling. Nothing seems more natural than that I should desire what pleases me, and that I should so so because it pleases me. And so, since a principle of correlation has so readily suggested itself to extratheoretical observation, one might suppose that it could only be a trifling matter for psychological theory to achieve a sufficiently strict formulation of this principle. However, the theoretical treatment of this matter has encountered unexpected obstacles. In particular, we have never yet succeeded in obtaining a satisfactory explanation of the relation in which feeling and desire are found together. Say that the feeling of pleasure is the only "true" object

[Objekt] of desire. Or say that whatever the nature of the object of desire is, the representation of this object must be accompanied by the feeling of pleasure, or by the prospect of the feeling of pleasure that will be present in the event that the object is realized. Or finally, say that we shall try to work with some sort of identity of the nature of feeling and desire. In every case we fall into conflict with legitimate claims, empirical or theoretical. Under such circumstances, the attempt to take a new path cannot be denied *prima facie* justifiability; there is no doubt about this. Ehrenfels actually made such an attempt, in formulating his "law of the relative enhancement of happiness"; and what we have to do now is to form an opinion on this attempt, regarding its inherent justifiability. To have a substrate for the following critical deliberations, I shall first of all put the relevant main ideas in the form with which I have had most success in making them my own. I hope I do not depart from the intention of the author in doing so. In case this does happen to me, let it be emphasized that in the following polemic I am as little concerned with the assessment of personal accomplishments as I have been in other written discussions of recent years.[6] My concern is exclusively with a knowledge of the matter at hand; so to the extent that there was any question of inaccuracies in the present rendition, these would just be inaccuracies through which the position under consideration was toned down.

What desire has to do with feeling, or how these two experiences show up in conjunction with each other—this receives the following formulation from Ehrenfels himself. Every act of desiring "in its arisal enhances the state of happiness in comparison to the state that would arise in the absence of that act."[7] By "enhancement of happiness"[b] we are to understand both the heightening of the desirer's state of pleasure and a lessening of his state of displeasure. The qualification "relative"—the law in question is called a "law of the relative enhancement of happiness"—is perhaps not very clear in itself. It is intended to call attention to the fact that the enhancement meant is not an enhancement in comparison with the desirer's actual state immediately preceding the desiring, but only an enhancement in comparison with a simultaneous but nonactual and purely hypothetical state of the desirer. It is the state that would have to arise in the absence of and in place of the desiring.

It wouldn't do too well to occupy ourselves with this law without bearing in mind the psychological perspective that it seems to open up, namely the prospect of a kind of analysis of desire and, resting upon this analysis, a deeper probing of the nature of desire. Deliberations like the following are supposed to lead to this goal.

First of all, following Ehrenfels's meaning, we can further characterize the factor in desires on which the felicific significance stated in the above law depends. What one desires is not "purely and simply" represented, but represented as actual or nonactual. More precisely, it is "incorporated in or eliminated from" the "causal fabric of subjective reality."[8] It is the representation of this incorporation or elimination that works felicifically. But that is not meant to preclude the possibility that "in positive desiring...a relative enhancement of happiness" is "usually already connected with purely and simply representing an object."^{C} Conversely, too, we can say: "Wherever the representation of the incorporation of an object in or the elimination of it from the subjective reality brings with it a relative enhancement of happiness, there is also a desiring present, positive or negative.[9] Coincidence of this sort permits one to surmise the identity of the coinciding states of affairs, and for this surmise there are also the following corroborating considerations.

It is not regarded as a case of desire if what is so termed does not maintain itself in consciousness in the face of competition. Also, the manner in which the conflict of motives reaches a decision is that the relevant object of desire either maintains itself or is dislodged.[10] But now, Ehrenfels is aware of principles of correlation that allow this self-maintaining capacity of desires to be attributed, on the one side, to the factor of incorporation or elimination, and on the other side, to the factor of enhancement of happiness; in that way, these two characteristics of desires are shown to be its essential core.

Ehrenfels affirms one of these principles of correlation as a "law of the relative enhancement of happiness,"[11] too, although it is wholly different from the above, similarly entitled law, notwithstanding the possibility that the domain of application of the two might partly coincide. In view of the theory of desire advocated by Ehrenfels, this difference is not so much clear from the fact that the new law presents itself as a law of representation as from the fact that this law, unlike the first law of this name, does not strike one as conferring the characteristic of being felicific on a definite class of facts. Rather, for certain felicific facts, namely the felicific representations, there is claimed the characteristic of being in a privileged position vis-à-vis other representations—and specifically, not so much with regard to their arising in consciousness as in regard to their remaining there. "The more pleasant representations receive an additional measure of power in the struggle for the narrow confines of consciousness."[12] This is not only shown by direct observation; "the law of the relative enhancement of happiness can also be comprehended physiologically, as being something inherent in the nature of the matter."[13]

Again, something quite similar to what holds true of felicific representations holds true of those representations whose objects are represented as actual or not actual—or in other words, as "incorporated in or eliminated from the causal fabric of subjective reality." To these representations, too, there goes the "additional measure of power." This is in accordance with the law "that the imagination adheres in a special way to something that is represented as standing in a causal relation to the always-present complex of the ego-representation."[14] It would be a mistake to see the effect of judgment there, since judgment can be lacking; but the influence of judgment proceeds "always by way of an incorporation in or elimination from the causal fabric of subjective reality."[15]

So speaking quite generally, both the enhancement of happiness and the incorporation or elimination always have the significance of an additional measure of power. And furthermore, we have met with both the enhancement of happiness and incorporation or elimination in the case of desires. Then it does not strike one as risky to give credit to these factors for the power of resistance that can likewise be shown in desires. But in seeing nothing short of the whole nature of desire in these factors, our author finds himself pressed by "almost insurmountable difficulties," difficulties that are supposed to stand in opposition to the acknowledgment of desire as a specifically distinct state of affairs,[16] as well as by the circumstance that inward perception fails to testify to such a state of affairs. Accordingly, Ehrenfels summarizes his standpoint in these words: "There is no distinct basic psychic element, 'desire' (wishing, endeavoring, or willing). What we call desire is nothing but this: a representation that establishes a relative enhancement of happiness and which is a representation of the incorporation or elimination of some object in or from the causal fabric at the center of the present concrete representation of the self."[17]

§49

The Testimony of Inward Perception

I shall begin the critical consideration of what has been set forth with a brief reference to the three "difficulties" just mentioned, which our author, by the way, grants only a quite passing treatment. As far as I can see, it is no difficulty, but only a fact, that the desiring of the means for the sake of the end is dependent on a judgment as to the connection between the end and the means.[18] Again, we may suppose that if desire is not, as regards part of its nature, a relative enhancement of happiness, as Ehrenfels would have it, desire is nevertheless dependent on this relative enhancement. Yet it may strike one as being strange that this merely relative enhancement of happiness, which is "the difference between an actual and a merely possible state of feeling, should lend existence and intensity to an actual element, to a present mental phenomenon."[19] But one is at a loss to see why the responsibility for this difficulty should have to be taken by the one who holds for the existence of distinct conative acts and not by the one whose explanations are supposed to make the "law" of the relative enhancement of happiness credible to begin with. In the same way, if the laws of happiness enhancement and power increment, in the sense set forth above, are regarded as proven, then one may ask one's self whether what is customarily taken as being a result of volition requires any further special cause at all;[20] but one whom Ehrenfels's remarks have *not* convinced will see no difficulty that is incumbent upon *him* to settle.

However, the testimony of inward perception is naturally not to be left out, and I must not fail to emphasize that this testimony sounds far different to me than it does to our author. To be sure, inward perception provides me with as little information about the simplicity or irreducibility of desire as it does anyone else. But it oughtn't to be left unsaid that astonishingly little of the "happiness-enhancing incorporation or elimination" is to be discovered in the picture of my desiring that inward perception gives me. For me, of course, this fact carries a good deal of persuasiveness. But I admit that there is little in the fact that could persuade the opponent; and to venture immediately on the strength of that fact to formulate the psychology of the opponent's error would seem to me to be a procedure that is admissible only in special exceptions.

In view of this situation, which is all too familiar to everyone as an insurmountable obstacle to agreement, it may be regarded as an exceptionally good stroke of luck if the appeal to inward perception does, nevertheless, exhibit a discussable side. This seems to me to lie in the fact that even the opponent will scarcely be inclined to deny—and in view of experience will not very well be able to deny—that inward perception normally informs us of the presence of our desires. But there could not be a single case of this, if Ehrenfels's characterization of desire turned out to be true, or more precisely, if the "relative enhancement of happiness" formed a constituent element of desire. Above,[21] I reproduced a passage from which it became clear how our author himself describes this enhancement of happiness as a difference between something actual and something possible. The "relative" nature of the advancement of happiness, in this special sense, is frequently and expressly pointed out elsewhere, too. But of course, inward perception provides no information about what is not actual but only possible, i.e., it provides no information about what would have to take place in circumstances that are in fact not realized.

And so the view in question precludes the possibility of perceiving desires. What does it have to substitute for that, then? In order to arrive at an opinion as to whether, in a given case, there is a "relative enhancement of happiness" or not, we shall require reflections that can easily be expected to turn out rather complicated, at least in many cases. Ehrenfels himself, who is no stranger to the question presently under consideration, answers it by pointing out "that on the occasion of the appearance in consciousness of the representations" constituting the relevant desires, "we observe a parallel alteration in the absolute, actual state of happiness." It is observed also on the occasion of "the fluctuations in vividness and intuitiveness to which these representations are exposed in virtue of continual disturbances of equilibrium in the other tendencies of the flow of representations."[22] But for one thing, the law of the "relative enhancement of happiness" for desire would thereby have turned into a law of the "absolute enhancement of happiness," at least for all instances of perceivable desire. And for another thing, one who wanted to know whether he was desiring or not would have to make a comparison between his present and his earlier state of pleasure. Yet normally no one is conscious of such or other reflections, though he is quite well aware of his desiring. I cannot help regarding the matter of the Ehrenfelsean theory of desire as already settled by means of what has been said.

§50

The Representational Law of the "Relative Enhancement of Happiness"

Let us now turn quite expressly to the two "happiness enhancement" laws; and let it first of all be the one that concerns representation, the one that could also, and in a certain sense more clearly, be spoken of as a "power increment" law. Here too, of course, the previously mentioned question as to how any "relative enhancement of happiness" is related to direct observation arises as a complicating factor in the attempt to pin down inductive instances. But here the question represents no more than a complication, since it is after all possible to obtain instances in an indirect way. The point Ehrenfels actually adduces is "that the more pleasant imaginative representations—or call them the less unpleasant ones—last longer than should be expected merely from the standpoint of habituation and fatigue." These representations "also maintain themselves longer and remain more vivid, without an inner volitional act directed to them, than do indifferent representations under the same circumstances, not to say unpleasant representations."[23] But if one would like to have a somewhat more detailed elucidation of this, which in itself is obviously not an altogether simple state of affairs, then one receives some advance information about it that is not exactly promising. "It would be superfluous," the author continues,[24] "to adduce examples for a law of such all-embracing significance. Examples will yield themselves in abundance to one who sees himself compelled to acknowledge this law in virtue of his overall psychological view, and one who denies the law will not be brought round by examples. For an individual case can do no more than show that this or that relatively pleasant representation remains in consciousness for such and such a length of time. That it could not remain as long if it were not pleasant—this conviction can be acquired only through the sort of induction that everyone has to carry out for himself, an extensive induction based on psychological imagination." With all due respect for "psychological imagination," the summary appeal to it might be all too summary in a case where the author himself subsequently has to call attention to counter-instances; and he will surely grant that there is at least room for dispute as to whether or not he has succeeded in disposing of these counter-instances.

Specifically, this too is a question about the evaluation of rather commonplace facts. Everyone has already experienced for himself how painful things, not just pleasant ones, can intrude quite forcibly in our thoughts and maintain themselves there. People of a melancholy disposition occupy themselves remarkably often and long with gloomy thoughts. Everyone has also rather frequently seen how one can be "bothered" by representations for which the adjective "painful" would be far too good, representations that were far better characterized as burdensome to the point of unbearability. The question of Ehrenfels's interpretation of the attitude of the melancholiac may be left undecided. He thinks that the gloomy thoughts of such a person are pleasant to him.[25] I cannot help suspecting that if the melancholiac could just get rid of the gloomy thoughts, he would find the more cheerful ones pleasanter. Yet, we cannot pass over Ehrenfels's opinion on the two other points without expressly pointing out the peculiarity of this opinion. For such cases, our author simply concedes that "the reactions deriving from the relative enhancement of happiness are often paralyzed," and he conjectures "that beyond the known partial causes there are other ones, probably purely physiological, that influence the course of representation."[26] Taking such possibilities into account is certainly quite unobjectionable in itself, when one is dealing with such firmly established laws as the law of gravitation or the law of inertia, which Ehrenfels adduces by way of analogy. If a stone flies upwards, then admittedly I shall not on that account begin to lose faith in the law of gravitation, especially if I have already heard something about throwing. But in the case of the "law of the relative enhancement of happiness," precisely what has to be done first of all is to determine whether there is any such law, and the present proof that there is can probably be condensed into the following formula. There are experiences that speak for such a law; there are admittedly also experiences that speak against it, but these latter experiences will have to be interpreted in a way still unknown to us at the present, and for that reason they do not matter. Under such circumstances,[27] however, it would seem that one should wait for more detailed investigation before deciding.

I note the beginning of such an investigation in the article "Über den Einfluss der Gefühle auf die Vorstellungsbewegung," by Robert Saxinger.[28] The author formulates his result in the sentence, "The longer persistence of representations and their more frequent arisal in consciousness always rests..., as far as feelings are involved at all, on the influence of actual feelings. This influence proceeds from feelings of displeasure as well as feelings of pleasure. That is, matters stand no differently for feelings of displeasure than they do for feelings of pleasure in this regard. The intensity of feelings, not their quality, is the decisive factor in the influence of feeling on the course of representation."[29] This statement presumably does not close the case; still, for the present I cannot help finding this result considerably more in accord with the facts known to me than the representational law of the "relative enhancement of happiness."

§51

The Desiderative Law of the
"Relative Enhancement of Happiness"

After the representational law of the relative enhancement of happiness, we must now subject the desiderative law of the relative enhancement of happiness to a brief critical consideration. Naturally, there is another instance here of what might be called the methodological difficulty—that we cannot strictly speaking be completely sure in any single case as to whether "relative" enhancement of happiness is really present. In this case, however, there may be a way out of the difficulty in the fact that we should be able to infer a relative enhancement of happiness from an absolute one. Thus, if we feel better as we desire than before we did, there may after all be little on the whole that we can plausibly urge against the conjecture that the relative enhancement of happiness may actually be a fact—i.e., that without the desiring, we should not feel as good as we do at the time in question. Indeed, we have already seen[30] that our author makes use of this point of view in connection with the perception of desire.

But then, if it actually is only absolute enhancement of happiness that we have empirically tangible instances of, why doesn't the law have to do with the absolute enhancement of happiness? Why does it instead have to do with the very thing that is not accessible to observation at all? No doubt it is easy to say what is gotten by means of this law: in any case where there is desire without any absolute enhancement of happiness, it will always be possible for one to surmise a state of affairs respecting the relative enhancement of happiness that is more favorable to the law. Actually, one is thereby secured against being refuted by observation. But would such a lack of counter-instances speak more emphatically in favor of the law than it would for a theory of color sensations, if a blind person could not produce any experiences that conflicted with that theory?

And so ultimately, the considerations in favor of our law can be expressed merely in the form of the following reflection. There are desires that are most likely accompanied by relative enhancement of happiness; these are the desires with absolute enhancement of happiness. On the strength of that, one may contemplate the possibility of a law of the relative enhancement of happiness. But there are also desires without an absolute enhancement of happiness. Of these, it is difficult to maintain that they are also without a relative enhancement of happiness, albeit the reason for this is mainly that at the present time we simply have no proper means at our disposal for knowing of a relative enhancement of happiness except the roundabout way via the absolute enhancement of happiness. Thus, the possibility of a law of the relative enhancement of happiness can still be taken into consideration; but to make it at all probable might at all events be rather difficult, under these circumstances.

For those who would still like to form some opinion, despite so unfavorable a situation, the relative frequency of the cases favorable to the supposed law in comparison with the uncharacteristic cases is naturally important. But our author, who is on the whole very reticent in the reference to concrete facts in this same matter, to my knowledge has failed to bring forward further information. Now, to attempt a rough estimate on the basis of the entirety of one's personal experiences, without any theoretical aids, is surely anything but a trustworthy thing in this matter. If I am nevertheless to hazard such a guess, then I cannot find the result at all favorable to the law in question. I certainly do encounter desires with "absolute enhancement of happiness"—or expressed in the customary manner of speaking, desires that are accompanied by a feeling of satisfaction or some similar feeling that one does not hesitate to connect with desire. The cases seem mostly to be ones where the usual way of thinking is to regard the desire itself as a step towards the fulfillment of one's desire, and on that account to hope for this fulfillment—primarily cases of confident willing, in other words. There is also a wishing^d that is accompanied by hope. The commonplace view does not allow that hoping can come from wishing, but we shall not press the point in the present place. Over against such desires with feelings of pleasure,[31] however, stand a quite considerable and, it seems to me, almost overwhelming number of volitions and wishes in which accompanying feelings are simply not observable, or where they are of an unmistakably displeasurable character. I don't think that a law can be legitimately grounded on favorable cases under such circumstances as these, where it also extends over so many unfavorable cases.

Until now, I have included desires accompanied by displeasure along with desires without accompanying feelings as being "unclear" cases, and I have taken only the number of cases into consideration. But in the end, one must also raise the question as to whether we have not already gone too far in meeting the theory of the "relative enhancement of happiness" half way. There are desires connected with displeasure that still must be given special consideration in this regard. In analogy to the repeatedly mentioned desires with "absolute enhancement of happiness," one can characterize the new ones as desires with "absolute impairment of happiness"; and then we can urge further analogies. That is, if it is correct to treat absolute enhancement of happiness as a sign of relative enhancement, then something similar for the impairment of happiness will be only fair. In that case, however, desires with absolute impairment of happiness will no longer be merely unclear cases; they are rather counterinstances to the law of the relative enhancement of happiness.

Under such circumstances, it becomes increasingly important as to whether there really are desires with absolute impairment of happiness. It seems to me that experience yields no reason for doubt in this regard, even under the most careful examination. Over against confident volitions, there are ones with little confidence. Or are we to suppose that when someone is faced with powers whose vincibility he can scarcely believe in and notwithstanding takes up the struggle against them, he is happier thereby than the one who resigns himself to the well-nigh inevitable? But wishing is still clearer on this point. One who is seized with longing for the unattainable is as a rule richer by a sorrow, not by a joy. Otherwise, why would people have so often attempted to see true happiness in the absence of wishes? I am by no means of the opinion that they have been right in doing so; but as applied to all desires, the law of the relative enhancement of happiness is the opposite extreme: It seems to me not only unproven and difficult to show probable, but directly opposed to the facts and for that reason unacceptable.

If what has been set forth about the two laws of the relative enhancement of happiness is correct, then along with these two laws there is a collapse of the two main supports of the reduction of desire, which has already proved itself to be unacceptable to us from another point of view.[32] Just in passing, I might add the following. In this reduction, desire's characteristic of "maintaining" itself in the "narrow confines of consciousness" also strikes me as having received more emphasis than it might deserve. In particular, it doesn't seem to me to be anywhere near in exceptionless accordance with the facts, to think of the resolution of the conflict of motives in such a way that the victor is the more persevering, as it were, and the vanquished simply the one crowded out. It is true that a child who has an unfulfillable wish can be most easily managed by "getting him to think of something else," as they say. But an adult certainly does not overcome contrary motives merely by "forgetting about it"; nor has someone really overcome a temptation, when he cannot look it in the face without becoming irresolute again.

§52
"Incorporation" in "Subjective Reality"

In our critical considerations up to now, there has been no discussion at all of the "incorporation in and elimination from the causal fabric of subjective reality." It seems to me that we might forego entering into this matter, if there were nothing to do but form an opinion in regard to the reductive analysis of desire. But this "incorporation and elimination" has to be brought up for special consideration in its own right, as being the point in Ehrenfels's presently considered arguments that stands in closest connection with the main object of the investigation directed to assumptions.

In the first place, I admit I have objections to raise in this matter too. In light of experience, I must most definitely deny that such "incorporation or elimination" is essential to every desire, at least as long as by "incorporation" and "elimination" we mean both what those words signify and what is in accordance with the description given by the author.[33] There are certainly cases where a desirer sees what he desires in some causal relation to himself. But for the average volitions of everyday life, let alone the wishes, it would seem to me to be extremely risky even to regard that as what happens as a rule. As for the exceptionlessness of any such rule, that is entirely out of the question, if I see the matter at all correctly. It is true that to someone who, say, wants to master a gymnastic exercise at which he has hitherto not succeeded, it is quite essential that *he* be the one who succeeds at it now. The case is otherwise, surely, with the experimenter who wants to turn on a gas-cock or reduce the force of an electrical current he is working with by introducing a resistance into the circuit.

It is even more clearly a different case, when someone wants something done, perhaps at his order—not to say when he simply has wishes, to whose fulfillment he is unable to contribute anything at all. In a thousand cases of this sort, the thought of any causal connection with himself will be furthest from his mind; and where he does think of one, it will rather often be inessential to do so. In appealing to examples like the following, our author appears to be abandoning the testimony of experience in a quite unmistakable manner. "If I wish that Socrates had been acquitted by his judges or that Beethoven could have gotten to hear the Ninth Symphony, then in representation I bring this occurrence into causal connection with things and events that I view as real. Either (as in the examples adduced) I regard these things and events as jointly determining causes of present realities that contain my own self, or I regard them at least as effects of common causes or as possible common causes of future effects, all understood in relation to the present subjective reality."[34] Causal relations of this sort may indeed be discoverable in all objects of desire; at least it has been fairly often maintained that, strictly speaking, everything necessarily stands in a causal relation with everything. In truth, I cannot see this necessity, either. Be that as it may, in a case like that of Socrates or Beethoven, the one desiring normally thinks just of Socrates or of Beethoven, and not of himself; and I would also be at a loss to see how the addition of the thought of myself could turn something into a desire, or even make it more nearly so, if it weren't already a desire.

There is another, second connection in which I must deny "incorporation and elimination" the significance that Ehrenfels accords it. As we saw, it is supposed to be what ensues when we do not "purely and simply" represent an object, but "represent it as actual or unactual." As things now stand, however, the investigations that we have carried out in the earlier chapters of this work may put us in the position of realizing, above all, that the contrast under consideration at this point cannot simply be a matter of representations. No doubt we shall have to grant right away that the qualification "actual" or "unactual" discloses no presence of a judgment.[35] But if "actual" amounts to factually "existing," then we have moved from an objectum to an objective anyway; and we now also know that an objective must be apprehended by means of an assumption, in the event that there is no judgment. We needn't consider the question as to whether there might be an additional step in thought through which what is "represented as actual or existing" has being assigned to it as an attribute (perhaps in the sense of the always rather strange "existential predication," mentioned more than once in the foregoing).[36] The essential thing consists in the assumption, which in any case suffices by itself. So to "represent as actual or not actual" is strictly speaking nothing but to assume affirmatively or negatively. But it is in itself a quite justified theoretical demand that made Ehrenfels think he had to accompany the representation of an object in the usual way, "purely and simply," with two other ways of representing the same object, and it is to be hoped that the author himself will find this demand satisfactorily answered by our reference to assumptions.

Along with this, there naturally ceases to be any reason to get involved with the expedient of "incorporation and elimination" in this matter—which expedient is, again, extremely questionable in the face of direct observation, too. But if those two things are replaced with the affirmative and the negative assumption, then one naturally might ask whether this replacement mightn't be able to make good the incongruities that just now prevented us from attributing desires a constant conjunction with "incorporation or elimination." Actually, if we try this replacement, we arrive at a result that is thoroughly correct and yet thoroughly familiar to us. A desire goes hand in hand with an assumption; this, we found earlier,[37] is practically the same as the fact that every desiring has its objective, i.e., that it is directed to the being or not-being of its objectum. As we already had occasion to mention,[38] this fact has not eluded our author, either.

§53
Assumptions and the Motivation of Desires

Thus, assumptions prove fit to accommodate the demands from which such a questionable conception as that of "incorporation and elimination" might have arisen. But I hope by all means to be able to show that through consideration of assumptions one can also close the gap that our foregoing rejection of the desiderative law of the "relative enhancement of happiness" now seems to have reopened in the understanding of the relation between feeling and desire. In the process, perhaps it will yet turn out that this law does, despite its other deficiencies, have an important contact with observation in one point—but that without resort to that law, this contact can be just as well established, and better established, by the enlistment of assumptions.[39]

In this matter we can perhaps best start again from the relation of feeling to desire that is taken for granted in prepsychological observation. This relation shows up in our approach to the question as to why someone desires this or that; the question is regarded as settled by the information, "because it gives me pleasure" or "because I find it pleasant"—and so forth, perhaps including also "because I set great value on it." On account of its obviousness, such a reply is not exactly regarded as informative; but by the same token it is regarded as unassailably correct. It might be very nearly as obvious to someone innocent of theory that when he says that he desires A because it is enjoyable to him, by this "it"—or the thing that is pleasant to him—he does not mean the desiring[40] and that what he means is most certainly in some manner that which is desired, or that which can be desired. And uneasiness about this approach surely never would have arisen, had the "manner" been easier to specify. But right there lies the old difficulty: What is desired cannot yet give me pleasure, since as that which can be desired it is not yet realized. Nor can we mean the pleasure in looking forward to it; for I first have to desire, specifically will, if I am going to look forward to what I desire. Pleasure in the mere representation does not do the job, either; and the various artificial expedients to which one is forced by the failure of the natural ones do not come off any better.

But we are able to set a further and as yet unconsidered possibility alongside the several possibilities we have already considered. In the first instance, after all, we are concerned with the psychological description of a person's psychological state before the desire comes about; and in this connection we already know, again by way of prepsychological past experience, that before we arrive at a decision we first of all think ourselves into the situation that is to be realized through our volition, i.e., we do so if we have any time at all to "think it over." We try to make clear to ourselves "how it would be if" the situation had already been realized, the situation whose realization is now within the scope of our will or at least seems to be so. If it is a case of mere wishing, instead of willing, then there will not so likely be an express "thinking it over," especially a deliberate one. But even in this case, a person must have already built a "castle in the air," if he is now wishing for one; and in building it he can hardly avoid the thought of "how it would be if..." Well, then, the nature of such a thought is already well-known to us. It is not a judgment, but neither is it a mere representation; in a word, it is an assumption. Above, we already saw that one who desires must not only represent what is desired but also make it the object of an assumption, the assumption being the means by which desire is given an objective, the object that is essential to it. It is quite in keeping with this if it now turns out that while the objective needn't under all circumstances be given in advance of desire, it is at least given everywhere that we have reason to speak of a motivational process that by nature precedes desire.

Of course, the matter is not finished with the assumption that the presumptive objectum of desire [Begehrungsobjekt] exists, or that it does not[41]—alternatively, in the case of an existing objectum, that it "is thus and so" or "is not thus and so."[e] It is natural to suppose that the assumption in question would have to be accompanied by a second one relating to the manner in which the assumed existence or non-existence, or the assumed so-being or not being thus and so, might engage the affective attitude of the subject. The two assumptions might then be connected with each other in a relationship of ground and consequent. But the whole would still be nothing but what has long been considered under the name of "hypothetical judgment," although without regard for the important role that assumptions have in this whole. In short, the motive of the desire would then be the reflection on how the subject might feel, in the event that what is willed or wished were achieved. Such reflections actually will occur, under special circumstances; but as a rule, what experience shows is the presence of feelings themselves, not reflections on feelings. And with that, it seems that we have finally been brought round to the old difficulty again, despite our recourse to assumptions.

This would actually be the case, and as far as I can see it would have to remain so, if the knowledge that there is something judgmentlike that is nevertheless not judgment did not suggest the question as to whether there might not also be something feelinglike that exhibits the qualitative opposition of feeling in the same way that assumption partakes of the qualitative opposition of judgment. Naturally, this is a question that requires as thorough an investigation as the one by means of which I hope I have proved the actuality of assumptions. The task would be too far-reaching for me to approach in the present connection. Nevertheless, even in the previous edition of this book, I did not think that I should omit some initial statements in this matter. Surely it was to be expected that if one could show the probability of there being something akin to assumptions in the extraintellectual domain, the significance of this for assumptions might not be altogether inessential. Today I am in a considerably more favorable position, in that I am already able to rely on more than one relevant investigation in other places.[42] It may be that through the following remarks, necessarily no more than sketchy this time, too, I shall succeed in being of assistance to further inquiry into a domain of fact that has been as neglected as that of assumptions, nay more neglected.

§54
Imaginative Feelings and Imaginative Desires. Empathy

In the attempt at an initial characterization of the state of affairs regarding assumptions, we found ourselves more than once compelled to describe assumptions as mental facts that occupy a kind of intermediate position between representations and judgments. I now believe I must assert, in a quite analogous way, that there are also mental facts that must be assigned a kind of mid-position between representations and feelings.[43] Experiences with works of art give us the clearest information on this. I am thinking of experiences which, if I am not mistaken, have until now remained an unsolved psychological and aesthetic problem, for all their ordinariness and familiarity. As such, these experiences invite the supposition that we are dealing with a peculiar specimen of mental reality and one that has not yet been adequately appreciated in its peculiar character. What are they, really—the "fear" and the "compassion" or whatever it may be that tragedy has the task of "evoking"? A fear in which one is basically not afraid at all, a compassion which, more closely regarded, is seen not to involve any sense of pain whatsoever—are they yet "feelings," as the psychologist is in the first instance accustomed to regard them? Naturally, it is not to be denied that many a theater-goer, in particular one who is as yet unfamiliar with such things, may now and then be seized by fear or, as is more likely, real compassion. But then, it is hardly likely that any of us will have trouble in determining that what happens to such a person is neither the normal reaction nor the one that could be said to be adequated to the work of art.[44]

In Stephan Witasek's contrast of the "empathetic feelings and sympathetic feelings"[45] which, under favorable circumstances, arise in the presence of the work of art, the twofold grouping of the experiences that are under consideration here shows up in a more clear-cut and general fashion than it does in the classical contrast of fear and compassion. If we may regard the matter of aesthetic sympathy as already being sufficiently elucidated by what has just been indicated about compassion, then it is quite instructive in regard to empathy to remember the fact that in an earlier work[46] Witasek found it possible to order the customary interpretations of empathy under the two concepts of an "actuality view" and a "representation view." According to the former view, the nature of empathy is the direct experiencing of the feelings in question; according to the latter view, empathy is the mere representing of these feelings. It is instructive, for these are the two extreme positions that almost immediately disqualify themselves empirically. The disqualification is especially clear in the case of the actuality view, if only one will think it through without the sort of illicit mitigating qualifications that would naturally enable one to bring this view closer to reality. Of the most moving tragedy, as opposed to the most gripping novel, anyone can ascertain the following for himself immediately: If things were different, if the enacted sufferings, which on all sides so heavily outweigh the enacted joys, were really personally experienced, then the serious art would have an incomparably smaller public, in the event that it had one at all. In light of that, one might attempt to work with the opposed view—a view which, strictly speaking, tends to resolve empathy into representations and thus to divest it of any character of feeling. The inadequacies of such an approach are unmistakably plain at the outset, quite simply in light of experience and without our going into the representability of feelings.[47] If in a certain sense the actuality view indubitably postulates too much, the representation view just as indubitably postulates too little.[48] That my attitude to the work of art should *only* be a representing and perhaps assuming attitude[49]—this is ordinarily in the most decisive contradiction to my clear-cut experiences. If in the second part of Björnsen's *Beyond Our Power,* for example, I coexperience how Elias Sang sacrifices himself and his opponents to his probity of will and to his drive toward the "immeasurable," I do not yet on that account feel that drive in me; less still does everything from heroic composure on down to the senselessly craven fear of death occur in me—the whole scale of feelings that the author wants to be exhibited to the onlooker in the different members of the doomed congregation. Yet there seems to be no room for doubt that besides intellectual processes, what is taking place in me includes something quite essential that cannot be classed anywhere but in the emotional domain. Even though we avoid, as we certainly must, a literal interpretation of "coexperiencing" ["Miterleben"], it is still going to be a much too highly colored metaphor for representing and assuming alone.

A less direct empirical objection to the "representation view" ought not to go unmentioned here, since the approach in back of this objection has been employed in the most diverse passages of the present book. If it is correct that inward perception is based not on perceptual representations of inner experiences, but on the experiences' self-presentation at the time of their presentness,[50] then the substitute for a self-presenting feeling on the other side of the boundary of presentness could hardly be a representation of this feeling. But the substitute could easily be something feelinglike which, having arisen by continuous transition from the feeling, is able to take over the self-presenting function of the original feeling, acting as a surrogate quasi-content.[51] Further, if the apprehending of mental experiences as a whole can be treated in analogy with the apprehending of one's own experiences, then it results first of all that the representation of the mental is, as such, entirely out of the question—and therefore also out of the question as a representing of feelings.[52] At the same time there is indicated, as a substitute for representations of feelings, something feelinglike that does in a certain sense have a representational function to perform, in that it is not primarily a matter of self-presentation in this case.

In the combined impression that they give, the representation view and the actuality view point to a certain mean between representation and feeling, although as we had occasion to say above, in a way the latter view asserts too much and the former one asserts too little. However high or low one may rate the cogency of our own statements, which certainly stand in need of verification in more than one respect, they do at any event point to a mean in quite the same way. Along with this, one is struck by an analogy to the first, still rather indefinite thoughts on the basis of which we assigned assumptions a position between representation and judgment. An assumption is something judgment-like that resembles judgment but is not a judgment. This leads to the idea of something feelinglike which, analogously, is not altogether a feeling, although it resembles feeling to some extent—and although, in particular, it partakes of the opposition of pleasure and displeasure in the way that the assumption partakes of the opposition of affirmation and negation. I confess that at present I do not know what to specify as the analogue to the "moment of conviction," the factor whose addition to an assumption makes a judgment of it, as it were. I can only hope that future analysis will be more successful in this.

It is not just in connection with the opposites of pleasure and displeasure that the existence of something similar to feeling begins to make itself apparent. The diverse experiences already treated in everyday psychology as "various feelings" are themselves accompanied by quite obvious parallel cases, their affinity being revealed in the applicability of the corresponding names. Thus, expressing himself in an altogether natural way, an ingenuous person will claim to experience joy and sorrow, fear and hope "with" the characters of a drama. The points of agreement between one's own intellectual presuppositions and those of the drama, along with the maintained parallel between assumption and judgment, doubtless afford no little justification for such assertions. But this is not enough; the spectator actually experiences something in himself. It is not literally joy or sorrow, fear or hope, but something similar; so that everyone can readily understand the use of the expressions in question, even if he immediately perceives it as being a nonliteral use.

But in order to preclude a misunderstanding that might arise at this point, let me expressly emphasize that what has just been said is not intended as a means of distinguishing the specific character of "aesthetic feelings." By no means do I want to deny such feelings the right to be regarded as feelings in the strict and literal sense of the term. But it is also easy to keep them distinct from the facts just mentioned.[53] For even today, in a time of such sweeping reformism in aesthetic matters, we speak of artistic enjoyment, pleasure in a work of art, and so on; and we also have no great scruples about attributing the capacity for evoking such feelings to, say, tragedy [Trauerspiel]. But what we aesthetically coexperience in the *"Trauerspiel"* are, after all, "sad things" ["Trauriges"]. And so artistic pleasure, delight in the work of art, and whatever else belongs in a group with these—in short, the previously mentioned "aesthetic feelings"—are something quite different from the facts whose theoretical recognition is being advocated in these discussions. Aesthetic feelings are genuine feelings in whose arisal the latter, feelinglike states of affairs along with assumptions have a quite prominent role, i.e., as the psychological prerequisites of those genuine feelings.

Facts entering into their first theoretical treatment as a rule present difficulties in naming, since language has usually not seen to their naming. In the case of assumptions, language has proved unusually accommodating. As concerns the feelinglike facts just affirmed, on the other hand, one has to rely on artificial naming. The term "pseudo-feeling" would not be entirely unsuited to this purpose, but we could hardly make do without a reinterpretation of the ordinary sense of the term. But it seems to me that what is primarily decisive for the choice of another term is this: that there is a point of view, one that is to be mentioned later on,[54] from which the designation "imaginative feelings" might seem to be especially appropriate. It is a designation that might already suggest itself on its own merits. At this point I must forego any further inquiry into this matter, too; for the immediate need, I shall just avail myself of the expression "imaginative feeling."

Yet even for an initial evaluation of the group of facts thus named, it seems indispensable to me to take one more circumstance into account, a circumstance that is not a part of the evaluation but nevertheless contains a sort of new guarantee for the correctness of the observations leading up to it. It is at least to be expected that we shall find ourselves less tempted to doubt the existence of imaginative feelings, if we have more cogent reasons for affirming something analogous in the domain of desires—something that would accordingly be entitled to the name "imaginative desires." The clearest proofs that there is such an analogue again arise from our attitude to art. Readers of "suspenseful" novels not infrequently tell us that they "wish" for a certain ending; desires of this sort occasionally find expression in connection with the action of dramas, too. In this latter connection they are readily scoffed at as a gross misunderstanding of the situation, and one may be fairly often right in scoffing at such desires. It must be conceded, though, that similar stirrings are by no means unknown to those who are in other respects far from ever confusing fiction with truth. Such a person realizes best the "unreasonableness" of a desiring that cannot be said to have the slightest orientation to actuality; but this realization is so little able to affect the arisal of the attitude described as desire, that it is no more than fair to ask whether in this case we do not again simply have to do with a desirelike state of affairs—a pseudo-desire, or rather an imaginative desire. I do not hesitate to answer in the affirmative here, either. The discriminating reader of a novel has wishes on behalf of the characters of the novel, just as he has feelings on their behalf; and these wishes are strictly speaking no more genuine wishes than the feelings are genuine feelings. What we thus learn from a relatively passive attitude to art can then easily be found confirmed in a more active attitude to it. In the case of the actor, especially, it will fairly often be too little for us simply to assume that he feels or desires. And as different from the spectator's position vis-à-vis the work of art as his own position may be in other respects, one point of agreement will still hold: In his case, too, not only imaginative feelings but also imaginative desires have their place. Of course, I am by no means unaware that in this matter, too, detailed investigation must first come into play. But for the present, I cannot rid myself of the suspicion that these imaginative desires will have to be credited with no small role in our attitude to works of art—and hence, no small role in "empathy." For the rest, imaginative desires have no relation to the immediate needs of our further investigations, and it is only at the end of this book that there will be occasion to return to them.

§55
Imaginative Feelings as Assumption-feelings

There will be no attempt to utilize the theses of the preceding section until we have given adequate consideration to the following. An inquirer to whom we attributed a special role in the development of the theory of imaginative feelings has objected to the basic theoretical conception of these experiences advocated anew in the foregoing. Stephan Witasek has given the most graphic delineation of the distinguishing characteristics of imaginative feelings that we possess today;[55] nevertheless, he thinks that he can dispense with any recourse to a special kind of emotional experience. For it suffices, he believes, to regard imaginative feelings as ordinary feelings whose peculiarity consists only in their psychological prerequisites; in the case of imaginative feelings assumptions are present, whereas in the case of feelings-in-earnest we have to do with judgments.[56] Imaginative feelings would consequently be assumption-feelings as opposed to judgment-feelings. An investigation of these feelings would accordingly be strongly suggested in a treatise on assumptions. But as far as I can see, this interpretation simply does not do justice to the facts. In any case, it might also turn out subsequently that a grasp of the parallelism of assumptions to imaginative feelings, i.e., the parallelism as I have attempted to explain it above, is not without importance for the knowledge of the nature of assumptions. So it will not be superfluous to give a brief account of why I must uphold my original view as to the nature of imaginative feelings in spite of Witasek's objections.

Besides appealing to the law of parsimony, which is certainly an unimpeachable move, Witasek appeals above all to this: that imaginative feelings are in fact always assumption-feelings and that assumption-feelings are themselves always imaginative feelings, the reason being that all feelings that have assumptions as their prerequisites are imaginative feelings and that, conversely, all imaginative feelings have assumptions as their prerequisites. Now, even if this should be entirely correct in itself, the coincidence still might just be of suggestive value, unable to prevail against the testimony of direct observation; and there doesn't seem to me to be any lack of such testimonies. Our attitude to the tragic heroine Margaret may be called compassion, but what I feel in regard to an unfortunate girl whose actually experienced fate becomes known to me in a sufficiently forcible manner—this is fundamentally different in quality from the former "aesthetic compassion," not just different in degree. Yet if such an appeal to one's own experiences can be quite persuasive under favorable circumstances, it is ill-suited for discussion when the circumstances are unfavorable. And so let us devote a few words to looking into the coincidence claimed by Witasek.

Does it correspond to the facts, that all imaginative feelings should have assumptions as their psychological prerequisites? If I have been right in describing the recollection of one's own past mental experiences as an extroversion of imaginative experiences,[57] then a present imaginative feeling will serve the specific purpose of recollecting a past feeling. If the feeling that I recollect was a sensory feeling, e.g., a toothache, then the imaginative feeling coordinated with it cannot possibly be an assumption-feeling. If it was a value-feeling, then I can recollect it even when, today, I still maintain the judgment that was at that time the psychological prerequisite of my gladness or sadness. For example, it can be the recollection of the initial pain at the report of someone's death, a report that I still regard as truthful today. Here too, we shall be unable to speak of an assumption as a prerequisite. In general, one may well have to say that assumption-feelings, as we have now called them, certainly do constitute an important kind of imaginative feelings. But if assumption-feelings are allied to judgment-feelings, other imaginative feelings are allied to other feelings-in-earnest, ones that are not judgment-feelings. Or if these feelings-in-earnest really are judgment-feelings, they do not pass from being feelings-in-earnest into being imaginative feelings by the judgment forming their psychological prerequisite changing into an assumption. The domain of assumption-feelings is consequently a far narrower one than that of imaginative feelings.

But at this point mightn't one at least maintain, conversely, that all assumptions acting as prerequisites of feelings bring imaginative feelings along with them? In view of instances that seem to me to refute even this thesis, I shall have to take a stand in opposition to a rather fundamental position of the Witasekean aesthetic—and indeed, in so doing, implicitly enter into opposition to Witasek's general characterization of aesthetic feeling. I think that I have an abundance of clear-cut experience to the effect that I can be "pleased with" simpler and more complicated situations and processes as with an ornament or a melody. In such cases we are dealing with objectives—ones that do not require any judgments at all for their apprehension, since the factuality of these objectives naturally plays no role in our attitude toward them. In this connection, one naturally thinks of our approach to the "discursive" arts. Here it would certainly seem that what makes an aesthetic impression on us are objectives apprehended by means of assumptions. On the strength of that, the aesthetic feelings in question might with justice be called assumption-feelings; but then, they are most assuredly feelings-in-earnest, not imaginative feelings.

As I intimated a moment ago, this view is opposed by a contention of Witasek, namely that objectives are not aesthetic objects at all, strictly speaking; so that no aesthetic feelings can be bestowed on them. True, he still includes objectives in the first provisional list of "aesthetic elementary objects";[58] but this is just so that he can more thoroughly justify their definitive exclusion from this list later on.[59] He derives a proof of the aesthetic indifference of objectives, albeit a merely formal one, from the possibility of transforming a sentence in poetic diction that is aesthetically effective into a wholly insipid sentence, without any change of sense and consequently without any change of objective.[60] Another argument goes deeper: Feelings that had objectives as objects could in the last analysis only be value-feelings.[61] To this we may add something which, to my knowledge, Witasek has not expressly formulated, namely that if objectives are aesthetic objects, his basic position that all aesthetic feelings are representation-feelings could no longer be maintained in its generality.

The first of these three arguments without doubt rests on a fact that has already undergone a thousandfold verification in the favorite classroom exercise of "translating the poem into prose." For the most part, there is nothing left of the poetic content of the poem, after this procedure. True, but has the objective really been left unchanged in each of these cases? In according an aesthetic dignity to certain objectives, one is assuredly not thinking of the objective after the deduction of its objectum-material; nor does one mean the objective in a certain passing treatment, where within certain limits one needn't speak of modifications regarding the material. It can very easily be that aesthetic significance exhibits a dependence on such determinations in the material, the very determinations to which Witasek appeals, and that the objective is nonetheless the true aesthetic object.

The second point compels me to move temporarily ahead along the path of discussion so far taken and to make use of something that will not be under consideration until section 57, below. Feelings that bear on objectives, Witasek thinks, are value-feelings—imaginative value-feelings in our case, where we are speaking of assumptions as prerequisites. Where is there any room left here for aesthetic feelings-in-earnest? Or what way is there to differentiate between these feelings and value-feelings? I confess that I am only able to meet this important question with a conjecture, and one that would have to be modified in accordance with theses I myself advocated earlier. I have often emphasized that value-feelings are existence-feelings, but I also thought that even objectives of so-being might be allowed to stand as value-objectives in the strict sense.[62] It is the same at present, except that one would have to be somewhat more precise in this connection and lay the following down as a fact. Value-feelings are of their nature directed entirely to being, in the first instance to existence. Of course, this is the existence of something that is thus and so [eines Soseienden]; great importance always attaches to its properties, and to that extent its so-being. But in the last analysis, existence is always the fundamentally important thing in the directedness of value-feelings. It is this very orientation that is altogether lacking in aesthetic feelings: They bear on so-being. *Per accidens* they doubtless also bear on the so-being of something existing, but primarily they always bear on so-being, and the fact of the matter is so unequivocal that the approach from which aesthetic feelings arise may be said to be quite fundamentally independent of existence. This independence of existence seems to me in quite striking accord with the facts. The circumstance that this or that exists is never a concern of the aesthetic attitude; rather the concern is always the converse: that a thing which may also be an existing thing is of such and such a character—whereas value-feeling is always turned toward the circumstance that a certain thing of such and such a character exists. If so, then the question raised by Witasek admits of the following simple answer. The mere fact of a judgment or an assumption does not of itself establish the character of a feeling as a value-feeling, even where act-feelings are left out of consideration; for the decision further depends on the nature of the objective. If the feeling bears essentially on being, then it is a value-feeling; if it bears essentially on so-being, it is an aesthetic feeling. And the same holds for an assumption feeling, *cum grano salis*. This said, it would still remain an important peculiarity of so-being feelings, albeit hardly a wholly incomprehensible one, that in their case the transition from judgment to assumption would not have the same import as in the case of being-feelings.

The foregoing would at the same time serve to open up a prospect of getting round the third difficulty, i.e., that of supporting Witasek's general characterization of aesthetic feeling where it deserves support. First of all, it is beyond question that there are fairly many aesthetic feelings that are directed to a color or a form or suchlike; they are directed to objecta (specifically properties), and they are thus far not directed to any objective. But above,[63] we saw instances of the implication of objectives of so-being in property determinations. If such instances of implication are expressly included, mightn't one on the strength of that say that all aesthetic feelings are, if not explicitly directed to objectives of so-being, at least implicitly directed to them? If it were possible to do justice to the facts of "inner beauty" without at the same time appealing to the intuitive representing of one's own empathetic and sympathetic feelings, this would appear to me to be an especially desirable gain.[64]

But returning to the question of imaginative feelings, I daresay I may draw this total: that the coinciding of imaginative feelings and assumption-feelings can scarcely be a fact. So in the case of assumption-feelings, and judgment-feelings as well, we shall have to distinguish expressly between feelings-in-earnest and imaginative feelings, wherever necessary. It is of course an entirely different question, as to whether the feelings that are, as I hope, verified in this way as being imaginative feelings stand in every respect in the same relation to feelings-in-earnest as assumptions do to judgments. The emotional domain certainly has its peculiarities. So it may well be, as I believe, that Witasek has succeeded in specifying an interesting point at which imaginative feelings fall out of analogy to assumptions;[65] yet this can scarcely be regarded as an argument against the interpretation of imaginative feelings advocated here.

§56
Imaginative Feelings as Motives of Desires

I can be brief about what led me into the foregoing discussions. As I see it, imaginative feelings in their peculiar character have always been overlooked whenever the question of the motivational relation between feeling and desire has been raised. If the desire for a certain objectum has been preceded by the representation of this objectum, together with an assumption devoted to the objective in question, then there will be a reaction to this assumption with an imaginative feeling, much as there is a reaction to the assumptions arising in the apprehending of a work of art. And it is first and foremost to this imaginative feeling that we must accord the power of "soliciting" desire, a power that has customarily been accorded to feeling, despite the difficulties one is always getting into in this way. It is now obvious at a glance that all these difficulties are obviated by the imaginative feeling. For it is a present feeling, and in its own way a quite actual one; yet it doesn't first depend on the realization of the objectum with which it is associated—a realization that is perhaps reserved for desire as its job.

Appearing almost of their own accord, also, are simple correlating principles that bring the quality of imaginative feelings into connection with the quality of the desires motivated by these feelings. In the simplest case, a pleasurelike imaginative feeling leads to a desire in the narrower sense, and a displeasurelike feeling leads to a reluctancy. Naturally, the matter takes on a more complicated form when more than one objectum offers itself for desiring, as it were. Actually, complications can even occur when there is just one objectum present. For the individual in question may, as it were, be thorough enough to take account of the possibilities of both existence and non-existence, so-being and not being thus and so with regard to the objectum. That is to say, he may be thorough enough to make affirmative as well as negative assumptions with regard to this objectum, in this way eliciting the imaginative feeling that goes with each of the assumptions. Such a procedure certainly wouldn't always merit the reproach of redundancy; for although attitudes toward existence and non-existence, so-being and not being thus and so^f are in no wise independent of each other, they are exposed to considerable variation by the mere fact that the objective "more customary" for the subject can be the positive objective on one occasion and the negative objective on another.

It is not likely that one will experience any real conflict thus far. But it is quite likely when several objecta enter into competition with each other, as it were. Here too, if it should be a question of choosing between A and B, the simplest but also the most primitive procedure will be to content oneself with the two existential assumptions and the imaginative feelings that go with them: One simply "thinks how it would be" if A were present and actual, and how it would be if B were. But again, it is more thorough to take into account, at the same time, the circumstance that the existence of A is tied to the non-existence of B and conversely. I daresay it must be left to a further special investigation to decide whether the imaginative feelings that then occur lead right away, just by the ratio of their intensities or also by some further circumstances, to a desire that is thenceforth directed only to one objectum. Alternatively, it may be that every imaginative feeling elicits its own desire and that the different desires (or desires and reluctancies) thus confronting each other then attempt to maintain themselves against each other. But this much appears certain to me, that the complications Ehrenfels has in the main correctly described, albeit in somewhat vivid colors,[66] are normally obviated. I mean the complications that would ensue if the conflict had to be settled exclusively before the forum of intelligence, without recourse to assumptions and imaginative feelings. If one does not even get involved in the deliberations in question, then these complications are obviated. With this, however, there ceases to be any purpose for one of the arguments that might otherwise incline one to accept a thesis like the law of the "relative enhancement of happiness"; indeed, this argument may have been the very inducement to such acceptance that was empirically best grounded.

§57
From the Law of Motivation to the Definition of Value

It would perhaps be unreasonably pretentious if my intention was to straightway elevate the principle of correlation in the preceding section to the status of "the law of motivation"; for it has been brought forward there merely in its initial outlines, and in addition the question as to whether and in what degree all desires conform to this principle remains fully undecided. The section heading that I have chosen for the following arguments is instead intended merely to make a connection, however external, with the polemical writing of Ehrenfels mentioned in the immediately preceding note. What has been set forth above seems to me to afford a natural point of departure for a brief assessment of the position regarding my fundamental theses which the author has adopted in that writing and elsewhere carrying on the work in the psychological foundations of value-theory. Here too, one should as far as possible disregard incidental considerations—and completely disregard matters of outward form, regarding which practically any opponent can be put in the wrong without much ingenuity. The reason is especially that in this controversy neither of us has prided himself in remaining as inflexible as possible in the standpoint originally taken; for the rest, there is little to be said for choosing a time when the opponent has presumably long since become mindful of certain difficulties to direct his attention to them in detail.

A question that I certainly cannot hope to settle here, but which might nevertheless be brought closer to settlement, concerns the nature of value, or at least^g the nature of the mental occurrences with which the idea of value is actually connected. I thought I had found the characteristic mental attitude for all value-facts in the way that someone orients himself, through his feelings, toward actuality as such. For that reason, I characterized this actuality-feeling as the true value-feeling, though I thought that value itself could be identified with an existing thing's ability to provoke such "valuings" under sufficiently favorable circumstances.[67] As against this, Ehrenfels advocated desires as the fundamental fact. According to him, having value was tantamount to being desired or at least being able to be desired.[68] And after the role in our valuing which the non-existence of value-objecta^h plays, in addition to their existence, had become clear to me,[69] I myself soon became attentive to the fact that value might be more closely connected with desire than I had originally supposed. On the strength of that, Ehrenfels regarded the definition "Value is the ability to be desired,"^{i} as accepted on my part, too.[70] Nevertheless, he accompanied this definition of value in terms of desire with a definition in terms of feeling[71] that exhibits certain modifications in comparison with my own. While he later changed his mind about these modifications in a few inessential points,[72] he has not done the same regarding the thing that strikes me as being the centerpoint of the whole question. Yet this juxtaposition of the two definitions has not been able to remove the impression that the desiderative and the affective theories are opposite theories of value and that one will have to come to a decision between them. And since that time, voices in favor of the one as well as the other manner of founding the theory of value have in fact made themselves heard.[73] For me, however, it was the present book (in its first edition) that provided the initial opportunity to state, first and foremost, that in writing the article "Über Werthaltung und Wert," nothing was further from my mind than the intention of making concessions to the definition of value based on desire. Along with this, I had the opportunity to explain what position the nature of the matter seems to afford me regarding the Ehrenfelsean double definition, especially as regards the alterations made in my precision of the concept of value, or as regards the objections constituting the basis for these alterations.

The question that requires answering, in view of the attempt at a double definition, takes only a few words: Aren't two definitions for the same thing one too many, in any case? When we consider the variety of things one can want to accomplish in formulating a definition, and also the variety of ways that can present themselves for the obtaining of a correct definition, we shall certainly not say "yes" as a general answer to this question. As early as the *Psychologisch-ethischen Untersuchungen,* I hope, I did sufficient justice to the possibility of an "artificial" definition of value.[74] But even as I did so, I expressed that I was primarily concerned with the "natural" definition—with *the* natural definition, not just with *a* natural definition. Or more precisely: If someone wants to ascertain what value *is,* then he must above all render an account of what it is that one actually thinks of, when one attributes value to things or denies it to them. If the word "value" is not ambiguous or otherwise uncertain in its use, then the question about what it is can have only one correct answer. Of course, this by no means rules out supplementary definitional modifications and precising steps, either for theoretical purposes or for practical ones. But the supplementary things must wait upon the answer. That is, the distinctive character of the domain of facts under investigation must first be made clear in its essentials, if one does not want to run the risk of having this distinctiveness slip through one's fingers. It was along these lines that I undertook the analysis of value in the first edition: The analysis can lead to feeling or to desire, but it can nowise lead to the one as well as the other.

Next, is the definition "Value is the ability to be desired," acceptable in itself? Actually, I took a position on this question in the previously mentioned place in the *Untersuchungen,* and it was by no means a flatly negative position.

But later on I was struck by an angle of approach from which the formula in question long afterwards impressed me as being unacceptable. And so this angle of approach shouldn't go unmentioned in the present context. Ehrenfels's use of the notion of the ability to be desired instead of the simpler notion of desiredness is occasioned[75] by consideration of the fact that one cannot make an object of desire of something that already has or had been actualized, but one can attribute value to existing things as well as to past things. So these things may have value without being desired. But if something is not in a position to be desired, on account of the circumstance just mentioned, can we nonetheless say that it is able to be desired? If not, then in such cases we are dealing with value-objects that are not only not desired, but are not even able to be desired. To that extent, the correction made by the introduction of "the ability to be desired" would be in vain.

Proceeding, we find the sense of this correction elucidated through the following interpretation. "We ascribe value to things that we either actually desire or would desire if we were not convinced of their existence."[76] There is actually nothing to object to this in a formal way, as far as the condition "if we were not convinced of their existence" is permissible. But can I still say that something is able to be desired, when it would be able to be desired only under a condition that is unfulfillable under the present circumstances? In granting the ability to be desired to something past, wouldn't it be quite as if one wanted to call a rhombus a square because it undoubtedly would have the properties of a square if its angles were right instead of oblique?

As mentioned, I long held this objection to be decisive; let me now briefly indicate why I no longer find it to be convincing today. The ability to be desired [Begehrbarkeit] is, of course, tantamount to the capacity [Fähigkeit] to be desired. Now if something has that capacity, then one can assuredly attribute this capacity to the thing in some way or another, as a sort of property of the thing. Yet with regard to the remaining properties, the ones that are in the first instance so designated, this capacity occupies a clearly exceptional position. In view of that, the comparison with the rhombus is not conclusive by any means. The thought of "Raphael without hands" provides a forceful example of how little one actually feels himself hindered in envisaging a disposition at a time when hindrances stand in the way of the actualization of the disposition—although in actual practice, one would hesitate to say of a cyclist, even after the permanent crippling of his legs, that he "can cycle." But the main thing to be taken into account in the present case is the following. The circumstance because of which the "ability to be desired" does not come to be actualized is the existence of the thing to which desiring could otherwise be directed. Given the discussions in previous chapters, there will surely be very little inclination to treat the objective "existence" as being on a par with some property of an existing thing, a property that would then act as a sort of impediment to the actualization of the disposition or capacity presently under consideration. So I may actually have to go along with Ehrenfels's *argumentum ad hominem*[77] and desist from a sort of a priori attack on the definition of value that he bases on desire.

Yet we may find that the situation alters when we take the empirical path. Even in daily life it is recognized that there are active and passive natures among human beings; in the emotional sphere, specifically, this difference shows up in the fact that there is a certain independence of variation in the general susceptibility to feeling on the one hand and desire on the other. Thus, for example, there are people who certainly feel the burden that life lays upon them but nevertheless refrain from making any objection to this burden. Are we to suppose that happiness has no value for such people and unhappiness no disvalue? But examples of this sort just give an especially clear indication of a fact that seems basically apparent to me through observation in the case of any attitude toward value-objecta, namely that it is primarily feelings that are involved and only secondarily desires. So to that extent, we find the facts again urging us toward a definition of value in terms of feeling, and we have to consider what Ehrenfels says by way of objection to the definition of value that I have attempted.

If we disregard certain incidental matters to which Ehrenfels himself no longer attaches any importance,[78] then it becomes a question of his attempt to reassign the role in value-feelings that I assign to one's conviction as to the existence or non-existence or the so-being[j] of the objectum. He wants to assign this role to "the maximally intuitive, vivid, and complete representation of the being or non-being of the object [Objekt],"[79] a representation to which judgment is indeed helpful, but in no wise essential.[80] In the face of such a formulation, with its recourse to the "representation" of being and non-being, one might feel strongly inclined to refer back to the investigations earlier carried out on assumptions and objectives. But even without appealing to the results of these investigations, we could prove the unsuccessfulness of the attempt in question if the following turned out to be the case: (1) that instances of valuing never do occur without judgment, whatever the situation may be regarding the "vividness," etc., of the available representations; (2) that instances of valuing can very well be encountered even where there is no particular vividness in the representations; and (3) that the basic character of a valuing—its plus or minus sign, so to speak—turns round into the opposite when the same sort of reversal occurs with respect to the judgment—whereas alterations in the vividness of the representations never lead to similar results.

§58
Imaginative Feelings Again. Valuation as Opposed to Valuing

I shall begin with the third point, taking experiences of the most commonplace sort for the proof of what is contained in that point. Suppose, say, that a collector of musical instruments has purchased a violin for a considerable amount of money. And suppose that, as is usual in such cases, what matters to him is not the tone quality of this violin but just its genuineness and possibly its well-preserved exterior. Proud of his possession, he shows it to an expert—only to have the expert tell him that he has accepted a new imitation as an old original. What alteration has taken place in the collector's valuing, supposing that he believes the authority? Until a moment ago, he thought that he possessed a genuine instrument; now he has suddenly realized that he does *not* possess such an instrument. This is surely not a mere *representing* of the being of his possession and then its non-being, even if there were nothing against such a representation. Even when he believed in the possession, he could have easily thought of the possibility of, say, a loss and accordingly of a "nonpossession," thereupon rejoicing more than ever in the possession. But now it's no mere "thinking of how it would be,"[81] but an all too distinct belief. Specifically, it is a belief opposed in quality to the belief that previously accompanied the valuing of the instrument. I think it will be evident that this latter belief must have been more than a mere concomitant fact, if one considers the change of feeling that has taken place. At the same time, the example has been so chosen that there is no reason whatsoever to suppose an alteration with respect to the vividness of the representations before and after the authority's momentous communication. During the entire discussion about its genuineness, the instrument was given in perceptual representations or was at least always accessible to such representations. But the genuineness—first affirmed and then negated—is not at all capable of conception by means of a perceptual representation.

To this example, with its maximally vivid and intuitive representations, we can add one in which the representations are primarily imaginative representations; they will not be very "vivid," then, and at least no guarantee could be made for their intuitiveness. In uncertain times, as we know, it rather often happens that a person will try to protect his money and other precious belongings by hiding them—burying them, let us say. Let us now consider the difference in the emotional state of the owner of such a hidden treasure as he thinks of it—on the one hand, as long as he believes it safe, and on the other hand, when he hears that it has been discovered and carried off. In this case, there would be the possibility of the report of the plundering making the representation of the lost property more vivid. But all we need do is assume also that the report turns out to be false, right after it comes in; we are then presented with a new veering round of feeling, and this time we cannot link the change to any instantaneous alteration in respect of the vividness of the representations.

The case just considered can at the same time stand as a proof of the second of the theses formulated above. One will be more able to concede this spontaneously, the more frequently one is actually concerned with goods, i.e., value-objecta, that are either difficult to apprehend with intuitive representations or not at all apprehensible that way, goods such as honor, public welfare, progress, and much else. Yet, the first of our three assertions, whose incompatibility with the Ehrenfelsean interpretation is especially striking, deserves especially careful consideration. For at first glance it does not appear to have experience on its side; indeed, it may be the more or less distinct sense of this discrepancy that has made the affective theory of value strike many a person as being in the first instance not quite trustworthy. My thesis, "Valuing is an existence-feeling," in the use that I have made of it in the *Untersuchungen zur Werttheorie* and afterwards, will in fact be met with the objection that there is, after all, a valuing also with regard to things that do not exist. Doesn't "feeling the want of" something consist precisely in this, that one "sets value" on something that does not exist—with the result that one desires its existence? This consideration needn't right away be regarded as an argument directly in favor of the desiderative theory of value. There are many things on which I set value, many things that I "rate highly," which I do not at all desire on that account. But from the foregoing consideration, it becomes clearly obvious how there is a falling asunder of value-feelings, on the one hand, and on the other hand existence, or at least presumed existence. To my knowledge, it has not been contested from any quarter that in the supplementary article "Über Werthaltung und Wert," I proved that the case of non-existence enters into consideration in the determination of the magnitude of value, and not just the case of existence;[82] and if I have succeeded there, then it seems that the falling asunder must have a perfectly obvious claim to acknowledgment. For if the question is at the same time one of non-existence as well as existence, then it surely cannot be requisite that the valuing subject be connected with the value-objectum by a single judgment as to these two eventualities, which are incompatible with each other. I certainly cannot at once believe in existence and in non-existence; but then, if conviction in regard to one of the two possibilities is dispensable, then it is natural enough to ask why it cannot be dispensable for both.

It is also plain that I myself was no stranger to the relevant facts at the time that I wrote my theses in the theory of value. In the supplementary essay just mentioned, I indicated that among the ways in which valuing and value fail to coincide, there is this: It is normally an out-and-out practical impossibility to apprehend an objectum's value in its totality by means of one valuing.[83] I indicated a sort of substitute for this apprehension in the judgment about the valuings that would occur in the respective cases of the objectum's existence and non-existence.[84] Today I must acknowledge that this position left a deficiency in my theses in the theory of value, a deficiency that was perhaps not the least contributing factor in making the construction of the theory of value on the basis of feeling appear unsatisfactory to many of those who have been more recently working on the problems of value.

But what has primarily led me to bring up these things right now is my belief that the reference to assumptions and the "imaginative feelings" following upon them under certain circumstances has placed me in a position to repair the deficiency, and thereby to give the affective theory of value all the substantiality that one could desire. For the moment, note that the following is certainly not in the nature of an experientially alien theorem; much to the contrary, it refers to a matter that is obvious to the point of triviality. When a poor man "sets value" on wealth or a sick man "sets value" on health, he not only feels the absence of this good, the absence with which he is so well acquainted, but he may even "put" himself in the position of a propertied or healthy man. Intellectually, as we know, this means an assumption; emotionally, it means one of the imaginative feelings discussed above. Conversely, a propertied or healthy man will be able to correctly apprehend the advantage that he has over so many people only when he emotionally, and not just intellectually, imagines himself in the position of the propertyless or sick man. But in the last analysis, there can also be an attitude of valuing towards "merely represented" objects, or more precisely, ones not judged about. In such an attitude, nothing is presupposed concerning the existence or non-existence that may belong to these objects, e.g., in the future, and yet there will be a view to existence as well as nonexistence. The objectum in question is assessed as to its subjective value in the most direct manner when one assumes both existence and non-existence and reacts to each of these assumptions with an imaginative feeling. The individual remains free, of course, to apprehend the state of affairs in a purely intellectual manner, by granting the objectum the ability to attract value-feelings or the imaginative feelings corresponding to these; still, this is a roundabout way that is probably only taken exceptionally.

So perhaps it is safe to conclude that in the sense just now explained I have secured an affirmative answer for the first of the preceding three theses, too. Then to that extent, as before, I find nothing to take back in my assertion "Value-feelings are existence (or non-existence) feelings." But what I was still unaware of in formulating this assertion, and what requires the most careful consideration, is the fact that objectives of existence and non-existence, or positive and negative so-being,^{k} can be apprehended not only by means of judgments, but also by means of assumptions. Accordingly, value-feelings present themselves not only as judgment-feelings, but occasionally also as assumption-feelings, or more precisely, feelinglike states with which the subject reacts to assumptions in cases where, given judgments, valuings usually arise.

In the face of these quasi-feelings, in which we have had to recognize a special case of "imaginative feelings," as it seemed best to call them earlier, the need for a new term naturally makes itself felt again, the sort of need that leads to so many difficulties in the face of newly observed facts. As pretheoretical linguistic usage does not afford me a word that is at all descriptive of the special state of affairs, I want to try just this once to draw a kind of advantage from the Babylonian confusion of tongues in philosophical terminology, from which all scientific work in the domain of philosophy still suffers in such great degree.[85] Starting with a mostly subjective opinion, I shall choose one of the relevant expressions that language offers, although I must thereby set a new usage against the one already introduced in practice by Ehrenfels and especially by Felix Krüger.[86] Three expressions enter into primary consideration, "valuation," "valuing," and "evaluation."[87] In my earlier publications, I have already attempted to define the latter two by suggestions as to their use. Expressly and on more than one occasion, I have characterized valuing [Werthalten] as the feeling elicited by the conviction of the existence or non-existence of an objectum. More in passing, I have characterized evaluation [Berwerten] as the merely intellectual apprehending of a value, in short, as value-judgment. Yet, the expression "valuation" ["Werten"] has for some accidental reason remained peculiarly foreign to my personal linguistic usage.[88] As a consequence, it has remained open for some new use,[89] and I now gladly accept it as the only term available for doing justice to the terminological needs created by the above statements, at least in a way that is not ungrammatical. So "valuation" is what I want to call the attitude of someone who reacts to an assumption of the existence or non-existence of an objectum with the imaginative feeling repeatedly mentioned above. Valuation is the counterpart to valuing, then; it is distinguished from the latter by the fact that the judgment essential to valuing is replaced by an assumption and by the fact that the judgment-feeling essential to valuing is replaced by an assumptive quasi-feeling, i.e., by an imaginative feeling. As mentioned, I do not delude myself that this arrangement is free of all arbitrariness. But if one is to try, in the interests of theory, to differentiate between three expressions that are so closely connected with each other pretheoretically, then it seems to me that in no case can things be brought off without some element of arbitrariness or convention. Moreover, it seems a reasonable hope that those who have been accustomed to employ "valuation" and "valuing" ["Wertung" und "Werthaltung"] indifferently, as has usually been the case until now, can more easily assent to my suggestion according as they find our description in terms of an assumption and an imaginative feeling appropriate to the facts that they have hitherto not given any separate name.

Given this terminology, I can now put the matter briefly. I was wrong when I thought that all value-feelings—or better, all ways of apprehending the value of something other than the merely intellectual way, i.e., by means of evaluation [Bewertung]—have their origin in instances of valuing, and therefore in judgment-feelings. Along with valuings there are valuations. And the latter even have a kind of advantage, in that they can never be wholly absent in the emotional apprehending of a value-fact, unless some essential factor has been overlooked. By contrast, valuings can disappear altogether under certain circumstances, circumstances under which valuations then prove to be sufficient by themselves. This is owing to the fact that the consideration of both existence and non-existence is required precisely for value, but that at a given time the subject can attempt to grasp at most one of these two objectives by means of an actual judgment. To this one objective there then corresponds a valuing; whereas to the other there can only pertain a valuation, which must occur in the place of the valuing that is inaccessible to the subject. However, it may well be that the subject has no conviction either as to existence or non-existence on hand: In this case, the subject always has assumptions and imaginative feelings—valuations—at his disposal for both eventualities. What we discussed above,[90] the motivational power of these quasi-feelings, is probably not the least important thing in making the connection between value and desire such a conspicuous fact.

After what has been said, it may seem strange if my contention that the fundamental experience of all value[91] is valuing, is not one that I am now likewise prepared to modify in favor of valuation. This is due to the peculiar relation in which imaginative feelings stand to the genuine feelings coordinated with them, a relation that is entirely analogous to that between assumptions and judgments, or to the relation between reproductive and perceptual representations. Assumptions and reproductive representations both play the role of surrogate facts in our mental processes. The ultimate meaning of such facts is above all derived from what they serve to replace, judgments or perceptual representations. Similarly, it seems to me that valuations and valuings[92] are not to be ranked on the same footing. For the very thing that justifies the occurrence of valuations is that valuings never have access to *both* existence and non-existence, and that it may even be impossible for the subject to get at either, due to lack of the requisite knowledge or at least the requisite judging. Thus, where valuations appear in the place of valuings, it takes place in the name of valuings, so to speak, and it is to valuings that the thought of value, by its very nature, always reverts in the last analysis.[93] A corroboration of this view shows up when reality does not fulfill what the imagination has promised, and the judgment does not elicit feelings that correspond to the imaginative feelings summoned up by foregoing assumptions. In such a case one speaks of delusion; this doubtless constitutes an acknowledgment that for all his imaginative feelings, meaning here his valuations, the subject really "had in mind" genuine feelings, i.e., in the first instance valuings.

For our present conclusion, it might help to clarify certain things as well as bring earlier theses into a summarization if valuings and valuations were again taken in juxtaposition with aesthetic feelings. Like valuings and valuations, aesthetic feelings are not act-feelings but content-feelings.[94] Also, aesthetic feelings are feelings-in-earnest like valuings, yet like valuations they are (at least in their immediate character) assumption-feelings. This peculiar intermediate position might well be connected with the fact that value-feelings seem to be primarily being-feelings and aesthetic feelings primarily so-being feelings.[95] As for the rest, it must not be concluded from what has just been said that imaginative feelings are not also to be encountered in the aesthetic domain.

For example, the suggestive influence that usually emanates from the aesthetic arrangement of one's spatial and temporal surroundings, or from personalities of especially strong suggestive power—this suggestive influence will doubtless always operate initially as a "suggestion to imaginative feeling." Finally, there are imaginative feelings not just in the domain of content-feelings, but also in the domain of act-feelings. This seems to me[96] to be proven by every case where we recall past physical pains or take note of such pains in the case of others. The contrast of feelings-in-earnest and imaginative feelings governs no less than the whole domain of feelings, in the same way that the contrast of judgments and assumptions governs the whole domain of those intellectual experiences that stand over against objectives as their means of apprehension. And on the other hand, though admittedly we cannot go further into this here, the contrast of desires-in-earnest and imaginative desires governs the whole domain of desires.

X

Results. Steps Toward a Psychology of Assumptions

A Description of the Assumption-experience. Act and Content

In the course of the foregoing investigations, it had to be pointed out more than once that the progress of these investigations necessitated the inclusion of rather diverse sorts of problems. Thus, a summary overview of the results of these investigations would itself have to record rather diverse sorts of things. The value of these things would not necessarily be dependent solely on the degree to which they served to advance the specific inquiry into assumptions. But in the present chapter, assumptions, as the true subject of these discussions, will gain our exclusive consideration. Thus, in the following there will be an attempt to survey, in subject matter sequence, the essentials of what may have been established with respect to assumptions in the foregoing, perhaps proceeding a bit beyond this. Our survey will exhibit a threefold aspect. First and foremost, there will be a compilation of the things that might subserve a definitive characterization of the new class of experiences. Then, the position that assumptions occupy in relation to their psychological setting will be given a closer precise description: on the one hand according to the way in which assumptions actually occur, but on the other hand also in accordance with the status and significance that would have to belong to assumptions in a systematic classification of mental events that was as natural as possible.

To begin with, I turn to the first of these three tasks. In the assumption we have become acquainted with a mental event that is by all means similar to the judgment in more than one respect. This circumstance seems to me to suggest a quite appropriate standpoint for seeking out the most important properties of the assumption. Of course, I think that the fact of judgment in its characteristic peculiarity is still far from commanding proper recognition in psychology. Yet as far as the assumption is concerned, there is no doubt that the judgment is by far the better known experience. So let us now take up one after another of the things essential to the judgment, in each case appending the question as to whether it is possible to meet with something analogous in the case of the assumption: It is to be expected that at least some of the things essential to the peculiar character of assumptions will come up for mention, if not absolutely the most essential things.

And as it turns out, several indubitable points of agreement can be noted at the very outset. This is apparent merely in connection with the psychological prerequisite, the experience that is as indispensable to the judgment as it is to the assumption, both of them being dependent experiences. In the case of the judgment, the representation has long been recognized as being such a prerequisite, and it seemed probable to us that the place of representations can be taken by other "presenting" experiences.[1] We have indeed had sufficient opportunity in the foregoing to satisfy ourselves that the situation is no different in the case of assumptions. More precisely, in the cases of judgments and assumptions alike, it is the function of the psychological prerequisite to present the "material" for processing, as it were. On the strength of that, we speak of judgment-about in the case of judgments. As for assumptions, we have thought that the designation "assumption-about" might not be altogether objectionable. The material is in one part or two parts, according to whether it is apprehended in an objective of being or in an objective of so-being; naturally, this is no less true of assumptions than it is of judgments. It is just insofar as what is presented is something factual and is supposed to be represented as such that the assumption is typically inferior to the judgment. We shall presently have occasion to mention this circumstance again, below.

Let us turn from the psychological prerequisite to the experience itself. For the present, at least, it would seem inevitable that the psychologist should give up hope of attaining a really satisfactory definition of judgment,[2] just as he has given up any idea of defining a representation, or any idea that he has hitherto succeeded in defining a feeling or a desire. And it would seem that circumstances are no more favorable for the definition of an assumption. For that reason, there is no way to provide preliminary information as to what an assumption is supposed to be except to refer someone to the direct empirical data of inward perception. This indefinability in practice, as it might very well be called,[3] in no wise prevents a psychologist from bringing out, by abstraction, certain factors in judgment that are typical of it and which vary in a definite manner; and it is to be expected that the situation will be no different in the case of assumptions. The psychologist has the advantage of a certain procedural canon here, by a fact that made itself plain to us even at the beginning of this inquiry:[4] the relation between a judgment and an assumption admits of a precisive formulation that is almost definitional in character. Thus, one can say, "An assumption is a judgment without belief"; and of course one can just as well say, "A judgment is an assumption with the addition of belief," or something similar. Strictly speaking, the assumption is no more defined in this way than the judgment is; but these formulations do give a rather clear advance indication of approximately how far similarity to judgment can go in the case of the assumption.

Judging is always a doing as opposed to an undergoing, i.e., as opposed to the passive attitude we meet with in, say, feeling—but in representation, too, strictly speaking.[5] The previously mentioned element of belief or conviction certainly plays a part in this active character, but not in such a way that the loss of that element entails the loss of the activity: assuming as well as judging is a doing. Nor does the absence of belief serve to prevent our distinguishing between a content and an act in the case of assumptions, as we do in the case of judgments—anyway, act has nothing to do with activity. For a general view of the state of affairs peculiar to such experiences, including assumptions, this contrast will actually prove to be our best vantage point.

To start with content, I needn't again state that by "content of a judgment" —or by "content of an assumption"—I do not mean the content by which the psychological prerequisites, the representations, present the material. Content of that sort is never anything but representational content.[a] But the analogy to representational content, on the part of the content of a judgment and the content of an assumption, still holds to the following extent. In representations, the content is what is closely correlated with the variable representational object, the objectum; in judgments and assumptions, similarly, the content is what is closely correlated with the object of these experiences, the objective. And just as the content of a representation is best characterizable via the objectum, so too the content of a judgment and the content of an assumption are best characterizable via the objective. In the most diverse contexts we have had occasion to satisfy ourselves that there is generally no difference between a judgment and an assumption as regards the objective; and so there would be no difference as to their content. Thus, there are assumptions of being and assumptions of non-being; assumptions of being and those of so-being, assumptions of existence and those of subsistence. However, matters are a bit more complicated in respect of factuality and the modality that is so closely related to it, possibility; as a consequence, it will be best to deal with these two things, along with the matter of evidence in assumptions, in a special section. Leaving these matters out of account for the present, we can say that on the side of the object, or the content, a rather thoroughgoing agreement between judgment and assumption is to be observed.[6]

We just now cited the contrast of objectives of being and objectives of so-being from the standpoint of content. This contrast may help us to achieve the transition from content to act, for I do not want the following to go unmentioned. I cannot altogether avoid thinking of this contrast as having some significance for the act, in addition to its significance for the content. And surely there is nothing against this further significance, as regards the possibility of it. In the first edition of this book,[7] I thought I might speak of a thetic and a synthetic function with respect to the judgments apprehending these two kinds of objectives. Applied to objects, the two figurative expressions thereby used, ones known to be anything but new, are actually rather misleading. It does not lie in the power of a judging person, as such, to "posit" objects. On the other hand, the fact that I judge something of the form "*A* is *B*," may actually constitute a kind of connection between the objects *A* and *B* that is for me to establish and interrupt; yet the word "synthesis" has hardly ever been intended so unpretentiously. Still, such figurative expressions serve to reveal a difference in the situations for which the content can hardly be solely responsible. But there is certainly nothing in this difference that would divide judgment and assumption from each other—for after all, a moment ago we had occasion to claim objectives of being and objectives of so-being for both modes of apprehension.

At any rate, apart from this still wholly unclarified point, in the act we have obviously arrived at that aspect of the fact of judgment or assumption where we may expect to encounter the real differences between these experiences. The first thing that strikes the eye is the quantitative factor in it. I do not mean the logical "quantity" that is customarily assigned the judgment, as opposed to its logical "quality." That "quality," as we know, concerns what is judged, and "quantity" concerns that which is judged about; so that both appertain to the domain of content—"quality" closely, "quantity" somewhat more remotely. In the present case, however, it is a question of the quantitative act-factor familiar to us as the more and the less of judgmental certainty. There can be no doubt about the variability of this factor. Then is there something analogous to this variability in the case of the assumption? Direct experience does not seem to reveal any of the variability in question on the part of assumptions. But what with the close relation between degrees of certainty and degrees of probability that can be found in the case of judgment, one can hope to arrive at an answer to this question by trying to see whether the domain of probabilities is somehow closed to assumptions. Actually, it would be an extraordinary thing, if it were; and it is in fact not the case, as can be easily verified.

This is seen at its clearest practically anywhere that someone is to some extent theoretically concerned with the determining of probabilities. In such cases, nothing is more natural than to say things like, "Suppose that from a sack of white and black balls, white has been drawn ten times in succession. Then under these conditions there obtains a certain probability of drawing white the eleventh time, too." The task may then be to determine this probability numerically on the basis of conditions further specifiable. Naturally, it is a question of the probability that follows from the given conditions. But what, if we may speak this way, does this probability adhere to? Perhaps one will immediately think of the judgment that would be valid under the given conditions, which judgment naturally could only be a surmise. But of course, this surmise is actually not present at all; the point is just that under the specified conditions it would be valid to make it. Obviously, reflections such as those that had to be carried out in the investigation of conclusions from suspended premises or of hypothetical judgments[8] have to enter in at this point, and they cannot be set forth anew. From a psychological standpoint, the premises are only assumptions. But so is the *conclusio,* and the conclusion-assumption is the very thing in regard to which there is a question of greater or lesser probability. The situation serves to epitomize the fact that these probability distinctions can be employed not just with reference to judgments, but likewise with reference to assumptions.

We can say, then, that probabilities are by no means inaccessible to assuming. But does this really permit us to infer anything as to the occurrence of different strengths of assumption? This is directly clear to begin with: that as easy as it is to establish the connection between degrees of probability and degrees of belief, or rather judgmental strength, just as difficult would it be to think out such a connection in respect of possible strengths of assumptions. Whatever the reasons are, it is perhaps not the least of them that in trying to think of "degrees of assuming," one cannot get anything at all intuitive, and this again for the reason that experience seems to leave us completely in the lurch as regards cases of different strengths of assumption. So in the end there will be nothing left to do except state, in accordance with experience, that the variability of strength in the judgment has no analogue in the case of the assumption. The bearing of assumptions on probability will come up again for discussion presently, below.

But of course, we shall not regard the judgmental act as having just quantitative characteristics; and without doubt, it will be permissible for us to use the distinction between judgment and assumption primarily with respect to act quality. It would be nothing remarkable if a closer description of this distinction should be impracticable. However, a prospect of getting another step closer is created by the fact that the judgment presents itself so naturally as a sort of richer state of affairs in comparison with the assumption as a poorer one. It has more than once proven natural for us to say, before any pretension to exactness, that in the assumption we have basically the same thing as the judgment, only somewhat less of the element of conviction or belief, as it were. Now, though, we might try to assert this more precisely in the following thesis. The assumption is a sort of limit-case of the judgment, characterized by the zero-value of the strength of conviction.[9] As part of this, we would also be asserting that judgment and assumption agree in respect of the act, too, and not just in respect of content. This agreement is not obvious, so that it would still stand in need of a more detailed proof.

§60
Continuation: Evidence

We now need to give careful consideration to the further question as to whether there is also something in the case of assumptions that is like the fact of *evidence,* which we know is so epistemologically fundamental in judgments. More precisely, the question is whether there is something in assumptions that is enough like judgment-evidence for us to be justified in speaking of assumption-evidence, too. At first glance, one may feel a very distinct inclination to answer "no" to this and to substantiate this answer by a reference to the fact that it is, after all, entirely a matter of my own discretion as to whether I make a certain object an object of an assumption or not and whether, in the former case, the assumption receives an affirmative or a negative quality. Indeed, if we have customarily accorded judgments a higher degree of independence from the influence of desire and will [Wünschen und Wollen] than corresponds to experience, this may in the first instance be because in the case of judgment one immediately thinks of knowing, which in the last analysis means evident judgment; the fact of evidence seems by its very nature to preclude the possibility that conative experience [Begehren] could have power over it in any way.

It is worth noting that an approach of this sort brings two quite different factors into play: On the one hand, there is a direct way of verifying evidence in a judgment, and on the other hand there is a very indirect way of verifying it. Under favorable circumstances, it is inward perception that tells me whether or not a present judgment has evidence. But frequently I can also ascertain something on this score if I hold to the fact, indubitable as it is important, that one cannot believe the contrary of what he sees or realizes to be the case [einsieht]. Implicit in this, of course, is that the contrary of what I believe can never be evident to me. If I could believe everything, then this would contain a proof that no judgment at all was evident to me.

Now, thoroughly in accord with the preliminary opinion expressed above is this: that whether one takes the path of direct empirical determination in regard to assumptions or the indirect path via the opposite, which has been confirmed in the case of judgments, we are altogether incapable of specifying any assumption-experience that could possibly be said to have, all by itself, anything like evidence or which, just by itself, would have some sort of advantage in evidence over its opposite. True, there is an abundance of assumptions that have true or false, evident or evidenceless judgments associated with them. But the fact that the judgment "A is B" is evidently true or is evidently false is entirely different from the question as to whether the assumption "A is B" has evidence or not. Bearing this in mind, we can then say: There is no assumption which, considered just by itself, could exhibit any evidential advantage over other assumptions; nor is there any assumption which, considered just by itself, would warrant objection from the standpoint of any evidential requirement. To that extent, our assuming does not have any sort of evidential bounds set for it: the situation is one of unlimited freedom of assumption.

Oddly, however, this freedom in isolated assumptions is matched by a quite unmistakable constraint when one regards one or more assumptions as already given and then makes further assumptions in relation to them. Once I have assumed that A is B, then it is no longer open to me to assume that one of these

A's is not *B*—provided that I have not yet abandoned the first-mentioned assumption or just ignored it. This fact might be expressed in the following proposition: It is true that assumptions are without exception free, absolutely regarded; but for all that, they can be constrained relatively. The only question now is how the fact of relative constraint is to be further described. We have come across it more than once in our investigations hitherto, and I daresay that on these occasions nothing has suggested itself to us so easily as the interpretation of this relative constraint as evidence, or at least as an evidencelike fact. But it would not be amiss to inquire expressly as to whether interpretations other than this might be enlisted with a reasonably satisfactory outcome.

To many a person it might seem manifest to the point of obviousness that this "constraint" could hardly be anything but a compulsion making itself felt under certain circumstances, so that once someone has assumed, e.g., that *A* is *B* and *B* is *C,* he simply cannot do other than assume also that *A* is *C.* Or it will be seen to be a compulsion such that in light of these assumptions he is at least quite incapable of assuming something like this, that *A* is not *B.* And then one could attempt further to subordinate this mental compulsion to a more general operative principle, to which the above-formulated principle of unlimited freedom of assumption would then have to fall a victim. Would it not be a quite appealing thought, to suppose that we are not at all capable of making assumptions against our better judgment, as it were—i.e., of assuming something of which we already know that it is false? The application to our syllogistic case would then be rather simple: we already know, surely, that it cannot be that *A* is *B* and *B* is *C* without also *A* being *C.* But the operative principle just now tentatively formulated is refuted by the simplest experiences. By making the attempt, anyone can satisfy himself as to how easy it is, say, during the dreariest rainy weather to think himself into the situation of a cloudless summer's day. Consequently, everyone is able to make an assumption of whose falsehood immediate inspection has only too compellingly convinced him, as we can say more concisely than precisely. In light of that, one might resort to a sort of limitation, maintaining that it is at least impracticable to assume something whose falsehood is clear from the nature of the objective or at least able to be made clear in that way, i.e., a priori. But even this thesis would come into conflict with experience: for I can also assume that there is a round quadrangle or that a circle is quadrangular, or suchlike. All standpoints from which one might attempt in another manner—an epistemo-teleological manner—to bring sense to the having-to or the not-being-able-to-do-otherwise fail in this way, it seems. But of course, the compulsion or the inability to make certain assumptions still could be a fact. Is it, though? And if it were, would it really be the place to look for what we just noted under the name of the constraint of certain assumptions?

To begin with, as concerns the first question, it might suffice for our purposes to point out the following. The sense of obviousness that may incline one to expect an affirmative reply does, in any case, have its origin in an error. True, it is understood that I shall not in one breath assume that all *A*'s are *B*'s and yet one of them not a *B*; but that is just because it would be palpably unreasonable. And to say the least, it is not at all certain that I could not manage this unreasonableness if I simply *intended* to be unreasonable; and it may well be that I wouldn't even need to have such an intention. If I may put any confidence in experiment, which is no doubt easy to arrange but difficult to interpret with sufficient reliability, then I would say that it requires no special effort to produce a real case of this unreasonableness. I can in immediate succession assume both that all *A*'s are *B*'s and that they are not. In this, I admit, it is doubtful as to whether the first of the two assumptions remains sufficiently present.

The situation of conjoint assuming, which may not always be clearly accomplished in the case of these (explicit) assumptions, in which a movement of thought abides for a relatively longer time, as at a goal or other resting place—this situation proves to be indisputably realized in the case of other assumptions. I mean assumptions that appear in thought only as points of transition, so to speak, e.g., where they function as means for the fastening upon or presentation of objectives. Typical of this is every case where one sees [einsieht] a contradiction. A person who judges with evidence, "It does not hold true that *A* is at once both *B* and not *B*," must of course apprehend the one as well as the other of the two mutually incompatible objectives. Consequently, unless he should happen to judge one of the two, he will have to assume them both.[10] And so one can say the following confidently: If what is meant by the words "freedom of assumption" is no more than the ability to make the assumptions in question under the given circumstances, then one may speak not only of the absolute freedom of assumption but also of the relative freedom—and thus, all in all, of a freedom of assumption that is in principle wholly unlimited. At any event, experience provides no really firm foothold for contesting this. But at the same time one can see that the above-formulated principle of absolutely free and relatively constrained assumptions, whose conformity with experience was immediately obvious, needed to be understood in another sense.

By this, as well as by the above reference to the factor of "reasonableness," our position on the second question is already determined. First of all, it is not amiss to point out that from the theory of judgment the notion of compulsion or inability has already acquired a certain prejudicial cast, by the fact that the notion usually goes into operation as a sort of emergency device in cases where a person would like to avoid simply acknowledging the fact of evidence. Of course, it can still happen even today that a person will regard himself as particularly free of prejudgment in being unable to see how necessity is different from compulsion. It would naturally take us too far afield to go into such misunderstandings in greater detail; yet it might not be superfluous to recall them, in cases where it is important to avoid analogous misunderstandings regarding assumptions. There actually will, undoubtedly, be assumptions that in practice cannot be conjointly made. Perhaps it will be because of their complexity; perhaps it will be because of a deficiency in the ability of this or that subject, or perhaps in all subjects. Nevertheless, this is something quite different from the fact that we had in mind in speaking of the constraint of one assumption by another. In full analogy to the case of judgments, the locution "I ought not to do otherwise" affords a much more relevant characterization of the constraint itself than one can find in the locution "I cannot do otherwise." But neither here nor in connection with judgments does this advertence to a type of imperative betray anything like a utilitarian consideration to the effect that such an intellectual procedure would be the one most conducive to this or that end. With assumptions as well as judgments, what comes to light here is instead a natural superiority in value. In the case of judgments, we know that it is based on the latter's evidence; as a consequence, it is easy for us to relate this superiority to something evidencelike in the case of assumptions, too. And it may be added that direct observation testifies clearly to the presence of such a factor.

Thus, in line with the many things that assumptions have in common with a judgment, including the fact that assumptions are without exception determinate in respect of the antithesis of yes and no, it seems that evidence can belong to assumptions. But if we now want to attempt a characterization of this assumption-evidence in accordance with the approach that has proven successful in the case of judgment, we are faced with the necessity of uniting the two principles expressed above, the principles of absolute freedom and relative constraint of assumptions, in the following proposition. All instances of evidence in assumptions are instances of mediate evidence. This there is, but there is no immediate assumption-evidence; for all assumption-evidence is evidence "in view of" other assumptions,[11] and these other assumptions are at most ones whose places can be taken by judgments—a posteriori, as it were.

We should not fail to recognize, of course, that there is an element of strangeness in such a thesis. We have, after all, seen that mediate evidence is not in its nature a different kind of evidence than immediate evidence and that it differs from the latter only by its origin.[12] Then how could immediate evidence be completely excluded from a domain of experience that does exhibit the mediate?

Even more important, though, is this: that the etiology of mediate evidence in a judgment leads back inevitably to other evidence that is in the last instance immediate. Hence, experiences whose nature precludes immediate evidence seem on that account just as incapable of exhibiting mediate evidence; indeed, in a certain sense they seem to a greater extent incapable of exhibiting the latter sort of evidence.

On closer inspection, however, these objections are seen to rest on presuppositions which, gotten primarily from judgment, are not immune to doubt as to whether they are strictly binding for assumptions. We saw that we might call a judgment mediately evident[13] in the event that insight occurred in view of objectives[b] alien to that judgment, but not in view of its own objective. To be sure, it was understood along with this that these other objectives themselves had to be judged, and judged with evidence, too. Naturally, in this case matters could not be carried through without appeal to instances of immediate judgmental evidence. For judgments, this yields the principle: no mediate evidence without the immediate. But must it inevitably be the same in the case of assumptions? True, according to the concept of mediate evidence, such evidence presupposes means; but it does not presuppose that these means are themselves instances of evidence. Suppose, then, that in assumptions there really is an analogue to what we know as mediation of evidence in a judgment. Then matters accord quite well if, on the one hand, this analogue ensues upon the choice of whatever objectives one needs as assumption-premises,[c] and, on the other hand, there is a complete absence of any distinction between assumptions that are immediately evident and those which are not. But in this case, a further doubt arises: May we call the conclusion of a correct assumption-inference evident, when the opposite of such a conclusion can always be assumed? In this case, too, we may suspect that the analogy to the judgment has received a wider application to assumptions than it will tolerate. Why shouldn't there be intellectual experiences whose realization is unhindered by the evidence of their opposites?

Of course, no secret should be made of this either: Once we have granted the possibility of assuming the contrary of something assumable with evidence, we have given up one of the arguments by which we just now derived the statement that no evidence belongs to an assumption all by itself. In that case, all that we would have left would be the testimony of direct perception against isolatedly evident assumptions—or as I suppose it is actually more precise to say, the lack of such testimony in favor of such assumptions. Then in addition we could recall the fact that a right triangle with two acute angles is more "reasonable" to assume than one with two right angles, and one could wonder whether this "reasonableness," already mentioned above, really makes its appearance only with the advent of judging. And then we would naturally have to see whether differences of this sort mightn't be found also in the evidential state of the assumption-conclusions inferred from such "reasonable" assumption-premises.

It must be left to future psychological investigation to make clear the value of such reflections. For the time being, it will accord best with our state of knowledge if we suppose that immediate evidence is not to be met with in assumptions, while there can no longer be any doubt as to the occurrence of mediate evidence on their part. There might still be a certain theoretical difficulty here, even for one who sees nothing inherently alien to discussion in the occurrence of mediate evidence without the immediate, in the sense of the above remarks. This would be the case if it were indispensable to treat evidence as a determination in the act, the act being the aspect of assumption-experiences in which they are experiences of different types. Then there might be a difficulty, although[14] there is ultimately nothing objectionable, in principle or in terms of possibility, in the idea of the judgment-act and the assumption-act having common elements in spite of their other differences. However, if evidence in judgment is already as much a part of the content as affirmative or negative character, say, then there is simply no way to create an initial presumption against assumption-evidence.

As the parallel between assumptions and judgments accordingly proves to be an even closer one, extending to evidence, another fact becomes all the more remarkable. And yet it is quite obvious in itself: Even in the most favorable evidential state, assumptions are never suited for the apprehending of factuality as such, in the way that evident judgments are. This is especially remarkable in view of the fact that the nonmodal determinations in an objective are not apprehensible only by means of a judgment; they are just as truly apprehended by means of assumptions. An affirmative assumption apprehends a positive objective, a so-being assumption apprehends an objective of so-being, and so forth. As against this, in advance of any special reflection on the matter we find the previously mentioned relation of assumptions to factuality so natural as to be a foregone conclusion. But then, the reason for this is that only evidence for certainty proved to be the means of apprehension adequate to factuality,[15] and this in the very case of judgments; assumptions, as far as could be ascertained above, cannot claim a determination in respect of the element of certainty. From this we may perhaps conclude that the modal contents of judgment, if that be acceptable as a brief designation for the contents coordinated with the modal properties of objectives, do stand in an especially close relation to the judgment-act. This relation would involve that if these same modal contents appeared in assumptions instead of judgments, they would be quite without the high standing [Dignität] of their analogues in judgment, exhibiting at most some sort of approximation to that standing—in virtue of which approximation they would perhaps be able to enter in as surrogates for the judgments in question.

But say that the statement just made stands, and that when modal contents make the figurative transition from judgments to assumptions, they are given a sort of poorer treatment than the nonmodal ones; does this statement, we must still ask, stand in accord with the facts at all points? Can't I assume the evidence of an objective, as well as its positivity? And what is especially important: did we not have to grant, in the preceding section, that degrees of probability and possibility are accessible to assuming?

Whatever we answer, there must be no misunderstanding as to the kind of cases in which modal and nonmodal contents really show up on a par with each other. If I assume that Julius Caesar died a natural death, then the objective apprehended by means of this assumption is positive; as against this, I could not by means of any assumption attain a similar result with respect to factuality, say. Assuredly, I can also assume that Augustus died a natural death, and the objective would be factual as well; but in this case I should have assumed something factual only *per accidens* (no differently than the way in which someone can see something sweet, to use the classical paradigm), which is nowise the case as regards positivity in the first example. Of course, there is also this: that I can include a modal property in the assumption, even in the case of the first example, by assuming, say, that it is a fact that Caesar died a natural death. But then, I could likewise assume that it is something positive that Caesar was not murdered. So to summarize we can say: Under favorable circumstances, the assumption-content apprehending an objective gives the nonmodal properties that this assumption-objective actually has; about the modal properties of an assumption-objective, one can at most make further assumptions—which is something that one can always do anyway, even in regard to nonmodal properties.

In this connection, one cannot help thinking of the contrast between the paradigm of the "red cross" and the "cross that is red,"[16] though this contrast was employed under quite different circumstances. Without dwelling on the possible consequences of this correspondence for the concept of intuitiveness and its domain of application, let us just point out a fact that seems to thrust modal properties into an analogy with the business of being nonintuitively apprehended. I mean the fact, briefly noted on the relevant occasion,[17] that modal contents are not "contents of judgment-of" but "contents of judgment-about." That which is the content of a judgment-of seems also able, without reservation, to be the content of an assumption-of (the expression, employed elsewhere, needs no interpretation). The case is not the same with what is purely the content of a judgment-about. The content of a judgment-about is no more able to be brought into a judgment-of than is the act; and in virtue of this, content shows a closer connection with act in the case of judgment-about. This connection makes it somewhat easier to understand the tendency, noted on the relevant occasion,[18] to ascribe evidence and such things to the act rather than the content of judgment. But by the same token, it is natural that the alteration of the judgment-act into an assumption-act will have a strong concomitant effect on factors in the content that are especially closely associated with the judgment-act. If something is not the content of a judgment-of, but solely the content of a judgment-about, then it is not only unable to stay on as the content of an assumption-of, it also cannot stay on as a content of assumption-about, at least not in that special way that permits us, in the case of a judgment, to directly see or realize the factuality, possibility and other such properties of the judged-about objective. Yet even with regard to their modal properties, there is still one way in which objectives of assumptions are just as accessible to assumption-about as objectives of judgments are. In accordance with the principle of unlimited freedom of assumption, I can assume of any given *negativum* that it is positive, of a factual objective that it is merely possible, and so on, just as long as I have first made the modal properties in question intellectually accessible, so to speak, by means of appropriate conceptualization.

Needless to say, degrees of possibility are also included in the present observation. While it is perhaps characteristic of the nature of degrees of possibility that they provide occasion for instances of mediate assumption-evidence, there is by no means anything in this that is in principle significant for assumptions themselves. In particular, we do not want to say that the ascertainment of degrees of possibility requires assumptions characterized by different degrees of certainty—or properly speaking, uncertainty. For then one might just as well be prepared to doubt that the apprehension of degrees of possibility through judgment was possible without reliance on different degrees of judgmental certainty. But there is a connection between known degrees of possibility, on the one hand, and justified surmises—and along with that, probabilities—on the other; and this connection obviously will, under the right conditions, be able to lend assumed degrees of possibility a certain significance for the determination of probabilities.

§61

The Relation of Assumptions to Their Mental Setting

Regarding basic mental facts that have long had their accreditation, as one might say—facts such as representation and feeling, to which conation [Begehren] and even judgment might be added—it is not exactly customary to raise the question as to when and where they make their appearance, not as a perfectly general question. This situation has different reasons in different cases. It obtains in the case of representing because the answer to the question as to when one represents would doubtless have to go, simply: always and everywhere that there are mental processes at work. In the case of the remaining basic classes, however, the reason that the situation is no different is that we do not yet have a sufficiently general answer to the question as it relates to these classes. Under such circumstances, should someone be advocating recognition of a hitherto unacknowledged mental fact,[19] it can scarcely constitute a source of objection if he himself has no perfectly concise formula ready in response to the question as to when and how this fact makes its appearance. But we ought to raise the question and offer an answer to it anyway, however imperfect the answer may be; for it is too obviously in the interest of our attempt at a recapitulation. So what we have to do now is to summarize, in whatever way makes for the easiest overview, the cases in which—or the circumstances under which —assumptions make their appearance in the processes of the mind. It is certainly to be hoped that the investigations of the foregoing chapters have placed at least the most important elements of the extant factual material at our disposal.

As I look for ways to bring some measure of order to the great variety of facts about assumption that we have encountered in these investigations, at first sight a quite heterogeneous assemblage of facts, three things suggest themselves to me as standpoints from which the cases of assumption known to me at present unite into three natural groups. Some assumptions are integral components of basic intellectual operations, and as such they help to form many of the most important simpler and more complex activities of our intellectual life. Again, there are assumptions whose function lies primarily in serving as a psychological prerequisite for extraintellectual activities. And finally, there are assumptions that exist by and for themselves, as it were. If it is found that upon examination these standpoints tend to assume a certain teleological cast, this should no more be attributed to an illicit prejudgment than should the custom of regarding the eye as the organ of seeing or the lung as the organ of breathing. But of the three groups, the third is naturally the group of the most obtrusive assumption-experiences. The first, in contrast, is probably the group of the most important and common of such experiences. From their standpoint, at any rate, our theoretical treatment can penetrate a bit deeper into the nature of the relevant facts than it could from the standpoint of the other assumptions; so it is especially to this first group that we must apply ourselves.

This will primarily involve the things investigated in chapters 5 through 8 above, in the first place the assumption's function of immediately apprehending an objective, or as it may be, mediately apprehending a presented objective (or presented objectum).[20] Again we are concerned with the supplementation of mere representation, which is passive, with intending by way of being or intending by way of so-being, the things that ensure assuming a fundamental role in our fastening upon objects.[d] Finally, we are concerned with the operation on objectives that has customarily, with more or less inexactness, been comprehended under the headings "hypothetical judgment" or "disjunctive judgment," as the case may be; "inference with suspended premises"; and so forth. In all this, as we cannot fail to recognize, the relation of the assumption to the objective stands before us as the basic fact. In the last-mentioned cases, this is already betrayed by the designation "operations on objectives," while the role of intending in our fastening upon objects goes back to the fact that it is only as the material of objectives that objecta can be said to be accessible to the intellect. But to properly appreciate these fundamental facts, as well as their consequences, we must take into consideration that it is not only the assumption that is capable of apprehending objectives, but also the judgment, and that a quite obvious position of advantage belongs to the judgment as opposed to the assumption. Without doubt, judgment owes this advantageous position to the value of knowing, which is always judgment, and to the value of truth. In the last analysis, the apprehension of truth does not always require knowing in the strictest sense, i.e., evident judgment,[21] but it does always require a judgment. As in so many other things, however, the advantage, the strength of judgment, is a disadvantage on the other side, and thus a sort of weakness. No one can believe, i.e., judge, without implicitly claiming truth for what has been judged; hence, in any case where what is wanted is an apprehension of objectives without this claim, judgment fails to work. In such cases, there is a need for a substitute that is more modest in its claims, so to speak, and it is the assumption that meets this need.

As to what these circumstances are, in which judgment is too much, the preceding investigations have thrown some light on this question, too. We have been led by these investigations to four main cases. (1) There can be no fastening upon an object otherwise than in an objective. In the first instance, an objective of being suffices for this purpose, when so-being is implicated by virtue of the content of the underlying representation.[e] But if I do not know whether the objectum in question exists or I know that it does not exist, then an existential judgment cannot be employed. (2) On the other hand, if even the so-being has to be apprehended in an explicit objective of so-being, then this cannot be an objective that is already judged; for it is only with respect to the nature of its material that a judgment can be true or false, a fact that we had occasion to verify quite clearly in the instance of definitions, which are never judgments. (3) Further, if it is a question of judging about [beurteilen] objectives, then as has become apparent, it is often in the nature of the objective of higher order to preclude the presentation of the objective of lower order by means of a judgment; and even where this is not the case, the presentation by means of a judgment at least gives the appearance of an unnecessary expenditure. (4) Finally, logical operations on objectives can actually be carried out to a large extent without any regard to whether the operator believes in the factuality of these objectives. It is easy to understand the significance of this when one puts oneself in the position of a person who is able only to connect believed objectives with each other, and who is unable to accomplish any of the work of thought even with these believed objectives, save at the time of need. Unable to do any such work in advance, put it into stock as it were, a person like that would be comparable to someone who, in order to send a telegraphic signal, was obliged to set up the telegraph at the time he needed it, if not indeed invent it then.

The points that have held up in the intellectual experiences somewhat schematically characterized here can now be carried over immediately into emotional experience as well as into the occurrences, on the whole more complex, that were the subject of special consideration in the ninth chapter. The same for the fourth chapter. Like value-experiences, desires inevitably approach objectives; but the nature of desires precludes the factuality of these objectives.

And as regards value, not only existence enters into consideration, but also non-existence—and under appropriate circumstances not only so-being but negative so-being;^{f} and in each pair, of course, no more than one member can ever be factual. Finally, we turn to those states of affairs in which the conspicuousness of assumptions enabled us to dispense with a closer analysis; here too it is easy to see the import of the typical mental situations in the main cases in question. Whatever a person says in lying, he believes the opposite of it; whatever a person asks about, he doesn't know it, and for that same reason he can't yet believe it; what a person understands, in hearing it or reading it, he is still quite a ways from surrendering himself to it as regards his opinion about it. Art and play, however, are those peculiar activities in which, naturally within certain limits, true and false are in principle devoid of any fundamental role. Seen against what we have so far considered, "explicit" assumptions offer nothing else that is peculiar; they are distinguished by nothing but their "explicitness," a feature that is indeed especially favorable for initial cognizance, but which is understood in the most obvious *prima facie* sense. As to the position that the relevant individual cases occupy in domains of intellectual or emotional fact already familiar to us in their own right, there is no chance of unclarity in this regard.

We may say, then, in summary: The position of assumptions in the processes of the mind is traceable to the significance of objectives as well as to a certain limitation that belongs to the judgment, which is to a certain extent the preferred means of apprehending objectives. The limitation develops out of the fact that the judgment always claims to apprehend something factual, even when it does not. By this, the judgment is deprived of access to all objectives of which it is known that they are false or, unless it is a matter of indifference, of which it is not known whether or not they are true. If such objectives nevertheless have to be approached, then it becomes significant that assumptions are capable of doing this and doing it without the limitation preculiar to the judgment. Thus, the function of an assumption consists essentially in serving as a surrogate for a judgment when the need arises. Naturally, this in no wise precludes the possibility that an assumption, by entering in as a surrogate for a judgment, might in a sense smooth the way for the latter. Nor does the fact of this surrogative function preclude the possibility that there is a sort of natural propensity for assuming, as well as something like a natural propensity to judgment.

§62
Assumptions and Language. Understanding Again

Perhaps it is not free of all violence to count the linguistic expression of an inner experience as part of the latter's "mental setting"; but in any case, it will be appropriate at this point if we can also make precise the position that assumptions have vis-à-vis language, in light of the investigations carried out in this work. Should it thereby turn out that these investigations have put us in a position to overcome difficulties in linguistic psychology that seemed insoluble before we introduced assumptions into the sphere of consideration,[22] then we might also be able to see new support in this for what has been set forth on assumptions here.

If one is trying first and foremost to make clear the relation of assumptions to the means of expression put at our disposal by language, then the oft-mentioned intermediate position of assumptions between representation and judgment again becomes important. We find representations expressed in single words or in word-complexes, judgments in sentences. By contrast, the expressions correlated with assumptions are words (including word-complexes) as well as sentences. Perhaps it would be more precise to say: sentences first and foremost, but also words. And there is an explanation for the occurrence of words in place of sentences; it lies in the ability of assumptions to offer their objectives as objects for further intellectual treatment. In that function, assumptions accomplish for objectives what representations themselves accomplish for objecta: If representations find expression in words, then the analogous functioning of assumptions makes it understandable that they, too, should come to be expressed by means of words. And aside from this, it is also understandable that in grammar, sentences that to a large extent serve for the expression of assumptions may themselves be treated in the manner of words or word-complexes. We have gotten to know "that"-clauses as such sentences, and consequently we can also understand the peculiar position that grammar teaches us to grant to "that"-clauses.

If we now start from the opposite side, assumptions, instead of from sentences, then the question that we abandoned in the second and third chapters, the question as to the functions of the sentence, can be answered without difficulty; and it can be answered from the standpoint of the speaker, as well as from that of the person who understands him. In the former regard, the difficulty to which we were led[23] consisted in the fact that we met with sentences that did not serve to express any judgment. Now we know that it is assumptions that are expressed in sentences of this sort. But as concerns the understanding of the sentence, we were able to see easily[24] that this does not require a judgment about the object represented by the speaker, i.e., a judgment that the speaker evokes by suggestion, and that it certainly does not require any judgment about the opinion of the speaker. To these negative determinations, the reference to assumptions once again affords the positive complement, as it were. Moreover, this reference admits of a quite simple formulation, if we also take the fact of sentence-signification[25] into account. As we noted, a sentence expresses either a judgment or an assumption; and for that reason, it always has a signification, which is the objective of that judgment or assumption. The understanding of a sentence consists, then, simply in the apprehending of this objective, and to that extent it makes no difference as to whether this apprehending takes place by means of a judgment or merely by means of an assumption.

Thus, as far as the question is one of specifying the minimum that must be present for us to be able to speak of the understanding of a piece of discourse, we may state simply: The listener understands if and when he assumes what the speaker says. So if the function of the spoken sentence normally consists in at least the expression of an assumption, then the function of the heard sentence normally consists in at least the arousal of assumptions in the person who understands the sentence. This may be compared with the relation by means of which we originally[26] tried to make the connection that generally obtains between sign and signification work for the case of the understanding of words and sentences; in the above way, this relation does, in a certain sense, reassert its importance. It remains clearer and more precise, however, to say: Understanding something spoken (or written, for that matter) consists in the apprehension of its signification. And although in this formulation it is once again quite explicitly a matter of "signification," the customary correlate of "sign," the very way in which we have put it shows quite clearly how little one really does justice to the most important functions of language by merely subsuming it under the concept of sign.

It seems that all the types of sentences mentioned in grammar can express assumptions; still, one will hardly scruple to ascribe the aptitude for that preeminently to dependent sentences in the broadest sense of the term. It is true that under special circumstances even these sentences can quite well be expressions of judgment. But as a rule they are not; and on the basis of the foregoing investigations, it is for the most part not difficult to account for the connection that obtains between assumptions and the distinctive grammatical character of the sentences in question. In particular, relative clauses point to the role of assumptions in the forming of complexes;[27] the compound sentences already characterized by grammar under the heading of "logical" connection point to judgments as to connection, hypothetical judgments, and assumption-inferences;[28] and "that"-clauses together with their equivalents point to mediately apprehended objectives.[g] Secondary expressions[29] constitute a special case of the last-mentioned group of sentences, of course; as we can now easily see, the essential thing about these expressions is that in them the directedness of the relevant mental happenings to their objectives moves considerably into the foreground.

It may be taken as a matter of course to begin with, that in the case of such secondary expression the "that"-clause is the primary expression of an assumption that is serving as "psychological prerequisite" for the secondarily expressed mental happening. If one regards the "that"-clause this way, then the particularly interesting thing for us about the case of secondarily expressed *judgment* is that we may in this case be confronted with an assumption as the psychological prerequisite of a judgment with the same objective. Of course, we shall have to take care not to draw too strict consequences as to what is going on in the speaker, from the fact that a judgment is once expressed primarily and again secondarily. On the contrary, it ought not to pass unnoticed how often stylistic and rhetorical needs contribute an element of their own toward making what is clear unclear and what is typical atypical. There are few people who have not at some time, for the sake of a good or supposedly good joke, adopted a seemingly frivolous attitude; and there are none who have yet to write or say this or that for no other reason than that it sounds good. But a person who is at all accustomed to "reflect" before he writes something down may easily be surprised when he first takes account of the changes that are usually undergone by the expressions in whose attire the thoughts originally made their appearance: transformations of affirmatives into negatives, existential assertions into categorical ones or vice versa, replacement of a relation or complexion by one of the surprising number of equivalents available—such are among the most commonplace changes. And just about as commonplace, I daresay, is an independent sentence turning into a clause with "that," where the sentence now shows up as dependent on the secondary expression of a mental state of affairs—which expression is altogether immaterial to the originally given thought. And who would hesitate on stylistic grounds to say or write, instead of the simple "*A* is *B*," "I say (maintain, insist, concede) that *A* is *B*," etc.; or again, "It is clear (obvious, incontestable) that *A* is *B*," and the like? Still, in such transformations of expression, the thought that is being expressed by no means proves to be something absolutely fixed; to the contrary, it follows the exigencies of expression, sometimes probably even at the expense of the point that is being made. But of course, there is only so much latitude for this, and occasionally rather little; so that in actual fact, a speaker as well as a writer rather readily perceives it to be a sort of forcibleness when he is "taken at his word" in an overly precise way. In short, then: The secondary expression of a judgment does not by any means guarantee, in the individual cases where one meets with it, that there is a mental state of affairs coordinated with just that secondary expression. Yet, a question arises when we take the fact that the transition from primary to secondary expression and vice versa is so easy to execute, and we consider this fact along with the hint that the secondary expression of judgment provides regarding the effective presence of an assumption. The question is whether this effective presence shouldn't also be seen in the primarily expressed judgment itself, and therefore in every judgment as the normal thing. This is a question to which we shall have to return briefly in the next section.

All the same, it should not be left unmentioned here that in some cases it would be at least a possible alternative for one to take the "that"-clause in the secondary expression of a judgment not as an assumption, but as a judgment. Actually, the notion that in some cases one and the same thing gains expression in the main and subordinate clauses is not to be rejected *a limine,* the reason being simply that such things most assuredly do occur occasionally in other domains. If someone says, "I insist, come in,"[h] then given the right intonation the insistence is in truth twice expressed, once indefinitely and once definitely; along with this, it is first secondarily and then primarily expressed. True, we do not have a sentence with "that" here; but why shouldn't something similar be able to occur with these "that"-clauses? Let us add immediately that it actually does occur in at least one quite definite case, even if the view set forth in the foregoing be the correct one. The locution, "I assume that it may well be so," scarcely admits of any natural interpretation other than this: that the assumption itself is gaining twofold expression here, once indefinitely and again definitely, secondarily in the former case and primarily in the latter. At the same time, we should consider that there is nothing new in the fact that language can be forced into pleonastic modes of expression in other ways besides this, as we can see from instances of so-called inner objects like "to do a deed," "to fight a fight," and so forth. But concerning such cases, no one has doubted that they are to be treated as exceptions, powerless to shake the rule that each of the individual components of a piece of discourse has its own special task to fulfill.

Finally, let us also return to a question that has remained unanswered ever since the second chapter: Is there something that one could identify as the characteristic function of sentences specifically, as against words or word-complexes? For the attempt to bring the question to an answer we have, as one specific basis, the expressive function of sentences and, as another specific basis, their significative function.

Let us begin, as would be natural, with sentences as expressions. Is there something that all sentences express, no matter what? The answer is simple: What every sentence expresses, i.e., if it does function as an expression at all, is at least an assumption. But may we also assert the converse? Is a thing that expresses at least an assumption always itself a sentence? Obviously not. For one to fasten upon an object in an intending manner, there must be at least an assumption,[30] but a word is perfectly adequate as the means of expression for this assumption. We may even ask, as will have to be done shortly, anyway, whether a sentence is at all able to provide expression for such a fastening-upon. One might better hope to get through to some result, following the path now taken, if one started from the aptitude that sentences have, circumstances permitting, for expressing not just assumptions but especially judgments. One could raise the question as to whether this ability, at least, shouldn't be reserved for sentences alone. Still, even here the answer proves negative if, as is certainly the case, there is a fastening-upon by means of judgments and this fastening-upon can be expressed by means of words of a nonsentential character. Such types of expression actually number among the most commonplace; in fact, it is not only exclamations like "Fire!" and "Land!" already theoretically well-exploited, that belong in this class. A person who is looking out the window and who says, "The sky is blue," does not at all need to have fastened upon the object "sky" by means of previous thoughts. But in that case, the words "the sky" express his fastening upon the relevant object, an object of which something is then predicated; and since the speaker wants to say something about the real sky, it is natural for this fastening upon to take place by means of a judgment or the "positing representation" that has more than once come under discussion.[31]

As to signification, the matter works out quite simply along the lines of what has been said. All sentences signify objectives; this we know. But does this sort of signification, objective-signification, belong only to sentences? Obviously not, as anything that expresses an assumption will thus far have to signify an objective, too.

Is it then a hopeless business to look for a function that is peculiar to the sentence? It still might not be, if we turn back again from signification to expression and we take into account not the distinction of judgment and assumption, but that of fastening upon an object and thinking something about the fastened upon. We just mentioned that the fastening-upon can find natural expression in single words. Now it may be added that a sentence, as far as I can see, is not at all able under normal circumstances to serve for the expression of a fastening-upon. In an independent sentence one sees this immediately; but a dependent sentence, too, is by nature always resorting to expressions for something one has already fastened upon, something that one "intends" in predicating something else of it. If this is correct, then we can simply assert the following: What a sentence as such expresses is thinking something about an object one has already fastened upon, whether this thinking be a judging-about or just an assuming-about.

§63

The Position of Assumptions in the System of Psychology.
Assumptions as Thoughts

Systematization is not an end in itself in any science or field of learning, but if one tries to do as much justice as possible to the requirements of systematic rigor, this can be of powerful assistance to the attainment of a true view of the nature of the facts to be investigated. For in the last analysis, the most important of the guiding principles for any systematic presentation remains this: that the things that bear an affinity to each other in this presentation should come into juxtaposition with each other; a juxtaposition, moreover, that should be closer in proportion as the affinity is a closer one. For that reason, the question as to what position is to be assigned to assumptions in the system of mental facts coincides in the first instance with the question as to the relation of affinity in which assumptions stand to the remaining, more closely investigated occurrences. In accordance with this, the latter question may be raised here at the beginning, too. It is possible, anyway, that the answering of these questions will suggest consequences that could make their influence felt even in the systematic grouping of experiences that are now quite inadmissible to the domain of things having any particularly close affinity to assumptions.

In assumptions, we have come to know a class of mental events with an extraordinarily rich representation in the processes of the mind. What position will we have to grant this class as regards the classes of representation, judgment, feeling, and conation, the classes more or less solidly accredited by tradition? We can take it for granted right away that the two classes appertaining to the intellectual life, those of representation and judgment, are the only ones that need enter into consideration. Also, the way in which assumptions first commanded our attention[32] forbids any doubt about this: that an assumption is more than a mere representation and is less than a judgment—or more precisely, less than a representation taken together with the judgment positioned on it. Thus, we have already more than once mentioned in the course of the foregoing investigations that assumptions occupy a sort of middle position between representation and judgment. Of course, this thesis was taken from the outward aspect of the facts; it was meant to serve as a description of that outward aspect,[33] and it was intended in a fairly primitive way. What the following three experiences do form is an ordered series of a rather striking sort: representation, representation with assumption, and representation with judgment (particularly when, as is so natural, one substitutes "assumption with belief" here for "judgment"). It is roughly like the complexes A, AB, and ABC, ignoring the nature of the components A, B, and C. But in our case, an ordered series, albeit one of a rather different sort, is also formed by the three components each considered by itself. Thus, in presenting an objectum, a representation apprehends its object in its own way. An assumption apprehends an objective in another way, at least to the extent that it is not committed to presenting that object. A judgment likewise apprehends an objective, and no less than an assumption, it does so on its own authority—but with the special nuance in virtue of which it is, as we saw, attuned to factuality, a nuance that is altogether alien to assumptions. And in the face of this new series, the question arises: How are the members of this series to be understood in relation to each other? Should we simply take assumptions in coordinate opposition to representations and judgments? Or do these intermediate facts, assumptions, stand so close to the one or the other of the latter groups that they were better united into a whole with it and taken in coordinate opposition to the remaining group?

As I see it, the whole course of these investigations suggests unequivocally that there is a far closer affinity between assumptions and judgments than there is between assumptions and representations. As paradoxical as it may sound, it really makes quite good sense to say this, that an assumption is a judgment without conviction;[34] whereas there would be no intelligible sense at all in defining an assumption as, say, a representation that is determinate in respect of the antithesis of yes and no.[35] The assumption's appearance as a judgment-surrogate,[36] so typical of it, speaks in no uncertain tones in this matter. And in reality, even the inadequacy of the term "assumption," mentioned on the relevant occasion,[37] points in the same direction: Aside from the experiences more closely investigated by us in this book, what this word signifies in use is a certain manner of judging, never mere representation in the strict sense. For all that, there will naturally be conceptualizations by whose aid one can embrace representations and assumptions in a single class and oppose them to judgments, if one does not stumble at the requisite artificiality. But if anything, we want even less to form class-concepts for their own sake than we do systems; all that is important to us is that the distinctive character of the facts should carry as much weight as possible in the framing of concepts. For that very reason, natural classes are the ones to which we have to hold fast. Accordingly, we can say the following: It is not judgments that constitute the class that can be naturally taken in coordinate opposition to representations, feelings, and conative experiences, but judgments together with assumptions.

Along with this result there naturally arises the vexatious need for a term that can be used as a name for the newly conceived class. The attempt to satisfy this need through a proposal normally cannot succeed without a certain element of arbitrariness or conventionalism; and then it is left more or less to chance as to whether one really finds the expression that the sense of language no more than fairly demands in the new application.

In the previous edition of this book,[38] with these reservations, I proposed taking assumption and judgment together under the heading of "thinking." I find it to be a quite felicitous modification, one that is only at first sight inessential, that Stephan Witasek[39] now introduces the designation "thoughts" for the new class of experiences to which assumptions as well as judgments belong. The value of the alteration lies in a fact which, though it has not escaped me, I have not rated highly enough: In the ordinary verbal usage one customarily designates not just judgment and assuming as "thinking," but practically all other intellectual operations, too—operations like comparison, abstraction, and so forth. In the case of "thoughts," these other operations are naturally out of the question. The problem is just that there is also an objection[40] to the previously mentioned proposal of mine, and this objection seems to remain in effect: that it won't do to exclude representation from the domain of "thinking," and that it seems unquestionable that building castles in the air and other activities of the representative imagination lead to "thoughts." I myself would not want to question this, either; but then, I am strongly inclined to question whether someone who is building castles in the air is merely representing in doing so. For we have seen that as something purely passive, representation does not yet apprehend an object, and that any intending is at least an assuming.[41] It is hardly likely that there is some need to call even purely passive, representational experiences thoughts. Thus, Witasek's precising remarks are far from giving the term "thoughts" any sort of seriously altered domain of application. But for the cases where it is better to speak of assuming and judgment than of an assumption and a judgment, a narrower sense of the term "thinking" can be derived from the term "thoughts"; then it might be regarded as unobjectionable to comprehend assuming and judgment under this term, if the sense is expressly designated as a narrower one.

Still, there is another way to overcome the terminological difficulty that we might have here. If assumptions and judgments belong together in one class of experiences, then in consideration of the position of judgment, which is in many respects a dominant one, we can treat judgment as the *potius* according to which the *denominatio* of the whole class is made. Or again, which in practice amounts to the same thing, a "judgment" in the broader sense can be contrasted to a "judgment" in the narrower sense, with the concept of a judgment in the broader sense comprehending assumptions. And it might become especially clear that we should proceed in this way; for as we yet have to see,[42] a quite analogous usage for "feeling" and "desire" is actually in full accord with the state of affairs actually prevailing in these domains of experience. That is why I thought[43] that I should adopt the position of not rejecting a form of expression that prefers to call assumptions a subspecies of "judgment" in the broader sense,[44] and I can only be amazed at the willingness with which this has been interpreted as a change in my fundamental views about the nature of assumptions.[45] I shall certainly change these views as soon as the facts teach me better; until then, however, it really should not be too difficult to distinguish terminological concessions from material ones.

At any event, making use of the mode of expression that seems descriptively adequate to me, I can summarize as follows. The nature of assumptions is also characterized by the fact that they together with judgments constitute thoughts in the technically specified sense of this word, and thinking (in the narrower sense) stands in a relationship of coordinate opposition to representation, feeling, and conative experience. At the same time, this formulation clearly suggests two questions, ones that I should not like to leave unasked, though I am not at present in a position to answer them conclusively.

First of all, mightn't the frequently emphasized affinity between assuming and judgment be due to what Stumpf once[46] called similarity by like parts? More precisely, isn't what we have in the judgment a complex state of affairs, in that it always contains an assumption and just one more thing, which we know as the element of conviction? By this supposition, at any event, the assumption's ability to substitute in various ways for the judgment would be brought considerably closer to complete intelligibility.

The second question would then go a step further: Isn't what we have in the assumption simply a sort of preliminary stage of the judgment, a stage that one normally has to pass in forming a judgment and which affords a certain chance of doing so when it is attained? In those cases where the material for the judgment is given beforehand, we have had repeated occasion to convince ourselves that judgments fairly often do have preliminary stages. But there we just saw a sort of advantage that an *affirmative* being-assumption has, insofar as it is the starting point even for the formation of negative being-*assumptions*.[47] As against this, affirmative assumptions could hardly be of use in readying negative *judgments*. This difficulty would not be insurmountable however; there would merely have to be reason to suppose that the qualitative veering round of affirmation into negation still falls in the domain of assuming. Thus, after the starting assumption of affirmative quality, there would first follow a negative assumption, and only then would a negative judgment develop out of the assuming. But that the assumption involves an improved chance at least for the like-qualitied judgment, i.e., for one directed to the same objective—this, at any rate, seems to be supported by the well-known experience of the liar who in the end believes his own lie, as well as the experience of the credulous person. For the sake of comprehension, the latter first had to allow the opinion of others to be evoked in him by suggestion as an assumption;[48] fairly soon, especially after repeated suggestion, he makes this opinion his own. In this way, there are not just assumptions evoked by suggestion, but also judgments evoked by suggestion.

As we can see, the situation is on the whole not unfavorable to an affirmative answer to the two foregoing questions; but at present the matter is in both cases far less ready for a pronouncement than it is worthy of a further careful investigation. And it may likewise be left undecided as to whether the relevant investigation belongs entirely in the context of the present section and not perhaps more in that of the preceding sections. However, there are problems involved here that go beyond the limits of elementary description fixed for the present investigations and which extend far into the domain of genetic intellectual psychology; we might add that J. M. Baldwin has now already entered successfully onto this path of research, giving particular consideration to assumptions.[49]

§64

On the Possibility of Assumptions

The reader may rightly be surprised if, at the end of a book in which assumptions have confronted him as an experience with the most diverse empirical confirmation, direct and indirect, he is now supposed to occupy himself with the "possibility" of this experience. He may also ask why we have to readdress ourselves to such a problem in a place where we were supposed to enter only upon a clarification of the relation between the assumption and the judgment. The reason lies in the fact that my very theses on the relation of the assumption to the judgment, apparent though it is that these theses have not gotten beyond the stage of a preliminary effort, have supposedly shown themselves useful for proving a priori that there cannot even be any assumptions.[50] In another place,[51] my opinion on the value of such an undertaking in general and of the particular one in question has been expressed clearly enough that I should not at this point have to concern myself anew with this proof of impossibility because of a reprise of it that has been made.[52] To my great astonishment, however, this proof has found a hearing and met with approval[53] even elsewhere than on the banks of the Moldau River, and this makes it seem appropriate to me, after all, to spend a few words in examining the rejoinder that has been bestowed upon my reply.

It will be best if I do not discuss certain embellishments that Marty bestows upon his new polemic, such as his reproaching me with a whole sin ledger of theses in which I am "at work subverting hitherto unquestioned truths."[54] It does not matter that the list contains a case in which I could have no part, as the enumeration is far from complete, anyway. It is to some extent understandable that Marty, on the basis of these samples, urgently warns against my way of carrying on the theory of objects;[55] and if I cannot mend my ways, then by the present reference to this warning, let me at least contribute my share to its propagation.

At any rate, as concerns the impossibility proof itself, the main idea of its consists in this: that the judgment and the assumption cannot be related to each other either as two different genera or as two species of the same genus and that they are, therefore, neither generically nor specifically different. In my reply, I had opposed to this the surmise that since there nevertheless are, as a matter of experience, both judgments and assumptions, there is doubtless something in need of rectification in Marty's presuppositions regarding genera and species. This is now entered in the previously mentioned ledger of sins as doubt about a thing that has been firmly established since Aristotle, wherewith it is determined that Marty has made his proof bear on the Aristotelian genus and the Aristotelian species. But inasmuch as in the first formulation of his proof, he spoke of genus and species without specifying things historically, it now turns out that whether deliberately or by oversight, he called just "genus" and "species" what he should have called "Aristotelian genus" and "Aristotelian species," respectively. Since as a rule it is not customary to use the terms "genus" and "species" in the strictly Aristotelian way, my surmise as to the need of a rectification is now verified by Marty himself. My objections in the reply were naturally not attuned to Aristotle; I doubt, however, that this has prejudiced their validity to any great extent. The best instances of a priori evidence, even when one can appeal in their favor to the authority of an Aristotle, can always fail in what is expected of them, when the right to apply them to the very case that is decisive has not been adequately secured.

The double thesis underlying the proof can be expressed with the minimum amount of erudition as follows: (*a*) The judgment and the assumption do not stand in regard to each other as color and sound do, (*b*) but they are not as green and red or any other two colors are to each other, either. The component thesis *a* is substantiated by pointing out common differentiations of the judgment and the assumption, ones such as affirmation and negation, to which several other things might be added, by reason of the above discussions;[56] by contrast, color and sound lack common differentiations. And this will be seen to be materially quite correct; as to whether, in contrast, the formal substantiation is adequate, this is perhaps doubtful. Marty is "astonished" at my counter-argument from intensity of sound and heat, but he cannot cope with it without appealing to Brentano's "differences of density in the filling of sense-space,"[57] which is of next to no use to me.

The substantiation of component thesis *b* resists any attempt to put it into plain words. The unnaturalness of this dialectical mannerism invites the same sort of thing in return, and it makes it unnecessary to go through the dreary business of a detailed criticism a second time here. Let us just note, then, that Marty is mistaken if he thinks that in my reply I had only wished to point out one *petitio principii*.[58] I have actually found two of them, or rather one of them twice, and I cannot see either that the appeal to "brevity" or "convenience" of expression[59] takes care of the one case, or that the appeal to the distinction between the "purely negative" and the "privative"[60] takes care of the other case. Yet I must confess that in my reply I did to some extent lose sight of the forest of the main idea for the trees of such details and that I did in this way fail to elucidate the very strange nature of this main idea. What is *supposed* to be proved, as Marty himself now expressly testifies,[61] is that "between the assumption and the judgment...there cannot be the relation" of "belonging...to the same genus." What *would* in truth be proved, if Marty's argumentation were open to no objection, is this: that when I opposed the judgment and the assumption to each other, I went about it in the wrong way, in that a contrast like "judgment with conviction" and "judgment without conviction" would have been more consistent. As could be seen above,[62] this idea has incidentally found a place in my thoughts, too, and demonstrably not just at the suggestion of the argument under discussion; and I have in no sense rejected the idea. But supposing that all this were not the case and that I had simply erred, what difference does my error make, when what matters is reaching a decision in favor of or against assumptions?

At the same time, once it is established that Marty is dealing with Aristotelian genera and species, a simple means of guidance is available to the person who rightly wants to be exempted from what I spoke of as being the less agreeable task, that of going into the above details. Suppose, namely, that Marty had succeeded in proving both components of the double thesis. It would consequently be established that the judgment and the assumption are neither Aristotelian genera nor Aristotelian species in relation to each other. What would this entail for the possibility of assumptions—or as we should say, against it? Even if the success in establishing something like this should be as certain as the failure at it is now, nothing in the slightest will follow in regard to assumptions as long as a principle like the following does not hold: "Objects that are not related to each other either as Aristotelian genera or Aristotelian species are impossible." The game of genus and species in the Aristotelian sense is an altogether idle one, as long as we do not know whether what we have are "strict" or "true" genera or species, let alone where we have reason to surmise the contrary from the empirical aspect of the subject matter.

Thus, Marty's "antecedent" proof of impossibility or improbability is actually no more than what it appears to be at first glance, to the cognitive instincts of an unbiased person. I myself would hardly be suspected of underrating the value of a priori modes of cognition. But no one can grant the authority to correct experience to an a priori wrangling that is quite devoid of any contact with experience. The question as to whether there are assumptions is one of empirical fact. To answer this question, one must first of all open one's eyes and only then spin out thoughts. When one has tried one's hand with living reality, and when, like ourselves in the foregoing, one has met with such great difficulties in trying to apprehend the relation of the judgment and the assumption even in the rudest of preliminary characterizations—then one loses any confidence in being able to master the facts of experience as easily as by the pretension to Aristotelian precising. Under such circumstances, I should naturally have preferred to spare myself as well as my readers the renewed treatment of this matter, a matter that seems to me to be so unpromising in every respect; at any event, it is only in the case of most extreme duress that I would take it up again, for a third time.

§65

The Outlook. Some New Considerations for a Definition of the Concept of Imagination

Without in any way anticipating future resolution of the questions raised in the section before the last, one can observe something like a two-stage character in the facts that have now been comprehended under the heading of thoughts. That is to say, one can find it to be intelligible and reasonable that judgments should in some sense serve as a sort of higher stage in relation to assumptions, the lower stage. The element of indefiniteness in such a thesis has the value of confronting us with the further question as to whether we might not somehow meet with such a two-stage character in one of the other three classes of basic mental facts, the classes that we have set in coordinate opposition to thoughts. It may be, however, that the question would never occur to anyone if the bipartition were not one of the most acknowledged and familiar facts in one of the three remaining domains. Naturally, I mean representation, with its contrast of perceptual representations and reproductive representations[63] [i]— the latter ones often designated as "recollective representations" ["Erinnerungsvorstellungen"] or "imaginative representations" ["Phantasievorstellungen"], as the case may be. The contrast is familiar to everyone,[64] and the familiarity scarcely begins in the days when Hume suggested the distinction between "impression" and "idea." To be sure, this contrast nowise governs all of representation, as long as one adheres to the domain of application for the terms we have just adduced; for it is only in association with objects that are perceivable in nature that one speaks of perceptual representations, or as opposed to them, of reproductive representations. The association is with real objects, then,[65] not with ideal objects like similarity, opposition, and the like.[66] In the case of the ideal objects, however, the bipartition or two-stage character of representation comes into its own again in the contrast of production and reproduction [Reproduktion].[67] And so actually, we find this character in the whole domain of representation; but it seemed to me so manifest that the members of the dichotomy stand in clear analogy to the judgment and the assumption that I regarded a special inquiry into this matter as dispensable in the first edition of this book.

Since, however, the analogy has in the meantime been called expressly into question,[68] let us in this matter[69] refer to the general aspect that makes itself apparent before any attempt at analysis.*j* From this aspect, as far as I can see, it results beyond a doubt that the judgment and the perceptual representation (or production-representation [Produktionsvorstellung], as the case may be) form a sort of pair, and that the assumption and the imaginative representation form another pair; surely, upon questioning, no one would opt for the opposite correlation. When one then attempts analysis, serious difficulties develop, as the case of imaginative representations has rather often permitted one to discover, and the result has been that even in the business of description it has been necessary to avail oneself of more or less figuratively intended definitions. But if we adhere to the characterization of imaginative representations which at the present time still comes closest to the facts, the characterization by emphasis on the "fleetingness" and "paleness"[70] of these representations, then as far as I can see there is again no doubt that properties of that sort could be better ascribed just to assumptions as such, not to judgments. But the relation becomes clearer yet when one takes the comparison of assumption and judgment made above[71] as a basis for the parallel.[72] We found these two experiences to be different not primarily as to the content but as to the act. What is judged can in principle also be assumed; but in respect of the act, the judgment exhibits a sort of overage in comparison with the assumption, whether or not this additional element can be apprehended and characterized independently. Perceptual and reproductive representations [Einbildungsvorstellungen] too (for the sake of brevity, we can let the cases of ideal objects be covered by this pair) are not distinct from each other as to their object or as to their content; for every representation of the one species there is, at least in principle, a representation of like content belonging to the other species. So here too, the difference lies in the act; and again the perceptual representation presents itself as the somewhat richer state of affairs, so that the notion that a perceptual representation might be an intensified imaginative representation (significantly, the converse notion seems not yet to have occurred to anyone) always has a certain naturalness in its favor. In another place, I thought that I should pronounce against the intensification-view;[73] if I am right there, then it is doubtless quite natural to surmise the additional presence of a *qualitative* factor in the case of the perceptual representation.

Of course, this is by no means to assert that the analogy will prove valid in absolutely every respect.[74] For example, there is actually no known counterpart in the domain of thoughts for the old principle *"Nihil est in intellectu, quod non prius fuerit in sensu,"* which concerns a sometimes overrated but in any case very important relation between perceptual representations and the allied imaginative ones.[75] And specifically, there might be more to the difference that has come to light in this example. We found it to be natural to contrast the assumption to the judgment not only as a sort of lower stage in the sense of perfection, but also as a preliminary stage in the sense of development.

In the previously given sense, the perceptual representation is, as we saw, a higher stage in relation to the reproductive representation; yet the principle of *intellectus* and *sensus* puts the perceptual before the reproductive—and not the reproductive first, as would certainly befit a "preliminary stage." But then who knows whether the principle in question can be so simply reinterpreted in genetic form? Furthermore, there is always room left for rather extensive differences when one states that the bipartite character (and, *cum grano salis* for the present, also the two-stage character) of thoughts has its counterpart in the case of representations and is therefore predicable of all intellectual activities; which suggests the question as to whether a character of this sort could be wholly alien to emotional experiences.

Some material for the answering of this question was gathered by us on an earlier occasion.[76] We had occasion to record facts that in regard to both their nature and the circumstances of their appearance could be called feelinglike, without really being what one customarily thinks of under the headings of pleasure and displeasure; analogously, we had occasion to set desirelike experiences alongside desires [Begehrungen] in the ordinary sense. And if in considering assumptions, admittedly in their outward aspect, we could ascertain that they were more representationlike than judgments are, then in between representations, on the one hand, and genuine feelings and desires on the other, there now appear these feelinglike and desirelike experiences. For the former, I have suggested the designation "imaginative feelings," and for the latter the name "imaginative desires," without right away going into detail on the motive for such a choice. It will become clear directly, in the present connection. If we accept these designations for the present, then it is clear right away that in relation to real feelings and real desires these imaginative feelings and imaginative desires respectively occupy a position quite similar to that of assumptions in relation to judgments; if it was quite in order to characterize the former as pseudo-feelings and pseudo-desires, so it will be with assumptions, when we call them pseudo-judgments. But although we juxtaposed thoughts with feelings and desires as a coordinate class in the section before the last, now we find a terminological asymmetry in this procedure. It consists in this: By "feeling" we have to understand pseudo-feelings along with the real ones, and by "desires" pseudo-desires along with real desires; whereas we make no use of this rather inexact terminological expedient in the case of "thoughts," but set two independent subspecies alongside each other under the independent titles "judgment" and "assumption." Needless to say, the latter procedure is by far the more correct one; but I have been unable, in respect of feelings or desires, to discover words that could accomplish something similar to what the word "thoughts" accomplishes in respect of judgments. And for the time being, we can let the matter of asymmetry rest at that. But of course, the asymmetry could be eliminated by extending the use of the less perfect mode of designation to the domain of thoughts and treating assumptions as pseudo-judgments in juxtaposition with real judgments or judgments-in-earnest. It is the verbal usage already mentioned above,[77] a usage that permits one to say "a judgment in the broader sense" instead of "a thought." In the following, we shall presently[78] see ourselves led to this usage from another side.

One can specify more than one aspect under which three classes of mental events—thoughts, feelings, and desires—are seen to be more closely related *inter se* than they are with the remaining class, the fourth or rather the first one, that of representations. Among such aspects is the peculiar lack of self-sufficiency in virtue of which every state of affairs belonging to these classes has, as its psychological prerequisite, a presenting experience on which it depends. Also among these aspects is the oppositional character prevailing within each of these three classes. This character manifests itself as affirmation versus negation in the case of thoughts, as pleasure versus displeasure in the case of feelings, and as desire in the narrow, positive sense versus reluctance in the case of desires. These and other features are without parallel in the case of representations; and so it is also not surprising if the bipartite arrangement that we are particularly concerned with here, and which confronts us in so much the same way within the three classes, evidently has a relatively peculiar character to it in the case of representation. It has already been pointed out, above, how little a reproductive representation can be regarded as the preliminary or transitional stage for the perceptual representation of the same object; and even terminologically it is noteworthy that the expression "representation" does not in the first instance mean "perceptual representation," so that one does not in the least feel compelled to designate reproductive representations as "pseudo-representations," e.g., in analogy to "pseudo-feelings." Rather, what is actually and in the first instance called a "representation," at least in extrascientific usage, is precisely the reproductive representation; thus, even many theorists, as is well known, cannot bring themselves to join in the broadening of the signification of the word "representation" into that of a class name comprehending both reproductive and perceptual representations.

However, such differences cannot change anything in the main point that the bipartition does obtain here, too. And whatever reproductive representations might lack in affinity to assumptions, pseudo-feelings, and pseudo-desires, it is in a way compensated several times over by the fact that the activities belonging to the lower stages of thinking, feeling, and desire are so frequently dependent on reproductive representations as their psychological prerequisite. It is not as though perceptual representations were once and for all incapable of entering into such a function; but as a rule they simply do not do so, and consequently the members of the lower stages of all four classes not infrequently afford the appearance of a homogeneous whole, in virtue of the relation of regular coexistence.[79]

This circumstance appears to me to be particularly worth noting, because if I see the matter aright, it holds the key to the understanding of an important psychological conception. True, it is in the first instance a conception of everyday psychology; yet any theory that is as attentive to strictness as is practicable has a well-founded interest in the proper comprehension of this conception. I mean the concept of imagination, to whose elucidation I have already made one approach in writing,[80] without the results thereby obtained being able to lastingly satisfy me or others. Of the factual presuppositions of my theses of that time, I shall scarcely need to retract more than what is entailed by the advances in psychology and the theory of objects that have occurred in the meantime, hopefully not wholly insignificant advances. Yet in the last analysis, the definition of imagination as "the spontaneity requisite for the intuitive realization of new forms"[81] or in some such way is in more than one respect much too narrow. Previous to this definition of mine, Witasek attempted to work out the concept of imagination as the "disposition to direct envisaging [Einbilden] of newly founded contents"[82] (or of founded objects, to put it in the more exact way that we have since learned). The approach had the considerable advantage of having pointed out an important factor for the first time, a factor that is also highly characteristic of artistic activity. But the shortcoming that this approach to a definition has in common with my own, and doubtless with most of the other ones now at hand, is that it does not reach far enough beyond the domain of representation. After all, in the course of the foregoing investigations we had sufficient opportunity to satisfy ourselves as to how intimately the way in which we approach art, indeed actively as well as passively, is as it were penetrated with assumptions—and with pseudo-feelings and pseudo-desires, too, for that matter. In fact, in the layman's understanding about someone who is attributed a lively imagination, the liveliness is understood as expressing itself not only in representation, but also in the other three domains of facts—not through convictions, and not through volitions and feelings in the strict sense, but through those peculiar manifestations that were more or less aptly described as belonging to the lower stage, as we have thus far called it. From that it seems to me to follow plainly that this whole lower stage, apart from whether representation, thinking, feeling, or desire appear in it, constitutes the domain in which imagination manifests itself.

Here we shall have to forego any inquiry into whether, on the strength of the preceding, we have the right to define imagination simply as a disposition to mental activities that belong to our "lower stage"—or in other words, whether the securing of theoretical or practical serviceableness for the concept of imagination mightn't depend on our restricting the concept in one or another way. It might be, anyway, that the notion of imagination is one of those lay notions that resist all but arbitrary precising. In that case, either the way this precising is to be undertaken remains ever controversial short of an explicit convention —as with the concept of attention—or else the theorist wholly renounces the use of the terms in question for exact purposes, as has happened in connection with "understanding" and "reason," the lay terms that are so common in everyday life. However, we have seen the connection between imagination, even in the lay sense, and our "lower stage," and this connection is enough to provide us with a comprehensive designation for the facts that belong to said lower stage. Given this designation, we can dispense with the makeshift expression "lower stage," an expression that is in no wise worth recommending. If my sense of language does not deceive me, even for prescientific observation it has some value as a description if all that we assigned to the "lower stage" is taken together as manifestations of the imagination—or more precisely, as manifestations of the intellectual imagination on the one hand and the emotional imagination on the other. As can now be seen, I anticipated this terminological approach above, in proposing the terms "imaginative feelings" and "imaginative desires" for pseudo-feelings and pseudo-desires. Perhaps we can now see more clearly why this proposal immediately had the sense of language on its side. If one carries this terminological choice over to the domain of thoughts, then one gets the designation "imaginative [Phantasie-] judgment" for "assumption"; and as far as I can see, this too is an expression that says something quite definite and correctly representative of the facts of assumption even to one who hears it for the first time; so the expression can by no means be regarded as unserviceable.[83] Finally, turning back once more to representations [Vorstellungen], we know that the compound *"Phantasievorstellung"* has long since been formed for us. What I urged against the comprehensive use of this term on the relevant occasion[84] loses its importance, looked at from the new standpoint of the foregoing investigations. The relationship of the two words entering into this compound is by nature a different one than in the other three cases, to the extent that in the present case it is far more likely that the signification of the "basal component," as the grammarians sometimes say, is interpreted by the "modifying component" than that it is modified by the latter; we have already alluded to this point, a few moments earlier.[85]

Thus, as one can see, the investigations that primarily aimed to elucidate a domain of facts virtually ignored by previous research lead far out beyond this domain. If assumptions have proven themselves to be important experiences and ones worth investigating, it is not just by shedding new light on the problems old and new to which psychology and the theory of knowledge have already applied themselves; it is also by showing the way to domains of fact that have hitherto been virtually unknown. Indeed, it seems to me beyond doubt that in connection with assumptions and, above all, imaginative feelings and imaginative desires, the investigations that have led to initial results in the foregoing, temporary or not, must be carried further before we have scantily repaired even the grossest deficiencies in our knowledge of one side of the manifestations of the mental life, the half that consists in the activities of the imagination in the broadest sense. Naturally, there is no telling what sort of light this will in turn shed specifically upon the theory of assumptions; but as earlier, it remains exceedingly improbable that every one of the above theses concerning assumptions should still come out justified. If, nevertheless, these theses should have proven able to direct psychological research into new and promising paths, then one may be able to pardon the deficiencies in what I have been able to set down in these investigations, deficiencies that even the most conscientious work is unable to get rid of. The teacher takes pride in educating students from whom he himself can learn something; so too, it is no humiliation for the inquirer if he has cleared the paths well enough for those following that they would not have to go on too much more to be confronted, in clearly delineated forms, with what hovered before the inquirer himself in vague remoteness.

Author's Addenda to the Second Edition

The following is a translation of the note slips from Meinong's working copy of the second edition of *Über Annahmen*. They have been made available for use in the English edition by the editors of the *Meinong Gesamtausgabe*. Rudolf Haller's treatment of these slips in his 1977 edition of *Annahmen* (*Gesamtausgabe* IV:509-517) is reflected in the present placement of Meinong's remarks on the theory of objects at the beginning, without page assignment. Also, as regards the internal grouping and ordering of the note slips for a certain location, there was nothing much to weigh against the advantage of easy reference to the Graz edition, and Haller's numbers have been assigned to the entries. Again, some of the bracketed insertions are taken from Haller's treatment of the slips. Finally, the place of each of his brief text-critical and supplementary notes has been marked with an asterisk (*) in order to facilitate reference to these notes in the Graz edition of *Über Annahmen*.

1. In Justification of the Theory of Objects*
   1. There is a need for a science of the totality of objects. One might regard metaphysics as such a science. But in that case, metaphysics would at least have to treat existing and nonexisting things on the same footing; i.e. it would presumably have to leave existence as such out of consideration, which would certainly run counter to the intentions of metaphysics. One might therefore divide metaphysics into 2 parts, existential metaphysics [Daseinsmetaphysik] and metaphysics independent of existence [daseinsfrei Metaphysik]. But in that case, all that it amounts to in regard to the theory of objects is a redesignation; adjustment would have been made to the notion of the theory of objects.
   2. There is a need for a science that puts objects* in the characteristic perspective of an a priori approach, a science whose main emphasis is on this approach, as opposed to the empirical attainment of knowledge, and which accommodates itself to the needs of such a distinctive approach—not only occasionally and according to incidental needs, as the empirical sciences have always done.
   3. On the tradition. Scholastics (Thomas?) speak of an *"ens latissimum,"* *ens rationis* being comprehended in that. But it is asserted that there can be no science of it. This is surprising, since it is precisely scholasticism that separates *essentia* and *existentia* and prefers rational methods of investigation. But it doubtless does this only with the instinctive presupposition that what is really

[275]

worth knowing is to be found only in reality [Wirklichkeit]; it is at most as means to an end that other things are to be given attention. But then, this is precisely [the] situation in which the theory of objects is something new. — After that, one might be able to estimate how the theory of objects stands in regard to ontology. Here it is surely questionable as to whether the latter is supposed to be more of a theory of being [Sein], or a theory of entities [Seienden]. Each by itself would be too little from the standpoint of the theory of objects. Main thing, though: it has always been understood as a part of metaphysics. If the latter* cannot be divested of the notion of reality without unnaturalness, then this tendency attaches also to the part of it that is taken separately as ontology.

4. Of course, there is nothing in the way of objective fact that can be brought against the designation of a thing by other names. But then, it is a question of objective fact, not one of names—and incidentally, a question about the correctness of the idea, not the originality of it.

Vokelt (*Gewissheit und Wahrheit,* between pp. 35 and 58) emphasizes that he wants to base the theory of knowledge on an empirical starting approach, not on the eidetic one of the *Wesensschau,* as in Husserl. If this opposition is justified, then one would have to inquire as to whether the starting point of the theory of objects, whose nature I have already called quasi-empirical, tended more to the one or to the other approach.

2. *For page 11:*

C. D. Broad /*Mind,* n.s., no. 85 (1913): 92 divides "assumptions" into "entertainment" and "supposition" /cf. also note slip below, for p. 100/. How does this relate to Mally's two types of assumption /"Gegenstandstheoretische Grundlagen," p.*/?

3. *For page 16:*

C. D. Broad /*Mind,* n.s., no. 85 (1913), p. 91/ thinks that he can produce an example of nonnecessary differentness, and that the application to negation is therefore unallowable.

Worthwhile objection against gradation-incapability of differentness /Which does not hold in every sense/ ibid., 92.

4. *For page 25:*

Instead of signification, K. Bühler says "portraying function" /"Kritische Musterung der neueren Theorien des Sätzes," *Indogermanisches Jahrbuch* 6 (1918). Separate print./.At loc. cit., pp. 9 f., he speaks of the primacy of the portraying function/in agreement with *Assumptions* p. 25, middle/.

5. *For page 27:*

According to lines 18 f. from the top, the experiences which on each occasion present objects to thought would always be representations. That is incorrect, since thoughts fall in this class, too. The indispensable presenting experiences are simply the intellectual ones, and the remaining ones the emotional.

6. *For page 30:*
Modern grammarians on sentence signification cf. Maier, *Psychologie des emotionalen Denkens,* pp. 5 ff.
7. *For page 49:*
According to Schmidkunz /"Lehre von der Evidenz" pp. 6 f.*/ objective requires a "subjective" and "judicative," on account of the correlation. Identity with Bolzano's *Satz an sich,* noted by myself below p. 75.
8. *For pages 52 ff.:*
For timelessness of truth, Bolzano, according to Bergman /*Das philosophische Werk Bernard Bolzanos*/ p. 24, things suggestive of persistence [Persistenz].

Timelessness of truth said to presuppose things' being determined. Thus ultimately Pichler, "Die Unverträglichkeit des Indeterminismus mit 'der' Logik" in *Die Geisteswissenschaften* I, issue 34, 1914, pp. 924 ff.
9. *For page 55,* [below the second] paragraph-break:*
Unclear formulation. The essence of it is that one can construct an indefinitely long series of superordinate positive subsistences without a resulting factuality. Nevertheless, negative subsistences are then also superordinated to the starting objective. Hence, the "only" at least unclear.
10. *For page 57:*
Gallinger seems to make the attempt at reducing so-being to being /*Problem der objektiven Möglichkeit,* p. 40/: according to it, so-being [Sosein] would be the being [Sein] of properties. The inadequacy of this is evident from the fact that the very thing in question is a connection of the property with something which is thus and so [mit einem Soseienden]. This cannot be accomplished through being alone.
11. *For page 62:*
Polemical material against absistence [Aussersein], cf. Bergmann in *Zeitschrift für Philosophie und philosophische Kritik,* 143, pp. 113 f.
12. *For page 71:*
What we have at [the place above] the subparagraphic dashes* is actually not a drawing in of the next higher objective, but just the fact already taken into consideration above with the concept of the content of a judgment-about. The fact is that modal properties never come to the fore just with judgment-of; they always wait on judgment-about. And for that matter, there are nonmodal properties not covered in judgment-of. If I judge "*A* is *B,*" it is just *A* and *B* that show up as judged-about in this, not positivity. Perhaps, then, the whole distinction is just one of degree.
13. *For page 71:*
Truth connected with factuality by Montague in *The New Realism,* pp. 252 ff., except that "real" said instead of "factual." The priority of the objec-

tive-based concept of truth over the experience-based concept, which priority I reaffirmed below in note 93, is given corroboration by Montague's comment that it is the mathematician whom one consults as to the truth of a proposition concerning triangles, not the psychologist /*New Realism,* p. 257 top.

14. *For page 73:*

Assignment of evidence to the judgment is said not to agree with earlier relating of same to objective, Schmidkunz, "Grundzüge einer Lehre von der logischen Evidenz" p. 6 /*Zeitschrift für Philosophie,* vol. 146.

15. *For pages 74 ff.:*

Mally treats of the name "Objectiv," "Gegenstandstheoretische Grundlagen," pp. 53 f.

16. *For pages 83 f.:*

K. Groos for "conscious self-deception" and to that extent against assumptions in the case of play, cf. note slips for *Assumptions* p. 118.

17. *For pages 89 f.:*

A. Stadler, "Die Frage als Prinzip des Erkennens und die 'Einleitung' der *Kritik der reinen Vernunft*"—11 pp. *Kant-Studien* 13, no. 3.

18. *For page 90:*

To Prof. Karl Groos, Giessen. 5-22-1911.

It certainly has the value of making clear a distinction which I should be inclined to overlook, that you connect the sentence "It is not known who the perpetrator was" with questions, although it contains no question. I mean the distinction between the above sentence and a case like "The one who was the perpetrator /I grant you, a German man—the one who did it/ is unknown." In your sentence, the unknownness is not that of "the one" determined by a relative-clause objective, but that of another objective, one not made to depend on an objectum. Now, this latter objective is doubtless a question objective—but as far as I can see, it is still not suited for characterizing the question as such. After all, I could also say, "I know who the perpetrator was." Or do you intend something different by your conjecture that a sentence with "who" is related to the question as the objective is to the judgment? At any rate, the matter does not come up for discussion in the assumptions book. But what is adduced there as to the nature of questions is so extremely imperfect that an attempt to make some progress in this connection could only be received with pleasure.

19. *For pages 91 f.:*

That Groos has rectified the position contested here, cf. review of *Annahmen* in *Deutsche Literaturzeitung* 1911, col. 2520 /cf. separate print/.

20. *For page 100:*

C. D. Broad /*Mind,* n.s., no. 85 (1913), p. 92/ contests the argument against Russell. Only, however, by reason of the possibility of the contrary; whereas my argument concerns only the improbability of the contrary. — Still, the difference of "content" seems to be granted for "suppositions" as well as for judgment. Distinction between "supposition" and "entertainment."

21. *For pages 118 f.:*

For "conscious self-deception" /though here, too, there is a reference to representational material and not to belief, as when one speaks of sense deception/ cf. Groos, *Seelenleben des Kindes,* 2d ed., pp 192 ff., also review of *Annahmen* in *Deutsche Literaturzeitung,* col. 2519, 1911 /cf. separate print/. Perhaps better treated under "play," despite the term "unconscious self-deception."

22. *For page 118:*

From letter to K. Groos, Tübingen, 10-11-1911.

.... "By 'judgment' I mean simply 'belief', 'being convinced', quite irrespective of the two-part or one-part character of the material. Now surely you, too, would not say that when I am at the window and see people or vehicles out in the street that my belief has no part in this. True, I do not have to believe in the seeing, but I do have to believe in the people and vehicles. On the other hand, I do not believe as I think of Hamlet, Faust, or an imaginary landscape. Yet even then I am not in an attitude of purely passive representing; I do intend these objects. But then, this is the counterpart to belief that I designate as assuming.* With this, I can now endorse practically all that you argue under the heading of 'self-deception.' For [it]* concerns a procuring of representational material that may, after all, be quite deliberate. But then, for me it is a decisive question as to whether the person who has procured the material thereby ends in believing, quite as one does who sees the people and the vehicles under normal circumstances. If he does not, then it seems to me that he has no recourse but to assume, if he is thinking of anything at all. If one thereupon still speaks of deception or self-deception, despite the lack of belief, then what you argue still agrees in the best possible manner with my position on the role of assumptions. But it would seem to me to be difficult to say of someone that he is deceived or deceives himself, if his state of conviction is not at all engaged. As far as I can see, sense-deception affords no analogue for such a verbal usage; for someone is deceived by his senses simply in that by the inducement of the senses he believes something that is false."

23. *For page 122:*

Overacute objections against role of the objective in desire, cf. C. D. Broad, review in *Mind,* n.s., no. 85 (1913), pp. 95 f. Devoid of subject-matter relevance, though could be taken into consideration anyway.

24. *For pages 126 f.:*

Statement of the question in this chapter has to be carefully reviewed. It seems that in the course of the discussions it has not always been adhered to. Cf. e.g. p. 131, at indentation.

Formal inference properly so-called, as opposed to merely reading things out of the intuitively given, cf. Störring, "Experimentelle Untersuchungen über einfache Schlussprozesse," *Archiv für die gesamte Psychologie,* vol. 11.

25. *For pages 144 f.:*

On the relation of hypothetical judgment and inference, cf. C. D. Broad's objections, *Mind,* n.s., no. 85 (1913), pp. 97 f.

The hypothetical judgment also has a negative form, "Although *p,* yet not *q,*" ibid., p. 98.

Against restriction and existential predication, ibid., 98 f.

26. *For pages 170 ff.:*

Objections of C. D. Broad /*Mind, n.s.,* no. 85 (1913), p. 100/ against intending: one objection seems to depend on a falling back into the "being-view" I abandoned, the second on neglect of the meaning of presentation [Präsentation].

27. *For page 188:*

Relation between relation and terms rejected on principle by Driesch /with literature/ on account of infinite series, *Ordnungslehre,* p. 51 top.

28. *For pages 189 ff.:*

Adequation as "ideal similarity," Marty, *Untersuchung zur Grundlegung der allgemeinen Grammatik und Sprachphilosophie* I, 406 ff., esp. 414.

Relevant material in *Über Möglichkeit und Wahrscheinlichkeit,* pp. 253 f.

29. *For pages 191 f.:*

C. D. Broad /*Mind* 1913, n.s., no. 85 (1913), p. 101, the ideal significance of really [real] complex contents as being out of the question.

30. *For page 194:*

Drobisch already used the terms "determinand" and "determinator" in *Neue Darstellung der Logik,* 1st ed., sec. 17*n* /i.e. in smaller print/ p. 13.

Term "Seinsmeinung" used /in passing, it seems/ by Husserl, *Logische Untersuchungen* II, p. 447, but specifically for judging or "positing."

C. D. Broad /*Mind* 1913, n.s., no. 85 (1913), pp. 101 f./ makes a sort of objection, though it consists merely in showing that intending by way of so-being is based on intending by way of being—which I daresay is already touched on in the following discussions.

31. *For page 205:*

Marty deals with naming and representation in their "strict and loose" senses, *Untersuchungen zur Grundlegung der allgemeinen Grammatik und Sprachphilosophie* I, secs. 109-112, pp. 455 ff.

For page 205, note 37: Bühler on direct and indirect intending, cf. *Zeitschrift für Philosophie,* vol. 51, p. 113.

32. *For page 221:*

Empathy as splitting of personality consciousness, R. Müller-Freienfels,

"Grundzüge einer neuen Wertlehre," *Annalen der Philosophie* 1 (1919): 335. Should not "splittings" conversely be mere cases of assuming? Cf. ibid., p. 346.

33. *For page 221:*

Literature on unrepresentability and unreproducibility of feelings /Wreschner/ cf. E. Landmann-Kalischer, "Philosophie der Werte," *Archiv für die gesamte Psychologie* 28: 46n.

What is in the text is also a possibility, and specifically for the following section.

M. Geiger "Über das Wesen und die Bedeutung der Einfühlung," *Bericht über den IV. Kongress für experimentelle Psychologie in Innsbruck* 1910 /to be sure p. 6 (note) reveals lack of acquaintance with the view of imagination already set forth in the first edition of *Assumptions/*.

Literature and discussion of relevant questions, cf. Urban, *Valuation,* 234 ff.

Literature on "empathy" ["Einfühlung"], cf. *Zeitschrift für Psychologie* 58 (1911): 309 ff.

Wilhelm Peters, "Gefühl und Erinnerung. Beiträge zur Erinnerungsanalyse," Kraepelin, *Psychologische Arbeiten* VI, 197 ff., 1911, — deals primarily with the influence of feeling on memory, but perhaps can also be consulted on reproduction of feelings and the like.

B. Erdmann, "Erkennen und Verstehen" /*Berliner Sitzungsberichte, philosophisch-historische Klasse Gesamtsitzung Dezember 1912**/ pp. 1257 ff., possibly also in earlier passages. /Separate print has come out./ "To understand" here seems to mean the apprehending of mental facts in others.

Not entirely worthless starts on new investigations concerning emotional /and also intellectual/ imagination, cf. course in general theory of value [allg. Werttheorie] II, quarto-sheet 15, pp. 2 ff.,* under the title "Wertungen."

Dilthey seems to lay stress upon *Nacherleben* /probably in opposition to mere representing/. References in Liebert, *Problem der Geltung,* pp. 86 f.

34. *For page 221:*

Feeling representations that have the tendency to become real feelings, "feeling hallucinations," as it were, Groethuysen, "Das Mitgefühl," *Zeitschrift für Psychologie* 34: 175 — Naturally, unintentional proof that a "feeling representation" can hardly be a representation. But against the principle of the realization of what is represented, there is what is recognized by me in "Zur Lehre von den Dispositionen," Martinak-*Festschrift,* p.*

Argument for representation of feelings: one can experience pleasure and displeasure at the same time, Groethuysen, loc. cit., p. 199, n. 5.

Representations of feelings (with literature, Groethuysen, loc. cit., pp. 201 ff., 206). Representation of a feeling = weaker feeling, ibid. 204 f.

Scheinaffekte as against *Ernstaffekte,* with reference to Witasek, cf. A. Boltunow, "Über den Strukturzusammenhang zwischen den ästhetischen

Wertgefühlen und seinen intellektuellen Voraussetzungen," *Berliner Diss.*, 1909, p. 25.

35. *For page 261:*

Satz defined as ultimate unity of sense, self-sufficient among the unities accomplished in discourse, Bühler, *Indogermanisches Jahrbuch* 6 (1919). Separate print, p. 18.

36. *For pages 266 ff.:*

On Aristotelian species and genus, cf. Husserl, *Logische Untersuchungen* II, p. 405.

Author's Notes

Preface to the First Edition

1. The page bore this inscription: "Dedicated in friendship to Miss Mila Radaković."
2. Now chaps. 3 and 5.
3. Now chap. 9.
4. Although the most important positions taken in the *System* saw publication in the *Vierteljahrsschrift für wissenschaftliche Philosophie*, a year before my *Untersuchungen zur Werttheorie*. On this, see Ehrenfels in the 1894 volume of that review, p. 96; also my foreword to the *Untersuchungen*.
5. Now secs. 48-52.

Preface to the Second Edition

1. "Meinongs Lehre von den Annahmen und ihre Bedeutung für die Schullogik," *Jahresbericht des Erzherzog Rainer-Gymnasiums in Wien*, 1903.
2. "Meinong's Theory of Complexes and Assumptions," *Mind*, n.s., 13 (1904).
3. *Über Annahmen. Eine Streitschrift gegen A. v. Meinongs gleichnamige Arbeit, nebst Beiträgen zur Bedeutungslehre und Gegenstandstheorie*, Ulm, 1910.
4. Cf. above, p. 3.
5. Cf. also the observations (certainly not arising out of any lack of sympathy for those people) in the *Deutsche Literaturzeitung*, 1909, col. 2645.
6. "As to the distinction between 'general' and 'schematic', between 'belief' and 'assumption'—that is one of the radical positions of my entire work, and I am glad to have it called attention to. It connects with and carries further the 'assumption'-theory of Meinong and the Austrian school." (*Thoughts and Things. A Study of the Development and Meaning of Thought*, London 1906-1908, vol. 2, p. 423.)
7. W. M. Urban, *Valuation, Its Nature and Laws, Being an Introduction to the General Theory of Value*, London, 1909.

I

1. Even now it is scarcely too early to point out that here and in the following, "judgment" is understood broadly enough to comprehend not only (subjective) certainty but also every degree of stronger or weaker surmise; and the same applies to "belief" and "conviction" ["Überzeugung"]. This has been felt to be especially forced in the case of the expression "conviction" or "the element of conviction" ["Überzeugtheit"]; cf.

Alois Höfler in the *Gottingischer Gelehrten-Anzeigen,* 1906, p. 210 n. However this may be, there are still degrees of conviction [Überzeugtheit] from the standpoint of linguistic usage. This seems to me to guarantee the applicability of the term beyond the case of certainty (in the strict sense, as the upper limit of surmise), even though I cannot deny that in daily life weak surmises would not be allowed to pass as convictions. I thought, therefore, that in this regard I could uphold the terminology of the first edition.

2. Cf. D. H. Kerler, *Über Annahmen. Eine Streitschrift gegen A. v. Meinongs gleichnamige Arbeit* (Ulm, 1910), p. 3.

3. This is, as far as I can see, one of the sources of the objections expounded by Kerler, ibid.; cf. pp. 33 f., perhaps also pp. 12, 14 ff., 30. Another source, which likewise is not independent of the term in question, will be taken up presently in the following, p. 12.

4. It will emerge later that this reference to an intermediate position, which is primarily intended to serve for preliminary guidance, admits of a more precise elaboration; cf. especially chap. 10, secs. 63 f., where there will also be occasion to take account of some basic objections.

5. Below, chap. 8, where admittedly it will turn out that even the examples of intuitive representations that we have chosen may not be free of inexactitude. Nevertheless, the serviceableness of these examples, especially for a beginning, should not be impaired by this.

6. Gottlob Frege has already turned the notion as well as the name to theoretical account and is doubtless the first to do so; this has been called to my attention by Bertrand Russell ("Meinong's Theory of Complexes and Assumptions," *Mind,* n.s., 13: 341, n. 1, also p. 206, n. 1). If there should someday be a history of the theory of assumptions, for which there is much to be said even now, then a sentence from Frege's paper on function and concept (*Funktion und Begriff,* Jena, 1891) will probably deserve to stand at the head of it. Let us reproduce the sentence word for word here: "This separation of the judging from that concerning which one judges appears indispensable; for otherwise we could not express a mere assumption—the putting of a case without any simultaneous judgment as to its arisal" (*Funktion,* pp. 21 f.).

7. This seems to me to be the deficiency, to some extent a terminological one, of D. H. Kerler's criticism; I have already touched on it above (cf. p. 10, n. 3). By way of "completion" of my above definition (D. H. Kerler, *Über Annahmen,* p. 4), he makes the following definition (*Über Annahmen,* p. 30): "To assume means to posit something as being, against one's better knowledge and against the facts of the case, or in ignorance of the latter"; without "disregard of the facts of the case" or without "falsification of same . . . one cannot speak of an assumption." The concept of the "assumption" that the following discussions are intended to legitimate is surely broader. How is the fact that Kerler makes a narrower definition supposed to provide the basis for an objection to these discussions?

8. Of course, I leave entirely out of account here the nonderivative, basic connotation of the word, according to which one "accepts" ["annimt"] gifts, favors, and the like.

9. It may be harder than one thinks to actually render this other sense of the word inoperative. If I am not mistaken, the opposition of D. H. Kerler is not entirely unconnected with the fact that he has not always managed to do this. (Cf. his *Über Annahmen,* pp. 13 f., 15 f., 17, 25, 27.)

10. In view of this, many a reader may find it better suits his needs to pass over the remainder of the present section (with the possible exception of the concluding remarks).

11. Below, chap. 8.

12. The differences that enter into the picture on this score, ones which Sigwart has justly emphasized (*Logik*, 2d ed., vol. 1, pp. 161 ff.), can be left out of account here.

13. The sense in which the theory of objects is concerned with it; cf. the *Untersuchungen zur Gegenstandstheorie und Psychologie*, edited by me (Leipzig, 1904), pp. 1 ff.—as well as chap. 3, sec. 8, below.

14. The concept and term "production of representations" is fixed for the first time in the first edition of this work, pp. 8 f.. Further information on the matter is found in Rudolf Ameseder's "Über Vorstellungsproduktion" in the Graz *Untersuchungen zur Gegenstandstheorie und Psychologie*, pp. 481 ff. More readily accessible information can now be found in Stephan Witasek's *Grundlinien der Psychologie* (Leipzig, 1908), pp. 99 f.

15. "Über Gegenstände höherer Ordnung und deren Verhältnis zur inneren Wahrnehmung," *Zeitschrift für Psychologie und Physiologie der Sinnesorgane* 21:189 ff.

16. Should someone call this into question, in view of the degrees of possibility (cf. below, chap. 3, sec. 13)—though this is hardly to be expected at this point—then it will probably suffice here to give attention to the fact that degrees of possibility, i.e., such cases of gradation, have nothing in the slightest to do with gradations of differentness. That black is more different from white than from grey surely does not mean that black's being white is more possible or, say, more probable than its not being grey.

17. The positivity of the notion of differentness, to which Bertrand Russell alludes ("Meinong's Theory of Complexes and Assumptions," pt. 2, *Mind*, n.s., 13:338), holds for this relation, but only for this one.

18. Cf. also Husserl, *Philosophie der Arithmetik* (Halle am Seder, 1891), vol. 1, pp. 57 f., where admittedly many a point might be quite assailable by itself.

19. Probably no express stand need be taken against such an unnatural interpretation as, say, "Everything that exists is different from the perpetual motion machine." Still, I had occasion to oppose a related notion in another place (*Über die Stellung der Gegenstandstheorie im System der Wissenschaften* (Leipzig, 1907), pp. 38 f.).

20. Cf. "Über Gegenstände höherer Ordnung," *Zeitschrift für Psychologie und Physiologie der Sinnesorgane* 21:200 f.

21. It need not be added that the simile underlying the term "founding" also could have been employed for the linguistic fixing of other concepts. However, no service to the aim of utter clarity and agreement in terminology was rendered by Edmund Husserl's subsequent attempt (*Logische Untersuchungen*, vol. 2, pp. 254 ff.) to give another meaning to the word that I put to scientific use, a meaning about which he does not convey what advantage it has over the one I proposed. For that matter, see also Rudolf Ameseder in the Graz *Untersuchungen zur Gegenstandstheorie und Psychologie*, p. 72, n. 2.

22. "Über Gegenstände höherer Ordnung," p. 202. As to Bertrand Russell's basic objections ("Meinong's Theory of Complexes and Assumptions," pt. 1, *Mind*, n.s., 13:208 f.), I have replied to them in *Über die Stellung der Gegenstandstheorie im System der Wissenschaften*, pp. 55 f., Cf. also below, chap. 3, sec. 13.

23. This disposes, I believe, of the arguments of D. H. Kerler on pp. 4 ff. of his pamphlet *Über Annahmen*, although on the face of it (cf. also ibid., pp. 18 f.) it must

be admitted that the account given in the first edition of the present work cannot really be sustained in all points. As to "object and content", pages 5 ff. seem to me to do justice neither to my view nor to the matter under consideration (cf. especially secs. 13 and 45 below). Moreover, Kerler himself remarks (pp. 9 f.), "the object of a representation would be . . . in Meinong's terminology what I call the 'in-itself' [das 'Ansich'backslash," except that he then reexpresses this as the "object" being "usually confused with the in-itself" by me (p. 11)—which would invite remarks like those above, p. 10, n. 3 and p. 12. Anyway, Kerler's "in-itself" is not my "object" at all, as his remarks on pp. 21 ff. show. Yet crudities in my first account are involved there, too, and an attempt to remove them will be made in chap. 7.

24. Cf. below, chap. 3.

25. "Über Gegenstände höherer Ordnung," pp. 186 f.

26. Of the third chapter.

27. Thus Bertrand Russell, "Meinong's Theory of Complexes and Assumptions," pt. 2, p. 338; and recently most likely Anton Marty, *Untersuchung zur Grundlegung der allgemeinen Grammatik und Sprachphilosophie* (Halle, 1908), p. 481.

28. Below, sec. 13.

29. Cf. below, chap. 8, sec. 45.

II

1. Leipzig, 1901.

2. Ibid., pp. 1 ff.

3. Cf. ibid., p. 12.

4. Probably in agreement with R. Gaetschenberger, *Grundzüge einer Psychologie des Zeichens, Würzburger Inaugural-Dissertation* (Regensburg, 1901), pp. 45 ff., as well as Edmund Husserl, *Logische Untersuchungen,* vol. 2 (Halle, 1901), pp. 25 ff.

5. Edmund Husserl, ibid., in addition emphasizes the lack of insight in this inference —and doubtless justifiably, as far as the insight that is meant is specifically a priori insight. A posteriori insight (surmise-evidence) would seem to me to be no obstacle, however.

6. It would be still more exact to include the case of the non-being of *B,* for which of course there can also be signs. Let me point out, by way of anticipation, that what becomes obvious in this is just the fact that the relation between ground and consequent is, strictly speaking, not something that concerns the objectum, but something that specifically concerns the objective. This latter contrast will be made clear in chap. 3.

7. On the contrast between real and final signifying, cf. Martinak, *Psychologische Untersuchungen zur Bedeutungslehre,* p. 12.

8. On this contrast, cf. also Martinak, *Psychologische Untersuchungen zur Bedeutungslehre,* pp. 19 ff.

9. What one may infer from *A* is really just the pseudo-existence of *C*—"pseudo-existence" being understood with the same meaning that I have used previously and which I assigned to the word in the essay "Über Gegenstände höherer Ordnung und deren Verhältnis zur inneren Wahrnehmung" (*Zeitschrift für Psychologie* 21:186 f.).

10. "Über Gegenstände höherer Ordnung," pp. 185 ff.; also below, secs. 13 f.

11. "Über Gegenstände höherer Ordnung," pp. 188 f.

12. Against Husserl, *Logische Untersuchungen,* vol. 2, pp. 46 ff. The difference of opinion probably originates in the fact that Husserl takes the concept of an object more

narrowly than would seem natural to me. Concerning this matter, cf. for the present, "Über Gegenstände höherer Ordnung," p. 188, n. The remarks in the text would appear to tally with Marty's (*Untersuchung zur Grundlegung,* pp. 285 ff., cf. p. 491, n.), except that—and this we shall have to come back to (cf. below, sec. 14)—the latter says "content" instead of "object." Moreover, he speaks of "signification" in a further, "broader" sense (cf., e.g., *Untersuchung zur Grundlegung,* pp. 291, 384). If this sense is needed, it would seem more appropriate to me to choose another word for it. The author never tires of pointing out (cf. pp. 284, n. 2; 286; 291; 490, *et passim*) that this (and some other things) is a "theory expounded" in his articles in the *Vierteljahrsschrift für wissenschaftliche Philosophie,* especially of the year 1884.

13. Further details on this will come under review immediately below (p. 26).

14. *Über die Erfahrungsgrundlagen unseres Wissens* (Berlin, 1906) pp. 72 ff.

15. I shall return to this below, in sec. 20.

16. As I have done in the first edition of this work, pp. 21 ff., on the basis of thoughts that the foregoing considerations attempt to simplify and set right.

17. For example, what one calls the object of feelings is really the object of the representations that form the basis of the feelings. It remains to be seen whether, in addition, there is still something proper to feelings, in the last instance, something that is traceable just to their nature as feelings and which, in an especially broad verbal usage, might still be called an object.

18. More exactly, on the side of what is either itself mental or at least connected by means of something mental with the physical component of linguistic events.

19. Leaving out of account such words as "yes" and "no" and ones like them, words which certainly have the ability to serve as expressions for judgments, but which in return leave it indefinite as to what the judgment is about.

20. Also cf., e.g., Sigwart, *Logik,* vol. 1, 2d ed., beginning of p. 25.

21. Whether the assertion itself is unobjectionable or not. I have taken the standpoint that it is not in *Über die Erfahrungsgrundlagen unseres Wissens,* pp. 72 ff.

22. It originates in the fact that belief is in no wise lacking here, either, but merely has a negative sign, as it were—just as one who says, "I don't want to," usually means to register anything but a lack of volitional experience. Cf. also below, sec. 21.

23. Cf. also my "Hume-Studien II," *Sitzungsberichte der kaiserlichen Akademie der Wissenschaften, philosophisch-historische Klasse,* vol. 101 (1882), pp. 108 ff.

24. Cf. sec. 3.

25. Cf. above, sec. 4.

III

1. Initially in the first article in the Graz *Untersuchungen zur Gegenstandstheorie und Psychologie* (cf. also the discussions by Rudolf Ameseder and Ernst Mally, published as the second and third article in the same collection) and then in *Über die Stellung der Gegenstandstheorie im System der Wissenschaften,* Leipzig, 1907.

2. In what follows, it will develop right away that these very objects actually have the best-founded claim to be called objects of judgment.

3. For some remarks in justification of the term "objective," cf. below, sec. 14.

4. In the Graz *Untersuchungen zur Gegenstandstheorie und Psychologie,* p. 54 and elsewhere.

5. Though admittedly not just these objects; for example, feelings are objecta, even

though it is not through representation but through self-presentation (cf. above, pp. 27 f.) or imagination that they become accessible to our intellect.

6. Over a period of years, experience has convinced me that this convention does not, practically speaking, lead to any incongruities.

7. An expression which, as it is, seems to be winning an ever greater domain of application in modern logic, albeit mainly in a somewhat more special signification. Cf., e.g., Benno Erdmann, *Logik,* vol. 1, 2d ed., pp. 475 *et passim.*

8. Our account in the first edition gave rise to justified objections in this connection; cf. especially Bertrand Russell, "Meinong's Theory of Complexes and Assumptions," pt. 2, *Mind,* n.s., 13:345.

9. Against Anton Marty, *Untersuchungen zur Grundlegung der allgemeinen Grammatik und Sprachphilosophie,* p. 481, and naturally also against a passage in the first edition of this book, the passage utilized against me by Marty.

10. Cf. chap. 7, sec. 38, middle.

11. Cf. p. 27.

12. Cf. above, chap, 2, sec. 6.

13. This is a thesis that Anton Marty (*Untersuchungen zur Grundlegung,* p. 483) is pleased to see as an "admission" made to him in my article, "In Sachen der Annahmen," on the occasion of a polemic to which I shall return below (sec. 20). He must have failed to notice that the relevant part of this formulation was dwelt on at great length from sec. 36 of the first edition of this work onwards. What I really "admitted" in the place cited was that the objective was given insufficient consideration in my first-edition investigation of the hypothetical judgment. I shall try to make good the omission below, in sec. 31.

14. Above, p. 38.

15. Cf. above, sec. 2.

16. Whatever is still missing will appear in due course in chap. 8, below.

17. Some further details will come up for discussion in sec. 20 of the fifth chapter, below.

18. Instead of "immediate" and "mediate," the terms "pre-given" and "post-given" were employed in the first edition of this work, pp. 164 ff. I hope that in the foregoing I have attached less cumbersome expressions to more correctly precised concepts.

19. It must be admitted that in this case one can say (rather stiffly, of course, but quite in line with the mode of expression I employed in sec. 8), "I judge the weight I first lifted as being heavier." Even by itself, the expression "being heavier" signifies an objective, as will appear presently in the following. And as to how often the "that"-clause concerns not something judged, but something judged about, sec. 21 below will attempt to offer a further look into that matter. In the present place, however, it might be advisable to leave this somewhat complicated matter out of consideration.

20. "Agreement or disagreement," says Bernard Bolzano (*Wissenschaftslehre,* vol. I, p. 96), "in and by itself can be called neither true nor false; rather, what can be called true or false is only the assertion that such an agreement or its opposite . . . exists." In my view, only the two words "the assertion" would have to be dropped.

21. Cf. "Über Gegenstände höherer Ordnung," *Zeitschrift für Psychologie* 21: 200 ff.

22. "Untersuchungen zur Gegenstandstheorie des Messens," in the Graz *Untersuchungen zur Gegenstandstheorie und Psychologie,* pp. 131 ff.

23. Cf. below, chap. 8, secs. 42 ff.

24. Cf. above, chap. 2, sec. 4, p. 27.

25. Cf. "Über Gegenstände höherer Ordnung," pp. 186 f.

26. Concerning the term "apsychological," cf. my paper "Über Urteilsgefühle, was sie sind und was sie nicht sind," *Archiv für die Gesamte Psychologie* 6(1905):34.

27. For more precise guidance, reference should be made to Rudolf Ameseder's "Beiträge zur Grundlegung der Gegenstandstheorie und Psychologie," (second article in the Graz *Untersuchungen zur Gegenstandstheorie und Psychologie*) and further to Ernst Mally's "Untersuchungen zur Gegenstandstheorie des Messens" (third article in the same collection). See also the relevant chapters of the writings of mine just cited: "Über Urteilsgefühle," pp. 30 ff.; *Über die Erfahrungsgrundlagen unseres Wissens,* pp. 18 ff.; and *Über die Stellung der Gegenstandstheorie,* etc., pp. 20 ff. Wilhelm Maria Frankl's "Gegenstandstheoretische Beiträge zur Lehre vom sogennanten logischen Quadrat," *Archiv für systematische Philosophie* 13(1907):346 ff., deals with more special matters, as do the two addresses of Ernst Mally, "Grundgesetze der Determination," *Verhandlungen des III. internationalen Kongresses für Philosophie,* Heidelberg, 1908, pp. 862 ff., and "Gegenstandstheorie und Mathematik," idem, pp. 881 ff.

28. Cf. my remarks, "Über Gegenstandstheorie," first article in the Graz *Untersuchungen zur Gegenstandstheorie und Psychologie,* pp. 3 ff.

29. Anton Marty's, in the *Untersuchungen zur Grundlegung,* p. 314. (Cf. also p. 293 *et passim.*)

30. Cf. my remarks, *Über die Erfahrungsgrundlagen unseres Wissens,* pp. 85 ff.

31. I don't think that it is part of the intention of the last-mentioned author to resolve being into possibility; but as far as I can see, there is no way to avoid this consequence. Add to this that, in my experience, it is only in the rarest cases that someone thinking of being is also thinking of judging. In what follows, it will develop in due course that the whole formulation is barred from any application to non-factual objectives by its limitation to correct judgment.

32. But again, as we shall see, not only by means of judgments; cf. below, chap. 5, sec. 20.

33. Cf. "Über Gegenstände höherer Ordnung," *Zeitschrift für Psychologie* 21: 189 ff.

34. *Über die Stellung der Gegenstandstheorie,* p. 29 et al.

35. Cf. "Über Gegenstände höherer Ordnung," p. 186.

36. It has emerged above (cf. sec. 10) that in reality, objectives are involved in cases of this sort, too. Here, however, it is not so much a matter of "being the same" and "being different" as of a certain "different" and "same," things that still clearly have the character of objecta—although on account of their ideal nature, they cannot exist and can only subsist.

37. Admittedly, there is no lack of necessity in this case, either, so far as every existent has its cause. But this necessity only beongs to the existent in light of the latter's cause; it does not belong to the existent all by itself.

38. By Anton Marty, *Untersuchungen zur Grundlegung,* p. 329.

39. Cf. below, sec. 12.

40. Marty, *Untersuchungen zur Grundlegung,* p. 329.

41. Which can be understood from the fact that objectives that have objectives rather than objecta as *inferiora* in truth always constitute exceptions.

42. Cf. below, sec. 13.

43. Marty, *Untersuchungen zur Grundlegung,* p. 328.

44. Ibid., p. 328.

45. Cf. below, pp. 59 f.

46. Cf. Rudolf Ameseder, second article in the Graz *Untersuchungen,* pp. 66 f.

47. The inexactness that remains in this "over itself" will be harmless in the present connection.

48. Cf. sec. 13.

49. My own choice of this term may be due to Christian Sigwart. But cf. even Schopenhauer, *Über die vierfache Wurzel des Satzes vom zureichendem Grunde,* sec. 15.

50. The German "verneinend" goes in analogy with "bejahend" and "affirmativ," so that we do not seem to have any German adjective characterizing the objective as negative.

51. "Über Gegenstände höherer Ordnung," p. 186.

52. Anton Marty's, in his *Untersuchungen zur Grundlegung,* pp. 323 ff.

53. Although the polemic fills more than four printed pages.

54. Ibid., p. 326.

55. In odd rhetoric, which has unfortunately gained a following (cf. below, p. 69, n. 85), Marty challenges me, "If, therefore, the distinction between 'subsistence of something' and 'existence of something' is situated in that" (in the mental attitude) "and not in the object, then let Meinong state it. What sort of distinction is it, between the mode of mental attitude that is present in the former case and the mode that is present in the latter?" (Ibid., p. 327.) It is unnecessary to comply with this invitation or challenge before Marty has legitimated the distinction between yellow and blue by pointing out the distinction in the "mode of mental attitude" that one has in representing these colors.

56. Cf. sec. 13.

57. Cf. "Über Gegenstände höherer Ordnung," pp. 198 ff.

58. Cf. pp. 52 ff.

59. In the sense specified above, p. 46.

60. From a time prior to the relevant discussions in "Über Gegenstände höherer Ordnung," etc., pp. 260 f.

61. Cf. above, pp. 52 ff.

62. In the essay "Über Gegenstandstheorie" in the Graz *Untersuchungen zur Gegenstandstheorie und Psychologie,* pp. 7 ff. For the history of the principle, cf. p. 5 of Hans Pichler's *Über Christian Wolffs Ontologie,* Leipzig, 1910. These investigations of Pichler's are also quite worthy of notice in other respects, and they may be welcomed as the first solid as well as clear-sighted monograph on the history of the theory of objects.

63. By Anton Marty who, on p. 340 of his *Untersuchungen zur Grundlegung,* kindly summarizes: "... all of what Meinong most recently proposes on behalf of it dissolves into nothing on closer inspection, and involuntarily it just serves to discredit the thesis completely." (Cf. also the polemic in connection with Descartes in Alfred Kastil's *Studien zur neueren Erkenntnistheorie,* vol. 1 (Halle, 1909), pp. 63 ff. Another occasion

must be reserved for a closer evaluation of this "closer inspection," which fills an imposing number of pages.

64. Nothing in this would be changed, even if one found the following interpretation natural: by a perpetual motion machine is meant something which, in the event that it existed, would have the properties customarily ascribed to a perpetual motion machine. For then this "something" would of course still have at least the property that found its characterization in the roundabout way via the hypothetical judgment.

65. Which of course can also temporally coincide in actual practice. We shall return to matters bearing on this in chaps. 7 f.

66. "Über Gegenstandstheorie," pp. 9 ff.

67. The acute remarks of Bertrand Russell in part 3 of his article, "Meinong's Theory of Complexes and Assumptions," probably also tend in this direction. (*Mind*, n.s., vol. 13, cf. especially pp. 521 ff.).

68. Cf. *Über die Stellung der Gegenstandstheorie,* etc., pp. 125 f.—also below, sec. 14.

69. Cf. p. 55.

70. Cf. Anton Marty, *Untersuchungen zur Grundlegung,* pp. 295 ff.

71. Cf. above, p. 50.

72. Cf. pp. 55 f.

73. On the authority of Grimm's dictionary, Spengler cites an interesting memorandum of Lessing's concerning the origin of this word; Spengler's article ("Zwei Termini der Grammatik, insbesondere der lateinischen, und ihre Verwendung," *Zeitschrift für österreichische Gymnasien,* 1896, p. 1058) stands in manifold relations to the main theme of our present book. Even at present, the word has had little theoretical use, and it is therefore particularly suited to take on the sense in which it will be used in what follows.

74. Concerning the indispensability of evidence, cf. *Über die Erfahrungsgrundlagen unseres Wissens,* pp. 31 ff. In connection with Leonard Nelson's noteworthy polemic, "Das sogennante Erkenntnisproblem" (in the *Untersuchungen der Friesschen Schule,* vol. 2, pp. 479 ff.), cf. for the present Alois Höfler's "Erkenntnisprobleme und Erkenntnistheorie" in the *Zeitschrift für Philosophie und philosophische Kritik* 137 (1910):1 ff.

75. Or ahead; cf. below, chaps. 7 f., especially secs. 38, 43, 45.

76. Cf. "*Über Gegenstände höherer Ordnung,*" etc., loc. cit., pp. 185 ff. If it is just a question of whether I did or did not ever regard the object as being a part of the representational experience or even (*qua* object) as being merely mental, the belief that I did is a misconception (e.g., Bertrand Russell's, cf. "Meinong's Theory of Complexes and Assumptions," *Mind,* n.s., 13:214 f., 218); nevertheless, this misconception is one which may have been incurred by me. It was possibly occasioned by the fact that I did not discontinue the use of the old term "immanent object" ["immanentes Objekt"]. Still, I have never conceived of this object [Objekt] otherwise than as "pseudo-existent." On this point I have become clear enough in the intervening time that even Anton Marty cannot have been directing his campaign against the "immanent object" with me in mind. (Cf. *Untersuchungen zur Grundlegung,* p. 761.) Only A. Kastil would prefer to believe otherwise of me (*Studien zur neueren Erkenntnistheorie* (Halle, 1909), pp. 208 f.) and to find that from my discussions it "does not follow . . . that" I have "appre-

hended the heart of the difficulties that have beset the fiction of an objective or intentional being which is different from that which is real."

77. Here we can disregard the fact that the rule has important exceptions; cf. below, however, secs. 38 and 45.

78. Cf. my article, "Über Urteilsgefühle, was sie sind und was sie nicht sind," in vol. 6 of the *Archiv für die gesamte Psychologie,* pp. 39 f.

79. For a reservation, cf. below, chap. 10, sec. 59.

80. *Über die Erfahrungsgrundlagen unseres Wissens,* p. 57.

81. It hardly need be mentioned that such a "thing" ["Sache"] is an objective, strictly speaking, and that it is by no means a thing in the precise sense.

82. On this matter, cf. below, chap. 6, sec. 26.

83. I shall have to reserve a detailed exposition of this for a following publication.

84. Cf. especially Johannes von Kries, *Die Prinzipien der Wahrscheinlichkeitsrechnung* (Freiburg, 1886). Kries's distinguished development of the conception of "objective possibility" here (and in his relevant articles in vol. 12 of the *Vierteljahrsschrift für wissenschaftliche Philosophie*) may have provided strong stimuli for the presently advocated interpretation of possibility as a property of the objective.

85. Concerning surmise-evidence, cf. for the meantime the discussions *Über die Erfahrungsgrundlagen unseres Wissens,* pp. 69 f. As for the not quite meaningful question that Alfred Kastil directs at me (*Studien zur neueren Erkenntnistheorie,* vol. 1 (Halle, 1909), p. 134, n. 2) in this matter (probably after the example of Marty, cf. above, p. 73), I shall "make up my mind" to answer it when it is put in a form which is less . . . unusual.

86. Cf. pp. 70 f.

87. Naturally, one must not think of the "understanding" of signs or words, in this connection.

88. Cf. *Über die Stellung der Gegenstandstheorie,* pp. 31 f.

89. Cf. Überweg, *Logik,* 4th ed., pp. 181 ff.; also the same author's translation of Berkeley's *Treatise on the Principles of Human Knowledge* (*Abhandlung über die Prinzipien der menschlichen Erkenntnis,* Berlin, 1869), p. 120.

90. Cf. *Über die Stellung der Gegenstandstheorie,* pp. 51 ff., where I also go into Bertrand Russell's rejection in principle of the notion of necessity. My employment of the concept of ground in those pages reveals the above presentation to be a superfluous complication. Still, this is a relatively inessential matter of interpretation compared with the attempt to analyze all necessity out of the world (first and foremost out of the world of the theory of objects, of course). Perhaps it serves some practical purposes of logistics to look for equivalents for necessity; even so, it remains a fundamental fact of the first order, and as far as I can see, one of the most immediately knowable facts, that there are necessary objectives. To secure this definitively against doubt, if possible, will not be the slightest occasion for the future theory of objects to practice what I have called respect for the facts. (*Über die Stellung der Gegenstandstheorie,* pp. 140 ff.)

91. Urged by Anton Marty against me, in *Untersuchung zur Grundlegung,* p. 313, n. But I have been unable to get clear as to why this author also maintains the objectivity of necessity against me (ibid., pp. 295 ff.), when in the first edition of this book (pp. 174, 193 f.), I already numbered necessity among the properties of objectives.

92. As I still did in the writing, *Über die Stellung der Gegenstandstheorie,* p. 53.

93. There seems to be an uncertainty in linguistic usage as to whether the judgment or

what is judged is better designated as the thing for criticism, and linguistic usage vacillates similarly with respect to the word "truth." In line with the thesis on p. 63, above, which has been carried over from the first edition, I hold to the statement that it is more natural to assert "true" of the objective than it is to assert it of the judgment. This, too, I maintain in the face of Marty's opposition, but the difference of opinion in this case is immaterial to what is to be set forth here.

94. A simile of Bertrand Russell's, "Meinong's Theory of Complexes and Assumptions," pt. 3, p. 523.

95. As maintained above, p. 81.

96. Also by Bertrand Russell, it would seem ("Meinong's Theory of Complexes and Assumptions"), though he might of course say in reply that it is easy to solve problems concerning truth when one has first heaped up all the difficulties into the concept of factuality. Perhaps, though, I can hope in that way to get a bit closer to the nature of these "last things" of epistemology.

97. Cf. also Ernst Mally in the second article of the Graz *Untersuchungen zur Gegenstandstheorie und Psychologie,* p. 201.

98. Cf. *Über die Stellung der Gegenstandstheorie im System der Wissenschaften,* pp. 114 ff.

99. Cf. Anton Marty, *Untersuchungen zur Grundlegung,* pp. 292 f.

100. Moreover—a fact that Marty has not recorded—this was immediately confirmed by me. Cf. "Über Urteilsgefuhle, was sie sind und was sie nicht sind," in the *Archiv für die gesamte Psychologie* 6:33.

101. Namely from "Erscheinungen und psychische Funktionen," *Abhandlungen der Berliner Akademie der Wissenschaften,* p. 30.

102. Alois Höfler in the *Göttingischer Gelehrten-Anzeigen,* 1906, no. 3.

103. Cf. *Untersuchungen zur Grundlegung,* pp. 304, 307 (twice), 308.

104. In the particulars I am now and then uncertain—as when Bolzano seems to identify his position with the following (Mehmel's): "Regarded objectively, i.e., in abstraction from the mind whose action it is, the judgment is called a proposition. There must necessarily be as many kinds of propositions as there are ways in which the mind can act to posit things." The objective is surely in no wise a "judgment" or "action." The following consideration might be much more important. If "propositions-in-themselves" are my objectives, then "representations-in-themselves" are doubtless my objecta. But now, Bolzano expressly opposes "objects" to "representations-in-themselves" (and doubtless also to "propositions-in-themselves"). (Cf. Gerhard Gotthardt, *Bolzanos Lehre vom "Satz an sich" in ihrer methodologischen Bedeutung* (Berlin, 1909), pp. 40 ff.—could it be that there is some connection between Bolzano and Edmund Husserl's view concerning the status of an object?) As against this, it seems to me that objecta and objectives together constitute the totality of objects known to us. (Cf. above, pp. 49 f.)

105. For divergent opinions on the subject, cf. Hugo Bergmann, *Das philosophische Werk Bernard Bolzanos* (Halle, 1909), pp. 17, n.; 41. Nevertheless, the interpretation to be touched on immediately below (pp. 76 f.) might present greater difficulties.

106. On the sweeping abstractive measures that Bolzano himself has to insist on, cf. Gerhard Gotthard, *Bolzanos Lehre vom "Satz an sich" in ihrer methodologischen Bedeutung,* pp. 7 f.; and on the misconceptions connected with these measures, cf. p. 17, ibid.

107. Cf. pp. 71 f.

108. "Über Urteilsgefühle," p. 33.

109. No one who has become attentive to its technical use will fail to observe that the word also finds extensive employment in Edmund Husserl's *Logische Untersuchungen*. From that it is perhaps even more clear than from the employment of the word "proposition," which I already mentioned in the first edition of the present book (pp. 195; 197, n.), how close at hand the problems of the objective are for the aforesaid writer, though he has not advanced any claim to priority.

110. Gerhard Gotthardt, *Bolzanos Lehre vom "Satz an sich" in ihrer methodologischen Bedeutung*, pp. 27 f.

111. In its first part, from which the above citations were taken, it is a Berlin doctoral dissertation.

112. Ibid., p. 26.

113. Anton Marty, "Über 'Annahmen,'" *Zeitschrift für Psychologie* 40:19, n.

114. *Untersuchungen zur Grundlegung*, pp. 292 f.

115. One of the reference sources has two authors.

116. Ibid., p. 293.

117. Especially since I myself have employed the expression, albeit with other meanings. Cf. "Über Urteilsgefühle: was sie sind und was sie nicht sind," *Archiv für die gesamte Psychologie* 6:40 f.

118. *Untersuchungen zur Grundlegung*, p. 293.

119. *Vierteljahrsschrift für wissenschaftliche Philosophie* 18:461, n.

120. *Untersuchungen zur Grundlegung*, p. 293.

121. Cf. also ibid., p. 306, bottom; perhaps elsewhere.

122. Ibid., p. 309, n. 1.

123. "Über Gegenstände höherer Ordnung," *Zeitschrift für Psychologie* 21:185 ff. Cf. above, p. 66.

124. Cf. also Stephan Witasek, *Grundlinien der Psychologie*, pp. 73 ff.

IV

1. Cf. sec. 1.

2. Alois Höfler in the *Göttingischer Gelehrten-Anzeigen*, 1906, pp. 212 ff.

3. Alois Riehl, "Logik und Erkenntnistheorie," in P. Hinnenberg's *Die Kultur der Gegenwart*, vol. 1, no. 6, p. 85.

4. Cf. chiefly chap. 6.

5. Cf. chap. 10, sec. 23.

6. Some of the positions rejected here and in the following have since found an advocate in Anton Marty; cf. his article "Über 'Annahmen'" in vol. 40 of the *Zeitschrift für Psychologie*, pp. 47 ff. and my reply "In Sachen der Annahmen" in the same journal, vol. 41, pp. 11 ff. Below, in sec. 64, I shall return to some controversial points, occasioned by further statements the same author has recently made in connection with this matter in his *Untersuchungen zur Grundlegung der allgemeinen Grammatik und Sprachphilosophie*.

7. Against this, D. H. Kerler (*Über Annahmen*, pp. 13 f.) writes: "One does not take oneself to be Siegfried, nor does one assume one's identity with Siegfried; on the contrary, one is conscious of portraying the hero, of representing him." What sort of

thought might that be—the thought of "representation" ["Repräsentation"] that no child could lack? I admit that one need not assume "identity," if only there be something analogous to the "positing representation" ["setzende Vorstellung"].

8. Interesting material on this theme is now offered by the article by Bernhard Groethuysen on sympathy ("Das Mitgefühl," vol. 34 of the *Zeitschrift für Psychologie und Physiologie der Sinnesorgane*, p. 209, but especially pp. 210 ff.). This article is also instructive in many questions fairly closely related to this one. But in using the data so assiduously brought together there, one must bear in mind that we are concerned with the intellectual side, whereas the author is concerned with the emotional side (and specifically that of sympathy). The question, in particular, as to "whether or not actors feel the feelings of the characters portrayed" (ibid., p. 211) would have to be answered yes or no according to whether or not one includes imaginative feelings (cf. below, secs. 54 ff.) among the feelings.

9. Understanding the word *"einbilden"* naturally not in the unpresuming sense in which the psychologist speaks of "reproductive representations" ["Einbildungsvorstellungen"], but in the popular and, at the same time, especially narrow sense which excludes "really believing" as well as the warrantedness of it.

10. This formulation is more popular than empirically precise, and it might thereby prejudice one against the interpretation being expounded here. It is not a matter of imagining a formal identity ("I am Julius Caesar," "I am Faust") but a matter of imagining the past, present, and future given by the role as being the past, present, and future of the one who has to play the role. Cf. also Bernhard Groethuysen, "Das Mitgefühl," p. 246.

11. Cf. below, chap. 9, sec. 54.

12. Cf. especially above, sec. 4, but also chap. 5, sec. 20.

13. Cf. sec. 19.

14. Strictly speaking, there is agreement with this even on the part of those writers who (as, say, Benno Erdmann, *Logik*, vol. 1, 2d ed., pp. 389 ff.) broaden the domain of application of the word "judgment" in such a way that the question finds a place in it along with the "assertion" ["Behauptung"]. Cf. also below, sec. 63.

15. After Delbrück, cf. Karl Groos, "Experimentelle Beiträge zur Psychologie des Erkennens" in the *Zeitschrift für Psychologie* 26:149.

16. Ibid., where reference is also made to the old distinction between erotematic and peistic questions.

17. On this and the following cf. now also Eduard Martinak, "Das Wesen der Frage" in *Atti del V. congresso internazionale di psicologia* (Rome, 1906), pp. 333 ff.

18. For this, cf. Heinrich Rickert, *Der Gegenstand der Erkenntnis,* 2d ed., pp. 99 f.

19. Groos, "Experimentelle Beiträge."

20. My attention was brought to this some years ago by Wilhelm Frankl.

21. Cf. Stephan Witasek, *Gründzuge der allgemeinen Ästhetik,* pp. 255 ff.

22. Cf. my article "Über Urteilsgefühle" in the *Archiv für die gesamte Psychologie* 6:36 ff.

23. Cf. below, ch. 5, secs. 24 f.

24. For the rest, cf. also below, sec. 23.

25. Cf. Stephan Witasek, "Zur psychologischen Analyse der ästhetischen Einfühlung," *Zeitschrift für Psychologie* 25:37 ff.

26. Abundant relevant factual material is afforded by Konrad Lange's observations

on "illusion" in art. Cf. *Das Wesen der Kunst,* 2d ed. (Berlin, 1907), especially pp. 65 ff., though the connection with assumptions is not taken into consideration here. This connection is treated by A. Möller, "Langes 'bewusste Illusion' und Meinongs 'Annahmen'," in H. Helbing's *Monatsheften über Kunst und Kunstwissenschaft* vol. 3 (1903): 230 ff. For the rest, cf. also below, sec. 23.

<h1 style="text-align:center">V</h1>

1. Cf. secs. 8 f.

2. "Meinong's Theory of Complexes and Assumptions," pt. 2, *Mind,* n.s., 13:348, 351 f.

3. Russell prefers to say "complexes"; he thinks that complexes coincide with objectives. I shall return to this point in chap. 8, sec. 46.

4. Cf. above, sec. 12.

5. He still coordinates the opposition of "true" and "false" with these two pairs; this is an assailable point (cf. above, sec. 13), but in the present context it is immaterial.

6. Which apparently Anton Marty managed to do in the zeal of his attack. Cf. *Untersuchungen zur Grundlegung,* pp. 480, n.

7. Cf. above, sec. 11.

8. Concerning the sense of this term, a term first employed in my "Hume-Studien," cf. below, sec. 46.

9. The question as to whether such a thought contains only representations or whether it also contains assumptions is incidental here. Cf., however, chap. 8, especially secs. 45 f.

10. Cf. above, sec. 2, pp. 19 f.

11. Cf. above, chap. 3, sec. 13.

12. Above, sec. 2.

13. Cf. secs. 11, 14.

14. Which will turn out to be false in chap. 8.

15. *Über die Erfahrungsgrundlagen unseres Wissens,* p. 72 ff.; cf. above, sec. 4.

16. Cf. below, secs. 54, 55.

17. Cf. Anton Marty, *Untersuchung zur Grundlegung,* p. 487.

18. By J. K. Kreibig, *Die Intellectuellen Funktionen* (Vienna, 1909), p. 59.

19. By contrast, the first-mentioned author's "grave doubts" are decidedly strange (*Untersuchungen zur Grundlegung,* pp. 487 f.). If the representation is replaced by the perceived experience itself, then, he thinks, why not the judgment, too? The answer, of course: because all perception is judgment, an experience which is not judged-about is one which is unperceived. As for the rest, I have already taken this matter into consideration in the *Erfahrungsgrundlagen,* p. 72 f. (as schema IV).

20. Kreibig, *Die Intellectuellen Funktionen,* p. 59.

21. Cf. below, sec. 65.

22. Anton Marty, *Untersuchungen zur Grundlegung,* pp. 482 ff.

23. Ibid., p. 483.

24. Cf. *Über die Stellung der Gegenstandstheorie im System der Wissenschaften,* p. 17. But I doubt that Anton Marty's panacea, the Brentanoan existential negation (*Untersuchungen,* p. 347), will carry much farther where the question is precisely one of existential affirmation. Of course, it is even less possible to join Bertrand Russell

(*Mind,* n.s., 16(1907):439) in questioning the very existence of the problem. A hypothesis along the lines of Russell's (ibid., p. 484, line 21 up from bottom) would seem to me to be neither required by the matter under consideration nor helpful to an understanding. For the rest, cf. also below, sec. 31.

25. Anton Marty, *Untersuchungen zur Grundlegung,* pp. 483 ff., 488.

26. I am unable to utilize Marty's substantiating arguments for the furtherance of comprehension. No sooner does my main thesis appear to be granted (ibid., p. 484, lines 21 ff. from top), than these remarks lead (in the way I have already noted in the article "In Sachen der Annahmen," *Zeitschrift für Psychologie* 41:8) to a polemical rejection of theses that no one postulates and which the author never collectively credits me with. Something is added about the "subterfuge" to which I must resort, because I "won't hear" anything of represented objectives. Going into this any further would probably take up a disproportionate amount of space.

27. Anton Marty, *Untersuchungen zur Grundlegung,* p. 485.

28. Anton Marty takes such great offense at this metaphor that he reproaches me with it five times on pp. 484-486 of the *Untersuchungen.* I didn't think that I should suppress it on that account.

29. In conformity, I should add, with the preliminary investigation already carried out on pp. 42 ff.

30. Cf. above, p. 45, n. 19.

31. By "quality," here, we naturally mean just quality in the logical sense—or in other words, the determination in respect of the antithesis of yes and no.

32. A case that is surprisingly seldom realized, we might add. The locution "I judge that. . . " is what would in the first instance be considered as such a clause; yet even this locution can hardly ever be divested of its affirmative character without violence.

33. Cf. also above, chap. 4, sec. 19.

34. Assumptions being included, of course, but only as consequences of the former.

35. Especially p. 95, above.

36. By Anton Marty, "Über 'Annahmen'," *Zeitschrift für Psychologie* 40, pp. 33 and 41 ff., as well as pp. 48 ff.

37. "In Sachen der Annahmen," *Zeitschrift für Psychologie* 41:9 ff.

38. Cf. sec. 20.

39. Anton Marty, *Untersuchungen zur Grundlegung,* pp. 260 f.

40. Ibid., p. 265.

41. In my rejoinder to Marty's first attack, I have already pointed out that there is usually no occasion for any conflicts; cf. "In Sachen der Annahmen," *Zeitschrift für Psychologie* 41:12. Marty notices this objection (*Untersuchungen zur Grundlegung,* p. 263), but as far as I can see, he does not even make the attempt to refute it.

42. Anton Marty, *Untersuchungen zur Grundlegung,* p. 263.

43. "In Sachen der Annahmen," *Zeitschrift für Psychologie* 41:12.

44. Thus Anton Marty, *Untersuchungen zur Grundlegung,* p. 261.

45. Cf. *Untersuchungen zur Grundlegung,* p. 265, lines 10 ff. from top.

46. *Das Wesen der Kunst,* 2d ed., p. 262.

47. Ibid., p. 253.

48. Ibid., p. 271.

49. Ibid., p. 283.

50. Ibid., p. 282.

51. Ibid., p. 274.

52. Ibid., p. 276.

53. By A. Möller in the article already cited on p. 96 above, "Lange's 'Bewusste Selbsttäuschung' und Meinongs 'Annahmen'."

54. Cf. p. 49, above.

55. Cf. Stephan Witasek, *Grundzüge der allgemeinen Ästhetik,* pp. 53 ff.

56. Ibid., p. 35.

57. Cf. chap. 9, sec. 55.

58. Concerning this concept, cf. my *Psychologisch-ethischen Untersuchungen zur Werttheorie,* pp. 31 ff., and especially "Über Urteilsgefühle, was sie sind und was sie nicht sind," in the *Archiv für die gesamte Psychologie* 6:22 ff.

59. An interesting as well as informative discussion of this basis of my statements in the theory of value is provided by W. M. Urban in *Valuation, Its Nature and Laws. An Introduction to the General Theory of Value* (London, 1909), especially pp. 41 ff. I must nevertheless refrain from entering into this subject here.

60. Here "existence" is to be understood in the way that it is normally understood in any other connection, namely as "factual existence." In "Über Urteilsgefühle," etc., I have already mentioned that the matter in question can just as well be the so-being of an existent as the existence of something which is thus and so [Existenz eines Soseienden]. Ibid., p. 36; cf. also sec. 55, below. Bertrand Russell ("Meinong's Theory of Complexes and Assumptions," pt. 2, *Mind,* n.s., 13:352, n.) rightly mentions the possibility that more than the existential sphere might be taken in. Naturally, the domain of the objective is not abandoned in any of these extensions of the sphere of consideration.

61. Cf. the beginning of sec. 10, pp. 45 ff.

62. Further particulars on this in "Urteilsgefühle," *Archiv für die gesamte Psychologie* 6:31 f.

63. Cf. sec. 10, pp. 46 ff.

64. Cf. also Ehrenfels, *System der Werttheorie,* vol. 1, p. 53, bottom. I am especially willing to emphasize the agreement in this matter, inasmuch as I shall be compelled further on to dwell at greater length on divergencies concerning other points of the theory of desire.

65. A kind of counterpart to the absent "that"-clauses is provided by cases in which such clauses, or something sufficiently similar to them, are indeed present, but desire remains entirely unacknowledged in the wording and its recognizable only from the construction. To be precise, in such cases desire is recognizable only from the connection of the dependent clause with a main clause that in the first instance expresses something quite different from desire. Such is the case with the purposive locutions using "in order that," "so that," and the like.

66. In opposition to Ehrenfels, especially in the *Vierteljahrsschrift für wissenschaftliche Philosophie* for 1899, pp. 278 ff. Against his comments there, I must adhere to my theses in the *Psychologisch-ethischen Untersuchungen zur Werttheorie,* p. 123. Cf. also Hermann Schwarz, *Psychologie des Willens* (Leipzig, 1900), pp. 160 ff. Not even in the case of desire for a counter-measure, a case which Ehrenfels (same article, pp. 280 f.) considers especially convincing, can I see that we would necessarily be confronted with desire for the non-being of something, i.e., so that reluctance to its being would be precluded. Desire for an end motivates desire for the means and reluctance to the hindrances: why should not desire for the hindrances be motivated also by reluctance to the end, as well as by reluctance to the means?

67. The word "object" of course being taken in its broader sense, the sense in which even a represented objectum can be called the object of a judgment, i.e., the judgment which concerns it. (Cf. sec. 8, p. 38 above.)

68. For the sake of simplicity, let us disregard the possible case of so-being; our remarks can easily be reapplied to this case, of course.

69. At least the sort of reluctance that in this domain would doubtless form the counterpart of willing.

70. Cf. above, chap. 4.

71. Cf. *Psychologisch-ethischen Untersuchungen zur Werttheorie,* p. 36, but especially Höfler, *Psychologie,* pp. 427 ff.

72. *Grundzüge der allgemeinen Ästhetik,* p. 181.

73. Ibid., n.

74. P. 211 of the first edition of this book.

75. Further on (cf. sec. 55) it will develop that according to Witasek's view, "assumption-feeling" would have to amount to the same thing as "imaginative feeling."

VI

1. Cf. *Über die Erfahrungsgrundlagen unseres Wissens,* p. 31 ff.; also above, sec. 13.

2. Which still might exhibit some very interesting roots here, as it fairly often does elsewhere; but we cannot investigate them in the present context.

3. Cf. Hillebrand, *Die neuen Theorien der kategorischen Schlüsse* (Vienna, 1891), pp. 4 f.

4. Cf. my observations in the *Göttingischer Gelehrten-Anzeigen,* 1892, p. 446.

5. Cf. above, p. 51.

6. The closeness of this interpretation to the one already expounded by Locke is shown by Eduard Martinak's observations on Locke's logical theory, observations that are also in other respects definitely oriented toward our present area of interest. Cf. *Die Logik John Lockes* (Halle, 1894), pp. 127 ff.

7. On p. 61 of the *Psychologisch-ethischen Untersuchungen zur Werttheorie,* it has already been urged that something similar also takes place in the case of feelings—or more precisely, in "mediated valuings," which I have opposed to "unmediated" valuings.

8. *Die Neuen Theorien der kategorischen Schlüsse,* p. 5. Husserl, *Logische Untersuchugen,* vol. 2, p. 28, claims it for Brentano.

9. *Göttingischer Gelehrten-Anzeigen,* 1892, p. 446; I must therefore yield to Husserl's polemical remarks, *Logische Untersuchungen,* vol. 2, p. 28.

10. "Hume-Studien II," pp. 108 f.

11. *Göttingischer Gelehrten-Anzeigen,* 1892, p. 445.

12. Hillebrand, *Die neuen Theorien der kategorischen Schlüsse,* p. 8.

13. *Logik,* 2d ed., vol. 1, p. 424.

14. I cannot deny that in choosing this example, I have implicitly taken a position in the matter of Euclid's eleventh axiom. Yet the position is not essential in the present connection; if it is found objectionable, one can easily replace the above example with another. Beyond that, cf. *Über die Stellung der Gegenstandstheorie,* pp. 77 ff.

15. Cf. my discussions, "Zur erkenntnistheoretischen Würdigung des Gedächtnisses," *Vierteljahrsschrift für wissenschaftliche Philosophie,* 1886, pp. 7 ff.; *Über die Erfahrungsgrundlagen unseres Wissens,* pp. 69 f.

16. Cf. *Über die Stellung der Gegenstandstheorie im System der Wissenschaften,* pp. 82 ff.

17. Cf. ibid., pp. 31 f. and elsewhere.

18. Cf. below, secs. 29 f.

19. Thus leaving out of account the possibility that what appears as a motivated judgment might, in addition, also be immediately evident or be derivable from other evident premises.

20. P. 68 *et passim.*

21. Cf. sec. 31.

22. Thus "Hume-Studien II," p. 107.

23. The case is otherwise when the conclusion makes its appearance really more *per accidens* as a conclusion, say in providing the requisite foundation for an operation of thought based on assumptions. "Grant that X be 20 years of age, Y 40, and Y therefore twice as old as X. Grant further..."

24. Here, of course, there will be no harm in disregarding certain things that are inaccurate from the standpoint of the theory of objects, e.g., inaccuracies such as can easily be proven against the venerable principle, *"Nota notae est nota rei ipsius."*

25. Cf. below, chap. 8.

26. Cf. below, chap. 10, sec. 60.

27. Above, sec. 29.

28. Cf. chap. 10, sec. 63.

29. The case is otherwise, though, with the counterpart of this that one encounters in "since"-clauses and their likes, e.g., in the locution "Although the sun is shining, it is not hot." But the adversative character that can be detected in such assertions does not primarily have to do with a connection implicitly negated in them; it relates merely to the consequent that has to be reckoned with in accordance with this connection, or with whatever this consequent might mean.

30. Bertrand Russell's polemic ("Meinong's Theory of Complexes and Assumptions," pt. 2, *Mind,* n.s., 13:342 f.) seems to me to misjudge the intention of these remarks. They do not at all deny that one can judge as to the connection (however the matter may stand with the necessity called into question by Russell). I wanted then and I now want to make plain only this: that the "If...then..." does not express such a judgment and that, for this reason, the hypothetical judgment correctly put into words by means of the "If...then..." is not a judgment as to a connection.

31. Cf. pp. 141 f.

32. D. H. Kerler, *Über Annahmen,* pp. 20 f.

33. Except that, as will presently become apparent, it requires some supplementation.

34. Cf. Gustav Spengler on p. 942 of the paper "Zur Grammatik der hypothetischen Sätze auf Grund neuerer psychologisch-logischer Theorien des hypothetischen Urteiles," *Zeitschrift für österreichische Gymnasien* 46 (1895), which brings forward much suggestive material.

35. Cf. *Über die Stellung der Gegenstandstheorie im System der Wissenschaften,* pp. 28 ff. Also see sec. 12 above.

36. *Untersuchungen zur Grundlegung der allgemeinen Grammatik und Sprachphilosophie,* pp. 340 ff.

37. Cf. sec. 20.

38. *Über die Stellung der Gegenstandstheorie,* p. 17. Cf. also above, sec. 20, p. 105.

39. *Über die Stellung der Gegenstandstheorie,* p. 17.
40. *Logik,* vol. 1, 2d ed., p. 577.
41. Ibid., p. 578.
42. Cf. ibid., p. 579.
43. Above, pp. 145 f.
44. *Logik,* vol. 1, 2d ed., pp. 585 f.
45. Chap. 3, beginning.
46. Cf. above, chap. 2, sec. 4.
47. Below, chap. 7.
48. Cf. above, sec. 2.
49. Cf. chap. 2, sec. 4.
50. J. K. Kreibig would be the one who deserves the credit for first having pointed out the specific character, as object, of what is apprehended in this case. Cf. *Die intellektuellen Funktionen* (Vienna and Leipzig, 1909), pp. 200 ff.
51. Especially pp. 87 ff.
52. "Meinongs Lehre von den Annahmen und ihre Bedeutung fur die Schullogik," *Wiener Gymnasialprogramm* 1903, pp. 28 ff. of the separate print.
53. In the place cited, p. 29, Spengler adduces the following examples: (a) Hypothetical sentences "of the form of reality": "You are at fault if you do not choose the lesser of two evils." (Possible assumption-inference: Granting that you do not choose the lesser of two evils, then it must be assumed that you are at fault.) Again— "A signal is given, if a train comes into the station." (The assumption of the train coming in legitimates the assumption of the given signal.) (b) The "case of eventuality": "If it should be a nice day tomorrow, I shall go out for a fairly long walk." (Here, of course, the assumption of fair weather legitimates the assumption of a carrying out of the decision that one has made for such an eventuality, unless the emotional side is involved in this case.) (c) For the "potential case": "Granting this case, that you made some error of mine plain to me, I should then be ready immediately to subscribe to your view." (Here the conditional clause already has the form of an "explicit assumption," in the sense of chap. 4 above. What would prevent one's deriving the consequent from this, as an evident concluding assumption?) For the same author's characterization of the main forms of hypothetical sentences, cf. the paper already mentioned, "Zur Grammatik der hypothetischen Sätze," etc. in volume 46 of the *Zeitschrift für österreichische Gymnasien* (1895), pp. 942 f.
54. Cf. My "Hume-Studien II," p. 108.
55. Cf. "Meinongs Lehre von den Annahmen," etc., p. 30.
56. *Logik,* vol. 1, 2d ed., pp. 579 f.
57. Ibid., pp. 559, 580.
58. Cf. above, chap. 3.
59. Concerning the relation of assumptions to the hypothetical and the disjunctive judgments, cf. also J. M. Baldwin, *Thoughts and Things,* vol. 2, pp. 108 ff.

VII

1. For the following, cf. my discussions "Über Gegenstände höherer Ordnung," *Zeitschrift für Psychologie* 21:183 ff.
2. In the Graz *Untersuchungen zur Gegenstandstheorie und Psychologie,* pp. 3 ff.

3. At present, the concept no longer seems to me to be unobjectionable in every respect; cf. *Über die Erfahrungsgrundlagen unseres Wissens,* pp. 83 f., and also below, end of sec. 36.

4. From here to the end of sec. 37, we are concerned with the object of a judgment only in the sense of that which is judged *about* [*be*urteilt] in the judgment in question. This is usually the only thing that one contemplates in connection with the words "object of judgment," prior to fuller acquaintance with the objective (cf. pp. 37 f., above). Even against the objective, that which is judged about maintains its position as the thing that is normally "intended" by the person who is judging (cf. below, sec. 38). Hence, earlier (pp. 39, 44), we spoke of it more than once as being the "main object" of a judgment, although the objective is in a way more intimately related to the judgment. So in the immediately following sections it would be not only clearer, but more correct, if we always said "main object" instead of "object." Yet the intentions of these discussions might come out more clearly if we adhered to the first-edition usage, which is still quite intelligible from the standpoint of that edition.

5. The theory of presentation advocated in the present edition requires a modification of this thesis.

6. Cf. my *Psychologisch-ethische Untersuchungen zur Werttheorie,* pp. 33 ff.

7. *Psychologisch-ethische Untersuchungen zur Werttheorie,* p. 41.

8. By Eduard Martinak in his "Psychologische Untersuchungen über Prüfen und Klassifizieren," *Österreichische Mittleschule* 14':7 ff. of the separate print.

9. Cf. Witasek, "Beiträge zur speziellen Dispositionspsychologie," *Archiv für systematische Philosophie* 3:273 f. Also Martinak, loc. cit.

10. Also in lectures.

11. Here D. H. Kerler (in his *Über Annahmen,* p. 26) correctly surmises an inexact choice of words. What is meant is the fittedness for serving as the psychological prerequisite of an affirmative judgment. But Kerler seems to misunderstand the sense of "psychological prerequisite," the term I coined. The psychological prerequisite is always an experience—thus, a representation in the present case—and never the object of the experience.

12. The aspect in which this principle bears on the theory of objects has now been contrasted to the psychological aspect by Jan Lukasiewicz with creditable acuteness in his article "Über den Satz des Widerspruches bei Aristoteles," *Extrait du Bulletin de l'Academie des Sciences de Cracovie,* November-December, 1909.

13. A decision to avoid any further connection of the adjectives "immanent" and "transcendent" with the substantive "objectum" or "object" now seems to me to be the simplest and most positive way to meet such difficulties, with all due respect for the historical importance of these adjectives. This decision will scarcely result in a terminological gap. Also, the danger (etymologically very close at hand, of course) of taking the "immanent object" to be something mental (cf. above, p. 66 f., n. 76) would thereby be removed once and for all. Beyond this, cf. also above, p. 219, n. 3.

14. Cf. especially Sigwart in the second edition of his *Logik,* pp. 150 ff., with particular attention to the note on pp. 154 ff. At the present juncture, there is no need for me to emphasize the specific points in which I am unable to agree with these remarks, since these points have probably already impressed themselves upon the reader. Accordingly, it is not specifically Sigwart's theses that are opposed in the following. (Against D. H. Kerler, *Über Annahmen,* p. 28.)

15. Anton Marty cites facts that diminish its value as a proof. "Über Annahmen," *Zeitschrift für Psychologie* 40:36.

16. In the sense of the remark above, p. 166.

17. Cf. above, pp. 61 f.

18. Now D. H. Kerler, too, correctly points out such things (*Über Annahmen,* pp. 23 ff.), though not without misapprehensions. In particular, the contention that I do not allow for negative objectives (p. 24) is erroneous even in connection with the first edition. It was just that I had by no means yet taken full recourse to the objective in that edition. We can forego consideration of further deficiencies in the relevant discussions of mine, deficiencies that the context alone made it impossible to remove on this occasion. Beyond that, cf. pp. 176, 198.

19. Cf. above, p. 166.

20. Concerning this thesis, which I have long advocated, there is now further information in Stephan Witasek's *Grundlinien der Psychologie,* pp. 84 f.

21. Stephan Witasek, *Grundzüge der Ästhetik,* pp. 36 ff.

22. For example, cf. B. A. Messer, *Empfindung und Denken* (Leipzig, 1908), pp. 40 ff. (also pp. 56 f.). It is true, however, that he actually has something other than the sense-object in mind, if I understand the railroad example correctly. The above book is referred to primarily as a particularly accessible summary of the position of Edmund Husserl, on the one hand, and on the other hand of the investigations on "thinking" carried out in Würzburg in recent years. The following discussions are indebted to these investigations for many different suggestions, although I should not know how to record these suggestions on each occasion and with the sketchy character of what follows, I should not be capable of an argumentative defense of the divergent elements in my own view.

23. Cf. Stephan Witasek, *Grundlinien der Psychologie,* p. 246.

24. Edmund Husserl, *Logische Untersuchungen,* vol. 2, pp. 40 ff. *et passim.*

25. As against this, cf. Messer, *Empfindung und Denken,* pp. 120 f.

26. Cf. above, p. 66.

27. Cf. *Über die Erfahrungsgrundlagen unseres Wissens,* pp. 58 f.

28. Ibid., pp. 96 ff.

29. Cf. sec. 20.

30. Above, pp. 61 f.

31. As far as the natural priority of affirmation to negation is implied by the present point, i.e., as a consequence restricted to objectives of being, I still think that the position that is reproduced in sec. 37 as part of the "being view," and which is connected with that point, is appropriate. But it seems just as certain to me now that it is not in every respect permissible to carry this position over to objectives of so-being. Cf. below, pp. 274 f.

32. Further on, we shall return to other things relevant to this point; cf. pp. 276 f.

33. Cf. sec. 4 *et passim.*

34. *Über die Erfahrungsgrundlagen unseres Wissens,* pp. 75 ff.

35. Against D. H. Kerler's *Über Annahmen,* pp. 28 f.

36. Chap. 8, sec. 45.

VIII

1. "Phantasievorstellung und Phantasie," in the *Zeitschrift für Philosophie und philosophische Kritik* 95:213. Cf. also Stephan Witasek, "Über willkürliche Vorstellungsverbindung," *Zeitschrift für Psychologie* 12:197 ff.

2. "Hume-Studien I."

3. I mean the abstract items that have other substrates—thus, in the example of the red cross, the form of the cross, which is incompatible with the spatial substrate of the red-representation, if., e.g., the representation of a red disc should happen to form the basis of this representation.

4. Cf. my discussions, "Über Gegenstände höherer Ordnung," in the *Zeitschrift fur Psychologie* 21:198 ff.

5. On the contrast of direct and indirect representing, cf. "Hume-Studien II," pp. 87 f., also below, p. 205.

6. Cf. "Über Gegenstände höherer Ordnung," pp. 200 ff.; there is now Rudolf Ameseder, "Über Vorstellungsproduktion" (eighth article in the Graz *Untersuchungen zur Gegenstandstheorie und Psychologie*), pp. 494 ff.

7. Concerning the principle of the coincidence of complexion and relation, cf. "Über Gegenstände höherer Ordnung," p. 193. It has been more precisely delineated by Ernst Mally in the "Untersuchungen zur Gegenstandstheorie des Messens" (third article in the Graz *Untersuchungen zur Gegenstandstheorie und Psychologie*), pp. 153 f.

8. Cf. "Über Phantasievorstellung und Phantasie," pp. 207 f.

9. Hans Cornelius, *Psychologie* (Leipzig, 1897), pp. 60 and 432, respectively.

10. "Hume-Studien II," p. 99.

11. A sort of counterpart to this contrast is afforded by the contrast of the directly and indirectly represented. Inasmuch as intuition provides only direct representations, one may be inclined to call the indirect representation, too, nonintuitive. In this sense, of course, it might then also be in order to call a simple representation—that of a certain pitch, say, or whatever else may answer to the demand for simplicity—intuitive. The possibility of such an extension of verbal usage may be ignored here, however.

12. It might seem strange that naming and expression come into a sort of opposition here, since it is customary to designate the names themselves as "expressions." But in the framework of the discussions of the second chapter, this is simply an inexactitude. It is an inexactitude that is removed only under special circumstances, namely those such as are usually present in the case of secondary expression.

13. For simplicity's sake, let us make the supposition, in itself a plausible one, that if *A* and *B* are in the relation *R,* then *R* stands in the same relation to *A* as it does to *B.* And of course, even if the situation should sometime be otherwise, this cannot possibly affect the cogency of the above reflections.

14. Cf. "Über Gegenstände höherer Ordnung," pp. 198 ff.

15. Cf. above, p. 182, n. 7.

16. "Über Gegenstände höherer Ordnung," pp. 187 f.

17. *Über die Erfahrungsgrundlagen unseres Wissens,* pp. 91 ff.

18. By Ernst Dürr in the review section of the *Archiv für die gesamte Psychologie* 13:30.

19. Ibid., pp. 64 ff.

20. The fact that contents appear here as objects could well puzzle someone who is

unpracticed in such investigations. But this fact constitutes neither an error nor a difficulty. For anything apprehensible is an object, and contents in particular are therefore objects. This will be especially clear in the present connection, where what we have to do, of course, is to occupy ourselves with the object "content" for a while and therefore apprehend it and make judgments about it.

21. Cf. Ernst Mally in the third article of the Graz *Untersuchungen zur Gegenstandstheorie und Psychologie,* p. 130.

22. A term coined by R. Bujas and communicated in the address "Sprachwissenschaft und Gegenstandstheorie"; cf. *Verhandlungen der 50. Versammlung deutscher Philologen und Schulmänner in Graz 1909* (Leipzig, 1910), p. 177.

23. Cf. *Über die Erfahrungsgrundlagen unseres Wissens,* pp. 26 ff.

24. Concerning how-being and what-being, cf. Ernst Mally's "Untersuchungen zur Gegenstandstheorie des Messens," in the Graz *Untersuchungen zur Gegenstandstheorie und Psychologie,* pp. 135 f.

25. And by this fastening upon it at the same time "predetermines" it. Cf. my paper "Über Urteilsgefühle, was sie sind und was sie nicht sind," in the *Archiv für die gesamte Psychologie* 6:48 f.

26. Above, chap. 1, sec. 2.

27. Of course, it has nothing in common with the *N* of our above paradigm; the agreement in the symbol chosen is an entirely coincidental one.

28. Such barbaric expressions will hopefully find some justification in their brevity.

29. Above, chap. 5, sec. 20; also chap. 8, sec. 43.

30. "Meinong's Theory of Complexes and Assumptions," pt. 2, *Mind,* n.s., 13:346 ff.; cf. also above, sec. 20.

31. In the Graz *Untersuchungen zur Gegenstandstheorie und Psychologie,* p. 142, n. 2.

32. "Differentness," so far as this means the same as "being different," as remarked above (cf. sec. 10), is the "relation" corresponding to this relatant.

33. Cf. Ernst Mally in the third article of the Graz *Untersuchungen zur Gegenstandstheorie und Psychologie,* pp. 135 f.

34. Ibid., p. 130.

35. After R. Bujas, cf. above, p. 194, n. 22.

36. "Hume-Studien II," pp. 87 f.; indirect representation has already come under consideration above, in sec. 20 and sec. 40.

37. Such being the case with Karl Bühler; cf. especially his inaugural dissertation *Über Gedanken* (1907), pp. 63 ff., where there is even (p. 64) a suggestion of my comparison of "indication" and "execution" (cf. above, p. 182).

38. As far as the decisive thing for him in this contrast is not just the normally complex nature of the concept-object, with the object being apprehended "nonintuitively" quite in the sense we have hitherto employed. Cf. Gustav Spengler, "Meinongs Lehre von den Annahmen," etc., *Wiener Gymnasialprogramm* 1903, p. 12.

39. "Hume-Studien I."

IX

1. Cf. my *Psychologisch-ethische Untersuchungen zur Werttheorie,* p. 34.

2. First in the writing *Über Fühlen und Wollen* (Vienna, 1887) and then in the revi-

sion of this writing, which is included in the first volume of the *System der Werttheorie*. It should suffice fairly well for all present purposes if we adhere to the second version, and I daresay it will also answer best to the intentions of the author.

3. Especially in the winter semester 1884/85.

4. *Psychologisch-ethische Untersuchungen zur Werttheorie*, p. 10 n.

5. In the meantime, a position that agrees with mine in its ultimate effect has been taken by Hermann Schwarz in the paper "Die empiristische Willenspsychologie und das Gesetz der relativen Glücksförderung," *Vierteljahrsschrift für wissenschaftliche Philosophie* 1899: 205 ff. Ehrenfels's "Entgegnung" is in the same volume of the *Vierteljahrsschrift*, pp. 261 ff. Now there is also Hermann Schwarz's *Psychologie des Willens*, pp. 155 ff. But in part and at least subjectively, concerning the things touched on in this controversy, those things would be less likely to enter my own mind as a basis for the evaluation of the Ehrenfelsean position. In part, also, Schwarz's attacks do not seem to me to be free of possible objections. But this is *not* true of the inapplicability of the Ehrenfelsean interpretation to instances of reluctance, the indication of which (cf. Schwarz in the *Vierteljahrsschrift* of 1899, pp. 220 f.) I consider to be as correct as it is important. Still, Ehrenfels himself, in his view of reluctancies (cf. above, chap. 5, n. 66) cannot see any shortcoming in this inapplicability.

6. Cf. "Über Gegenstände höherer Ordnung," *Zeitschrift für Psychologie* 21:183, 205; to which we might add "Abstrahieren und Vergleichen," in vol. 24 of the same journal, p. 35, along with *Über die Stellung der Gegenstandstheorie*, preface.

7. *System der Werttheorie*, vol. 1, p. 32. Taken in its entire wording, the cited sentence admittedly deals only with "endeavor and volition," whereas the author justifiably includes also wishing among the desires. It is expressly emphasized later, though, that the law also holds for wishing and, hence, for all desire. Ibid., pp. 39 f.

8. Ibid., pp. 217 f.

9. Ibid., p. 219.

10. Cf. ibid., pp. 231 ff. and farther on.

11. Expressly so designated, e.g., pp. 191 f.

12. Ibid., p. 190.

13. Ibid., pp. 195 ff.

14. Ibid., p. 205.

15. Ibid., p. 207.

16. Ibid., pp. 245 ff. We shall return presently to the nature of these difficulties; the author enumerates three of them.

17. Ibid., pp. 248 f.

18. Cf. ibid., pp. 245 f.

19. Ibid., p. 246.

20. Ibid., pp. 247 f.

21. P. 209.

22. *System der Werttheorie*, vol. 1, p. 252.

23. Ibid., pp. 189 f.

24. Ibid., p. 190.

25. Ibid., p. 194.

26. Ibid., p. 194.

27. Naturally, the physiological hypothesis on pp. 195 ff., in itself rather attractively

formulated, is not a proof. Also, I would rather leave the evaluation of this hypothesis to the expert in physiology.

28. *Zeitschrift für Psychologie* 27:18 ff.

29. Ibid. p. 28.

30. Cf. above, p. 212.

31. A superfluous reduction of the force of these instances is made by Ehrenfels himself; cf. *System der Werttheorie*, p. 37; also Hermann Schwarz in the *Vierteljahrsschrift für wissenschaftliche Philosophie* 1899:222 f.

32. Cf. above, sec. 49.

33. The case is otherwise when what one has in mind as incorporation and elimination is something that really has no claim to these designations. We shall return to this presently.

34. *System der Werttheorie,* vol. 1, p. 218.

35. Cf. ibid., p. 202 f.

36. Cf. especially p. 105.

37. Cf. above, chap. 5, sec. 25.

38. Above, chap. 5, n. 64.

39. Cf. below, sec. 56, at the end.

40. To that extent, pretheoretical thinking is itself providing rather emphatic testimony against a motivation along the lines of the "enhancement of happiness."

41. The time-determination in this case needn't always be the present; in the case of volitions, it can never be that. I can will only something in the future, future existence or non-existence. Accordingly, the relevant assumption must likewise relate to the future—the future to which volition can then be directed. As against this, wishing can relate also to something in the present or past, and for that reason wishing can also be motivated by assumptions that bear on the present or past.

42. Among such investigations, I daresay I may in the first instance include Stephan Witasek's lucid discussions in his *Ästhetik,* pp. 110 ff., as well as in his *Psychologie,* pp. 329 ff., quite apart from a rather fundamental difference in interpretation, to which I shall return below (sec. 55). Cf. moreover: Robert Saxinger, "Über die Natur der Phantasiegefühle und Phantasiebegehrungen," in the Graz *Untersuchungen zur Gegenstandstheorie und Psychologie,* pp. 579 ff.; Robert Saxinger, "Beiträge zur Lehre von der emotionalen Phantasie," in the *Zeitschrift für Psychologie und Physiologie der Sinnesorgane* 40:145 ff.; Ernst Schwarz, "Über Phantasiegefuhle," in the *Archiv für systematische Philosophie* 11:481 ff.; also to some extent my discussions in the writing *Über die Erfahrungsgrundlagen unseres Wissens,* pp. 75 ff. Again, there are now Hermann Siebeck's subtle discussions concerning music in *Grundfragen zur Psychologie und Ästhetik der Tonkunst* (Tübingen, 1909), from p. 14 on; here I find more worthwhile in the way of observation than in the way of basic theoretical interpretation that is prejudiced as little as possible with forethought. Entirely new paths (in particular, for genetic consideration) are indicated for the theory of imaginative feelings (and the theory of assumptions closely connected with it) by W. M. Urban in his *Valuation, Its Nature and Laws* (London, 1909), a book that is noteworthy in respect of both exposition and criticism. (For the basic questions, cf. especially pp. 48, 115 ff., 133 ff., 137 ff., 245 ff., 250 ff.) Fifteen years before the publication of the first edition of *Assumptions,* as I discovered only after that edition had come out, Wilhelm Dilthey had main-

tained that there is no purely representational "copying of acts of feeling and will." (This was in his essay "Die Einbildungskraft des Dichters," p. 345 of the *Philosophischen Aufsätze, Eduard Zeller zu seinem 50 jährigen Doktorjubiläum gewidmet* (Leipzig, 1887). Cited by Bernhard Groethuysen in the *Zeitschrift für Psychologie* 34: 202, n. 7. The aforesaid book of Hermann Siebeck's seems to refer to related things in Eduard von Hartmann; I cannot look into them at the present time, however.

43. Cf. also below, sec. 65.

44. As Bernhard Groethuysen rightly observes, "It results in a great difference among individuals, that some should be easily moved by the content of mere assumptions, while others should find a judgment necessary as the psychological prerequisite of sympathy. In general, the rule holds that the more highly educated a person is, the less he will allow a feigned state of affairs to move him to feelings of compassion and to excite these feelings in the way that reality does." ("Das Mitgefühl," *Zeitschrift für Psychologie* 34:263.)

45. *Ästhetik,* p. 148 and elsewhere.

46. "Zur psychologischen Analyse der ästhetischen Einfühlung," *Zeitschrift für Psychologie* 25:1 ff.

47. On "representations of feelings" cf. the very meritorious compilation of the literature in Bernard Groethuysen's "Das Mitgefühl," *Zeitschrift für Psychologie* 34:201 ff., also pp. 193, 248, 262 f.

48. Cf. also Karl Groos, *Der ästhetische Genuss* (Giessen, 1902), p. 209.

49. Here let us expressly leave out of account the genuine "aesthetic" feelings of pleasure and displeasure and what goes with them; we shall return to this presently below.

50. Cf. *Über die Erfahrungsgrundlagen unseres Wissens,* pp. 72 ff.

51. Ibid., p. 75.

52. Doubt in this regard is expressed also by Karl Groos, *Der ästhetische Genuss,* p. 209.

53. Cf. Witasek, "Zur psychologischen Analyse der ästhetischen Einfühlung," *Zeitschrift für Psychologie* 25:44 ff.; *Ästhetik,* pp. 99 ff.

54. Cf. below, chap. 10, sec. 65.

55. *Ästhetik,* pp. 115 ff; *Psychologie,* pp. 330 f.

56. Cf. especially *Ästhetik,* pp. 120 f., n.

57. *Über die Erfahrungsgrundlagen unseres Wissens,* pp. 75 ff.

58. *Ästhetik,* pp. 53 ff.

59. Ibid., pp. 67 ff.

60. Ibid., pp. 169 f.

61. Ibid., pp. 176 f.

62. "Über Urteilsgefühle," etc., in the *Archiv für die gesamte Psychologie* 6:34 ff.

63. Cf. secs. 45 f.

64. Cf. my review of Witasek's *Ästhetik* in the *Deutsche Literaturzeitung* 1904, cols. 2727 f.

65. *Ästhetik,* pp. 118 f., n.

66. "Von der Wertdefinition zum Motivationsgesetz," *Archiv für systematische Philosophie* 2:114.

67. *Psychologisch-ethische Untersuchungen zur Werttheorie,* p. 25.

68. First in the articles "Werttheorie und Ethik," in the *Vierteljahrsschrift für wissenschaftliche Philosophie* 1893: pp. 89 and 209, respectively.

69. Cf. my remarks "Über Werthaltung und Wert," in the *Archiv für systematische Philosophie* 1:340 f. especially.

70. *System der Werttheorie,* 1:53, n. 2.

71. Ibid., pp. 54 ff.

72. *System der Werttheorie,* 2:262 ff.

73. Cf. the survey and opinion on the matter in Max Reischle's *Werturteile und Glaubensurteile* (Halle am Seder, 1900), pp. 27 ff.; now especially in W. M. Urban's "Recent Tendencies in the Psychological Theory of Value," *Psychological Bulletin* 4 (1907), no. 4. The standpoint taken in the present book has found especially effective representation through the paper of Wilhelmine von Liels, "Gegen eine voluntaristische Begründung der Werttheorie," tenth article in the Graz *Untersuchungen zur Gegenstandstheorie und Psychologie,* pp. 527 ff.

74. In p. 25, n. of that work.

75. Cf. *System der Werttheorie,* 1:52 f.

76. Ibid., p. 26.

77. *Archiv für systematische Philosophie* 2:106 bottom.

78. *System der Werttheorie,* 2:262 ff.

79. *System der Werttheorie,* 1:62.

80. Ibid., pp. 57 ff.

81. More precisely, of course, "assuming."

82. "Über Werthaltung und Wert," in the *Archiv für systematische Philosophie* 1: 332 ff.

83. Ibid., p. 342.

84. Ibid., pp. 343 ff.

85. And naturally will suffer ever more, until a change has been brought about through a convention by all or at least most members of the professional community, creating the sanction of an individual's inevitable alienation of himself from that community. Today the relevant resolutions of the Sixth International Congress of Psychologists in Geneva may be safely welcomed as a first step in the approach to this goal.

86. *Der Begriff des absolut Wertvollen* (Leipzig, 1898), especially pp. 30 ff.

87. Cf. the little survey in Ehrenfels, *System der Werttheorie,* 1:70 f.

88. Hence also n. 1 on p. 343 of my article, "Über Werthaltung und Wert."

89. To that extent, Max Reischle does not report quite exactly when he characterizes my view as being "that valuations themselves can come about only by means of a value-judgment" and cites as proof of this characterization the following assertion of mine: "If I evaluate an object, this occurs through my conferring value on it, or in other words, making a value judgment." (Max Reischle, *Werturteile und Glaubensurteile,* pp. 20 f.). This oversight is unimportant in itself; but in the place cited, where the writer has immediately beforehand identified valuation with valuing, it can give rise to a misunderstanding of the basic thought of my theory of value.

90. Cf. sec. 56.

91. At this point, I do not think that I should withhold the confession, albeit a quite subjective one for the time being, that the transition from the basic experience to value itself no longer seems to be to be as easy to effect as it still did at the time of the writing

of the first edition. If one has become accustomed to see intellectual psychologism in a clear light by the approach that is characteristic of the theory of objects, then one can no longer ignore the question as to whether there is not also an emotional psychologism. However, to alter the theses of the first edition on the strength of that seemed to me to be premature, again speaking subjectively.

92. On the surrogative significance of imaginative feelings in play, cf. Konrad Lange, *Das Wesen der Kunst,* 2d ed., pp. 628 ff., also pp. 618 f.

93. As one can see, I am quite far from wanting to loosen the natural connection between "true value" and true objectives or judgments. Bertrand Russell's reference to this connection ("Meinong's Theory of Complexes and Assumptions," *Mind,* n.s., 13: 352, n.) constitutes a very noteworthy reminder that in the case of value-experiences assumptions cannot enter in as replacements for *all* judgments, but it proves nothing against assumptions having the role in value-experiences that is characterized above.

94. Cf. Witasek, *Ästhetik,* pp. 195 ff.

95. Cf. above, sec. 55, towards the end.

96. Against Witasek, *Ästhetik,* pp. 199, 202.

X

1. Cf. secs. 4, 20.

2. As to whether for all time, this will have to be left undecided at present.

3. It would be theoretical if the nature of judgment or assumption precluded a definition; which is possible, but which I cannot undertake to prove.

4. Cf. above, chap. 1, sec. 1.

5. Cf. Höfler, *Psychologie,* p. 16; Witasek, *Psychologie,* pp. 81 ff.

6. The agreement appears so great to Carl Stumpf that on the strength of it he questions the whole class distinction of judgments and assumptions ("Erscheinungen und psychische Funktionen," *Abhandlungen der königlichen preussischen Akademie der Wissenschaften zu Berlin,* 1907, p. 30, n. In contrast, Anton Marty declares, "I understand only what is supposed to distinguish so-called assumptions from judgments, not what is supposed to be common to them as their generic character" ("Über 'Annahmen'," vol. 40 of the *Zeitschrift für Psychologie,* p. 17).

7. In sec. 34 of that edition—a section which, it seems to me, has now become superfluous.

8. Cf. above, chap. 6.

9. Cf. Efraim Liljeqvist, *Meinongs allmänna värdeteori* (Göteborg, 1904), pp. 105 f., n. To be sure, Anton Marty asserts, "With that, the character of conviction would cease being a mere element in an act; it would itself have to be an act, a real accident of the soul, or rather an act in the act—all of which is quite unacceptable" ("Über 'Annahmen'," in vol. 40 of the *Zeitschrift für Psychologie,* p. 11). In the end, though, such difficulties might still be surmountable.

10. This was brought to my attention by Bertrand Russell, "Meinong's Theory of Complexes and Assumptions," pt. 2, *Mind,* n.s., 13:343.

11. On the analogous state of affairs in the case of mediately evident judgments, cf. above, chap. 6, sec. 28.

12. Cf. above, pp. 135 f.

13. Cf. above, p. 131.

14. As emerged at the end of the preceding section.

15. Cf. above, chap. 3, pp. 69 f.

16. Cf. above, sec. 40.

17. Above, p. 68.

18. Cf. above, p. 67.

19. Sec. 63 will attempt to bring forward more precise information on this.

20. For the sake of simplicity, let us leave out of account the peculiar fact that extroverted assumptions serve for the apprehending (not of their objectives but) of nonpresent judgments (cf. above, pp. 103 f.), although even this readily admits of subordination to the general point of view presently to be shown.

21. Cf. above, p. 72.

22. Cf. above, chap. 2.

23. Cf. above, chap. 2, sec. 6.

24. Cf. above, chap. 2, sec. 7.

25. Cf. above, chap. 3, p. 48.

26. Cf. above, chap. 2, pp. 34 f.

27. Cf. above, chap. 8.

28. Cf. above, chap. 6.

29. Cf. above, chap. 2, sec. 4.

30. Cf. above, secs. 38, 45 f.

31. For the first time, p. 10 above, with reference to D. H. Kerler.

32. Cf. above, sec. 1, also chap. 5.

33. Cf. also my article "In Sachen der Annahmen" in vol. 41 of the *Zeitschrift für Psychologie,* pp. 6 ff.

34. Benno Erdmann speaks simply of "judgments without force" ["geltungslose Urteile"] (*Logik,* vol. 1, 1st ed., pp. 271 ff.), among which he classes questions, for example. I should not like to make this term my own today, either; but since knowing about assumptions, I can no longer deceive myself about this: that the conception itself has a sense that is well-founded in the facts. And I believe that I should acknowledge this in the face of my negative opinion in the *Göttingischer Gelehrten-Anzeigen,* 1892, p. 447.

35. The fact that Bertrand Russell judges to the contrary ("Meinong's Theory of Complexes and Assumptions," pt. 2, *Mind,* n.s., 13:351) is traceable to a view that I have attempted to refute above (chap. 5, sec. 20, pp. 99 f.).

36. Cf. above, sec. 61.

37. Cf. above, end of sec. 1.

38. P. 278.

39. On pp. 79 and 279 of his *Psychologie.*

40. Cf. Alois Höfler in the *Göttingischer Gelehrten-Anzeigen,* 1906, p. 226.

41. Cf. above, chaps. 7 f.

42. Cf. below, sec. 65.

43. Alois Höfler in the *Göttingischer Gelehrten-Anzeigen,* 1906, p. 226.

44. *Über die Erfahrungsgrundlagen unseres Wissens,* p. 60, n.

45. Anton Marty, *Untersuchungen,* p. 245, n.; but even then there was Carl Stumpf's "Erscheinungen und psychische Funktionen," *Abhandlungen der königlichen preussischen Akademie der Wissenschaften zu Berlin,* 1907, p. 30, n.

46. *Tonpsychologie,* vol. 1, p. 113.

47. Cf. above, chap. 7, sec. 38.

48. Cf. above, chap. 4, sec. 19.

49. Cf. the work mentioned above (in the preface to the present, second edition), *Thoughts and Things*, especially vol. 2.

50. This being a main task of Anton Marty's article "Über 'Annahmen'," in vol. 40 of the *Zeitschrift für Psychologie*, especially pp. 7 ff. In place of "impossibility" (cf. ibid., p. 6) he also speaks of "improbability."

51. In the article "In Sachen der Annahmen," *Zeitschrift für Psychologie* 41, chiefly pp. 3 ff.

52. Anton Marty, *Untersuchungen zur Grundlegung der allgemeinen Grammatik und Sprachphilosophie*, pp. 247 ff.

53. Cf. Carl Stumpf, "Erscheinungen und psychische Funktionen," *Abhandlungen der königlichen preussischen Akademie der Wissenschaften zu Berlin*, 1907, p. 30, n.

54. *Untersuchungen zur Grundlegung*, p. 250.

55. Ibid., p. 250, n., p. 255.

56. Particularly in the introductory sections of the present chapter.

57. *Untersuchungen zur Grundlegung*, p. 251.

58. Ibid., p. 253.

59. Ibid., pp. 252 f.

60. Ibid., pp. 253 f.

61. Ibid., p. 252.

62. Cf. p. 264.

63. Cf. my remarks, "Über Begriff und Eigenschaften der Empfindung," in the *Vierteljahrsschrift für wissenschaftliche Philosophie*, 1888, pp. 478 ff. Also "Beiträge zur Theorie der psychischen Analyse," *Zeitschrift für Psychologie* 6:373.

64. Except Marty, who has only now been trying to find the meaning of the expression "imaginative representation," as became apparent after the publication of the foregoing in the first edition ("Über 'Annahmen'," *Zeitschrift für Psychologie* 40:26 f.; cf. my rejoinder, "In Sachen der Annahmen," *Zeitschrift für Psychologie* 41:8. In the end, it seems, he arrives at the result that a perceptual representation is a representation with belief, an imaginative representation a representation without belief (*Untersuchungen*, pp. 259 f.). As a counter-instance to such a view, I would have to adduce the imaginative representations with belief that we experience when we recall things or in some other way make judgments that are not perceptual judgments. For the description of imaginative representations, cf. now especially Stephan Witasek, *Psychologie*, p. 250 ff.

65. "Über Gegenstände höherer Ordnung," *Zeitschrift für Psychologie* 21:198 ff.

66. Cf. as far back as my "Beiträge zur Theorie der psychischen Analyse," *Zeitschrift für Psychologie*, on pp. 441 f. and beforehand.

67. Cf. above, pp. 15 f.

68. By Anton Marty, "Über 'Annahmen'," *Zeitschrift für Psychologie* 40:26.

69. Cf. secs. 54 f. above, incidentally.

70. Stephan Witasek, *Ästhetik*, pp. 111 f.

71. In secs. 59, 63.

72. Cf. also Stephan Witasek, *Ästhetik*, pp. 111 f.

73. "Beiträge zur Theorie der psychischen Analyse," *Zeitschrift für Psychologie* 6:374, n.

74. Cf. also above, end sec. 55.

75. Cf. my remarks on "Phantasievorstellung und Phantasie" in the *Zeitschrift für Philosophie und philosophische Kritik* 95:166 ff.

76. Cf. above, chap. 9, secs. 54 ff.

77. Cf. sec. 63.

78. Cf. p. 273.

79. Concerning the lower stage's substituting for the higher stage, cf. above, sec. 58, towards the end, as well as sec. 61.

80. In the essay on "Phantasievorstellung und Phantasie," *Zeitschrift für Philosophie und philosophische Kritik* 95, especially pp. 234 ff.

81. Ibid., p. 236.

82. "Beiträge zur speziellen Dispositionspsychologie," in the *Archiv für systematische Philosophie* 3:283.

83. Through this expression, assumptions would naturally also be subsumed under the "judgments in the broader sense" mentioned on pp. 264 and 270 f. above.

84. "Über Begriff und Eigenschaften der Empfindung," *Vierteljahresschrift für wissenschaftliche Philosophie*, 1888, pp. 479 f.

85. Above, p. 271.

Editor's Notes

I: Initial Theses

a 'Verschiedenheit' is rendered as 'differentness' in the following argument and wherever Meinong means to give an example of an ideal relation or to look into the objective signification of the German word (hence, also in chapters 3 and 8). The more natural 'difference' is rejected in these contexts because of its tendency to denote a *fundamentum relationis* rather than a relation. The problem of an appropriate English word is tacitly acknowledged by Bertrand Russell and J. N. Findlay, who also pass over 'difference', but in favor of 'diversity' rather than 'differentness'.

II: The Characteristic Functions of the Sentence

a For 'Begehren', one can occasionally use 'conation' or 'conative experience' instead of 'desire'. The reason will be apparent from the following note.

b Here 'desires' is used for 'Begehrungen', but in some places the difference in naturalness between 'desires' and 'conative experiences' will be so slight that the ready generality of the latter expression makes it the preferable one. It gives us a chance to remind ourselves that for Meinong, along with Ehrenfels and some earlier writers, any experience that involves an endeavor or counterendeavor qualifies as a *Begehrung*. Thus, dreamy wishes and determined volitions qualify as *Begehrungen,* because they are conative in that sense. Most of the *Begehrungen* that Meinong discusses under that name are of an intermediate sort (e.g., the desire to know something). He lets them have the generic name, instead of calling them *Wünsche.* The abundance of these examples of "desires" in the ordinary sense with no other name than 'Begehrung' for themselves compels one to forgo the more general expressions 'conation' and 'conative experiences' except in cases where Meinong is clearly using the German expression in a general way, or where he might just as well be using it that way. See Editor's Introduction, p. *xii,* and notes *c* and *d* for chapter 4; note *i* for chapter 5; and notes *a* and *d* for chapter 9.

c 'Reproductive representation' is used (instead of 'imaginative representation') for 'Einbildungsvorstellung'. Our rule, which Meinong sometimes breaks, is that *Phantasievorstellungen* constitute a proper subclass of *Einbildungsvorstellungen,* viz., the imaginative rather than the recollective subclass. Just the *Phantasievorstellung* is the "imaginative" representation, then. See Editor's Introduction, p. *xii,* and note *i* for chapter 10.

d 'Introversion' is used for 'Einwärtswendung'; similarly, 'extroversion' is used elsewhere for 'Auswärtswendung'.

e 'Sentence' is used (instead of 'proposition') for 'Satz', and 'independent sentence' for 'abhängige Satz'. No recourse is made to 'clause' except in ' "that"-clause', 'main clause', and 'subordinate clause'.

[314]

f See notes *a* and *b* for this chapter.

g The German for Meinong's preceding specimen sentence ('. . . is not connected. . .') is actually in the subjunctive somewhat as is the relative clause in 'There is not an automobile on the lot that would have all the extras you want'.

h 'Nonsimple' is sued for 'zusammengesetzte' with the meaning of "compound or complex."

III: The Objective

a The locution 'allows of correct acknowledgment' is used for Anton Marty's 'mit Recht anerkannt werden kann'. Elsewhere, 'correct acknowledgment' is used for 'berechtigte Anerkennung'. When Meinong used the word 'berechtigte' in the first edition to express his own views, he had long been accustomed to treat it as an evidence word. Consequently, in the older part of chapter 7 (see the second paragraph of section 34, for example) it is 'justified' rather than 'correct' that appears in the translation. The *Berechtigung* of an affirmative existential judgment was for Meinong its internal justification, its evidence. Not so for Marty. For him it was just the rightness or correctness (or if you will, external justification) of the judgment, the judgment being a simple affirmation (acknowledgment, acceptance) of something represented. Marty's reflex conception of existence does not have much to do with possibility, much less the possibility of an evident acknowledgment. It is instead just a conception that identifies the existence of a thing with the thing's meriting acknowledgment. So it is in the second and sixth articles of Marty's "Über subjektlose Sätze," *Vierteljahrsschrift für wissenschaftliche Philosophie* 8 (1884):174; ibid., 19 (1895):32, n. 3. Allowing of correct acknowledgment is no more or less than meriting acknowledgment.

b The concept of mediate apprehension is yet to be introduced, notwithstanding page 44. Mediate apprehension will turn out to be apprehension "in" or "through" an objective. See note *g* for chapter 5.

c For an example of an infinitival phrase that designates an objective (of reluctance), Meinong gives the following sentence in chapter 5: 'I do not want to leave the interests of the whole community out of consideration' (p. 121). When infinitives were first mentioned (p. 46), there was a slight suggestion that Meinong doubted their suitability as objective-expressions.

d Concerning existences, Meinong means that it is occasionally allowable in German to speak of persons or things as "existences."

e 'Fastening upon' is used (instead of the insight word 'grasping') for 'Ergreifen'. The word is important only in connection with intending (*Meinen*) in chapters 7, 8, and 10. There are some remarks on *Ergreifen* in the Editor's Introduction, pp. *xxxii-xxxiii*, and in note *d* for chapter 10.

f 'Absistence' is used for 'Aussersein'. See Editor's Introduction, p. *xxxii*.

g 'Evidenz' is given the usual rendition of 'evidence'. The occurrence of 'evidence' and 'evident' in the present text will always signal the presence of their German cognates in the original text. The one exception is with 'einleuchten' (verb) and 'einleuchtend' (the derived adjective). These show up respectively as 'to be evident' and 'evident'. All the "evidence" sentence specimens in this (the first) paragraph of section 13 are *einleuchten* expressions in the German.

h Concerning the narrower sense of factuality, Meinong means the *rejected* narrower sense, in accordance with which nothing necessary would be called factual, not the *proposed* narrower sense, according to which no objectum is to be called (f)actual, i.e., *tatsächlich*.

i See the preceding note. The allusion here is to the following more or less traditional approach to modality:

A problematic judgment is a judgment of possibility.

An assertoric judgment is a judgment of (f)actuality.

An apodictic judgment is a judgment of necessity.

From here on, *Assumptions* is free of the historical allusions that would interfere with our adherence to J. N. Findlay's 'factuality' as the regular rendition of 'Tatsächlichkeit'. See note 10 to the Editor's Introduction.

j Concerning 'Einsicht': We can assign to it an English word later on, when it occurs more often. For the time being (and once in a while later on), we can use the fixed locutions 'see or realize' and 'seeing or realizing'. The word 'insight' is brought in at the end of section 26.

IV: Most Obvious Cases of Assumptions

a Aside from counter-to-fact conditional clauses, all of the nonsubordinate subjunctive sentences Meinong adduces get themselves into nonsubjunctive English forms. Thus, in the following 'Let there be...' (for 'Es sei...'), there is an infinitival rather than a subjunctive 'be', and Meinong's preceding remark about the subjunctive mood is left unsupported.

b The unavoidable use of 'imagine' for 'sich einbilden' should be compared with note *c* for chapter 2, as well as with the system of classification given in the Editor's Introduction, p. *xii*.

c For 'Begehrende', 'conative subject' instead of 'person desiring'. See note *a* for chapter 2, as well as the system of classification mentioned in the foregoing note *b*.

d In his treatment of questions, Meinong avails himself of two different senses of the verb 'begehren'. The sense that easily fits the topic of questions is "expressing one's desire or will, in order to have something done." The other sense, with which we are familiar now, is "desiring or willing." The first sense would be seen in "craving an immediate reply" from a correspondent; the second sense would be seen in the craving to hear from someone. They sometimes call that an inner craving, and so the first craving must be an outer craving. Asking a question would therefore be like an outer craving. But good sense says we should go no further in the present vein, and this sentence and the section heading have been given a literal, unrationalized translation.

e 'Second' is used even though the German word is 'vorigen'.

V: The Objective and Assumptions

a Concerning mediate apprehension, see note *g* below for this chapter.

b A ist. The sense of this paradigm is not "*A* exists" but "*A* exists or subsists." One can mentally substitute that reading for the "*A* is" reading.

c Concerning Anton Marty's *mit Recht anerkannt werden können* or (second sentence, next paragraph) *mit Recht affirmiert werden können,* see note *a* to chapter 3.

d Not so correct in English. If one has 'Irate subscribers get attention', then with retention of grammaticality one can substitute 'Irate subscribers are attention-getting'. But one may not proceed analogously from 'The paper is white' to 'The paper is white-being'. See *Über Möglichkeit und Wahrscheinlichkeit, Gesamtausgabe* 6:279-280 (sec. 37, par. 7).

e In the German, the two pairs of sentences are, first, 'Dass *A B* ist, das ist' and 'dass *A* ist, das ist', and then 'dass *A B* ist, ist *C*' and 'dass *A* ist, ist *C*'.

f The English rendition of the first sentence obviously invites the remark that *being the case* is predicated of :that *A* is *B*:.

g Mediate apprehension has already been mentioned by Meinong in the second paragraph of this chapter, with a note referring the reader to sections 8 and 9. The next-to-the-last paragraph of section 8 (p. 40) contains the hint of mediate apprehension as it will appear in the last section of chapter 7, viz., as the apprehending of an objectum in or through an objective. But section 9 (p. 44) provides us merely with the idea of a judgment having one of its objects "mediately," i.e., through the assistance of a prior, presenting experience. One cannot go from that to the chapter 7 idea so easily. Given just the hint in section 8, we are not yet in a position to understand references to mediate apprehension of an objectum, much less of an objective. The preceding discussions of approached objectives have provided nothing to prepare us for the later development.

h Meinong has "ich lege Wert darauf, dass ich dieses Buch besitze."

i 'Desires' is used for 'begehrungen', as usual; still, this time the general sense of "conative experiences" (volitional or specifically desiderative) might better have been made explicit. See notes *a* and *b* for chapter 2.

j 'Conative domain' is used for 'Begehrungsgebiete'; the reason can be seen in the foregoing note.

k The allusion is to the first-edition axiological material in chapter 9 (first-edition chapter 8), as though we had to get ready for it now. The present paragraph served as the conclusion of first-edition chapter 7 (the heterogeneous and latecoming chapter on objectives). The occasion for an introduction to the chapter on the psychology of desire and value has disappeared, but instead of removing this introduction Meinong adds a general introduction to the intervening chapters 6, 7, and 8. Because of this, the reader might be misled into thinking that these three chapters in intellectual psychology represent some preliminary work that must be done before the main course of the inquiry can be resumed.

VI: Operations on Objectives

a 'Evidence' is used for 'Evidenz'. See note *g* for chapter 3.

b 'Insight' is used for 'Einsicht'. See note *j* for chapter 3. Whenever 'insight' is inconvenient, as it is with the verb 'einsehen', one can revert to the stereotypes 'see or realize' and 'seeing or realization' used earlier. When a judgment is simply said to be evident, and there is nothing said about a lower order of evidence, then the implication is that it is a seeing or realization (*Einsehen*), but that need not be an instance of a priori evidence. In other words, there is insight without comprehension.

c 'Inferential judgment' is used for 'Schlussurteil'. Meinong alludes to section 6 of chapter 5, part 2, of his "Hume-Studien II: Zur Relationstheorie," *Sitzungsberichte der philosophischen-historischen Klasse der Kaiserlichen Akademie der Wissenschaften in Wien* 101 (1882), in *Gesamtausgabe* II. An inference is said to be a judgment. It is a judgment that the premises (or their truth) are incompatible (*unverträglich*) with the negative (or the falsity) of the conclusion. The premises and the conclusion are themselves judgments, but they need not actually be made, for there to be an inference. What is indispensable is just that judgments be represented as the terms of a relation of incompatibility. Needless to say, Meinong in 1882 did not have the dislike of appeals to occult reflective operations that is the hallmark of his mature philosophy. In the present passage from the 1902 edition of *Assumptions*, the question about the nature of inference is reopened, though there is not yet any sign that Meinong will get the mind's own premising out from in front of the mind and put premise-objectives there instead.

d 'Schlussgesetz' (Christian Sigwart) is untranslated here, but is later translated with 'universal-hypothetical major regulating the inference'. The *Schlussgesetz* was conceived by Sigwart as an a posteriori or a priori law for an area of inquiry or action, but also as a judgment (hypothetical, conditional) that regulates one's inferences in that area. Such "inferential laws" correspond to the major premise of the *modus ponens* form of inference. Meinong sees his earlier "inferential judgments" here.

e 'Intuitive' is used for 'anschaulich', with the usual understanding that the intuitive is to be opposed not to the discursive (as is normal in English) but to the abstract or conceptual.

f The reader of the second edition of *Assumptions* is faced with the problem of whether premises, conclusions, antecedents, and consequents are being treated as linguistic entities (sentences, coordinate clauses), objects (objectives), or experiences (judgments, assumptions). Although this third, psychological contender for the logical designations drops out, it is strong in the first-edition paragraphs that have been by far the predominant ones up until now (henceforth, second-edition paragraphs far outnumber the first-edition ones). It is worth noting, then, that Meinong is so far ruling out only the view that premises and conclusions are *represented* judgments (see note *c* for this chapter), not the view that they *are* judgments or assumptions.

g It appears now that the hypothetical antecedent (*Vordersatz*) and the hypothetical consequent (*Nachsatz*) are sentences—i.e., coordinate clauses—that have objectives as their significations. (See also page 145.) The signification of the antecedent is the antecedent objective (*Vorderobjektiv*), and the signification of the consequent is the consequent objective (*Nachobjektiv*). There is fair adherence to this usage in the following pages; yet there are exceptions, in which the *Vordersatz* and the *Nachsatz* themselves are plainly regarded as objectives, e.g., on page 148 in section 31. Also, at the end of that section, Meinong appears to be content with this conflicting understanding about a *Satz*. Thus, with the same intent, Meinong will speak of a *Vorderobjektiv* restricting a *Nachobjektiv* and of a *Vordersatz* restricting a *Nachsatz*. The less important effect is to crowd the sentence, the linguistic thing, out of consideration; the more important effect is to encourage the treatment of an objective as a proposition. (See note *i* for this chapter.) Meinong's passing reference to a restricted *Nachsatzurteil* (page 149) need not be taken too seriously.

If there is any confusion, it is undoubtedly the result of objectives (the subject of the first-edition seventh chapter) now appearing in a position (the revised first-edition fourth chapter) where they were once absent. Whatever might have been the disadvantages of having a discussion of inferring and hypothetical judgment come before a discussion of objectives, this arrangement did give Meinong the logician's prerogative of ignoring the ontological status of his antecedents, consequents, premises, and conclusions. Now that prerogative has disappeared, and it becomes important, so far as Meinong wants to designate objectives as antecedents, etc., that he not designate sentences or experiences (judgments and assumptions) in the same manner. Otherwise, allowing either that the linguistic things may be designated as antecedents, etc., or that the psychological things may be designated in such a way, Meinong must forbid himself to speak of the "assuming" and "judging" of premises, conclusions, antecedents, and consequents. For only objects (i.e., objectives) may be assumed or judged.

h See note *a* for chapter 4.

i 'Propositions' is used (instead of 'sentences') for 'Sätze'. The restricted *Nachsatz* and the restricting *Vordersatz* are *Sätze*, anyway; in the present case the problem of propositional consequents and antecedents merely surfaces. It is especially interesting inasmuch as the restricted and the restricting things will be called "objectives" in the passages immediately ahead. Since this is a second-edition section of *Assumptions,* one may suppose that Meinong had in mind his view of propositions as pseudo-existent objectives, and that there is not really any occasion for him to pause with "in-between" things like propositions, as he passes from antecedent and consequent experiences to antecedent and consequent objectives. Their present designation as *Sätze* is merely casual. It occurs again on page 148, however.

j 'In view of' is used for 'im Hinblick auf'. The *Hinblick*-thesis, as one might call it, is being reformulated, here and in the next paragraph. The earlier formulations of it, which are taken from or are in conformity with the first edition (they start at the top of page 130) are not compatible with what is now being done. According to the present formulation, a judgment gains mediate evidence by being made "in view of" (*im Hinblick auf*) an objective already apprehended; according to the first-edition formulations, the phenomenon of mediate evidence is the result of a judgment's being made in view of a prior judgment, not an object.

k In conformity with the change just noted, Meinong now speaks of a judgment being motivated by an *objective* already apprehended, instead of by an earlier *judgment.* This dismissal of the causal in favor of the rational ground makes for a striking contrast with the first-edition remarks on inferential motivation (pages 130 and 136). Last but not least, notice the sentence that now follows.

l In the second edition of *Assumptions,* Meinong adopts the distinction that Ernst Mally makes between complexes and complexion in his "Untersuchungen zur Gegenstandstheorie des Messens," in *Untersuchungen zur Gegenstandstheorie und Psychologie,* ed. Alexius Meinong (Leipzig: Barth, 1904), pp. 147-155. In the immediate context, the importance of the distinction is just the flexibility of interpretation that it gives us. One might insist that all complexes are objecta and that therefore a "complex" of objectives would have to be an objectum. But one would still have to concede that their "complexion" or being together in that complex was an objective, along with every constitutive "being related thus and so."

VII: Assumptions in Apprehending What Is Presented—Intending

a 'Objective' is used (adjectivally) for 'gegenständlich', notwithstanding its existing use (substantively) for 'Objektiv'. Within sections 33 through 37, we can consider the question as to what makes representations and judgments "objective" in their appreciable psychological character. In that space of consideration, there will be no "objectives" to cause confusion. When these objects return for consideration in section 38, there will be no more discussion of the "objectivity" of representations and judgments. Thus, the two usages will not run into each other, and there need be no worry about the possibility of a confusion of the adjectival and substantival senses of 'objective'. The former sense does show up one or two times more, after section 37, but the issue of the objectivity or objective quality of representations is in the main a superseded issue in the present edition of *Assumptions.* It is superseded by the theory of intending.

b 'Object' is used (instead of 'objectum') for 'Objekt'. Meinong uses the expression 'Objekt' here because it is the word customarily used in repeating the Brentanoan contrast between that which is immanent and that which is transcendent. In writing this passage in 1901, or earlier, Meinong most likely did not have the distinction between an objectum and an objective at hand. For these two reasons, his deviation from 'Gegenstand' is ignored.

c 'Fastening upon' is used for 'Ergreifen'. See note *e* for chapter 3.

d 'Reproductive representations' is used (instead of 'imaginative representations') for 'Einbildungsvorstellungen'. See note *c* for chapter 2.

e 'Intend' is used (instead of 'refer to') for 'meinen'. The effective reason for rejecting 'refer' is implicit in the discussion of *Seinsmeinen* in the Editor's Introduction (pp. xxxii-xxxiii). There are three further considerations that might be found persuasive. The first is this: *Meinen* pertains to the person, unlike *Gegenständlichkeit*, which pertained to the representation. Referring pertains to the person, too, if it is referring with a sign instead of the sign's referring. But personal referring *must* be referring with a sign, and *Meinen* needs no sign at all. The second reason is this: C. D. Broad uses the expression 'intending' for 'Meinen' in his 1913 review of the second edition in *Mind*. The third reason one might find most persuasive. 'Meinen' does appear in one passage of the first edition (p. 132), and there it is provided with a synonym: 'Intentioniren'.

VIII: Assumptions and Complexes—More on Intending

a 'Intuitive' is used for 'anschaulich', and 'nonintuitive for 'unanschaulich'. See note *e* for chapter 6.

b 'Object' is used (instead of the regular 'objectum') for 'Objekt'. In the first edition, the chapter on objectives is still to come, and the present context does not suggest any intent, or conscious intent, to use 'Objekt' in a more specific sense than 'Gegenstand'. In essentials, the same reasoning applies as in note *b* for chapter 7.

c For 'rot seiendes Kreuz'. Like the "white-being" piece of paper in chapter 5 (see note *d* for that chapter), our present "red-being" cross cannot be justified by analogy, i.e., not with 'red-colored mouthwash' or any other grammatically correct English construction. As before, best not to attempt anything.

d 'Fastening upon' is used for 'Ergreifen'. See note *e* for chapter 3. The meaning will alter from what it was in chapter 7. There, the predefinition of the character of the object was taken for granted and was tacitly credited to the representational content. *Ergreifen* first appeared as the apprehending phase or aspect of *Seinsmeinen*. Now it will associate itself with *Soseinsmeinen*, and it will appear anew as "fastening upon a thing by predefining its character actively." The theoretical position vis-à-vis *Meinen*, intending, is somewhat more unstable than allowed in the Editor's Introduction (pp. xxxii-xxxiii). See note *d* for chapter 10.

IX: Psychology of Desire and Psychology of Value

a The allusion is to what Meinong said in section 25, paragraph 3. He has now recalled that a state of affairs that one "definitely doesn't want" need not always be an assumed state of affairs. Reluctance (*Widerstreben*), the negative form of conation, or *Begehren*, can sometimes operate in the face of a known state of affairs, even volitionally. It is not "psychologically prerequisite" that the state of affairs be assumed.

b 'Enhancement of happiness' is used for 'Glücksförderung'. The English may be taken elliptically: enhancing (the feeling of) happiness. One feels happier with this representation than one would without it. As to 'enhancement', see Howard O. Eaton's *The Austrian Theory of Values* (Oklahoma: University of Oklahoma Press, 1930), pp. 131 ff. 'Felicific' in the present chapter is just an alternative to the unwieldy 'happiness enhancing' (*glückfördernde*).

c 'Object' is used (instead of the normal 'Objectum') for 'Objekt'. By now, in the first edition, Meinong had accomplished the division of objects (*Gegenstände*) into objecta (*Objekte*) and objectives (*Objektive*). But he was now resuming an earlier controversy in which 'Objekt' had just been another way of saying "object" in German. It is treated that way here, until Meinong reintroduces the objective on page 218.

d 'Wishing' is used for 'Wünschen', but one might alternatively use 'desiring' here and in the next paragraph, with an accommodating shift of 'Begehren' out of 'desire' and 'desiring' and into 'conation'. That would accord with Meinong's and Ehrenfels's understanding of volition as a kind of *Begehren*. See page 211 (first paragraph) and page 216 (last paragraph).

e The so-being expressions and the following references to so-being are added in the second edition. A few other such occasions are pointed out in notes *f, j,* and *k* below. Except in note *k* ('negative so-being'), 'not being thus and so' is used for 'Nichtsosein'. The 'negative so-being' of note *k* is used again in chapter 10, page 256.

f See the preceding note *e*.

g The "or at least" is substituted for a first-edition "more precisely" (p. 241 of the first edition). The change gives a quite graphic representation of the new axiological antipsychologism that is merely hinted at in the portentous note 91 for this chapter.

h 'Value-objecta' is used (instead of 'value-objects') for 'Wertobjekte'; it no longer sounds anachronistic. See note *c* for this chapter.

i 'The ability to be desired' is used (instead of 'desirability') for 'Begehrbarkeit'.

j See note *e* for this chapter.

k Again see note *e* for this chapter.

X: Toward a Psychology of Assumptions

a The content of a judgment or assumption is not a representational content. The opposite belief is expressed at a comparable point in the concluding chapter of the first edition (p. 257). There we read that content can be disregarded as a basis of comparison for assuming and representation, and for judgment and representation as well. The reason given for this is that the representation supplies everything in the way of a content.

b See note *j* for chapter 6.

c 'Objektive als Annahmeprämissen': Here and earlier in the paragraph one can see the nonpsychological characterization of premises as *objectives* "in view of which" one assumes or judges something. But the older, psychological manner of speaking of premises survives into chapter 10, too (see pp. 244-245). This survival probably should not be taken very seriously; by now the question about premises is just a question of whether 'premise' shall mean the premise-experience or the premise-objective.

d See note *e* for chapter 3. Fastening upon (*Ergreifen*) has at this point lost the inceptive aspect that it had when we met with it on page 171, and intending (*Meinen*) even seems to be instrumental to the fastening upon. Later on, on page 261, Meinong seems to shift back to the view of *Ergreifen* as an inceptive "bringing an object into consideration," as it were—with *Meinen* being the resultant "having it under consideration" as we think whatever we think about the object. Then *Meinen* would, of course, be what one meant in speaking of a "mental referring." But in Meinong's subsequent writing, *Meinen* is always treated as an inceptive fastening upon an object, and it is no longer thought necessary to use another word, i.e., one that connotes that "fastening upon."

e Implicit intending by way of so-being was also mentioned on pages 198-199. The notion probably concedes too much to the representational content, because later on Meinong welcomes the notion that there are "shadowy" assumptions, ones whose presence can be ascertained only indirectly. Moreover, he introduces the second notion in connection with intending. See Meinong's "Über emotionale Präsentation," *Sitzungs-*

berichte der philosophisch-historischen Klasse der Kaiserlichen Akademie der Wissen-schaften in Wien 183 (1917): 48-51. (In *Gesamtausgabe* III.) [*On Emotional Presentation,* trans. Marie-Luise Schubert Kalsi (Evanston, Ill.: Northwestern University Press, 1972), pp. 42-45.] Whatever may be the value of the notion of implicit intending by way of so-being, it is clearly an attempt to explain why perception seems to require only an existential judgment as its active component.

f See note *e* for chapter 9.

g See note *g* for chapter 5.

h Instead of translating "Ich bitte, Komm her."

i 'Reproductive representations' is used for 'Einbildungsvorstellungen', following note *c* for chapter 2. It might be added that Meinong's own terminological reasoning appears in "Über Begriff und Eigenschaft der Empfindung," *Vierteljahrsschrift für wissenschaftliche Philosophie* 12-13 (1888-1889): 479-483. (In *Gesamtausgabe* I.) One sees the result in the words that now immediately follow.

j The "general aspect" appears from the following to be *comparative intensity of the act.*

Index